Build Your Own .NET Language and Compiler

EDWARD G. NILGES

D1595098

Apress™

Build Your Own .NET Language and Compiler
Copyright © 2004 by Edward G. Nilges

ISBN (pbk): 1-59059-134-8

Printed and bound in the United States of America 12345678910

Trademarked names may appear in this book. Rather than use a trademark symbol with every occurrence of a trademarked name, we use the names only in an editorial fashion and to the benefit of the trademark owner, with no intention of infringement of the trademark.

Lead Editor: Dan Appleman

Technical Reviewer: William Steele

Editorial Board: Steve Anglin, Dan Appleman, Ewan Buckingham, Gary Cornell, Tony Davis, John Franklin, Jason Gilmore, Chris Mills, Steven Rycroft, Dominic Shakeshaft, Jim Sumser, Karen Watterson, Gavin Wray, John Zukowski

Assistant Publisher: Grace Wong

Project Manager: Beth Christmas

Copy Manager: Nicole LeClerc

Copy Editor: Marilyn Smith

Production Manager: Kari Brooks

Production Editor: Kelly Winquist

Compositor: Linda Weidemann, Wolf Creek Press

Proofreader: Elizabeth Berry

Indexer: Bill Johncocks

Artist: Kinetic Publishing

Cover Designer: Kurt Krames

Manufacturing Manager: Tom Debolski

Distributed to the book trade in the United States by Springer-Verlag New York, Inc., 175 Fifth Avenue, New York, NY, 10010 and outside the United States by Springer-Verlag GmbH & Co. KG, Tiergartenstr. 17, 69112 Heidelberg, Germany.

In the United States: phone 1-800-SPRINGER, email orders@springer-ny.com, or visit http://www.springer-ny.com. Outside the United States: fax +49 6221 345229, email orders@springer.de, or visit http://www.springer.de.

For information on translations, please contact Apress directly at 2560 Ninth Street, Suite 219, Berkeley, CA 94710. Phone 510-549-5930, fax 510-549-5939, email info@apress.com, or visit http://www.apress.com.

The information in this book is distributed on an "as is" basis, without warranty. Although every precaution has been taken in the preparation of this work, neither the author(s) nor Apress shall have any liability to any person or entity with respect to any loss or damage caused or alleged to be caused directly or indirectly by the information contained in this work.

The source code for this book is available to readers at http://www.apress.com in the Downloads section. You will need to answer questions pertaining to this book in order to successfully download the code.

Contents at a Glance

Contents

About the Author

Edward G. Nilges has programmed since 1970, when he learned machine language for an 8KB IBM 1401 as part of an elaborate draft-dodging scheme that appears to have gotten out of hand.

Early on, Edward discovered the power of languages and their translation in "ordinary" management information systems (MIS) applications. He consolidated several applications into one by creating a specifications language within the 1401's constraints, and he also provided his university with a working Fortran compiler. Some of his early adventures are relevant to today's challenges, and this book contains some of Edward's unexpurgated war stories.

Edward has developed millions of lines of code for MIS, telecommunications, naval architecture, and education applications. He has developed several compilers, including internal compilers for telecommunications applications at Nortel, the QuickBasic compiler of this book, and a compiler for the Mouse language that fits in 1KB of storage. He has taught at Roosevelt University in Chicago and DeVry University, and delivered training classes at Princeton University.

At Princeton, Edward was honored to assist the real-life protagonist of the recent film *A Beautiful Mind*, John Nash, with a bug in the old Microsoft C compiler. Edward was also privileged to meet Cornel West, the noted American philosopher, and Ralph Nader. He took classes in philosophy and computer science, and gained access to Firestone Library (and has since paid fines accrued).

Currently, Edward is working in China on methodologies for transferring client/server applications to the Web, while also studying written and spoken Chinese.

Edward has two grown children and a former wife who he honors as the mother of those children. Indeed, he calls himself Edward G. Nilges to disambiguate himself from his eldest son, Edward A. Nilges, who is studying philosophy at the University of Illinois and has contributed errata to Bjarne Stroustrup's book, *The C++ Programming Language*. His other son, Peter "Chauncey" "Zeit-Bug" Nilges, recently graduated *cum laude* from DePaul.

Edward has published material on computer and general topics since 1976, when he suggested in *Computerworld* that it was possible to write structured code in assembly language, and got yelled at by Ed Yourdon. Recent articles include utilities for string conversion and display in Visual Studio, and a critical assessment of the language we use in speaking about database theory, published in the Austrian journal *Labyrinths*.

Current interests include .NET, art, running, reading, China, and world philosophy.

Acknowledgments

THIS BOOK IS DUE to a suggestion of David Treadwell of Princeton and Microsoft, because he suggested a list of potential languages for .NET implementation, including QuickBasic. Initial impetus was provided by Josef Finsel, author of *The Handbook for Reluctant Database Administrators*, and I am in Mr. Finsel's debt for this reason.

Dan Appleman's support and patience during the excitements of its development is most appreciated, as is that of Marilyn Smith, Beth Christmas, Grace Wong, Nicole LeClerc, Kari Brooks, Bill Johncocks, Kurt Krames, and Kelly Winquist, as well as the accounting team at Apress.

Dan Appleman in fact volunteered his valuable time for a developmental edit and put up with some of my deeper nonsense with a great deal of patience.

I need to thank the gang at the Evanston YMCA, as well as the operators of various executive stay places around the world for providing working space at various times, for my day jobs have taken me to the far corners of the world.

The Silicon Valley "out-to-lunch bunch," including Rick, Ragu, William, Bill, and Jason, are also owed a debt of gratitude for their assistance, including Rick's wireless card, Ragu's thoughtfulness, William's unfailing kindness and Jason's laptop, which is toast, I'm afraid.

Helmut Epp of DePaul University, Max Plager of Roosevelt University, the late E. D. Klemke of Roosevelt University and Iowa State University, and Gilbert Harman of Princeton University are all academics from whom I have learned a prior dedication to the truth of the matter.

Long-suffering managers to whom this book is dedicated include Rita Saltz, Robert Geiger (a Visual Basic authority in his own right from whom I learned much), Jeff Burtenshaw, and Monsieur Hugh Levaux.

Tim Tyler was and remains a source of spiritual guidance before, during, and after the writing of this book.

Lee Thé at Fawcette assisted with an earlier release of part of the software in an article on Visual Studio and was a most patient and learned editor.

My strange friend Alex, "Sasha Alexandrovich" Gaydasch, is also owed a debt of gratitude for his support and advice over a period of many years.

Of course, we all owe Edsger Wybe Dijkstra a debt for showing how integrity goes a long way.

But the main dedication of this effort is to Darlene Nilges, Eddie Nilges, and Peter Nilges (junglee Peter), for in dreams begin responsibilities.

Introduction

I mean, if 10 years from now, when you are doing something quick and dirty,
you suddenly visualize that I am looking over your shoulder and say to your-
self, "Dijkstra would not have liked this," well, that would be enough
immortality for me.
—*Edsger Wybe Dijkstra*

Let us not speak falsely now, the hour is much too late.
—*Bob Dylan, "All Along the Watchtower"*

DIJKSTRA DIDN'T PLAY for the Chicago Cubs baseball club, to my knowledge, nor
did he play for the Arsenal, Chelsea, Antwerp or Eindhoven football organizations
(nor did Dylan, but you knew that). Instead, Edsger Wybe Dijkstra was a found-
ing computer scientist who was involved in the early Algol language and either
invented or reported the invention of structured programming.

And since Dijkstra passed on in August 2002, he is rolling in his grave. Here
is a book on how to write a halfway decent compiler, using object-oriented techniques (about which Dijkstra was skeptical) to compile Basic (which he felt was
a mental mutilation) that has the gall, the side, the cheek ... to quote the guy!

That is because Dijkstra was also one of the few computing scientists to keep
steadfast in his mind the true proposition that computing science is applied science, and that is because Dijkstra refused to divorce theory and practice.

Furthermore, I cannot believe that Dijkstra would dislike the desire to know
how compilers work. I have set myself the task of communicating this, at a basic
level, to a wide audience of "ordinary" (ordinary?) programmers.

These are the numerous hard-working programmers who have written code,
probably, for Visual Basic and C++ COM and now are working, probably, in C#
and in Visual Basic .NET. I would like to show that a responsible compiler can be
written in Visual Basic. I would like to provide the complete, runnable, and modifiable, source code at the Apress Web site. I would also like world peace and
harmony, but I digress.

Why not C#? I didn't choose C# because of a simple theory of mine. All, or
nearly all, C# programmers know Visual Basic, but not all Visual Basic programmers have made the transition to C#. And despite the flash and glamour of C#,
there is nothing doable in C# that cannot be done in Visual Basic.

My goal is to demystify and to deconstruct a skill set that can be of actual
use in .NET and Java. Write-once, run anywhere is a goal that entails a need for
more compilers, and more generally, greater portability and ease of modification, not only of code, but also of business rules, stored as data.

To set the scene, Chapter 1 provides an overview of the history of compiler technology, and Chapter 2 describes the .NET background.

Chapter 3 is a fun and exciting chapter, if I do say so myself. That chapter builds a simple "flyover" compiler to demonstrate the key concepts in a lightweight form. This will prepare you for subsequent chapters, which build a compiler of more than 10,000 lines of code for a significant part of the old QuickBASIC language, a Microsoft forerunner of Visual Basic.

In Chapter 4, you will learn about the indispensable formal notation Backus-Naur Form for designing the syntax of a language in the context of the bnfAnalyzer tool, for which, as is the case with all software in this book, source code is provided.

Then, in Chapter 5, you'll learn the basic "lexical" level of parsing, in which we recognize the elements of the language.

Chapter 6 shows a complete, object-oriented approach to storing variables and their types in the Basic language. This is extensible to other languages. In fact, it uses parsing to design an internal language for "serializing" data types and values, thereby showing one way in which this information can be stored.

Chapter 7 is the high point, for in it, I will show you how to build the actual parsing front end of the compiler, where the source code is translated to an interpreted language.

Chapter 8 shows how any computer (given enough time and memory, of course) can simulate any other computer, based on an important early result of hero computer scientist Alan Turing. You'll see how we can use this result to test compiled Basic code while visually displaying, step by step, its execution.

Chapter 9 introduces techniques for taking this process one step further, and translating compiled code to Microsoft Intermediate Language (MSIL) for execution in the Common Language Runtime (CLR). This translation makes the formerly slow, interpreted code run much faster.

One concern of mine is how compilation techniques can make life easier for the end users who are charged with keeping business rules up-to-date in credit, banking, law, and other applications. Compiler technology can be used to represent these rules as ASCII data suitable for storage in a database. Chapter 9 shows how this could be accomplished for a small loan company, Loans for the Honest Poor, which uses flexible rules to find good risks among "ordinary" (ordinary?) working people.

Chapter 10 winds up by discussing some of the issues that can arise in designing a language, including political and business issues.

Appendix A provides a comprehensive and geeky reference manual for the language of the representative QuickBasic compiler, and Appendix B provides another reference manual for the objects used to build the compiler.

The comprehensive source for all software and tools is available to purchasers of this book at the Downloads area of the Apress Web site (http://www.apress.com), along with Apress forums in which you can meet authors, ask questions, and, within reason, schmooze and socialize. You will need Visual Basic 2003 Professional or Enterprise to run all of the code.

I am also available at spinoza1111@yahoo.com should you have any questions.

Thanks for buying my book, or, at least, taking it down from the shelf at Borders, Barnes and Noble, Page One (at Festival Walk in Kowloon Tong), or wherever. If your bookstore has a café, grab a latte, sit down, take a load off fanny, take a load for free, and peruse. I hope you will get excited at the prospect of actually being able to walk through the basics of compiler design theory while running practical examples on your .NET system.

That's because, if you are like me, and indeed like the mighty Dijkstra, you don't divorce theory and practice. Dijkstra's pronouncements have a common theme, and they are that he never thought himself above getting down into the actual code—whether program code or the equally demanding codes of formal, if applied, mathematics.

Programmers get irritated, on the one hand, by academics who rattle on about arcane proofs and theorems with no apparent connection to the real world of schedules and deadlines (as well as sick children and cars that don't start), and on the other hand, by managers who sketch out vast ambitions that must then be wearily constructed in reality, by programmers with little say in the end product (for let us not speak falsely now, the hour is much too late).

But in honor of the late, hero computer scientist Dijkstra, and indeed for the dear old schoolhouses (in my case, St. Viator High School, Roosevelt University, DePaul University, and Princeton as a sort of midlife crisis, for both me and dear old Nassau), I will now attempt to steer a course between the rocks of academia and management-o-rama, and sail true toward your mastery of something new that will make you feel like a devil of a fellow or a hell of a gal, at a minimum. For, the boss, in today's Big Chill, groans at us on the job to only learn the essentials, and ultimately, this is stunting. Let's learn something almost (but not quite) for its own sake.

Let's dweeb out.

CHAPTER 1

A Brief History of Compiler Technology

I would therefore like to posit that computing's central challenge,
viz. 'how not to make a mess of it,' has not been met.
–Edsger Dijkstra

THE LATE, HERO COMPUTER SCIENTIST, Edsger Dijkstra, was rather confident. He seemed to know that computing's central challenge is not messing up. Some programmers and their managers might contend that the main challenge is achieving user satisfaction.

In either case, writing parsers and compilers will be a challenge!

You can learn much about compilers from their history. Therefore, this chapter describes the mainstream history of compilers and follows up with a look at the sidestream history of Basic compilers.

The Mainstream: From Fortran to C

In the 1950s, the earliest programmers prided themselves on doing their work without any assistance, and their work was tedious—in the extreme.

Of course, older people always like to say that they had to walk to work after school in the snow uphill both ways to support their aging mother. But it does appear that below the level of people like John von Neumann or J. Presper Eckert (two early inventors of modern digital computation), the actual work of creating programs was simultaneously invisible, brutally tedious, and sexist.[1] However, the big shots soon found that they and the programmers were up against what hero computer scientist Edsger Dijkstra shortly thereafter called a "radical novelty."

The difference between writing a proof on a blackboard and writing a program is that the mathematician is able to appeal to the shared understanding of a rather close-knit mathematical community, but the programmer must account

---

1. In the 1940s and 1950s, the presumption on the part of the big shots was that some "girl" could prepare programs for their hardware and perhaps find an up-and-coming graduate student to wed. (I'm not making any of this up.)

for everything. If something goes wrong with his or her program, a programmer is expected to fix it quickly and accurately.

John von Neumann thought that any use of the computer to assist in programming was a waste of a valuable resource by lazy programmers. But one early programmer, Grace M. Hopper,[2] discovered that the computer itself could be an aid in preparing bug-free programs. Her work led to the first two major computer languages: Fortran and Algol.

Fortran, Algol, and Beyond

At first, the programming community resisted the use of computers for program development, perhaps for the same hard-wired reasons some guys don't ask for directions when they're lost. However, the benefits of Hopper's "autocoding" were clear enough. In 1954, IBM[3] had a team of mathematician/programmers develop one of the first compilers and languages: Fortran.

This team was led by IBM Fellow John Backus and did a terrific job with very limited hardware. A bit later, a European/American group, which included John Backus, developed a more ambitious language: Algol.

Fortran supported a style of programming in which a program is conceived as a series of instructions to which control flows by means of the infamous goto command. Algol, on the other hand, introduced the notion of block structure, in which the programmer could group lists of statements, effectively creating one instruction out of a list of instructions. In this structure, control flows much more readably into and around the blocks.[4]

In general, the Fortran compiler writers and the actual Fortran programmers, who wrote code for science and engineering, delivered useful results faster. The Algol compiler writers, and eventually the Algol programmers, delivered more useful and more accurate results, but more slowly. This, as many programmers know, can be a serious problem in the real world.

It was easier to write Fortran compilers that generated efficient code, and the Algol team ran into problems in compiling efficient programs. Programmers of the 1950s were defensive about their skills in translating mathematical and business requirements into assembler and machine languages, and their requirement was that a useful compiler generate faster code than a skilled programmer could

---

2. At the time Grace M. Hopper began exploring the use of the computer for programming (in the late 1940s), she was a lieutenant in the United States Navy. She later became an admiral in recognition of her accomplishments.

3. At the time, IBM was competing with Univac, now Unisys, for dominance of the computer industry.

4. Edsger Dijkstra was an early Algol programmer. He noticed that Algol programmers could use block structure to avoid goto statements, and he wrote a famous letter to the editor of a computer journal, "Go To Considered Harmful."

produce. Fortran met this requirement, but Algol did not until about 1960, when the Burroughs Corporation provided a machine whose hardware was able to run Algol efficiently.

An Early Fortran Adventure

In 1970, I was a long-haired kid in a computer science class at Roosevelt University in Chicago, taught by the great Max Plager, who is still teaching math at Roosevelt. At first, we programmed in basic machine language, and I wrote my first program in Northwestern University's new library. It worked fine the first time, except for the fact that it loaded itself on top of Max's loader, causing the printer to go berserk for reasons too horrible to detail.

Max had us then write in assembler, and thus re-created the entire history of software, as we realized the key concept that we could use the computer, as did Grace Hopper, to enhance our productivity. Through Max, we learned the "DNA" of computer science, not "computer literacy" (whatever that is).

However, Max was stymied by the fact that the Fortran-II compiler in our small university data center did not work and could not be fixed, because IBM had abandoned support. He had us use an IBM 1620 at a service bureau for Fortran programming because of this problem.

Meanwhile, most of the faculty and students at the university went on strike when Nixon invaded Cambodia and four students were shot at Kent State by National Guardsmen. Max allowed those of us who joined the strike to submit programs in lieu of attending his class, but I received only a B in the class, in these days prior to grade inflation, since I did not do all the work.

Nonetheless, I was enthusiastic about the way in which Max taught us computer science. Shortly thereafter, I got a job in the university computer center and, after hours, I decided to see what was wrong with the Fortran-II compiler.

The compiler existed as a deck of 2,000 punched cards, and the operator inserted the punched cards for the source code after an initial loader phase. Then, within only 8,000 seven-bit (don't ask) bytes, 99 "phases" of the compiler would run to gradually parse, and change, the source, creating an intermediate language, a distant ancestor of .NET's Common Language Runtime (CLR).

In my analysis of the compiler's failure, I used John A. N. Lee's 1969 book, *The Anatomy of a Compiler*, as a guide.

One night, I triumphantly discovered the problem. The compiler had been altered by an IBM customer engineer who had been retained on an hourly basis, since IBM software support had been ended for this older platform. Thinking that the university's mainframe did not include optional hardware for multiplication and division, the customer engineer had inserted a subroutine to do multiplication and division. However, the compiler was running on a minimum amount of memory, and this subroutine overlaid needed instructions.

In this era, IBM would agree only to have a customer engineer show up in a white shirt and tie, and make a "best effort" to solve the problem.[5] In this case, the customer engineer did a credible job without seeing the real problem and without knowing the configuration of the machine. This was, in fact, a best effort.

Max had shown us that the machine included the optional hardware, and I simply removed the subroutine (working completely in machine language) and replaced its call by instructions to multiply and divide. The machine then compiled and ran several programs through to completion.

This ranks with my discovery of Visual Basic 3 as a true Eureka moment. Max nearly fell out of his chair when, at the next meeting of the university computer committee, I announced the fix. H. Chang Shih of the Physics department bought me a drink at Jimmy Wong's watering hole, which was then across the street from Roosevelt.

We used the Fortran compiler continually for teaching and support. Although it did not generate very fast code, it was a great way to solve problems quickly. For example, Fortran-II had a very complete Print statement with a format feature that supported both multiple lines and replacement of control sequences by data. This made it easy to elegantly format reports. In contrast, coding reports in assembler was very tedious.

Fortran and Algol were followed by a plethora of compilers, both famous and infamous, and initially in the tradition of Fortran. For example, early Cobol programs, like early Fortran programs, were primarily single main procedures with goto commands for flow control.

Cobol raised and then dashed some management expectations. An Air Force general was overheard to say, "Now that we have Cobol, can we get rid of all those beatnik programmers?" (In the early 1960s, "beatnik" meant "slacker.") But managers have continued to depend on programmers throughout the beat, hippie, Generation X, and slacker eras.

IBM introduced an ambitious programming language, Programming Language One (PL/I) in 1964, when it introduced its System/360 line of mainframes. This language owed much to Algol because it was fully block structured. However, PL/I's scale and scope exceeded the capabilities of its designers and compiler writers, and it wasn't until 1974 that truly useful compilers became available for PL/I.

---

5. This "best effort" approach has been replaced by the vow to solve the problem no matter what. The benefit is that, perhaps, more problems are solved. The downside is that many "solutions" are hacks.

Reacting perhaps to the overly ambitious goals of PL/I, a small group of programmers, centered around Bell Laboratories and Princeton University, and including Brian Kernighan and Dennis Ritchie, designed the C language in 1971. C was terribly important, but it was also rather dangerous.

C used Algol-like block structure but gave the programmer an assembler language level of control over the machine. For example, the machine address of a variable could be accessed using the same facilities as could be used for ordinary arithmetic. This feature was known as *aliasing*.

Because of aliasing, C was rather dangerous. Efficient but delicate and hard-to-maintain software could exploit machine peculiarities in undocumented ways. Indeed, C programmers (like the assembler language programmers who resisted Fortran in the 1950s) to this day speak of the added efficiencies they are able to derive by staying "close to the machine." (My suspicion is that close to the machine is warm and toasty in the winter, and nice and air-conditioned in the summer.)

Today, C is ever so slightly out-of-date, but it won't be completely out-of-date until another language manages to dislodge it. C predominates in system programming along with C++. However, C doesn't "do" objects, and for this reason, it doesn't provide the benefits of closer and more logical association of code and data. Its lack of safety means it's a dangerous choice for mission-critical and important management information systems (MIS) projects.[6]

C was the basis of many subsequent languages, including Java, Perl, and JavaScript, because of its very clean syntax. However, Algol and Algol's block structure were the real intellectual innovation, not C. Despite the fact that C is regarded with some awe, Brian Kernighan and Dennis Ritchie simply wanted a tool. For this reason, they based much of C on Algol and PL/I, while simplifying the design.

The Origins of Basic

Basic was invented in 1964. By the 1960s, compilers for high-level languages were in common use, although many programmers still preferred assembler, both for its speed and for its cachet (pardon my French). It was in 1964 that mathematics professor John Kemeny of Dartmouth developed the language and the compiler for what was called Beginner's All-Purpose Symbolic Instruction Code, which was similar to Fortran but intended for a much wider audience.

---

6. Of course, many C programmers have a variety of personal standards that prevent the choice of C from being as dangerous as it could be. The problem is that, in general, they don't have the organizational clout to enforce these standards over the complete system life cycle.

Both the Fortran and the Algol teams wanted to write compilers that would generate highly efficient and optimized code. Their motto was "you compile once, but you run many times." But Kemeny, and a separate group at Purdue University, noticed that this is not true for student programs, which compile many times and bomb out often.

Kemeny reasoned that a compiler for nonprofessionals should be fast and should accurately link runtime errors to source code. His compiler, and the Purdue University Fast Fortran Translator (PUFFT) system, used an "interpreter" language and an interpreter to change instructions on the fly to actual machine code at runtime.

Interpreters, as code that converts special codes to actual machine instructions every time the object code is run, are slower, by definition, than pure object code. But because the special codes can be directly tied to source lines, error reporting in interpreters can be highly accurate and understandable.

Just-In-Time Compilation

Just-In-Time, or JIT, compilation is sometimes confused with the older technique of interpretation in which the source program was converted to an intermediate form and then "executed" by the interpreter. The interpreter needed to translate the intermediate form each time an instruction was executed.

The similarity is that processing of the "object" code representation occurs after compilation. The difference is that JIT compilation, unlike interpretation, generates actual machine code for reuse. Interpreters produce machine code for immediate consumption each time an interpreted instruction is executed, and this magnifies the effect of any preexisting loops in the interpreted code. No such magnifying effect appears in JIT compilation.

The conventional wisdom is that interpretation is slow. Therefore, the JIT compilation used with .NET and Java creates a perception that such environments might run code more slowly.

However, the use of object-oriented programming (OOP), as you will see in this book, means that the "data" (the source code) and the procedures (the JIT compiler routines) are close together, and this avoids unnecessary sequential passes over large amounts of code. The result is that JIT compilation to .NET's CLR creates code that is often somewhat slower than raw, native COM applications, but those applications are not as flexible as .NET applications.

Earlier interpreters, because of the cost of storage, had to "pass over" source code and translate it entirely to the interpreted special codes. Then the interpreter needed to modify each special code into machine language repeatedly throughout the execution of the program, magnifying the effects of loops.

Suppose instead that the interpreter could save its work in the form of the compilation of special code to object code, on the fly. In a procedural language, this opens a can of worms, in which tables must be efficiently constructed and searched. OOP provides a straightforward association of code and working data.

OOP's tighter linkage of the compiler's instructions with its data (the source and interpreted code) means that both compilation and interpretation can be performed incrementally, or "just in time," and the output of the compilation in the form of binary machine code can be saved with specific instances of executable objects. This is because the data is, by definition, inside the object instance. For this reason, there is far less overhead in finding the data.

For example, the compiler that I present in this book stores all the information about a variable in an object. The procedure responsible for accessing a variable no longer confronts, on entry, a huge table of variables—by definition, more than it wants to know. This procedure does not need to search a table because it is presented with one handle to all the information about the variable, including its name, value, and type.

Of course, the compiler does have a table of the variables. However, other procedures are responsible for obtaining the variable using its name. It's true that the basics are the same,[7] but overall, in a well-designed OOP solution, there tends to be less rummaging around, because once the object is found, a rich set of data is linked to it.

Lexx and Yacc

In the late 1960s, a number of computer scientists noted that, because computer languages had to be strict and formally specified (unlike normal human languages), not only was the process of writing a specific compiler itself the development of an algorithm, it, in turn, could be algorithmically specified in a *compiler generator*. However, this idea strained the capacities of mainframes and the abilities of earlier programmers. Instead, two spin-offs from the overall effort became widely used. These were the lexx and yacc programs of the Unix operating system. lexx accepts a definition of the low-level syntax of the language, and yacc accepts a definition of its high-level syntax. Together, they generate C or C++ code to parse the language.

The lexx and yacc programs dominate good compiler design practice today. However, effective use of lexx and yacc requires knowledge of compiler internals, since these are "white box" tools.[8]

---

7. As you will see in Chapter 8, the Collection object provides a convenient hash-based search to map variable names to variable objects.

8. White box tools assume that users know basically what the tools are doing on the users' behalf.

Today, the Java and .NET "compile once, run anywhere" credo has created some innovation in compiler development because this portability creates demand for compilers. In addition, the increasing use of object-oriented development and programming has produced compilers of higher quality, since the tighter coupling of data and software means that the compiler developer no longer needs to build enormous tables for the entire source.

Basic Compilers

As I've mentioned, the Basic language was invented by a group at Dartmouth University in the 1960s. It initially targeted General Electric time-sharing machines, but a few years later, programmers of Digital Equipment Corporation (DEC) hardware (the progressively more powerful systems DEC PDP-8, DEC 10, and DEC 20) developed a number of time-shared Basic compilers.

Early Basic

In the early 1970s, in Menlo Park, California, a group of visionaries provided storefront access to inexpensive DEC computers in the form of The People's Computer Company, and they found Basic to be of broadest appeal. This might be why Bill Gates and Paul Allen chose Basic as the first high-level language for the first microcomputer, the MITS Altair.

Early Basic compilers were "hacks," because of the small amount of memory available to Basic compiler writers. Most followed the lead of the PUFFT and IBM Fortran-II compiler, because it saves memory to generate packed code that is executed by a software interpreter. As noted earlier, using an interpreter takes more time than running pure object code.

However, in the 1970s, compiler runtime developers discovered a technique for saving some time inside a commercial interpreter known as *threaded* code. With threaded code, each action of the interpreter takes responsibility for branching to the next action indirectly through a register.[9] This technique was invented for the Forth language developed by Calvin Moore and was adopted by some Basic developers.

Another issue in early Basic was the representation of the source code in memory for large programs. As you know, code contains characters that the compiler and computer do not need, including programmer comments and white space (blanks, tabs, and other nonprintable characters). While such excess

---

9. I encountered an elegant implementation of threaded code in a version of the SL/1 compiler's target machine, in use at Nortel Networks to provide a flexible range of private branch exchange systems. My own SL/1 compiler for a 24-bit (sic!) machine compiled to this environment.

characters were not a problem in toy and demo programs (like Print 'Hello world'), they made large programs for user solutions impossible to develop because the Basic compiler was not able to read the entire source.

As you crazed coders out there can imagine, there were workarounds for handling large programs, including using a disk to save part of the source code. But consider that waiting for even a modern form of virtual memory to catch up can be very irritating. Another approach was to reduce the usable symbols of the Basic source code to the smallest possible code. For example, if there were only 256 different identifiers—such as PAYRATE, GROSS, NET, and so on—in a Basic program, you could save a lot of space in the interpreted code by replacing the identifier with its position in a 256-position list. This index would take only 1 byte.

Basic in Two Kilobytes

One of the most brilliant examples of space saving was authored by Clive Sinclair (now *Sir* Clive Sinclair, so there) of the UK, in his Sinclair personal computer. This device included an implementation of Basic in only 2KB. Its physical design, with a two-dimensional pad style keyboard, was rather charming. It looked like a computer you might get in a box of cereal. Its power design was less charming. It was shipped to American customers with an adapter for American voltages. When I plugged in the machine, it started a small American fire. After the smoke cleared, however, I was able to bring this system up using a safer voltage adapter, and then write small-scale Basic programs. My total investment was about $150.

By the early 1980s, many desktop developers had already used various hacked Basic compilers to create quite a lot of business and other support for real users. IBM shipped a solid Basic, GW-Basic, with its very rugged IBM PC in 1981. Microsoft offered the QuickBasic compiler and interpretive runtime, which was used heavily on MS-DOS systems.

Visual Basic

During the 1980s, as desktops became powerful enough to support bitmap graphics, developers discovered the graphical user interface (GUI). At that time, there were two common ways of adding a GUI to a program. The most popular way was to spend a small amount of time on hacking. However, this created considerable inflexibility and unneeded complexity. The other way was to spend a lot of time on the careful design of an underlying reusable engine for the GUI. With luck, this would result in code that could be reused by different applications and perhaps plugged into different systems.[10]

The need to generate custom graphics engines was largely eliminated in the 1980s with the introduction of Microsoft Windows (the notable exception at the time being games, which demanded better access to the hardware than Windows could provide). Windows 3.1 provided considerable additional power in the form of forms and controls for display and entry of data—at a high and somewhat hidden price. To create the simplest command button, programmers in C and assembler had to write large amounts of repetitious code.

Perhaps for this reason, Alan Cooper developed and sold an engine for drawing forms and controls, known as the Ruby form engine, which was usable as a set of Application Programming Interfaces (APIs) from a variety of languages. He sold this product to Microsoft, who integrated Ruby with QuickBasic. In 1990, Microsoft announced the stunningly high-quality product, Visual Basic 1.

I like to code. But I do not like to code the same instructions repeatedly. Therefore, I was thrilled, when I adopted Visual Basic 3 in 1993, to be able to summon up simple forms and their controls, even with a language I considered clunky compared with C.

Why Use Visual Basic to Write a Compiler for Basic?

As you will learn in Chapter 4, the clunky, old-fashioned, and keyword-intensive surface syntax of Visual Basic—with its Ifs, Thens, End Ifs, and Do Whiles—hides a rather elegant subsurface. You will discover that it isn't necessary to hack compilers, even for languages with an older (or legacy) syntax.

C# has a classier syntax, fully based on C. So why do the code examples in this book use Visual Basic .NET rather than C#?

While nearly all C# developers know Visual Basic, not all Visual Basic developers have made the transition to C#. I wanted the widest possible audience to be able to read and modify the source. I wanted to write clear code, maintainable by readers with access to the code at the Apress Web site. I avoided anything like unmanaged code or void pointers. Therefore, there was no reason for using C# or C++.

---

10. My experience is that this type of approach drives hard-working managers crazy. One reason is that it's an investment not justified by most business cases. Also, in practical terms, it is a license for ambitious programmers to spend too much time on the interesting, fun, and possibly renumerative development of the GUI as a product they could, in some scenarios, resell.

From the standpoint of compiler writers, Visual Basic releases 1 through 4 were interpreters. The compiler generated symbols, which were translated into special codes. These codes were translated on the fly and "just in time" by a proprietary interpreter, written in C++, unique to Visual Basic.

Visual Basic 5 introduced the ability to compile Visual Basic to actual Pentium, Cyrix, or other machine instructions, and it officially avoided the need for the Visual Basic interpreter (while, as many Visual Basic programmers can confirm, not avoiding the need for shipping the Visual Basic runtime). However, although the Microsoft developers of the Visual Basic 5 compiler did a great job, actual results in the field were disappointing. At best, the CPU speed improved only by 20% when Visual Basic 5 code was shipped.

Visual Basic 6 was an incremental release, which perhaps lulled Visual Basic programmers into a false sense of job security. Then came .NET.

.NET, as you will learn in the next chapter, completely changed the ground rules. And while it actually removed some facilities, it added powerful interoperability and flexibility. This includes the ability to use Visual Basic .NET to write true compilers. In this book, I will make the business case for giving .NET systems the flexibility and ease of maintenance that compiler technology adds.

Summary

This chapter provided some historical background. At the bottom of the "dark chasm and abyss of time," we don't see C. This is because time did not start in January 1970 (nor will it end in 2034 when Unix runs out of bits to track time since January 1971).

Brian Kernighan, the author of the basic book on C, *The C Programming Language*, actually uses Visual Basic to teach introductory computer science to non-majors at Princeton. Brian reasons that America's "best and brightest," who will go on from Princeton to run the country in some cases, need to know about *real* programming, much of which is MIS programming. MIS programming can be intellectually challenging, but is thought to be For Dummies, with the result that the challenges aren't adequately met, or are met by Dummies, who are Dummies because of low self-esteem. Compiler design in Visual Basic is one excellent way to master Visual Basic for other challenges.

Algol, not C, was truly groundbreaking, while Fortran showed it was possible to develop a compiler that could outperform human programmers. Algol's key concept—that a list of statements can, in turn, be a statement—generated structured programming, which Visual Basic inherits.

I conclude that programming is a human adventure and only accidentally about programming languages and computers per se. Indeed, see Chapter 4's introductory material for an alarming if not gnomic quote from a hero computer scientist in this regard, which will help us to focus on the right stuff.

Challenge Exercise

Crazed coders like challenges. Using your existing programming experience, consider tackling the following challenge. Otherwise, return to it after reading Chapter 10.

Your end user's system is characterized by the need to enter and frequently change business rules such as:

```
if income>20000 And homeOwner then give credit with an APR of 8%
```

Justify developing the code for the business tier in Visual Basic, knowing that you will need to frequently change the rules. How much time will be spent in maintaining the code? What will happen if contradictory or conflicting rules exist in the code, such as the sample rule, plus the following:

```
if income>20000 and homeOwner then deny
```

Resources

If you are interested in learning more about compiler history, I suggest the following resources:

"Revised Report on the Algorithmic Language Algol 60," CACM, Vol. 6, No. 1, January 1963, page 1; by J.W. Backus et al. This article describes the Algol language. It is in the public domain and available at a number of sites on the Web. CACM is the professional journal, Communications of the Association for Computing Machinery.

"On the Cruelty of Really Teaching Computing Science," CACM, Vol. 32, No. 12, December 1989, page 1404; by Edsger W. Dijkstra. This article gives a good idea of Dijkstra's contention that computer science really is rather different and why it is hard.

"Go To Considered Harmful," CACM, Vol. 11, No. 8, March 1968, page 147; by Edsger W. Dijkstra. This article is a bit difficult to read but worthwhile. It ranks as Dijkstra's invention of structured programming, although he was too humble to say so.

The Anatomy of a Compiler, by John A. N. Lee (Wadsworth Publishing, now Thomson-Wadsworth, 1974). Still available through Amazon, this book is only of historical interest. It is the book I used as a reference for IBM Fortran.

"The History of Visual Basic and BASIC on the PC," by George Mack (2002), `http://dc37.dawsoncollege.qc.ca/compsci/gmack/info/VBHistory.htm`. This Web site describes the background of early Basic. Bill Gates will be the first to admit that he did not invent Basic.

The First Computers: Histories and Architectures, edited by Paul Rojas and Ulf Hashagen (MIT Press, 2000). This book describes the early discovery that software matters.

Programming Systems and Languages, by Saul Rosen (McGraw-Hill, 1967). This book describes early practice (so you can see that I didn't make stuff up!).

CHAPTER 2

A Brief Introduction to the .NET Framework

Every few years, the modern-day programmer must be willing to perform
a self-inflicted knowledge transplant to stay current with new technologies.
—*Andrew Troelsen*

All that is solid melts into air, all that is holy is profaned...
—*Karl Marx*

WHEN MICROSOFT BROUGHT OUT the .NET Framework, it was a radical shift and a wake-up call. This chapter describes the basics of this Framework.

According to people I've met at Microsoft, the Framework adds a computer science level to Visual Basic. However, this doesn't mean that you need to return to school. Instead, I recommend you refuel in flight. This book will help you to do so.

This chapter is an introduction to some of the issues that arise, in practice, when code (including, of course, code inside compilers) is reused and how .NET addresses some of the problems in reuse, including the infamous "DLL hell" problem. This chapter will explain how the Common Type Specification (CTS) and Common Language Specification (CLS) provide write-once, run anywhere interoperability for code in multiple languages. We'll also take an in-depth look at the Common Language Runtime (CLR) and identify the base class libraries that support a large .NET toolkit.

.NET binaries provide a layer of information that avoids DLL hell. At the end of this chapter, we'll briefly examine their structure to see how they accomplish this.

Code Reuse and DLLs

One thing that C and C++ have always had going for them is code libraries. However, libraries do have some problems. If there is a bug in the library that is later fixed, all of the programs that use the formerly buggy module must be recompiled. The solution for this problem is dynamic linking libraries, or DLLs.

Dynamism in programs is nothing new. It was a common way to fit a 1MB program into 640KB of memory. Consider an accounting package. You might separate the Accounts Receivable and Accounts Payable sections into their own dynamic libraries, but they remain a part of the program. When the program loads, it gets enough memory to load the largest dynamic library. Then when you want to run the Accounts Receivable functionality, it loads the Accounts Receivable library and uses it. When you need Accounts Payable, the program unloads the Account Receivable library and loads the Accounts Payable library. These dynamic libraries, however, are closely tied to the program, providing half of the solution.

The second half of the solution comes from device drivers. In the past, if you were lucky enough to have one of those RGB monitors that could do color graphics, and you wanted to write a program to use it, you either had to write directly to the hardware (not pretty) or write to a device driver.

Writing directly to the hardware isn't ugly because it is hard to do and requires knowledge. Rather, it is ugly because successful use by your software depends on a large number of preconditions, which have nothing to do with the needs of the user. It is very annoying for the end user to need to keep old hardware alive just to run needed packages.

Of course, just because your code worked with one company's device driver was no guarantee it would work with someone else's.[1] This led to more dynamic libraries, less for memory than to load the code that worked with the driver you specified.

Driver troubles began to be resolved with Windows, which introduced *virtual hardware*.[2] Rather than writing to the driver for the hardware, Windows allows the programmer to write a consistent interface and let the operating system handle writing to the hardware. This means that you need to write the code only once, and it will work with any monitor, printer, keyboard, and so on.

It wasn't long before this idea spread beyond hardware, and all kinds of DLLs were being written that provided some consistent interface for doing tasks. This made many tasks easier. Rather than becoming a data-access expert, you could use Open Database Connectivity (ODBC) or later, Active Data Objects (ADO). Learn a few basics of how to connect, how to request data, and how to update data, and you could access any ODBC-compliant database.

Of course, ODBC and ADO provide new complexities and new issues, and they do not always make your job easier. However, improvements in technology improve your programs, without the need to change code. If the ODBC driver is improved, then upgrading the driver makes your program work more efficiently. The database system isn't locked to old hardware and operating systems. On the

---

1. Nonprogramming computer users are often astonished by the need to acquire new drivers for new hardware. They are not amused by device driver conflicts, a consequence of the original (1980s) vintage design of PCs.

2. Nonprogramming computer users may be ROTFL (rolling on the floor laughing) because they still have problems with Windows drivers. However, they may fail to realize that driver problems are an inevitable consequence of the new stuff they have to play with. Newer software always tends to be more buggy, even though Plug and Play now works in the vast majority of cases.

other hand, accessing the new goodies does impose a converse requirement: the forced upgrade when the new feature requires a current operating system. On the whole and from a business perspective, however, this is much easier than operating museums of computing legacy arcana just to support users.

DLL Heaven and DLL Hell

There she stood in the doorway;
I heard the mission bell
And I was thinking to myself,
'This could be Heaven or this could be Hell'
—The Eagles, Hotel California

With the introduction of DLLs and all the derivatives (COM, COM+—the alphabet soup can be dizzying), programmers became more efficient. But most managers didn't notice, since the programmers were asked to do more work.[3]

No longer did programmers need to deal with the underlying plumbing. Microsoft continued to make their jobs easier by introducing technology like Microsoft Transaction Server (MTS) to handle transactional processing. Yes, life was good as long as a few rules were followed.

The 11 Commandments for DLLs

1. Thou shalt create an interface, which shall be a standard, which can be added to but not taken away from.

2. Thou shalt version thy DLL consistently.

3. Thou shalt maintain backward compatibility.

4. Thou shalt write installation routines correctly, so that older versions shant overwrite newer ones.

5. Thou shalt keep all internal functionality private and not expose it to the world.

6. Thou shalt create properties using GET/LET/SET rather than PUBLIC variables.

---

3. In my experience as a programmer, which stretches from the ancient, second-generation (1959) IBM mainframe 1401 to Web development in the dot.com mania, today's programmers work much harder than in the past. Offshore developers, in particular, work terribly hard. I worked with them in Fiji, and they shared a single room with a wheezing air conditioner. Despite the heat, they worked very hard without coffee or Internet breaks, because the alternative in Fiji is cutting sugarcane.

7. Thou shalt put error checking within all thy code and handle any errors thou can.

8. When thou encounters an error thou cannot handle, thou shall pass it up with correct and documented error codes.

9. Thou shalt not change thy error codes, though thou may add new ones.

10. Thou shalt generate a complete executable for the entire system, starting at day one of coding

11. Thou shalt play nicely with other DLLs.

As long as you follow the rules for DLLs, everything works, and you save vast amounts of programming resources. And following the rules isn't too hard, unless you happen to live in the real world of users, operating systems, and third-party controls. Then you could easily find yourself transported into DLL hell. Let's take a simple (and all too common) example.

You have a project that uses version 1.5 of a common third-party widget from the Acme Novelty Company. The widget is used a lot in your program, which is used consistently by the president of your company to keep her fingers on the pulse of the company.

Your company isn't a software company, and the president, like many other managers, is focused on her job of running a company. She neither needs nor wants to understand the minutiae of programming. However, she has enough technical know-how to be able to download and install software. One day, a peer recommends a demo program. He has the demo from when he installed it last year, so he gives it to her, and she installs it.

And that program, during the installation, installs version 1.3 of the widget your program relies on. Now it shouldn't have, because that violates one of the 11 commandments of DLLs. But it does. And the president doesn't notice anything wrong while she's exploring this new software package. In fact, she doesn't notice anything wrong until that afternoon, when she decides to run your program, to check the pulse of the company; in other words, to do her job. And she gets an error.

The egg hits the fan. She calls your tech support team because your software is broken. Time, energy, and resources go into finding the cause. And how do you explain that someone else broke your software? You sound like a weasel.

This brings us to .NET.

.NET—Beyond DLLs

One of the goals of .NET was getting rid of DLL hell. Another was making coding and program interaction easier. And thus was born the .NET Framework. To understand the Framework, you need to look at what it's made of, and that would be the four Cs: CTS, CLS, CLR, and class libraries.

In later chapters, you'll explore the Framework pieces in detail, because the QuickBasic compiler that we're going to build will use the four Cs. Here, you'll just get an introduction to how these parts work. However, we'll spend some time examining the CLR, because that will help you to understand the design decisions in our compiler.

The CTS

The CTS is the Common Type Specification. This defines all of the possible data types and constructs supported by the runtime environment. This means that a 32-bit integer is a 32-bit integer everywhere. Providing the definitions of the data types allows everyone to work together. Think of it as the metric scale for programming languages—a way to standardize.

The CTS is, unfortunately for Visual Basic programmers, based on the C language. In consequence, an Integer data type in Visual Basic .NET is a 32-bit integer in the range -2^{31} to $2^{31}-1$, not a 16-bit integer in the range -2^{15} to $2^{15}-1$.

Arrays in Visual Basic .NET can no longer start at any index other than zero. When you declare an array, such as strArray(5), you are specifying not the number of elements, but the upper bound of the array. strArray(5) declares six elements now numbered in .NET, at all times, from 0 through 5.

Strings in the CTS are updated differently than strings in Visual Basic 6. Visual Basic 6's runtime manages strings in their own region because, traditionally, Basic languages have treated the string as an independent data type and imposed no fixed limit on strings.

In .NET, Visual Basic strings are implemented using the .NET String object. In .NET, when the string is altered, the alteration makes a copy of the original string, throwing away the old string.

> **TIP** *In cases where you need to frequently alter the contents of a string, consider using the .NET* System.Text.Stringbuilder *object, which allows for more efficient modification.*

The CLS

The CLS is the Common Language Specification. This part of the framework defines what every language must implement to be a .NET language. It's a subset of the CTS, because not all of the types defined in the CTS are in the CLS (for example, Visual Basic .NET does not have the ability to declare an unsigned number). However, as long as the code you write sticks to the CLS-defined types, it will interact with code written in any other language without any problems.

The CLR

The CLR, or Common Language Runtime, is the heart of the .NET Framework. The CLR handles loading your code, managing variables and objects, and providing the interconnectivity between all .NET programs.

The CLR is structurally a simple virtual machine definable by an interpreter. The CLR, however, doesn't have the performance penalty of classic software interpreters, because on first execution the code is compiled, "just in time," to native code.

The confusing fact is that while you can and should think of the CLR as a traditional slow interpreter for a virtual machine, it actually converts to native code behind the scenes. Individual compilers act as if they were creating purely interpreted CLR code, but behind the scenes, JIT compilers tailor the instructions to the platform. In this way, the compiler does not need to be rewritten to generate code for a new or different machine.

> **NOTE** *In this book, you'll see two programs (the runtime of Chapter 3's product* integerCalc *and the testing runtime of the* quickBasicEngine *compiler itself) that show how to develop a virtual machine, similar to the CLR but much less efficient.*

The Stack and the Heap

In the abstract, the CLR supports a machine with a last-in, first-out (LIFO) stack and a heap. The stack contains *value objects*, which are referred to this way because they are fully described at any time by identifying their value. Value objects are typically numbers, and they take up fixed amounts of storage. The heap supports objects of variable size and shape, including strings and user objects. These objects are represented by pointers in the stack. Figure 2-1 shows the stack and the heap.

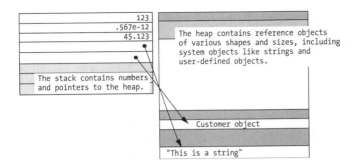

Figure 2-1. The CLR stack and heap

As you can see in Figure 2-1, the numbers are represented directly in the stack. Visual Basic strings, which can have widely varying lengths, are represented by pointers to the heap. Value objects can also be stored on the heap, using a process called *boxing*.

The heap is somewhat like your garage, before your significant other gets you to clean it up. The garage is where you put objects that don't fit neatly in the house. The major difference is that the objects in the heap are accessed more frequently than the foam plastic things that hold electronic equipment, out-of-date computers, out-of-date computer books, infant carriers for infants who are now anguished teens, and back issues of *National Geographic*.

Objects that use the heap are subject to a process known as *garbage collection*. Regularly, and at an interval not under your control (unless you force garbage collection by calling GC.Collect), the Framework sweeps through the heap and deletes objects that are no longer referenced by your program.

When You Might Need to Expose Dispose

There is one case where garbage collection is a serious problem. That's when you create an object that declares and creates references to objects that correspond to or tie up limited system resources, such as window handles, system objects, database connections, and so on. For these objects, you should implement the IDisposable interface and code a dispose method, which should call the Dispose methods of any objects it references and release any system resources used by the object.

Expose dispose only when necessary. If the object's variables in the General Declarations section are numbers and strings, dispose isn't necessary. You may wish to expose a dummy dispose in your class if you anticipate the addition of reference objects at a future date and you need to ensure that the object's users use dispose.

My own practice is anal, since I want to make sure, as far is possible, that the callers of my object dispose of instances. I expose dispose for all objects with state in the form of variables in the General Declarations section.

The alert reader may have a question here. If, as I said, a string is a reference object, then if a string appears in the General Declarations section, shouldn't this force the conscientious programmer to implement dispose? The answer is that the string object does not and will not itself create "open-ended" reference objects in the heap. The string will be in the heap, but it will never create any reference objects on its own. The string is a "closed" object, which, as a string, can be left on the stack for the garbage collector.

But a true reference object is permitted, now or after being modified, to create reference objects as part of its state. If you do not implement a dispose for a true reference object (or fail to call dispose when you're finished), runaway use of the heap is possible.

It might be the case that you know a reference object is very simple and safe, and you know that it does not create any further references. However, real experience in real development teaches you to also know that this situation might change.

The goal of a team standard dispose is to avoid open-ended situations that result when a more complex reference object is not destroyed by executing its own dispose, leaving it and any objects it declares (directly, or indirectly by creating other open-ended reference objects). The heap becomes cluttered with dead soldiers, which appear, to the CLR, as needed objects. If you do not implement a dispose, reference objects will clutter the heap until the system gets around to freeing their storage.

Portability

A major design objective of the CLR was to enable "write once, run anywhere." For example, you may want your software to run on the Web, on different servers, and even on different hardware platforms (and your manager may want this even more than you do). There are many cases where the cost to create software that runs on more than one box can't be justified.

However, software should be designed whenever possible to run on more than one box. This is natural in the university environment, for example, where faculty members do not want to submit to the rules of a centralized facility. In industry, we don't talk as much about this need, but the business reality may create it anyway. We don't control, for example, an upper management decision to change platforms or demand that the software run as a Web service.

The CLR deconstructs the idea that computing power takes a positive amount of extra thinking time, proportional to the power increment. If you follow the rules, and in a Microsoft turn of phrase "let go and let the CLR," the code will be transportable for free.

Of course, we've heard this before. There have been cases where the promise wasn't fulfilled. But in significant areas, as long as the platform supports the Framework (which happens to be free), transportability exists to a much higher degree than it did with COM.

Reliability

A second major design objective of the CLR was to make operations predictable and to avoid bugs based on creative abuse of data types. A classic example is using string data for a numeric operation and forcing overflow deliberately for a result that you "know" will occur. The problem arises when the overflow does not occur as planned when the software runs on a new machine or in a different environment.

For example, a poorly written program might read a text field from a SQL database and immediately try to do arithmetic on the field, creating a crash in the field. Or the programmer might add one to a number such as 32,767 (the maximum value of a Short integer) just to transfer control out of a deeply nested set of procedures.

Respect the CLR, for it encapsulates years of knowledge about how to create reliable software, on schedule. Lessons learned by Microsoft and incorporated by the developers of the CLR include the lesson of the stack, the lesson of typing, and the lesson of just-in-time.

The lesson of the stack is that for solving problems, a machine or paradigm with a stack is better than a machine or paradigm with a small number of general-purpose registers. This is because even simple problems can and should be broken down into simpler subsolutions. Not all managers see this, and this may be why there has been some resistance to stacks. The stack, despite its inefficiency (the admitted fact that it is a single bottleneck from the standpoint of multiple parallel threads) represents a problem that has been modularized.

The lesson of data typing is that sometimes your need in C for a void pointer (a pointer that points to untyped data) or in Visual Basic for a variant represents poor design. What you really need is code that, if it compiles, will probably work. If all your variables are of the precise type needed by the solution, you shorten the time between a clean compile and a correct result.

Class Libraries

The final component of the .NET Framework is the base class libraries. You can think of these as similar to the operating system DLLs prior to .NET, but they provide access to all of the basics that you need:

- Data access

- Security

- XML/SOAP

- File I/O

- Debugging

- Threading

- User interface

All of this comes together to create the .NET Framework and to change how your programs work. In VB.Classic, you might create an executable that uses the VB*.DLL to run or VC++ to create a stand-alone executable. In the .NET Framework, you create a binary file that sits and waits until you run it. It's the same binary file, regardless of whether it was written in Visual Basic .NET, C#, J#, Cobol .NET or Eiffel .NET. And although they may have a DLL or an EXE extension, they look nothing like the pre-.NET files of the same type. Instead, they contain a quiet revolution. In the next section, you'll see what I mean by this.

Inside a .NET Binary

Open a .NET binary file, and you won't find a fortune, but you will find `Microsoft Intermediate Language (MSIL)`. MSIL is kind of like a tokenized version of your code that looks like assembler, but it has a very different purpose.

This binary file, called an *assembly*, contains `MSIL` code and metadata that describes the characteristics of all the types and interfaces within the assembly. When you want to use the assembly in your own programming, this interface information is read and processed, and then handed up to the calling program. Then when the assembly actually needs to be run, the `CLR` takes the `MSIL` and creates a compiled program specific to that operating platform. That means that a .NET assembly can run, without programming changes, on any .NET platform that supports the four *C*s.

Performance Penalties in .NET

One objection Visual Basic 6 and COM programmers in general have about .NET is, "All this loose talk about storing type information in assemblies *means* that things will run slower, and a performance penalty will be incurred."

The quick response is that .NET does the extra work once and not continuously. Its design lends itself to "just-in-time" processes. Missing is the redundant and behind-the-scenes work traditional interpreters (including the Visual Basic 6 interpreter) had to do continuously while an application program was running.

There is a performance penalty in both .NET and the Java environment, although it is not nearly as great as that of traditional interpretation. In return, we get code that can run as a Web service (allowing authorized remote users and remote software to use code on any platform). Additionally, DLL hell, as we know it, goes away.

Summary

This chapter explained how modular libraries of code were necessary for reusable code, but also created problems. Those problems motivated, and indeed explain, the features of the .NET Framework. My experience as a programmer and mentor is that the deepest appreciation of a feature comes through awareness of its absence.

As Andrew Troelsen implies, the Framework is a major change, which devalues deep hacker knowledge of the specifics of things like variants and the details of the Visual Basic 6 runtime. The Framework is actually an artifact of computer science. It uses tested but advanced techniques to enable us to write once, run anywhere.

As Marx (Karl, not Groucho) saw, we make progress by means of "creative destruction," and this is why we can't get comfortable with the deficiencies of Visual Basic 6. Marx said, "All that is solid melts into air," which means that job you had in COM has gone with the wind.

My advice, harsh as it may seem, is this: suck it up. Learning new stuff is a great way to stay young.

We're now ready, in Chapter 3, to address another computer science artifact: a simple front-end compiler, as a flyover of terrain we must walk over, starting in Chapter 4.

Challenge Exercise

What are the 11 commandments for DLLs? Can you suggest any additional commandments?

Resources

The following are some resources for more in-depth information about the Framework.

"Common Type System," *.NET Framework Developer's Guide,* `http://msdn.microsoft.com/library/en-us/cpguide/html/cpconthecommontypesystem.asp`. This is the main CTS documentation.

"What Is the Common Language Specification?" *.NET Framework Developer's Guide,* `http://msdn.microsoft.com/library/en-us/cpguide/html/cpconwhatiscommonlanguagespecification.asp`. This is the main CLS documentation.

Visual Basic .NET and the .NET Platform: An Advanced Guide, by Andrew Troelsen (Apress, 2001). This book gives a good overview of the .NET platform as it relates to Visual Basic .NET. Consider reading it and working through Andrew's code.

CHAPTER 3

A Compiler Flyover

For insofar as we understand, we can want nothing except what is necessary,
nor absolutely be satisfied with anything except what is true.
—Baruch Spinoza, Ethics, Of Human Freedom

BEFORE I VISIT A NEW TOWN on business, I often use Microsoft Flight Simulator to buzz the city to get a general idea of the lay of the land. This chapter will constitute a "flyover" of compiler theory and the hands-on application of the theory.

You will learn about the phases of a compiler and the three formal approaches used by compiler developers to complete those phases: regular expressions, Backus-Naur Form, and Reverse Polish Notation with stacks. To "keep it real," you will see how these approaches are applied in working code, the integerCalc application. Understanding integerCalc is an excellent preparation for understanding the more complex quickBasicEngine described in Chapters 5 through 8.

The Phases of a Compiler

It is generally agreed that a typical compiler for a standard, procedural language like Basic should do its work in three phases:

- **Scanning:** Divide the source code into tokens above the level of a character but below the level of statements and expressions.

- **Parsing:** Use the tokens developed in the first phase to parse identifiers, expressions, statements, methods, and so on. This phase should create either object code or an intermediate language.

- **Object code optimization:** A commercial-grade compiler (as opposed to a student or free compiler) should optimize the object code or intermediate language by removing common constructs and making safe rearrangements of code to reduce the code size or improve its performance.

These three compiler phases are conceptual. Early compilers were often constructed of separate programs, each of which executed a separate pass. In these passes, the compiler would read the entire source text to create a table or file of tokens. Then the compiler would read the token file or table and parse the tokens to generate object code.

Although the `quickBasicEngine` compiler we will build in later chapters uses the serial approach, it is not necessarily the best approach. For a production-quality compiler, in place of each pass, you can use object-oriented design to fully encapsulate the result of any phase.

Our goal, in writing a compiler, is not to pass over the source code for the sake of it. Instead, the phase one goal can be an object, a "scanner server," which keeps track of its current state and can be called to get the next token. The state of the scanner server can be an input file and a position in the input file.

However, for now, you can think of each phase as reading a large file. In the scanning phase, this is raw source code (in some instances, preprocessed, perhaps by the C++ preprocessor or the more limited pound-sign statements found in Visual Basic). In the parsing phase, this is a token file. In the optimization phase, this is a file of object code.

As a final phase, many compilers (such as Visual Basic releases 1 through 6) include an interpreter, which executes the compiled code in an intermediate form. Although interpreters can be slow, their interactive nature and ability to modify code and values on the fly make them useful for quick results and offer easy debugging.

> **NOTE** *The .NET CLR is not an interpreter. The intermediate code produced by .NET compilers is further compiled into native code, as noted in Chapter 2, by a separate step called JIT compilation.*

Three Theories, and Keeping It Real

In order to understand how a simple compiler is constructed, we need to turn to three theories and three formal notations: regular expressions, Backus-Naur Form, and Reverse Polish Notation.

- Regular expressions are associated with phase one of a compiler: the scanning (lexical analysis) of source code.

- Backus-Naur Form (BNF) is associated with parsing and the initial object code creation.

- Reverse Polish Notation (RPN) helps with a compiler's phase three, creating, without making hardware, a computer on which to run your code.

To keep it real, let's take a look at a very small compiler, integerCalc, which uses the theories in code to do simple integer calculations. The source code and object code for integerCalc are available from the Downloads section of the Apress Web site (http://www.apress.com). You will find the code in the egnsf/apress/integerCalc folder.

Open integerCalc/bin/integerCalc.exe and run it. Type a math expression, calculating with integers only, and click the Evaluate button to see its calculated value. Your screen will look something like Figure 3-1.

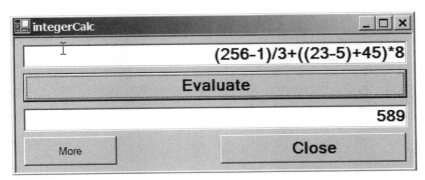

Figure 3-1. The integerCalc application is a simple compiler for integer expressions.

> **NOTE** *If you check* integerCalc's *work with your Windows calculator, you will find that it works with integers only. For the expression shown in Figure 3-1, your Windows calculator would return 36.8235....*

The source code of this application, in integerCalc/form1.VB and related files, uses lexical analysis with regular expressions, parsing based on BNF specifications, and an RPN interpreter. To understand how it works, read the code along with the rest of this chapter.

Lexical Analysis with Regular Expressions

Both phase one and phase two of a classic compiler do essentially the same thing—parsing. However, the parsing of raw character data is significantly different from the parsing of higher-level constructs, in much the same way as the spelling checker and grammar checker are different levels in Microsoft Word.

In Word, many users spell-check their documents. A more advanced check is done with the grammar checker, which looks for common blunders in putting words together, such as dangling constructs, passive voice, and run-on sentences. The grammar checker must use the spell checker's ability to form individual words.

Job one in a good compiler, or grammar checker for that matter, is *lexical analysis*. The input of lexical analysis consists of the raw stream of characters, including newline characters. The output consists of a stream of tokens. Each token is a small data structure, indicating the start, length, end, type, and value of a meaningful "word" in the text or programming language.

Consider, for example, the Visual Basic statements in Figure 3-2, over which I have placed column numbers.

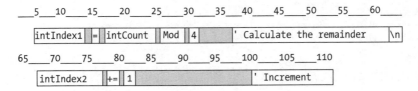

Figure 3-2. Scanning, also known as lexical analysis

This code can be tokenized by a lexical analyzer. Let's go through some of it to see how this works.

- `intIndex1` is an identifier. It starts at column 5 and is nine characters long.

- One blank white space character starts at column 14. (White space is actually shaded as gray space.)[1]

- One operator (the equal sign) starts at column 15.

- One blank white space character starts at column 16.

- `intCount` is an identifier starting at column 17 for a length of eight characters.

- From the point of view of lexical analysis, `Mod` is an identifier (that later will be classified by the parser as an operator). It starts at column 26 and is three characters.

- One blank white space character starts at column 29.

- A number starts and ends at column 30.

---

1. *White space* is a C language word that refers to the characters from 0 to blank (ASCII 32).

- Six blank white space characters start at column 31.

- A comment starts at column 37 and is 25 characters in length.

- On Windows systems, a newline starts at 62 and is two characters long (it is represented as \n).[2]

- Four blank white space characters start at column 64.

- intIndex2 is an identifier starting at column 68 and is nine characters long.

You can watch the integerCalc application tokenize its source code by running integerCalc.exe and clicking its More button to see an additional display, as shown in Figure 3-3. Enter an expression and click Evaluate to scan, parse, and evaluate the expression. The expanded display identifies (by type, start index, and length) the position of each token in the source code on its left side.

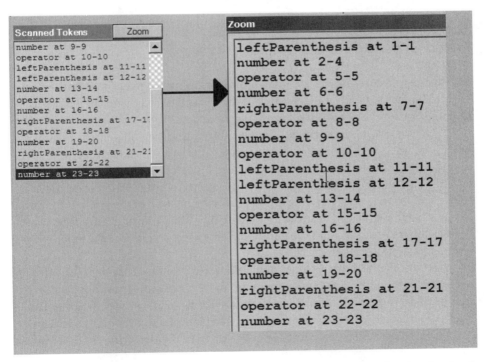

Figure 3-3. The More display of integerCalc shows how the expression is tokenized.

---

2. Windows newlines consist of the carriage return (hex D) followed by a newline (hex A). On the Internet, this would be a single newline character.

Lexical Analyzer Construction

A lexical analyzer can be built in three ways:

- Brute-force coding

- Using regular expressions

- Using a lexical analyzer generator

Before deciding to use brute-force coding (as is used in integerCalc), it is important to be very clear on what you want to accomplish! In integerCalc, I wanted to partition the source code into mutually exclusive tokens and identify each token's start index, length, and type.

You can use regular expressions to specify the low-level syntax of your language and as a basis for writing brute-force code. Therefore, let's start with regular expressions. You may have already played with them, since Microsoft supplies a regular expression object (Regex) in the .NET Framework.

Components of Regular Expressions

Regular expressions are not so much a programming language as a mathematical and logical notation. In fact, this notation was devised by mathematicians and logicians before computers were in general use.

As a programming language, regular expressions are deficient, as I think you'll see. For one thing, they look like explosions in a gnome factory; some regular expressions can look like messages from foul trolls from the Dark Ages. They can be difficult for programmers to debug and to maintain. However, they are invaluable for the understanding and formal specification of the goals of the code.[3]

A regular expression is a rule for specifying a simple formal language, and it defines the set of strings that are part of the language. It consists of a series of data characters and metacharacters.

Most ordinary characters are data characters, and their appearance in the regular expression means "at this location, these characters must appear." A regular expression that contains no metacharacters whatsoever specifies that the language defined consists of one string. For example, the regular expression Authors press specifies the language consisting of only the string "Authors press."

---

3. Don't inflict regular expressions on end users, but keep them handy for a fully precise specification, and use them in code when you are confident that your maintenance programmers will be comfortable with their use.

The power of regular expressions lies in metacharacters, a rather large collection of special characters such as the asterisk, plus sign, and slash. (Don't blame the gnomes of Unix for the use of a large number of metacharacters; mathematicians used these to save space on blackboards.)

The asterisk specifies a repetition of a string or subexpression zero, one, or more times.[4] For example, a* (lowercase *a*, asterisk) specifies that "the valid strings in my language consist of zero, one, or more copies of the letter *a*." Using the asterisk provides the capability of specifying languages with an infinite number of symbols. The regular expression (Author's press)* represents the set of strings "" (the null string), "Author's press," "Author's pressAuthor's press," and so on. This set consists of an empty (null) string, because the asterisk specifies *zero* or more. The plus sign in a regular expression specifies one or more repetitions.

Why Worry About Null Strings?

The null string is mystery meat. There is only one null string, and it contains no characters. In business, it seems useless, and it's one of those marvelous mathematical constructions that gives geeks a bad name. But it is useful for the same reason that zero is handy.

Zero is handy in business when you are broke; the null string is useful in business when you have nothing constructive to say. Zero was, in fact, introduced from Arab countries into Europe at that point where European merchants needed to borrow capital for long voyages of trade, conquest, and discovery. They needed zero and negative numbers to track the inevitable losses.

A compiler should be able to compile null strings and even null programs.

Any metacharacter, including the asterisk, can be preceded by a backslash *escape* character, which changes the metacharacter into an ordinary character. For example, * represents the language consisting of a single asterisk, and ** represents zero, one, or more asterisks. This latter regular expression should use parentheses for clarity: (*)*.

---

4. You have seen a form of this in file identifiers such as a*.txt, which defines a "language" consisting of every file beginning with the letter *a* and ending with the extension .txt. However, MS-DOS never really supported regular expressions, aside from a limited form apparently based on a misunderstanding of the Unix grep command.

Regular expressions have a number of limitations. Without extensions, they are unable to parse even balanced parentheses properly, and they cannot completely parse most real programming languages. Parsing based on BNF is needed for full-scale compiling of real languages.

Regular Expression Tools

There are many more things to learn about regular expressions, and complete documentation is available from your Visual Basic .NET CD-ROMs. At this point, however, you can get started learning about regular expressions using the relab tool. The code for relab is available from the Downloads section of the Apress Web site (http://www.apress.com), in the egnsf/relab/bin folder.

Open relab/bin/relab.exe and run it to see the screen shown in Figure 3-4.

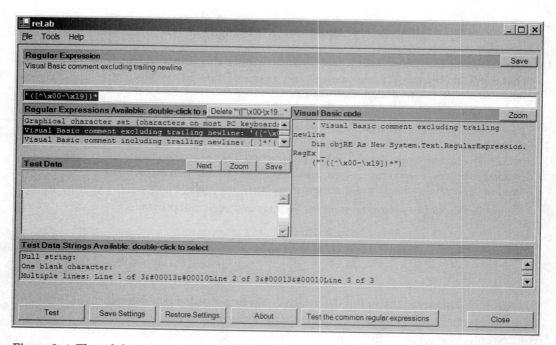

Figure 3-4. The relab.exe program provides a tool for evaluating a set of prewritten regular expressions, entering your own regular expressions, and converting them to Visual Basic declarations.

This tool provides several canned regular expressions for your use; it documents the most popular symbols; it allows you to create, document, and save America's Funniest Regular Expressions; and it can convert regular expressions with special characters (such as newlines) into readable Visual Basic expressions. Most important, it allows you to test regular expressions, which prevents bugs in the code where you use them.

Another tool in the source code is located in egnsf\utilities\bin\utilities.dll. This DLL is a collection of shared, stateless utilities for common tasks. The utilities.commonRegularExpressions file provides a series of regular expressions as strings, which you can use to drive the Regex object.

A Sample Regular Expression

For an example of a regular expression, take a look at the code in integerCalc (integerCalc/form1.VB). Find the private function named scanExpression, in the Scanner region.

Although I did not use the Regex object, I was thinking hard about the following regular expression in writing the code of scanExpression:

\+|\-|*|\/|\(|\)|[0-9]+

Note the following about this regular expression:

- The vertical bar separates alternative possibilities.

- Each operator is preceded by an escape backslash to avoid treating it as a metacharacter.

- Square brackets in regular expressions surround character *sets*. These represent any one of an alternative set of characters. They can be listed by brute force (for example, [abc] specifies the possible appearance of *a*, *b*, or *c*) or as ranges separated by dashes (as in the example, [0-9]).

The regular expression is confusing—certainly more so than well-written code. However, it specifies precisely what is parsed, whereas code specifies nothing but unverified behavior. While your users won't understand the regular expression, it can form a basis for a discussion of what is expected.

> **NOTE** *My experimentation has found that code is somewhat faster than using the* Regex *object provided with Visual Studio .NET, but your mileage may differ.*

Parsing and BNF

Parsing takes the chunks produced by the lexical analyzer, which you can consider to be individual words of your language, and builds sentences and paragraphs.

Parsing is usually based on the representation of the language in BNF. The BNF of a language is a series of productions, of the form `nonterminal := grammarSymbols`. In each production, `nonterminal` is normally a single word that identifies a grammar category, such as "noun" in a grammar for English or "statement" in a grammar for Visual Basic.

Grammar Categories

There are two types of grammar categories: *nonterminals* and *terminals*. Nonterminals are like sentences in the grammar for English, because a grammar for English must provide productions that explain what a sentence is (such as *subject verb object*.) Terminals need no further explanation, and they are detected not by the parser, but by the lexical analyzer. In English, they would be words. In Visual Basic, they would be identifiers or numbers.

In a massively oversimplified grammar for English, we might have the following productions:

```
sentence := noun verb
sentence := noun verb noun
noun := John
noun := Mary
verb := likes
verb := sees
```

In this grammar, the nonterminals are sentence, noun, and verb. The terminals are John, Mary, likes, and sees. The power of BNF is that this oversimplified grammar for a Dick-and-Jane level of English nonetheless allows us to parse a number of different sentences, such as "John sees" and "Mary likes John."

In a grammar for Visual Basic, the nonterminal statement might look like this.

```
statement := assignmentStatement
assignmentStatement := lValue = expression
```

Note that lValue is either a simple variable or a reference to an array in Visual Basic. I call it an lValue as shorthand for location value. This is because in Visual Basic, the left side of an assignment must refer to a storage location.

BNF Tools

Unlike for regular expressions, no object is shipped with .NET to transform the BNF to code or interpret the BNF. However, such software exists for a variety of platforms. The oldest example is the Unix program yacc. The problem with these tools is that their effective use demands that you have written some parser code by hand to get a feel for its complexities.

Yacc: Not Another Compiler-Compiler

Yacc stands for Yet Another Compiler-Compiler. This title is both apologetic and inaccurate. At the time yacc was written, a number of researchers had written programs to create compilers from their language specification.

The name apologizes for reinventing the wheel, but in fact, yacc is not a compiler generator; it is just a parser generator. It does not address either lexical analysis or code generation. Calling yacc "yet another compiler-compiler" is lamentable and like a caveman calling a wheel "yet another Ford Fairlane."

Nonetheless, as is the case with many Unix commands, the gnomic name yacc stuck.

Many Visual Basic .NET authors encourage you to create .vb files with a simple text editor outside the GUI to get a feel for the way in which forms and classes are constructed. Similarly, I recommend that you write a parser that implements the BNF to understand how to construct a BNF for a language.

BNF Design

Take another look at the source code in form1.VB for integerCalc, in the Parser region. The parser is a series of recognizers for grammar categories of a simple math grammar. Here is that complete grammar:

```
expression := addFactor [ expressionRHS ]
expressionRHS = addOp addFactor [ expressionRHS ]
addOp := +|-
addFactor = term [addFactorRHS]
addFactorRHS = mulOp term [ addFactorRHS ]
mulOp := *|/
term := INTEGER | ( expression )
```

Note the following about this grammar:

- Unlike parentheses, which are terminals and correspond to the appearance of parentheses in the source text, square brackets in BNF mean that the bracketed grammar symbols are optional.

- An informal regular expression notation is used to explain nonterminals; see the addOp and mulOp definitions. This is because all regular expressions can be translated to BNF (but not the other way around).

- In typical BNF, a name in uppercase represents a self-explanatory terminal, which, being self-explanatory, does not need to be further defined, such as INTEGER in the example. The lexical analyzer has already isolated tokens.

The first line declares our goal, which is to parse an expression, such as 1+2–3*4.

```
expression := addFactor [ expressionRHS ]
```

It divides the expression in this example between 1 (the addFactor) and the right side (the expressionRHS), which is +2–3*4.

An addFactor is anything that can be a part of an addition operation. The expressionRHS is anything that starts with a plus or a minus sign and appears on the right-hand side (RHS) of an expression.

Now consider this BNF line:

```
addFactor = term [addFactorRHS]
```

The brackets mean that an add factor can be, but does not have to be, terminated by an "add factor right-hand side." But let's set that aside for now, because it looks like 1 does not have a right-hand side (the plus sign after 1 starts an expressionRHS).

And, if you look at the BNF rule that defines term, you can see that a term is an integer or an expression in parentheses.

```
term := INTEGER | ( expression )
```

1 is an integer, therefore, we have a term, which is also (going back up the tree) an add factor.

Let's return to the top of the BNF. Since we have found an integer, which is a term and which is a full-bodied addFactor, we can move to the right in the expression.

Is the string "+2–3*4" an expressionRHS? It does begin with an addOp, because a plus sign is an addOp (see the rule addOp := +|-). The addOp seems to be followed by an addFactor, the number 2. Therefore, it looks like it starts with the expressionRHS +2.

We then see another call for an optional expressionRHS in brackets inside the rule for expressionRHS, which means that any expressionRHS can embed one or more smaller expressionRHS instances at their end.

So, we look for the addOp, which must start any expressionRHS according to our rules, and find a minus sign. We find in the definition for addOp that a minus sign, like a plus sign, is considered an addition operation.[5] Then we look for the smallest add factor and find the number 3.

However, take a look at the definition of addFactor. In the expression, 3 is not followed by a plus sign or minus sign; it is followed by an asterisk. In the definition of an addFactor, a term (such as the integer 3) may be followed by a different type of RHS construct. This is the addFactorRHS, the right side of an add factor, which may start with a multiplication or division symbol (see the rule mulOp := *|/). Since 3 is followed by an asterisk and the integer 4, the 4 constitutes an addFactorRHS, and 3*4 is the addFactor that follows the plus sign.

In applying the BNF, we are in effect making a tree of strings with longer and more comprehensive strings at the top, and smaller and less comprehensive strings at the bottom. Figure 3-5 illustrates this tree of strings.

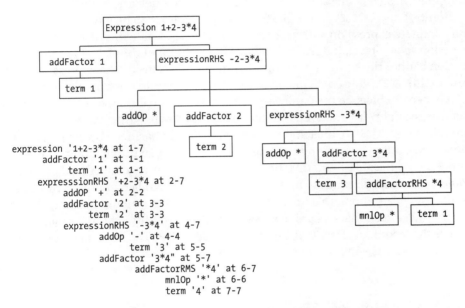

Figure 3-5. The tree and the outline representation of the parse of 1+2–3*4

Figure 3-5 also shows that the tree can be alternatively represented in outline form. This outline view of integer expressions is provided when you click the More button on the integerCalc screen, in the Parse Outline box, and this box can be zoomed (see Figure 3-6, later in this chapter).

The application of BNF described here may seem a little imprecise. This is because BNF, in general, does not show you how to write code. The BNF must be

---

5. It makes sense, when you think about it, to treat subtraction as syntactically like addition. As you know, in common programming languages, subtraction and addition have the same precedence and are evaluated left to right.

designed with care. The problem is that more than one BNF specification for a language can be valid. Some BNFs make it easy to parse; other mathematically valid BNFs create parsers with loops and ambiguity.

The ideal approach is to find a BNF specification for a language you would like to convert to CLR code. If you must design a BNF specification, it is wise to keep it simple. Try to find nonterminals that start with a small number of possible symbols, as do both expressionRHS and addFactorRHS in the example shown here. Find nonterminals that reduce to a single, smaller nonterminal, with an optional trailer, such as expression and factor.

Another key concept in the BNF is the way in which we support parentheses. It does leave one hole in the BNF considered as a design for coding, which we do need to address. Parentheses, fortunately, are parsed at only one point. To support nested expressions such as ((1+1)*3)/4, we declare, in the last production term := INTEGER | (expression), that a term can be either an integer or a complete expression surrounded in parentheses. While this nicely plugs in recursion to any level, it does have a flaw: the right parenthesis inside the production cannot be confused with the right parenthesis inside the expression. In term := INTEGER | (expression), expression can contain right parentheses.

We need to balance the parentheses to the left of the expression. We handle this with straightforward code (see the procedure findRightParenthesis). For example, in ((2+1)*3)–5, the leftmost parenthesis is not balanced by the first right parenthesis, but by the second right parenthesis. Now, in a production compiler it may not be feasible to do this, because it would involve a lookahead, which would cause multiple reads to input code. This can be handled, however, by using a buffer or cache, and in this example, this consideration is not important.

So, you've seen that designing a usable BNF can be a little bit tricky, but you can use the technique described here to avoid headaches. The key is to write some sample parsers, as you'll see in the next section.

Transformation of BNF to Code

In order to make the code as readable as possible, we assign a private method, returning True or False, to each nonterminal.

These methods are provided with four parameters: the current index (not in the raw source code, of course, but to our table of scanned tokens), the table of tokens, the data structure (usrRPN) for the output object code, and an end index. The end index is normally the number of tokens in the source code, but, in this case, will be the position of a right parenthesis when we are parsing a term surrounded by parentheses.

Extending Scanning and Parsing to Threads

Because of the simplicity of our requirements, the table of scanned tokens is a simple, static data structure, not in the Visual Basic sense of being in static memory, but in the sense that we know, at parse time, that this structure is complete.

For a larger project, consider making both the index to scanned source and scanned tokens properties of an object that hides the details of how tokens are retrieved. This object may very well be "lazy," using the scanner logic described here not in a loop, but one token at a time. Such an object can be used with the .NET threading model to run the scanner and the parser side by side, with the parser chasing the scanner in its own, separate thread.

This is very cool, but it's overkill for simple languages, including the language of integerCalc, the example used in this chapter. Solid design that avoids coolness forms a basis for extension to coolness.

The mission of each nonterminal recognizer is to move left to right through tokens, trying to parse lower-level nonterminals, reporting True on success and False on failure. By design, we always expect the intIndex parameter of each recognizer to leave intIndex one token beyond the last token of the source code that corresponds to the nonterminal.

Take a look at the simple expression method:

```
Private Function expression(ByRef intIndex As Integer, _
                    ByRef usrScanned() As TYPscanned, _
                    ByRef usrRPN() As TYPrpn, _
                    ByVal intEndIndex As Integer) As Boolean
    If Not addFactor(intIndex, usrScanned, usrRPN, intEndIndex) Then Return(False)
    expressionRHS(intIndex, usrScanned, usrRPN, intEndIndex)
    Return(True)
End Function
```

Since an expression must start with an addFactor, if expression fails to parse an addFactor in its first step, it returns False. But it then can call expressionRHS, which returns a Boolean value, as a subroutine and ignore the result. As you can see in the BNF rule for this procedure, we do not care if the RHS expression fails to appear; it is "gravy."

Suppose the expression in this example is passed something simple like 1+1. intIndex is 1; usrScanned contains the three tokens 1, plus sign, and 1; usrRPN is empty; and `intEndIndex` is 4. The first line of code checks for an `addFactor` at `intIndex` (at 1) and increments `intIndex` past the largest `addFactor` it finds at index 1, which is the number 1. It cannot go any further because an `addFactor` is either a term or a term followed by an `addFactorRHS`, which starts with a multiplication operator, and a multiplication operator is not found. Therefore, `addFactor` returns to the second line, which calls `expressionRHS`. This is successful at finding the expression RHS +1, and as a result, it increments `intIndex` past the end of the expression RHS, setting it to 4, the end of the expression.

Two lines of code do all this work (take a look at the source), because they both call routines that call other routines in a rather deep nest.

An obvious question at this point would be, "Well, there might not be an `expressionRHS` after the `addFactor`, but what if there is garbage and line noise?" Take a look in the source, above the `expression` method, and at the method `parseExpression`. It contains a check of the index (named `intIndex1` here) passed by reference among the compiler procedures when the top-level recognizer `expression` claims to be done. We report an error if that index is less than the length (token count) of the source code.

Read the remaining source code to confirm that this code works. Also, note the support routines, not only `findRightParenthesis`, described already, but also `checkToken` and `genCode`.

`checkToken` is our workhorse interface to the scanner data structure. It is overloaded because it has two jobs. The first is to check for any integer and return its value by reference to the caller, and the second is to check for a specified string operator or a string parenthesis. `checkToken` enforces an important rule, where a grammar category, like the expression, is something capable of appearing on the left side of an expression:

- On recognition of a grammar category, the parse index must always point one token past the last token corresponding to the grammar category.

This is because a grammar category always ends with some specific token. Once `checkToken` has confirmed that the expected token (any integer, a specified operator, or a parenthesis) occurs at the current position of `usrScanned` as indexed by `intIndex`, it can increment `intIndex`. This enforces the general rule.

In the much larger parser for the `quickBasicEngine` compiler we will build in later chapters, this rule takes on added importance, because we want to report precisely error and other information that pinpoints offending, or merely interesting, source code.

Therefore, here and in `quickBasicEngine`, a single interface is always used to the scanner data structure, and all code makes a blood oath never to look at the scanner data structure without going through `checkToken`.

Enforcing the Rules

Rules about access are easy to follow for a single programmer responsible for an entire compiler. They are harder to enforce on a team. And a common fact of life in programming is the programmer, working on deadline, who uses her "own" code to access a data structure in her "own" way, causing her "own" bugs.

Unfortunately, the technical leaders most familiar with the damage that this can cause are most often soft-spoken philosopher kings, who don't want to lecture the team on checkToken-style routines that are supposed to be used to access their associated data structure.

But as we will see in the next chapter, use of object-oriented design makes it much easier to naturally enforce these types of rules.

Finally, genCode generates the code. For now, think of it as a black box, because understanding genCode requires us to move on to our third and final theory, in the next section.

But first take a break from slogging through the theory and run integerCalc again. Click More and evaluate a complex expression. Look at the list box in the middle of Figure 3-6. It presents the parser results as the list of nonterminals parsed, which, as shown earlier in Figure 3-5, is just another way of representing a tree.

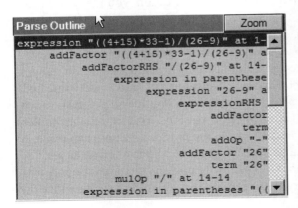

Figure 3-6. The list box shows the nonterminals as a nested outline, because unlike scanning (which scans for nonoverlapping tokens), parsing looks for nonterminals and terminals that nest and overlap each other.

The list box is an indented outline because, unlike the tokens produced by the scanner, the grammar symbols nest. Everything in our simple language is an expression. Expressions consist of addOp, addFactor, expressionRHS, and other elements. Therefore, a tree-like display is best.

Interpreters and RPN

If we were compiling for a chip in the embedded systems world, or for the Reflection object and the CLR, we would be finished. However, for later chapters, we need to understand some of the ideas behind the CLR and software emulation and interpretation of code.

Since the CLR is not a classic interpreter, but rather a large set of object-oriented JIT compilers, it is not slow. The CLR is independent of underlying hardware, and it meets its goal of write once, run anywhere. Reverse Polish Notation (RPN) underlies many of the ideas implemented in the CLR.

RPN Construction

Most logicians and mathematicians use, instinctively, the language that is compiled by integerCalc, where operations appear between operands. However, in Poland before World War II (a period in which that country enjoyed brief freedom from Russians and Germans, and flourished as a result, as it has flourished since the end of communism), a group of logicians discovered a more elegant notation, which is named in their honor.[6] In this notation, you just write the operands before their operator. This means that 1+1 becomes 1,1,+, where the comma separates the operands.

You never need parentheses! 3*(4+1) is 3 (write operand), 4 (go to the next operand, just noting the presence of multiplication), 1 (go to next, again remember add), + (the add is next, obviously since 4 and 1 use it), and * (we're finished).

Early computer designers realized that evaluating Polish expressions is much simpler than evaluating non-Polish, or *infix*, expressions. Infix expressions (unless you use a careful BNF structure, as designed in the previous section) can result in complex code, which needs to move back and forth in source to finish its job.

Suppose you have a table, accessible only on one end by means of only two operations: push will add an entry to the top of the table, and pop will remove the

6. One reason guys like Jan Lukasiewicz (the inventor of Polish notation) and Alfred Tarski (the leading Polish logician before WWII) should be honored is that some of them were interned and suffered during the war, along with other smart people, who totalitarian governments don't like. Nazis appear to have been, among other things, guys who flunked math.

most recently pushed entry.[7] Perhaps surprisingly, this simple gimmick handles parentheses logic well, because parentheses in infix expressions essentially prioritize the contained operators, making operators of lower precedence wait until the parenthesized operators complete.

Take a look at genCode, in the Parser region of integerCalc. This builds an RPN expression in the usrRPN data structure. It is passed an enumerator of type ENUoperator, which can have the values add, subtract, multiply, divide, and push. It is also passed an operand that is zero for all operators, except push.

When the parser recognizes a term that is an integer, in the method named term, it calls genCode to append a push operator and the integer value of the term to the end of the usrRPN data structure. usrRPN is not a stack, but rather an array that represents the RPN of the expression to be evaluated.

When the parser recognizes the right side of an arithmetic operation, the operands have already been "pushed" by the lower-level methods that recognize the nonterminals in the operation. So, all the parser needs to do at recognition time is call genCode to append the right operator (with a dummy and unused operand) to the end of usrRPN.

Stack Use

Now, take a look in the Interpreter region of integerCalc, at the interpretExpression method. It declares a stack as a local variable of type Stack, and then uses a very simple For loop to index left to right through the usrRPN data structure.

When the interpreter "sees" an operator of type Push, it uses the push method of the stack object to place the value on the stack. It does so in the pushStack method using a Try..Catch block, because at this point, we are leaving our code and asking a system facility to accomplish something for us. We need to make sure the external facility succeeds.

In the code for this book, I will always use this rule:

- When using a facility whose code is outside your code, check its result.

Just because you're paranoid doesn't mean you aren't being followed.

When interpretExpression sees an opcode,[8] interpretExpression must "pop" the two operands and, using the facilities of Visual Basic .NET, perform the operation. The only complexities here are that we need to check for stack underflow,

---

7. Many Visual Basic .NET and C# developers will be familiar with the Stack collection now available, but it was quite simple to make stack-like arrays in older Visual Basic versions, or to use collections as stacks.

8. This opcode is known as a *zero-address opcode* in some contexts, because the opcode, unlike a typical Pentium opcode, does not need to find anything in memory. Its operands are already in the stack.

and we need to properly order the operands. For example, stack underflow occurs in the (invalid) sequence of commands push 1, add, which doesn't specify what to add 1 to.

If the parser phase has no bugs, it will always generate a correct RPN expression in usrRPN, and no valid expression will cause stack underflow (1,+ is invalid). However, we are paranoid and being followed, as noted earlier, so another rule is as follows:

- Never be reluctant to add checks, in major subsections of code and objects, on the work of your other sections, even if you wrote them yourself (you might be following yourself).

Therefore, in the same manner as pushStack, popStack is in a Try..Catch block, which mostly will catch stack underflow, if the parser is changed in a buggy fashion.

We also need to remember that operands in the stack for division and subtraction (but not addition and subtraction) will be out of order, and we cannot code popStack-popStack or popStack/popStack. Since 1–2 will translate to the RPN 1,2,–, popStack-popStack will actually calculate 2–1!

This is an annoyance if, like me, you do not like temporary variables and prefer to call functions for values directly. But since the Stack object fails to provide a way of exchanging stack entries, we bite the bullet on this one and use temporary variables in interpretExpression for the nonsymmetrical operators—subtraction and division.

Also note that interpretExpression contains a virtual or potential bug in the way it performs addition and multiplication. A *virtual bug* is a bug that might be activated by a probable modification to code. Here, the virtual bug is the fact that in using function calls of popStack without temporary variables, we execute addition and multiplication in the wrong order: the user codes 1+2, but we execute 2+1; the user codes 3*4, but we execute 4*3. This is a virtual bug because it won't happen unless the code is changed to operate with real numbers with signs. Then certain addition operations will be subtraction, and the result may differ if either operand is small. Therefore, in a production compiler, addition and subtraction should use temporary variables and execute the operation in the user-specified order.

Run integerCalc again and click More. Type a reasonably complex expression and click Evaluate. You'll see the expression in RPN, as shown in Figure 3-7. The More display also shows how a stack is used, as shown in Figure 3-8.

TIP *If the display is too fast, you can check the box labeled Replay, click Evaluate again, and then use the Step and Back buttons to review the steps.*

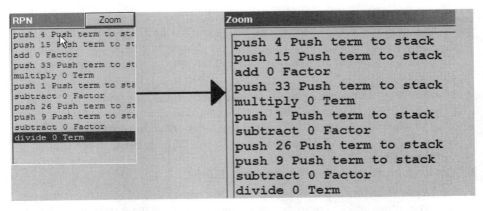

Figure 3-7. The RPN box of the More display shows how the parsed input expression has been converted to RPN.

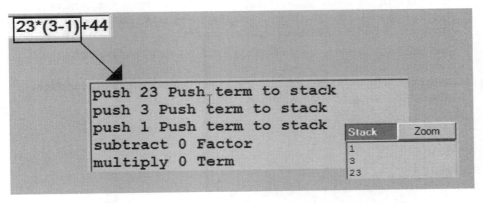

Figure 3-8. The right side of the More display shows how a stack is used to evaluate an arithmetic expression in RPN.

Stacks: Great, Wonderful, or What?

Stacks are great but not wonderful, or perhaps vice versa.

Whereas hardware designs exist based on stacks, especially for programmable calculators, reduced instruction set computing (RISC) designers tend to dislike stacks, because it is harder to optimize stack code.

The most famous example is lazy Or and lazy And.

In RPN, a And b becomes a, b, And. The problem is that an RPN-based machine cannot easily recognize, without more code, a False value of the variable a, which means that there is no need to evaluate b. A corresponding problem exists with the Or operator. In a Or b when a is True, there is no need to evaluate b.

Perhaps because of this limitation in simpler interpreters, many Basic compilers have enforced the rule to evaluate both a and b in both And expressions and Or expressions. This can be an important consideration whenever, in legacy code, the b expression is a function call that has side effects, such as actually updating a database.

This problem has been elegantly addressed both in the Visual Basic .NET language and in the CLR by the new operators AndAlso and OrElse. a AndAlso b is False when a is False, and b is not evaluated in this case. c OrElse d is True when c is True, and d is not evaluated here. Support exists in the CLR, and I urge you to abandon the old operators And and Or, because code using AndAlso and OrElse is more reliable and efficient.

Stack code as encountered in the CLR can be tricky to debug. Sometimes the debugger must build a complex mental model of stack structures of a great deal of depth. The more step-by-step nature of register machines makes their object code somewhat easier to follow. But it does appear from the software history record that stacks make for rather reliable architecture, not prone to the security flaws of register machines. This is because stacks avoid unnecessary temporary variables, which are a security exposure.

The Tandem architecture used stacks to provide a notably highly reliable minicomputer still in use in banking. In general, Algol and later C programs were more reliable than Fortran code, all other things being equal, due to the use of stacks in the runtime of both Algol and C.

Summary

This chapter has introduced three core theories that you can apply to developing compilers for the CLR: scanning and regular expressions, parsing and BNF, and interpreters and RPN.

We've had an almost complete flyover of the entire process of crafting a small compiler. Although this compiler is of limited practical use, it could be expanded to parse and evaluate business rules.

At this point, we haven't addressed compiling to the CLR, because witnessing the internals of a very small runtime is excellent preparation for Chapter 9, where we send some object code for QuickBasic to the CLR.

The next chapter describes the front-end scanning and parsing of the complete quickBasicEngine example, which scale up from the methods demonstrated in this chapter.

Challenge Exercise

As supplied, integerCalc calculates only with integers. In order to understand how it works, consider updating it to calculate with real numbers.

Your most important task will be to change the lexical analyzer of `integerCalc` to scan real numbers. This is the method named `scanExpression` in the code.

For best results, construct a regular expression that correctly scans all real numbers, where a real number consists of the following parts:

- An optional plus or minus sign

- An optional sequence of decimal digits

- An optional decimal point

- An optional second sequence of decimal digits to the right of the decimal point

- The letter *e* (uppercase or lowercase)—for mad scientists and disturbed engineers, we need to support floating-point expressions for very large and very small numbers, such as 1,000,000 (.1e7) or .0000001 (.1e-6).

- After the letter *e*, an optional plus or minus sign

- Then the value of the *e* exponent, which you can think of as the number of positions an implied decimal point, located to the left of the leftmost nonzero decimal digit at the beginning of the floating-point number, should move. By default, and if the letter *e* is followed by a plus sign, the implied decimal point moves right. If the letter *e* is followed by a minus sign, the implied decimal point moves left.

Since the lexical analyzer represents the source code in the `USRscanner` data structure, and since scanned values are represented in an object, you probably do not need to alter anything other than comments in the regions named `Scanner` and `Parser`. The `interpretExpression` procedure needs some modification in the way it performs arithmetic, since, as delivered, it uses integers.

When you complete this challenge, you will have experienced modifying a simple front-end compiler in the .NET platform, and you will have a full calculator for numeric expressions.

Resources

For more information about compiler theory, refer to the book *Compilers: Principles, Techniques and Tools*, by Alfred Aho, Ravi Sethi, and Jeffery Ullman (Addison-Wesley, 1985). This is the famous "dragon" book, which shows the compiler developer, armed with theory, defeating the dragon of complexity. While academic in its tone, it does constitute an excellent reference. In particular, it contains information on the use of `lexx` and `yacc`.

The Syntax for the QuickBasic Compiler

The use of Cobol cripples the mind, and its teaching should be regarded as a criminal offense.
—*Edsger Dijkstra*

It is practically impossible to teach good programming style to students that have had prior exposure to Basic; as potential programmers, they are mentally mutilated beyond all recognition.
—*Edsger Dijkstra (in a foul mood)*

THE LATE, HERO computer scientist was just wrong about Basic. Dijkstra's comment is academic sociology at its worst. It creates the illusion that programming skill derives from the use of politically correct platforms and languages.[1] Dijkstra was wrong because Visual Basic is Turing-complete, and it has a formal and sensible syntax. Visual Basic is Turing-complete because you can use it to write any program, as long as you disregard resource consumption.

I would revise Professor Dijkstra's aphorism. The use of Basic or Cobol as representative of a good programming language in and of itself cripples the mind and rots the teeth because Cobol and Visual Basic preserved (until Visual Basic .NET) some standards and practices created in the Fortran era, which simply did not allow for effective problem breakdown. This was less a scientific fact and more a result of a management illusion that programmers should merely code specifications provided by the "real" experts, and not factor the problem into subroutines, functions, and objects. Much sloppy programming results from this false view of the field and the low self-esteem it creates in programmers, who believe that a disreputable language permits mindless coding. In actuality, the

---

1. In an interview, Peter Neumann, long the hard-working moderator of the comp.risks newsgroup, told me that Dijkstra struggled with depression most of his life. Many bright people are depressed because they are powerless to stop other people from making mistakes. Dijkstra, unlike many successful corporate MIS types, never restrained himself from speaking his mind. His attempts at constructive criticism sometimes bothered people who had heavily invested in a paradigm Dijkstra did not like. Paradoxically, all who knew Dijkstra personally said he was easy to get along with.

reverse is true: we should compensate for the deficiencies of the language by mindful coding.

In the 1970s and after Dijkstra made these comments, Basic compiler developers added structured constructs to the language, and commencing with Visual Basic 4, Microsoft has been adding object-oriented tools.

Dijkstra said and wrote a lot of things, all of which are thought-provoking, but not all of his views have stood the test of time. One strange aphorism that still holds is that "computing science is no more about computers than astronomy is about telescopes."

Dijkstra meant that it's a mistake to focus on tools rather than the job at hand. Don't forget that the computer and the programming language are your telescope, and the stars are the user's problem and your solutions. The programmer's job is to bring the stars down to earth.

Basic has a reputation as being vague in syntax and not formalizable, as are more recent languages like Java and C++. As you'll see, this isn't so. Underneath its clunky, wordy, and keyword-intensive syntax, Basic can be completely and formally specified using Backus-Naur Form (BNF), and a tool for analyzing BNF can be written in Visual Basic itself. This brings the stars down to earth, as long as we cease fussing about the deficiencies of the telescope, stop hacking at it, and grow up and get to work. I will also show you how to convert BNF to Extensible Markup Language (XML), which gives another sensible view of BNF syntax.

In this chapter, I will discuss the rules for coding BNF by actually applying an analyzer, the `bnfAnalyzer` program, to the syntax for BNF itself. Then I will describe the construction of the BNF for our version of QuickBasic. We will then run the syntax of our QuickBasic through an analyzer and examine the output. We need to verify that it is analyzed without error and forms a solid basis for the compiler we will start to build in Chapter 5. As a summary, we'll look at eight guidelines for effectively developing BNF. This chapter will conclude with a special section on `bnfAnalyzer` internals, best read after you've read Chapters 5 through 8.

BNF is a valuable tool for specifying sensible .NET languages. Don't skip this chapter. If you propose to design a language for business rules, text processing, or making home movies, always create a solid BNF as your detailed requirements analysis.

A Tool for Analyzing BNF

In this chapter, we'll use a program called `bnfAnalyzer` to load and analyze the syntax of QuickBasic, expressed in BNF. The `bnfAnalyzer` executable program is available from the Downloads section of the Apress Web site (http://www.apress.com). You'll find the code in the egnsf/bnfAnalyzer folder.

The best way to understand the examples in this chapter is to run bnfAnalyzer while you're reading it. As long as you have the Visual Basic 6 runtime on your machine, you'll be able to run the program. To compile the source provided at the Apress Web site, you'll need Visual Basic 6 Enterprise or Professional, or if you have the Learning edition, you can organize the two projects shipped into a single project.

bnfAnalyzer reads a text file containing the BNF grammar of a language. It analyzes the BNF specification, finding many errors that would prevent you from using the specification to write, or automatically generate, a compiler or that might cause serious bugs. This tool produces a language reference manual, which includes the following:

- A list of the nonterminals, which are the categories of the language (such as *expression* in QuickBasic) that need to be defined in terms of smaller sequences

- A list of the terminals, which are the categories of the language (such as *string* in QuickBasic) that do not need to be broken down further

- The rules for forming language constructs as a numbered outline or as an XML tag

You can use this tool to analyze your own .NET language. bnfAnalyzer uses many of the compiler techniques discussed in Chapters 5 through 8 of this book. A final section of this chapter, "bnfAnalyzer Technical Notes," will discuss this topic, but I suggest you read that section after you've studied Chapters 5 through 8.

Why Is bnfAnalyzer a COM Executable?

You can run the bnfAnalyzer.exe file on any platform that has Visual Basic COM or most versions of Office. You can compile it with your edition of Visual Basic 6.

bnfAnalyzer is a COM executable because my .NET development laptop was resident at the pawnshop for a brief time while I was writing this chapter. I used Visual Basic 6 on my old system to write a somewhat nonreusable product (for which you can get the free source at the Apress Web site) that bases its objects primarily on complex collections, as described in the last section of this chapter. This product will run and compile on modern systems, since it uses no special or legacy features.

Analyzing and Coding BNF

BNF can be specified as a formal language, although it is not a programming language. As you saw in the compiler flyover in Chapter 3, BNF does not show the computer how to parse. Instead, it simply declares, formally, the valid constructs in the language. Those constructs might be the familiar sentence, noun, and verb of English or the statement, expression, and identifier of Visual Basic.

BNF is a powerful notation. For example, any regular expression can be recast in BNF, although the reverse is not true, and BNF is far more readable than regular expression notation.

BNF is specifiable in BNF. This means it is one of those somewhat confusing closed systems: a mathematical concept that can be applied to itself (just as a database can record all databases in a shop's inventory).

BNF Syntax

Figure 4-1 shows the syntax of BNF. It is available in the file named bnfAnalyzer test 6 (BNF of BNF).txt that comes along with the downloaded code for the analyzer.

```
bnfGrammar := production +
production := [ nonTerminal ":=" productionRHS ]
             (NEWLINE|EOF)
production := NEWLINE ' Allows for empty lines
nonTerminal := IDENTIFIER
productionRHS := sequenceFactor [ sequenceFactor ]
sequenceFactor := mockRegularExpression
                  [ alternationFactorRHS ]
mockRegularExpression := mreFactor [ mrePostfix ]
mreFactor := nonTerminal |
             UPPERCASESTRING |
             STRING |
             "(" productionRHS ")" |
             "[" productionRHS "]"
mrePostfix := "*" | "-"
alternationFactorRHS := "|" mockRegularExpression
                        [ alternationFactorRHS ]
```

Figure 4-1. The syntax of BNF

Now, this is confusing. Figure 4-1 shows the syntax of BNF, a formal syntax for programming languages, although I just told you that BNF is not a programming language. To make things worse, I am presenting the rules of BNF in BNF, as if you knew BNF all along or in a former life.

BNF isn't a programming language, but all programming languages are formal languages (but not the reverse). The syntax of all formal languages, by definition, can be specified in a formal notation like BNF.

Let's walk through some of the rules to get a feel for the use of BNF. The first line says, when read properly from left to right, that a `bnfGrammar` is *one or more* productions, where a `production` specifies possible components of a grammar category. (The plus sign in `production` + means one or more repetitions, just as it does in regular expressions.)

Okay, cool. What's a production?

Glad you asked. Go to the second line. A production is normally a nonterminal, followed by a colon and an equal sign (:=), followed by a production on the right-hand side (RHS), followed by either a newline character or end of file (EOF). Note that the nonterminal, :=, and RHS are optional, which means that blank lines are allowed.

A nonterminal is an identifier as seen in Visual Basic. An RHS is more complex. It is a sequence factor, perhaps followed by another sequence factor.

Okay, what's a sequence factor?

A sequence factor is a mock regular expression, followed by an alternation factor RHS. A mock regular expression (so-called because it isn't a full-scale regular expression) is a simplified regular expression that consists of a mock regular expression factor (`mreFactor`) followed by a mock regular expression postfix (`mrePostfix`). An `mreFactor` can be one of several things: a nonterminal, a completely uppercase string (which, in our language, represents a terminal symbolically), a quoted string using Visual Basic conventions, a parenthesized production RHS, or a left bracket.

As this example shows, you read BNF by following branches of a tree (and if you examine the code of `bnfAnalyzer`, you'll see that it represents the source BNF in a tree data structure). Each branch is less an instruction than a timeless law, which is always true no matter if the cows come home or not, as we say on the farm. The comfort of this is that the rules never change.

But let's step back a bit.

Like a programming language, BNF has operators. These include the alternation stroke | and the mock (as in not complete) support for the regular expression operators asterisk (*) and plus (+). Oddly, when white space occurs on the RHS of a production, between two grammar categories, it is an operator that specifies that the material on its left is followed by the material on its right. Also, a grouping of square brackets is an operator, which specifies that the material it contains is optional.

As in a programming language, these operators have precedence. The sequence operator (consisting of blanks or white space) has lowest precedence, followed by the alternation stroke, and then the mock regular expression operators. However, parentheses can be used to group operations and change this precedence. For example, if in your language, an a nonterminal consists of a b or the sequence c d, the production is a := b | (c d). The square brackets change precedence in the same way, while also specifying that the bracketed material is optional; a:= b | [c d] specifies that an a is a required b or optionally c and d. Note that this production allows a to be a null string.

Rules for Coding BNF

The following lexical rules apply specifically to coding formal BNF as far as the analyzer is concerned. Note that different rules will apply to BNF as supported by other tools, including yacc on Unix.

Comments: Completely blank lines and lines that commence with an apostrophe are treated as comments. Lines may also end in comments; any characters after the leftmost unquoted apostrophe, including the apostrophe, are treated as comments.

Continued lines and new lines: Lines that contain individual productions (definitions) may be continued, simply by making sure that the first character of the continuation line is a blank. A newline suitable for the environment in which the analyzer is run (carriage return and linefeed on Windows; linefeed on the Web) is a "real" newline only when it is followed by a nonblank character or end of file. Suppose a Windows newline is the NEWLINE terminal of your language. In your lexical analyzer, this would correspond to a small routine that checks for the proper newline at the current position and advances a scan pointer.

Identifiers: Identifiers follow Visual Basic 6 conventions: starting with a letter, they should contain letters, digits, and the underscore exclusively. There is no limit to the length of identifiers, except common sense. However, unlike Visual Basic identifiers, identifiers are completely case-sensitive, as in the case of C++. The case of the first letter of the identifier shows its type.

- Identifiers that start with a lowercase letter are assumed to be nonterminals of the grammar. These identifiers must appear as defined on the left side of at least one production.

- Identifiers that start with an uppercase letter are assumed to be symbolic grammar terminals (note that strings may also be terminals). These identifiers may not appear on the left side of a production.

- For best results, symbolic grammar terminals should be exclusively UPPERCASE, but they may also be Proper case, with only the first character in uppercase.

Nonterminal definition: The := (colon and equal sign) operator is the preferred production operator to separate a defined nonterminal from its definition. The plain equal sign may also be used for this purpose, but := is less apt to confuse the reader. Note that you should not expect to be able to enter special characters to represent themselves in the right side of a production. `assignmentStmt := rhs = value` should be coded as `assignmentStmt := rhs "=" value`, with the second equal sign in quotes.

Quoted strings: Quoted strings follow Visual Basic conventions (double quotes are delimiters; internal double quotes must be doubled) and are used to specify exact character sequences as terminals. Sadly, Visual Basic's limitation applies: nonprinting characters cannot be specified in strings. You should make nonprinting sequences into terminals, named in proper case or uppercase, and your lexical analyzer should take care of their recognition.

A Grammar Test

We'll now test (if you are following along with downloaded software) the grammar for BNF using the `bnfAnalyzer` program. Open the bnfAnalyzer.vbp file using Visual Basic 6 Enterprise or Professional and compile this project, producing VBPanalyzer.exe. Run bnfAnalyzer.exe.

The first screen presented when you run `bnfAnalyzer` will be a general announcement screen, as shown in Figure 4-2. Most of the software in this book will include these "about" screens, which appear the first time the software is run. Subsequently, they are available using a button and/or a menu item labeled About.

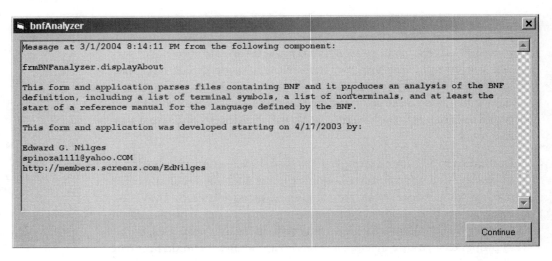

Figure 4-2. bnfAnalyzer's About screen

Then you will see the main screen of bnfAnalyzer. In the list of directories on the left side of the main screen, find and double-click Test Files, as shown in Figure 4-3.

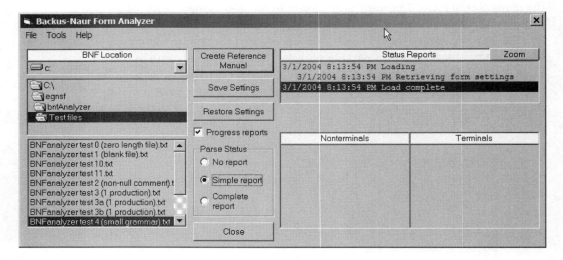

Figure 4-3. bnfAnalyzer's main screen

In the list of files in the lower-left corner, find and select the file named BNF analyzer test 6 (BNF of BNF).txt. Click the Create Reference Manual button. After a sequence of progress reports, you'll see the Reference Manual Options form. Enter **BNF** as the language name, as shown Figure 4-4.

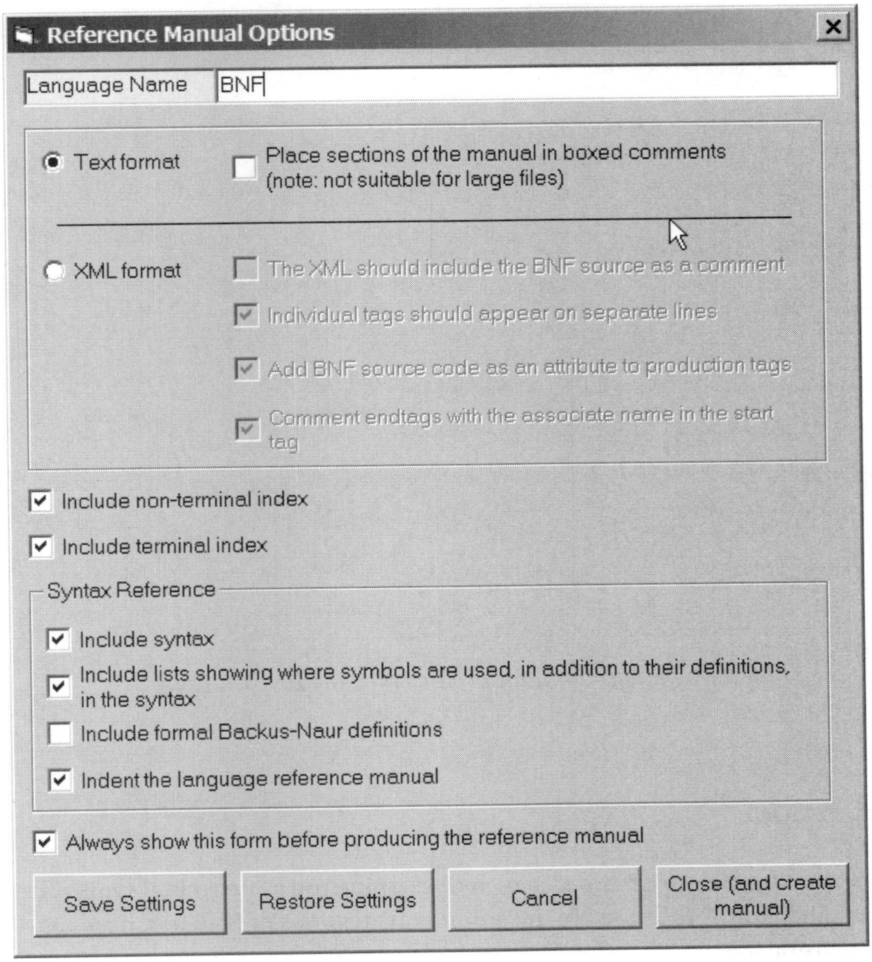

Figure 4-4. Reference manual options

This form allows you to tailor the reference manual. bnfAnalyzer supports two formats for the reference manual. The default text format uses the monospaced Courier New font to format the manual. An option is also provided to create an XML reference manual.

Click the button labeled Close (and create manual) to see the reference manual, as shown in Figure 4-5. This report can be selected, copied, and pasted into a Notepad or Word file.

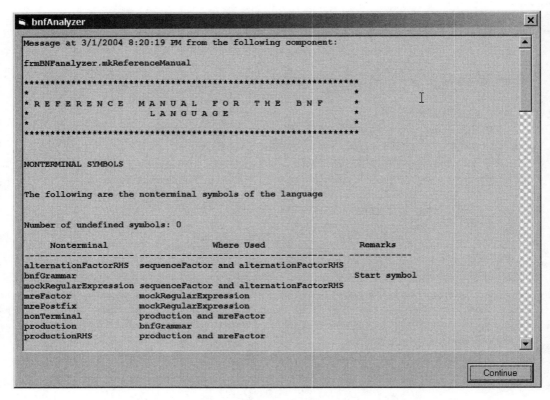

Figure 4-5. Start of the language reference manual produced by the BNF analyzer

Nonterminals

Scroll down the reference manual screen to examine the nonterminal symbols, as shown in Figure 4-6. These are the grammar categories of BNF that have further expansions.

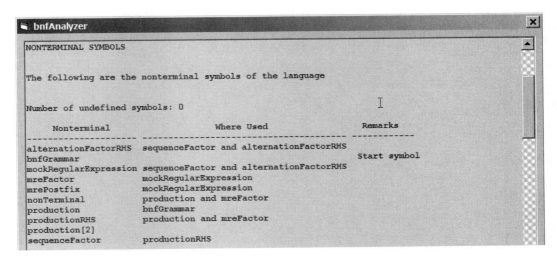

Figure 4-6. List of nonterminals

The first column identifies the nonterminals in alphabetical sequence. The second column identifies the nonterminals that use the nonterminal in the first column. The third column will identify undefined terminals (not shown) that are used but do not appear in the left side of any production, as well as start symbols that are not used on the right side of any production. These are typically the most important constructs of your grammar. For English, a start symbol might be a sentence; a start symbol in a programming language might be a complete program.

> **NOTE** *If a nonterminal has null in the Where Used list, it is a start symbol. The reverse is not true. If your language defines the major construct recursively as smaller instances of itself, the start symbol column will be blank. For this reason, I suggest you do not define the start symbol recursively.*

Terminals

Scroll down further to see the list of terminals, as shown in Figure 4-7. Terminals in our BNF are of two types: strings and symbols that at least start with an uppercase character.

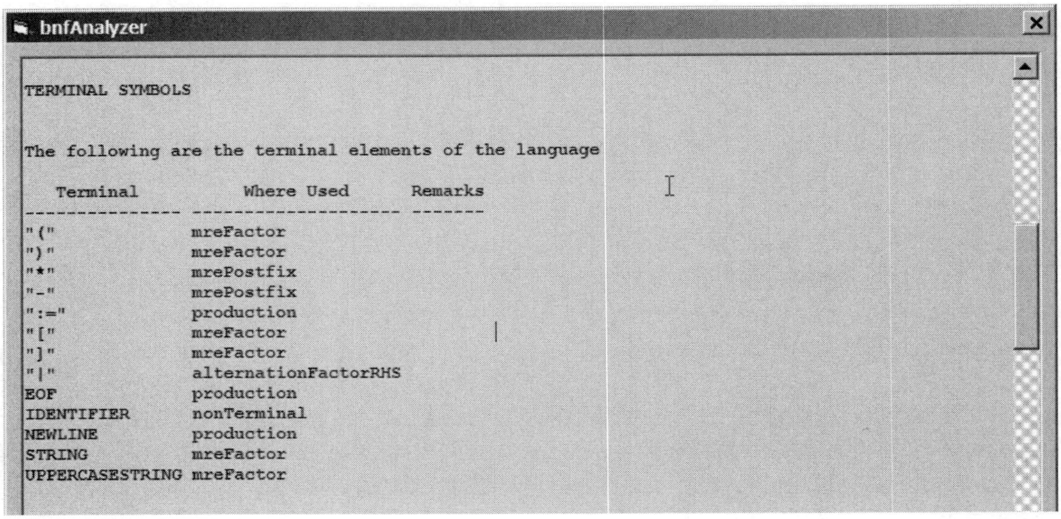

Figure 4-7. List of terminals

Like the nonterminal list, the first column in this list identifies the terminals in alphabetical order. Note that several strings are terminals and operators of BNF. We've also identified some terminals as symbols.

Because they start with uppercase, the identifiers EOF, IDENTIFIER, NEW-LINE, STRING, and UPPERCASESTRING are treated as symbols in the grammar that will be understood by the lexical analyzer. These follow the convention that symbolic terminals should be in all uppercase characters, for maximum visibility in a medium or large BNF.

These symbolic terminals can be used to express the fact that a terminal that will be recognized by the lexical analyzer is a potentially infinite number of symbols, such as IDENTIFIER, STRING, or UPPERCASESTRING; or a nonprintable string not expressible as a Visual Basic string; or a condition that is not a string at all, such as EOF (at end of file.) In fact, NEWLINE, in the parser for BNF, is both a string and a condition. When the BNF lexical analyzer (in the procedure BNFcompile_scanner_findNewline) finds a newline, it then checks to see if the newline is followed by a space and an underscore (the continuation indicator), and if so, it cancels the newline.

The lexical analyzer's mission in life, which we will revisit in the next chapter, is to make life easy for the parser in any way it can. Here, it does this by replacing funky terminals by simple symbols.

Recall that regular expressions represent the *conditions* "start of input line or string" and "end of input line or string" using the *characters* caret and dollar sign. In general, conditions and sequences of characters can be usefully considered by the lexical analyzer as simple characters and abstracted as simple tokens.

Syntax Outline

Scroll down to see the (pardon my French) *pièce de résistance*, or reference manual outline of BNF (or any other language expressible in valid BNF), as shown in Figure 4-8.

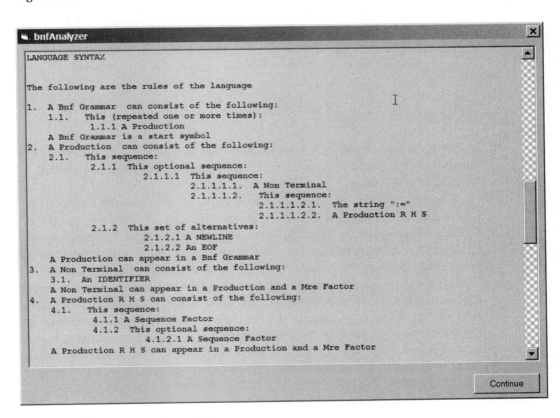

Figure 4-8. Language syntax outline

Any valid BNF can be transformed into an outline of the language, suitable as a basis for a complete reference manual. This overcomes a major, and quite valid, managerial objection to the very idea of forming our own language for business rules, by providing accurate documentation of the language.

Reference Manual Display

One potential problem with the reference manual's nonterminal and terminal lists and the outline is that they are in a fixed format, which is suitable only for a monospaced font such as Courier New, because the format uses blanks for formatting. In fact, an option in the Reference Manual Options form, Place sections of the manual in boxed comments (see Figure 4-4), will transform the material into a boxed comment, suitable for inclusion in program text. This option works if you prepend each line with the comment symbol of the language (such as apostrophe in Visual Basic) or surround the comment with balanced comment tags (such as /* and */ in C or the XML comment tags).

If word wrapping in any of your BNF files creates an unreadable reference manual in the display, copy and paste the reference manual into a Word document. Set Page Setup to landscape printing and the font to Courier New. Make the font size small enough for you to see the output properly formatted.

XML Reference Manual

We need a less proprietary and more flexible way to format the output, so we can use Visio and other tools to create documents based on our reference manual. XML is the best choice.

Click Continue on the reference manual outline screen, and then click Create Reference Manual again on the main screen. This time, the Reference Manual Options form will appear immediately, since the manual has already been parsed. Click the XML format radio button. Make sure the first XML format option, labeled The XML should include the BNF source as a comment, is unchecked. The other three options—Individual tags should appear on separate lines, Add BNF source code as an attribute to production tags, and Comment end tags with the associate name in the start tags—should be checked. These choices will avoid replicating the BNF source in a leading XML comment, place newlines between XML tags, and enhance the tags with source BNF. Click the button labeled Close (and create manual) to see the screen shown in Figure 4-9.

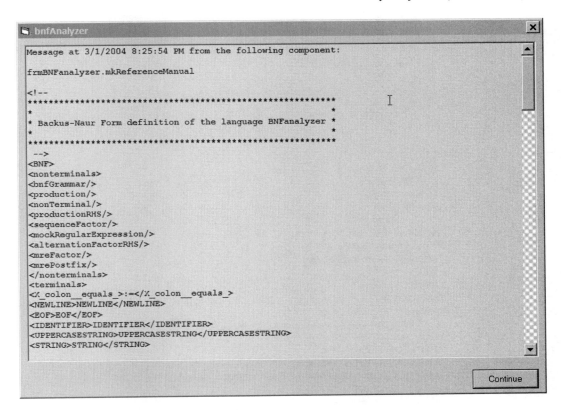

Figure 4-9. The XML reference manual screen

You can format this XML. Using Visual Studio .NET, create a new Windows application and choose to add a new item. At the prompt, select XML file and paste in the XML, commencing with the comment tag <!--. Click Browse with, save the file, and select Internet Explorer. You will see the formatted XML, as shown in Figure 4-10.

```xml
<?xml version="1.0" encoding="utf-8" ?>
<!--

    **********************************************************
    *                                                        *
    * Backus-Naur Form definition of the language BNF        *
    *                                                        *
    **********************************************************

  -->
<BNF>
  <nonterminals>
    <bnfGrammar />
    <production />
    <nonTerminal />
    <productionRHS />
    <sequenceFactor />
    <mockRegularExpression />
    <alternationFactorRHS />
    <mreFactor />
    <mrePostfix />
  </nonterminals>
  <terminals>
    <X_colon__equals_>:=</X_colon__equals_>
    <NEWLINE>NEWLINE</NEWLINE>
    <EOF>EOF</EOF>
    <IDENTIFIER>IDENTIFIER</IDENTIFIER>
    <UPPERCASESTRING>UPPERCASESTRING</UPPERCASESTRING>
    <STRING>STRING</STRING>
    <X_leftParenthesis_>(</X_leftParenthesis_>
    <X_rightParenthesis_>)</X_rightParenthesis_>
    <X_leftBracket_>[</X_leftBracket_>
    <X_rightBracket_>]</X_rightBracket_>
```

Figure 4-10. The formatted XML reference manual

Figure 4-10 shows the beginning of the XML reference manual, which lists the nonterminals and then the terminals of your language. Scroll down to see the actual BNF productions, as shown in Figure 4-11.

```
- <bnfProductions>
  - <GS name="bnfGrammar">
    - <OP name="production">
      - <OP name="oneTripRepeat">
        <production />
      </OP>
      <!-- End oneTripRepeat -->
    </OP>
    <!-- End production -->
  </GS>
  <!-- End bnfGrammar -->
  - <GS name="production">
    - <OP name="production">
      - <OP name="sequence">
        - <OP name="optionalSequence">
          - <OP name="sequence">
            <nonTerminal />
            - <OP name="sequence">
              <X_doubleQuote__colon__equals__doubleQuote_ />
              <productionRHS />
            </OP>
            <!-- End sequence -->
          </OP>
          <!-- End sequence -->
        </OP>
        <!-- End optionalSequence -->
        - <OP name="alternatives">
          <NEWLINE />
          <EOF />
        </OP>
        <!-- End alternatives -->
      </OP>
      <!-- End sequence -->
```

Figure 4-11. The BNF productions in the XML reference manual

Note that each production will start with a GS (grammar symbol) tag and contain one or more OP (operator) tags. Each GS tag will name the grammar symbol and show its BNF (if the appropriate Reference Manual Options setting is in effect). Each OP tag will identify the operator. For example, the first OP tag identifies the production operator :=. The ending OP tag will identify the start tag in a comment if the corresponding Reference Manual Options setting is in effect.

You can use the XML format with a large variety of formatting tools to view the language reference. The basic text format is more suitable in simpler documents.

In this section, you've learned quite a lot about BNF, in the way in which many programmers want to learn—by getting your hands dirty. You've learned how to use the free tools provided with this book to get started with language design.

In the next section, you'll see how the much larger grammar for our QuickBasic was built.

Building the BNF for Our QuickBasic

Using bnfAnalyzer, we can analyze the BNF or our QuickBasic compiler. Figure 4-12 shows the beginning of this larger syntax, available as BNF analyzer test 5 (quick basic).txt in the Test Files directory. Since the complete file is available for download, in this section, I will restrict the detailed forced march to just three areas, to give you a feel for what it is like to construct a large BNF.[2] The three areas we will look at are the start of the definition (the big picture, so to speak), the important definition of the assignment statement, and the equally important definition of the expression.

```
' --- Immediate commands
immediateCommand := singleImmediateCommand (":" singleImmediateCommand)*
singleImmediateCommand := expression | explicitAssignment
' --- Source programs
sourceProgram := optionStmt
sourceProgram := sourceProgramBody
sourceProgram := optionStmt logicalNewline sourceProgramBody
optionStmt := Option ( "Base" ("0" | "1") ) | Explicit | Extension
sourceProgramBody := ( openCode | moduleDefinition ) +
openCode := statement [ logicalNewline sourceProgram ]
logicalNewline := Newline | Colon
statement := [UnsignedInteger | identifier Colon ] statementBody
statementBody := ctlStatementBody | unconditionalStatementBody |
                 assignmentStmt
ctlStatementBody := dim |
                    doHeader |
                    else |
                    endIf |
                    forHeader |
                    forNext |
                    if |
                    whileHeader |
                    loopOrWend
unconditionalStatementBody := circle |
                              comment |
                              data |
                              end |
                              exit |
                              goSub |
                              goto |
                              input |
                              print |
                              randomize |
                              read |
                              return |
                              screen |
                              stop |
                              trace
```

Figure 4-12. Start of the BNF for our QuickBasic

2. For the same reason a film can't show all the action and lack of action in a person's life, a metaprogram discussion cannot reproduce, at base, the writing of each line of code, its debugging, and its modification. Before "extreme programming," this was endured in isolation by the programmer. Today it is, in extreme programming, a sort of MTV *Real World* or *Survivor* show, with the boring parts left in, and fewer hotties overall.

Are Formal Definitions Necessary?

It is an urban legend that languages like Java and C++ have a clear syntax, while languages like Visual Basic cannot be formalized at all. This is not true, because were it not possible to formalize Basic, then it could not be compiled.

Indeed, the Java programmer's cubicle is decorated with beautiful syntax charts, typically produced from formal BNF, of the entire language. The Visual Basic programmer's cubicle is, we suppose, littered with Jolt Cola empties, pawn tickets, and back issues of *Motor Trend*. There is no law of nature that this needs to be so.

Many compilers for older Basics were, in fact, coded in the 1970s by noble savages who were innocent of academic computer science. This was true for other old languages as well, including the old Fortran compiler I mentioned in Chapter 1. But for the same reason different cultures do the same abstract math with the same results in wildly different notations—from the abacus to knotted strings to Visual Basic and C—the noble savages were able in most commercially viable instances (including a small company operated out of a motel in New Mexico) to produce in actuality what were formal definitions of Basic, whether on diskettes or on paper tape.[3]

I have near-zero tolerance for compilers hacked above and beyond the language definition, as you will learn in Chapter 5, where each parser procedure must quote the BNF justifying its code. Compilers hacked beyond the formal definition of the language are very dangerous tools. Especially in the case of an "inside job" (a compiler written for internal use), the developers and users relying on the compiler may develop programs and business rules that exploit undocumented extensions and compiler bugs. This means that the compiler, and not its formal specification, becomes the law, and the compiler cannot be repaired!

The Big Picture

Designing a BNF is a top-down process. We start with a goal: to write a compiler that can evaluate immediate expressions for calculator-style solutions and more complex programs with state, just as the original Basic authors wanted to support engineering and scientific needs for a handy calculator and more extensive modeling.

Referring to the start of the BNF analysis (see Figure 4-12), take a look at the definition of an `immediateCommand`:

---

3. Microsoft operates a Microsoft Museum in Redmond, and while waiting for my ride after the 2001 author's event, I was able to see the paper tape Bill and Paul created for their Altair Basic compiler.

```
immediateCommand := singleImmediateCommand (":" ImmediateCommand)*
```

This declares the "what" and not the "how." It says in English, "An immediate command is a single immediate command, followed by zero, one, or more occurrences of a colon, followed by an immediate command." It is a recursive but not circular definition, because we can tell, by just looking at it, that the immediate command on the right side of the production is shorter than the immediate command being defined, by at least one character—the colon.

We then define a single immediate command:

```
singleImmediateCommand := explicitAssignment | expression
```

This declares that a single immediate command can be either an explicit assignment or an expression. An expression will support our responding to the entry of formulae with the value of the formula, but we also, in the immediate command mode, need to allow the user to enter variables, as in the case of the entry Let a=4: a*32.

If you look up the productions for explicit and implicit assignment, you'll discover that they differ only in that explicit assignment starts with the keyword Let. As it happens, we cannot support implicit assignment in immediate command mode, since it would not be possible to tell the difference between "assign 4 to a" and "return true if a equals 4." Therefore, a single immediate assignment must start with Let.

We then need to define a source program. Where there is more than one production for a given nonterminal, the multiple productions are Or'd, and any one can be satisfied by a particular input string. a:=a|b is equivalent to a:=b followed by a:=c.

A source program is a single option statement; a source program body; or an option statement, followed by a logical newline, followed by a source program body. This apparently complex definition expresses the fact that you cannot put Basic's Option statement anywhere but at the beginning of your code. This is only the first example of how what seems to be a rather ad-hoc rule can be formalized. Yes, it's still ugly compared with C, which abandoned the very idea of header statements, but it isn't vague.

The Option statement, in turn, can be easily defined as the sequence consisting of the terminal Option and the terminal Explicit.

The definition of a source program body is more complex. This is because we allow functions and subroutines, in addition to global definitions (which are at the module level in Visual Basic). Unlike Visual Basic and C, we also allow open code. *Open code* consists of global variable declarations (known as module-level declarations in Visual Basic) and instructions that are part of a main procedure, which receives control initially.

Therefore, a source program body is a series of one or more occurrences of either open code (data and instructions) or the definitions of functions and subroutines, expanded much later in the BNF file.

Next, we define the logical newline, which is used at several points. A logical newline is either a real newline or the colon, which allows multiple statements per line. We make a mental note to use the Visual Basic .NET reserved word vbNewline for the actual newline, rather than a ChrW function using linefeed, because the reserved word makes the newline correspond to the runtime environment. On Windows, it is carriage return and linefeed, which we use to rile Unix people, but on the Web, it is linefeed.

Next, in defining a statement, we need to account for another ugly feature of our language that might be considered unformalizable. This is the presence of statement numbers and symbolic statement labels, which opens the entire can of worms around the question of Go To.[4]

It's a snap to formalize. A statement is an optional unsigned integer or an optional identifier, followed by a colon, followed by the body of the statement. A body of a statement can be a control flow statement, an unconditional statement commencing with a keyword, or an assignment statement.

These definitions at the start of the file give you an idea of how the BNF is built. Let's now move to the important definition of the Basic assignment statement.

The Assignment Statement

Figure 4-13 shows the assignment statement definition. An assignment statement is either explicit or implicit. As already mentioned, it is explicit if it starts with Let, and implicit otherwise.

```
' Assignment
assignmentStmt := explicitAssignment | implicitAssignment
explicitAssignment := Let implicitAssignment
implicitAssignment := lValue "=" expression
lValue := typedIdentifier [ "(" subscriptList ")" ]
subscriptList := expression [ Comma subscriptList ] |
```

Figure 4-13. The definition of assignment

---

4. As early as Microsoft's release of QuickBasic in the 1980s, Go To was useless to skilled programmers except in error handling. This has been only recently fixed in the provision, in Visual Basic .NET, of Try..Catch..End Try error handling.

To understand the syntax of an assignment statement, we need to be careful not to make the grammar ambiguous with respect to the equal sign, because unlike C, we do not have different terminals for assignment and equality. We need to avoid allowing expressions to occur on the left side of the assignment; a+1=b+1 is math, not code.

Therefore, I have swiped an important concept from C, that of the LValue, or location value. An LValue refers to, or can be made to refer to, a named piece of storage, whether the name is a simple identifier or an identifier along with its subscript.

All LValues are expressions, but not all expressions are LValues, because the value of any complex expression like a+1 refers to a nameless quantity that appears on the stack at runtime only when it is needed. Therefore, an LValue is an identifier with type, optionally followed by a subscript list. We need to use the annoying nonterminal typedIdentifier, because this is an identifier (look up its definition in the file) that is optionally followed by a special character indicating its type. (I do not use this feature, which produces ugly variables such as uglyString$, where the dollar sign implicitly says "uglyString is a string," and it is my sad duty to implement it.)

Finally, let's proceed to the way in which we define expressions.

Expressions

We need to define the precedence of operators from the very low-precedence operators And and Or to the very high-precedence multiplication, division, and exponentiation operators, and we need to account for parentheses.

Figure 4-14 shows how we define expressions. There are a lot of "gotchas" here, so pay attention.

```
' --- Expressions
expression := orFactor [ orOp expression ]
orOp := Or
orOp := OrElse
orFactor := andFactor [ andOp orFactor ]
andOp := And
andOp := AndAlso
andFactor := [ Not ] notFactor
notFactor := likeFactor [notFactorRHS]
notFactorRHS := Like likeFactor [notFactorRHS]
likeFactor := concatFactor [likeFactorRHS]
likeFactorRHS := "&" concatFactor [likeFactorRHS]
concatFactor := relFactor [concatFactorRHS]
concatFactorRHS := relOp relFactor [concatFactorRHS]
relFactor := addFactor [ relFactorRHS ]
relFactorRHS := relOp relFactor [ relFactorRHS ]
addFactor := mulFactor [addFactorRHS]
addFactorRHS := mulOp mulFactor [addFactorRHS]
mulFactor := powFactor [mulFactorRHS]
mulFactorRHS := powOp powFactor [mulFactorRHS]
powFactor := ("+" | "-")* term
term := unsignedNumber |
        string |
        lValue |
        True |
        False |
        functionCall |
        ( expression )
functionCall := functionName "(" expressionList ")"
functionName := Abs | Asc | Ceil | Chr | Cos | Eval | Floor | Int |
                Iif | Isnumeric | Lbound | Lcase | Left | Len | Log |
                Max | Min | Mid | Replace | Right | Rnd | Sin |
                Sgn | String | Tab | Trim |
                Ubound | Ucase | Utility
unsignedNumber:= ( UnsignedRealNumber | UnsignedInteger )
                 [ numTypeChar ]
typedIdentifier := identifier [ typeSuffix ]
typeSuffix := numTypeChar | CurrencySymbol
numTypeChar := PERCENT | AMPERSAND | EXCLAMATION | POUNDSIGN
identifier := Letter LettersNumbersUnderscores
string := DoubleQuote AnythingExceptDoubleQuote DoubleQuote
relOp := "<" | ">" | "=" | "<=" | ">=" | "=" | "<>"
addOp := "+"|"-"
mulOp := "*"|"/"|"\"|"Mod"
powOp := "**"|"^"
```

Figure 4-14. Expressions definition

It is one thing to define an abstract BNF that validly expresses the set of possible sentences in a language, but early compiler designers found that it is quite
another to design BNF from which actual debugged code can be generated,
whether by hand or by using a parser generator. As I mentioned in the previous
chapter, you need to design a real-world BNF with care.

Expression Operators

In defining the typical binary operator of an expression, such as the Or operator, we must be careful to avoid left recursion. We cannot define an expression in the obvious way—as expression := expression Or Expression—because to get started with parsing an expression, we would need to parse the lowest precedence production (Or), and to do this, we would need to parse an expression. This would cause an immediate loop, since we would always start parsing an expression in the same place!

> **NOTE** *Remember that looping isn't recursion. Recursion is applying the same code to a smaller integer or a smaller set of data. Looping is getting stuck so that no matter what your code does, it re-creates the same state, including the position in the parse.*

Therefore we could define (but we won't) Or as an *or factor* (an expression that contains no Or operators), followed by an Or, followed by an expression. This avoids left recursion because an or factor can be parsed, and by the time we get to a recursive parse of the expression, we know we have eliminated some tokens—at a minimum, an Or operator. Because the length of the input string is smaller, this is recursion and not looping.

Typical code generators will generate valid code for Or operators in this scenario. However, they will generate very bad code using this same approach for any operator that is not symmetrical, such that a *Op* b equals b *Op* a, and fully associative, such that a *Op* (b *Op* c) is the same as (a *Op* b) *Op* c.[5] In particular, they will generate code that evaluates subtraction and division operators to the right of other operators of the same type, which will give wrong answers.

Therefore, we instead decide on the same pattern for addition and subtraction operators. They start with their factor (the longest expression type that doesn't contain the operator or any operator of lower precedence) and end with an RHS consisting of the operator, followed by a recursive and a smaller instance of the left-side production.

For example, we need to parse a–b–c–d as a, followed by the subtract RHS –b–c–d. We need to parse the subtract RHS as the minus operator, followed by

---

5. Some of my students complain I use math too much. This isn't math. It's symbolic logic. That is even worse. However, symbolic logic, unlike traditional math, does not require an extensive background to understand. To understand college calculus, you need to have succeeded at four years of high school math. To understand these formal notations, you need only read this book, do the examples on your computer, and, like Billy Crystal's Second Gravedigger in the Kenneth Branagh film of Hamlet, "cudgel thy brains."

a subtract factor, followed by the smaller subtract RHS -c-d. This is the best sequence because it simplifies generating subtraction operators left to right, as you'll see in Chapter 5.

Were we to parse a-b-c-d as a factor, a minus sign, and an expression, something unexpected would happen. In the first parse, the a would be the or factor, and the expression would be b-c-d. We could generate code to get the value of a, but we could not generate code to subtract! That's because we first need to generate code to calculate the value of b-c-d. But if we generate code to calculate b-c-d, the two subtractions to the right of the first subtraction will be generated *before* the leftmost subtraction, and this is *wrong*. The second subtraction will happen *after* the third subtraction. Suppose a=1, b=2, c=3, and d=4. Properly evaluated, a-b-c-d is –8. But if the subtractions are executed right to left by an incorrect parser, c-d is calculated first, giving –1. This value is then subtracted from b to give 3, since the value of c-d is negative. This is then subtracted from 1, giving –2!

Similar problems happen in real and integer division. Basically, subtraction and division are left and not right associative; therefore, for the productions corresponding to these, we define the RHS as starting with the operator.

The attractive feature of defining the RHS of a binary operator in this way is that the production on the right side has a very simple *handle*, which is the symbol with which it must begin. We only need to look for the symbol to see, moving from left to right in the source code, whether the entire sequence is present. This avoids a bane of early compiler developers called *backtracking*,[6] which is retreating from right to left in the source text, because the parser has realized that what it thought it had does not occur. Backtracking is a problem because we want the parser to be responsible for various tasks, including the generation of object code, all of which would have to be undone. This gets nasty.

In general, and in parser theory, the handle is the set of terminal symbols that can occur validly at the start or end of a nonterminal. The left handle is the set of terminals that can occur at the beginning. The right handle is the set that can occur at the end.

In producing a pragmatic production, a rule of thumb is to watch for ambiguity, in the form of adjacent nonterminals, whose right and left handles are sets of symbols that intersect. For example, expression orFactor is an ambiguous sequence. An expression's right handle happens to be the set consisting of all identifiers, the right parenthesis, and all numbers. An orFactor's left handle is the set consisting of all identifiers, the left parenthesis, and all numbers. Since these two sets have a large intersection, there is no easy way of telling where the or

---

6. Backtracking was a bane of early compiler developers, both on mainframes of the 1950s and micros of the 1970s, because whenever the input text was on a serial medium such as magnetic or even audiocassette tape, the medium had to rewind. The rewind had a high "fwizz" factor in that it was fun to watch but it wasted time.

factor begins! For example, a+1 and b might be the expression a and the or factor 1 and b, or it might be the expression a+1 and the or factor b. You might object that we know that and has lower precedence than +, but we cannot use this "knowledge," because we're constructing it as the BNF itself.

Compiler generators such as yacc are developed to efficiently determine sets of handle symbols in order to find out whether the grammar is ambiguous.

Parentheses

Finally, let's look at the way in which we support parentheses. This is a topic we touched on in Chapter 3.

Look at the definition of a term. A term is the smallest component of an expression, and typically it is an identifier, string, or number. However, what parentheses do in a language like Visual Basic is make a simple term out of complex expressions; therefore, a possible term is left parenthesis, expression, and right parenthesis.

The ambiguity here is that working from this definition alone, an expression such as (a*(b–c)) with nested parentheses would be parsed improperly. This is because a typical implementation in code of a BNF grammar would find the leftmost parenthesis and conform to the BNF, because BNF, by itself, does not specify where to stop.

The BNF definition for term shows the alternatives unsignedNumber, string, LValue, True, False, functionCall, and the parenthesized (expression). If the candidate string for a term starts with a left parenthesis, we know that the only valid possibility is a parenthesized expression, because, as we can see by examining the BNF, no other candidate starts with a left parenthesis. The left handle of an unsignedNumber is plus, minus, and the digits. The left handle of a string is a double quote, and so on. None of these left handle sets include the left parenthesis.

The problem, as we've seen in the miniparser of Chapter 3, is that we need to pass a *substring* to the expression parser. If we pass the entire source program one character beyond the left parenthesis, it will be rejected as a valid expression because it will end with unbalanced material, as in a+1) –b.

Just as we did with integerCalc in Chapter 3, in Chapter 5, we will implement a simple code workaround as a submethod in the term recognizer, and search ahead for the balanced right parenthesis.

We've reviewed the critical parts of the BNF. You've seen that with only one exception—the use of code as a workaround to balance parentheses (a strategy that can also be used with languages of the C family)—our version of QuickBasic can be formally specified. Let's now take the complete BNF and run it through the analyzer to see what happens.

Analyzing the BNF of Our QuickBasic

Let's rerun bnfAnalyzer.exe. Click the file BNF analyzer test 5 (quick basic).txt, and then click Create Reference Manual. The processing will be more intense as the application progresses through the large file.

When the Reference Manual Options form appears, set it up as shown in Figure 4-15. The large amount of output will exceed the capacity of the text box used to display the results, and the boxed, monospace comments are inappropriate for large outputs.

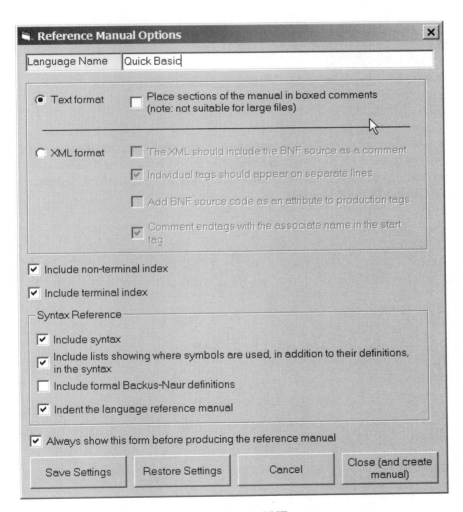

Figure 4-15. Options set up for QuickBasic BNF

The output with these options is just too large to fit in a text box. Therefore, you will see the prompt shown in Figure 4-16. This will allow you to also store the output in the named text file.

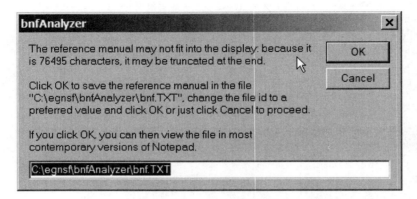

Figure 4-16. Saving the reference manual for QuickBasic as a text file

You will then see the reference manual, commencing with the nonterminals, as shown in Figure 4-17. Note that to obtain the properly formatted effect, you will need to copy the text from the (pink!) dialog box and paste it into Notepad, because it wraps in the dialog box.

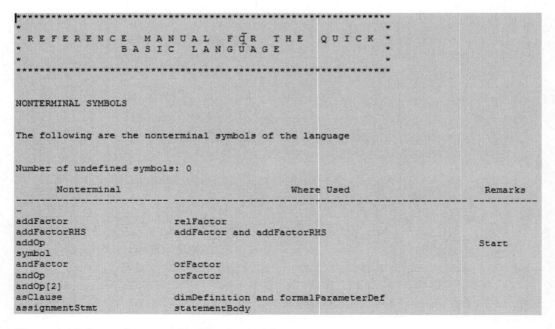

Figure 4-17. Start of nonterminal list for QuickBasic

This lists the grammar categories of QuickBasic. Notice the appearance of the nonterminal andOp twice, with the second occurrence containing a sequence number.

This occurs because I could not resist adding Visual Basic .NET's AndAlso as a new operator. As explained in Chapter 3, AndAlso allows a lazy And, which does not evaluate the right side of the And when the left side is False. Our implementation also contains OrElse. Therefore, there are actually two productions for andOp: andOp := And and andOp:=AndAlso. When multiple alternative productions appear, they will create multiple lines in the nonterminal list, as in Figure 4-17. The Where Used column information, however, will be provided for only the first line, because it applies to all forms of that production.

Scroll down to see the terminals, as shown in Figure 4-18. The list starts with all terminals specified, in the BNF, as strings. Scrolling down in the list, you will find a complete list of reserved words associated with this language, specified using proper case.

```
TERMINAL SYMBOLS


The following are the terminal elements of the language

         Terminal                           Where Used                      Remarks
   ----------------------------    ---------------------------------------   --------
   "&"                             likeFactorRHS
   "("                             lValue and functionCall
   "()"                            formalParameterDef
   ")"                             lValue and functionCall
   "*"                             mulOp
   "**"                            powOp
   "+"                             sign, powFactor and addOp
   ","                             formalParameterListBody
   "-"                             sign, powFactor and addOp
   "/"                             mulOp
   "0"                             optionStmt
   "1"                             optionStmt
   ":"                             immediateCommand
   ";"                             print
   "<"                             relOp
   "<="                            relOp
   "<>"                            relOp
   "="                             implicitAssignment, forHeader and relOp
   ">"                             relOp
   ">="                            relOp
   "Base"                          optionStmt
   "End"                           subDefinition and functionDefinition
   "Function"                      functionDefinition
   "Inst"                          trace
   "Line"                          trace
   "Memory"                        trace
   "Mod"                           mulOp
   "NoBox"                         trace
   "Object"                        trace
   "Source"                        trace
   "Stack"                         trace
   "Sub"                           subDefinition
```

Figure 4-18. Start of terminal list and part of the reserved words for QuickBasic, including extended reserved words for the trace instruction

Finally, scroll down further to see a complete syntax reference for our version of QuickBasic, synthesized in English from the BNF alone. Figure 4-19 shows the beginning of this reference. This is a comprehensive outline for QuickBasic programs, organized as a sequence of rules.[7] For example, the first rule declares that an immediate command (used to type an expression for immediate evaluation as seen in the Immediate window of Visual Basic) is a single immediate command, followed by zero, one, or more sequences of the form *: immediate command.*

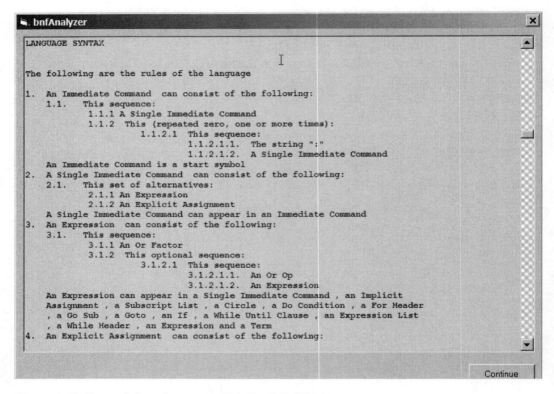

Figure 4-19. Start of the reference outline for QuickBasic

Take a look at outline item (3). It claims, truly, that an expression can consist of an or factor, followed by an optional sequence consisting of one of the or operators (Or or OrElse) and an expression. It claims, truly, that an expression

---

7. As a "word" person, who went into computing as part of an elaborate draft-dodging scheme that got completely out of hand, I have always been underwhelmed, to say the least, by the absence of truly automatic documentation from source code. This is my two cents.

can appear in many contexts, including single immediate commands such as `Let A=1+1` (where `1+1` is the expression), implicit assignments such as `A=1+1`, lists of subscripts as in `array(A,B+1)`, and so forth.

This is useful information, although the raw outline needs to be "decorated" with tutorials, examples, illustrations, and witty remarks to be an actual reference manual. If you want to enhance the reference outline extensively, you should use the option to convert it to XML.

Eight Guidelines for Effective BNF

You've seen how to use BNF in the requirements phase of our language, as a formal language that is not a programming language, and we have some tools for documenting the language. Here are some general guidelines for creating good BNF:

1. Create the valid BNF before you code the compiler.

2. Validate the BNF by making sure that `bnfAnalyzer`, `Bison`, or `yacc` processes the BNF completely and without any errors, before you code the compiler, or expect to use the output of `Bison`, `yacc`, or any parser generator.

3. If the BNF tool you are using supports comments, comment the BNF with descriptive information. Consider accompanying each rule with a complete explanation in your natural language.

4. In general, nonterminals that are sequenced (as in `a b`) should have disjoint sets of handles (possible terminals) in the right handle of `a` and the left handle of `b`. For example, the sequence `identifier identifier` should never occur if `identifier` has Visual Basic syntax, because the right handle of the first `identifier` is the set of all letters, numbers, and the underscore, while the left handle is the set of all letters (for .NET format identifiers, the left handle also includes the underscore). This means that unless blank is also defined as having a syntax role in your language, you literally don't know where the first identifier ends and the second identifier starts.

5. In general, nonterminals that are alternated (as in `a|b`) should have disjoint sets of handles in the left handle of `a` and `b`. For example, `number|identifier` is probably okay, because `number` can start with a digit only, while `identifier` can start with a letter only.

6.   When coding BNF, take your special programmer hat off and wear your special requirements hat. BNF is a formal language, rather than a programming language. It specifies the set of possible sentences in your language, not how to parse.

7.   In spite of rule 6, develop the BNF for the programmer of the parser and not for posterity.

8.   Don't show the user the BNF. Instead, use bnfAnalyzer to create the basis of a rules manual. Don't show the user this manual. Instead, use it as a basis for a presentation that shows you have done your due diligence and a reference manual is available for posterity.

bnfAnalyzer Technical Notes

As I mentioned earlier in this chapter, this section is best read after you've read Chapters 5, 6, and 7, since it discusses how bnfAnalyzer was developed as a small compiler for BNF.

Like our flyover compiler of Chapter 3, and like quickBasicEngine, bnfAnalyzer is a scanner that outputs individual tokens to a table (USRscanned, defined in the General Declarations section of frmBNFanalyzer.frm). Then a recursive, top-down descent parsing algorithm is used to convert the scanned code.

We need to scan because the input to bnfAnalyzer is free-form, consisting of white space, comments, and tokens similar to a Visual Basic or QuickBasic program. However, we do not parse to object code as in the case of integerCalc or quickBasicEngine. Instead, a tree structure is created, showing all the rules.

Recall, however, that my very cool Vaio laptop was briefly resident in the pawnshop during the initial development of the software for this chapter alone, in April 2003.[8] For this reason, I had to use Visual Basic 6 on my older Compaq Presario laptop to develop bnfAnalyzer. I also wanted to develop a solution in a hurry as exclusively form code.

It is generally better to factor large projects into objects: objects for scanning, objects for representing variable types, objects for representing variables, and so on. As is shown in Chapters 5 through 7, this allows us to ruggedize the objects by creating a comprehensive test methodology and test the GUI for each object. But often enough, schedule pressures don't permit this. However, you can take lessons from genuine object-oriented development and apply them to procedural development, and this has been done in bnfAnalyzer.

---

8. Many pawnshops will no longer accept old laptops and will make loans only for contemporary laptops that can show DVD movies, since their clientele will often want to watch movies.

The tree that represents the compiled BNF (in COLparseTree inside General Declarations, inside frmBNFanalyzer.frm) is just a Collection. But while most vanilla collections are simple one-dimensional arrays and hash tables, COLparseTree exploits the fact that any collection item can be a variant, and in particular, it may be a collection!

This means that recursive data structures can be, without too much loss of efficiency, represented as collections that contain subcollections.

For example, item(1) of COLparseTree is a one-dimension collection of all non-terminals found in the BNF. Item(2) is a similar collection of all terminals. Item(3) is the root of a tree, as described in a comment header placed in the code before COLparseTree, which represents the compiled BNF.

COLparseTree is, in fact, a virtual object, since, for all intents and purposes, it encapsulates the complete parse in one place that is easily passed between routines. When a new input file is selected, it is set to Nothing, and then rebuilt when the user chooses to create a reference manual. However, I was far more concerned with the reliability than the efficiency of this approach.

The problem with legacy, plain vanilla collections in Visual Basic 6 is that they can contain any variant value in any item. The parallel problem in .NET is that plain collections can contain any object in any item. This means that the language and the Framework won't enforce any rules on our behalf, and if we mess up, incorrect results will occur without warning!

The Inspection Report

Years ago, starting to use more and more complex user defined types (UDTs) in the C language, I found myself developing two routines rather consistently for those data types. I needed a routine to print the UDT so I could check it for validity, and, for advanced applications, I needed a routine to audit or inspect the UDT for correctness, over and above the rules enforced by the compiler and operating system. These later became a core object methodology, which I describe in the next chapter, because objects also need these tools.

This is why you may have noticed, during the parse of your BNF files, a series of progress messages claiming to "inspect" the parse tree in COLparseTree. After creating the parse tree, a series of rules is applied to the collection, and the program prints an error message if they are violated.

Of course, if I've done my job, these rules, which have strictly to do with the internal structure and not with user error, will always be satisfied. However, they are not quite a complete waste of time, since I've provided source code, and they comprise a check on changes to the source code.

Run bnfAnalyzer.exe on any input file and go to its Tools menu on its main screen. Choose Inspect the parse tree. Part of the resulting inspection report is shown in Figure 4-20.

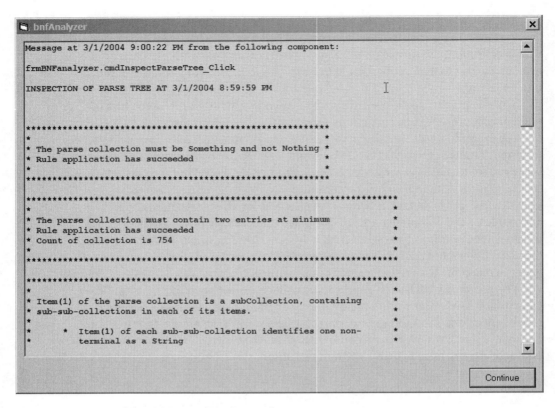

Figure 4-20. Part of the COLparseTree inspection report

Notice that the inspection report explains in painful detail what it needs to find, as you will see as you scroll.

Am I going overboard? No, I'm not.

A large object, whether it is a true object or a UDT that dreams of being an object, is something with a determinate state, and that state is either correct or bad. A bane of maintaining legacy, non-object programs was the way they, as large collections of disconnected variables, could easily get into a bad state, never to return.

The inspection routine is not only accessible from the menu, it is also called when bnfAnalyzer parses an input file. This provides valuable ongoing quality control. We are, in other words, doing real quality control on the ground.

Collection to String Conversion

Another way to check the parse tree is to see the data structure as a collection. The bnfAnalyzer project includes clsUtilities, which is an embedded utilities class (a more ambitious .NET utilities class, implemented as Shared methods, is used in our .NET projects). `clsUtilities` contains a tool for converting any collection to a readable string called, unimaginatively, `collection2String`. To see how this displays `COLparseTree`, open the Tools menu and select Dump the parse tree. The result is shown in Figure 4-21.

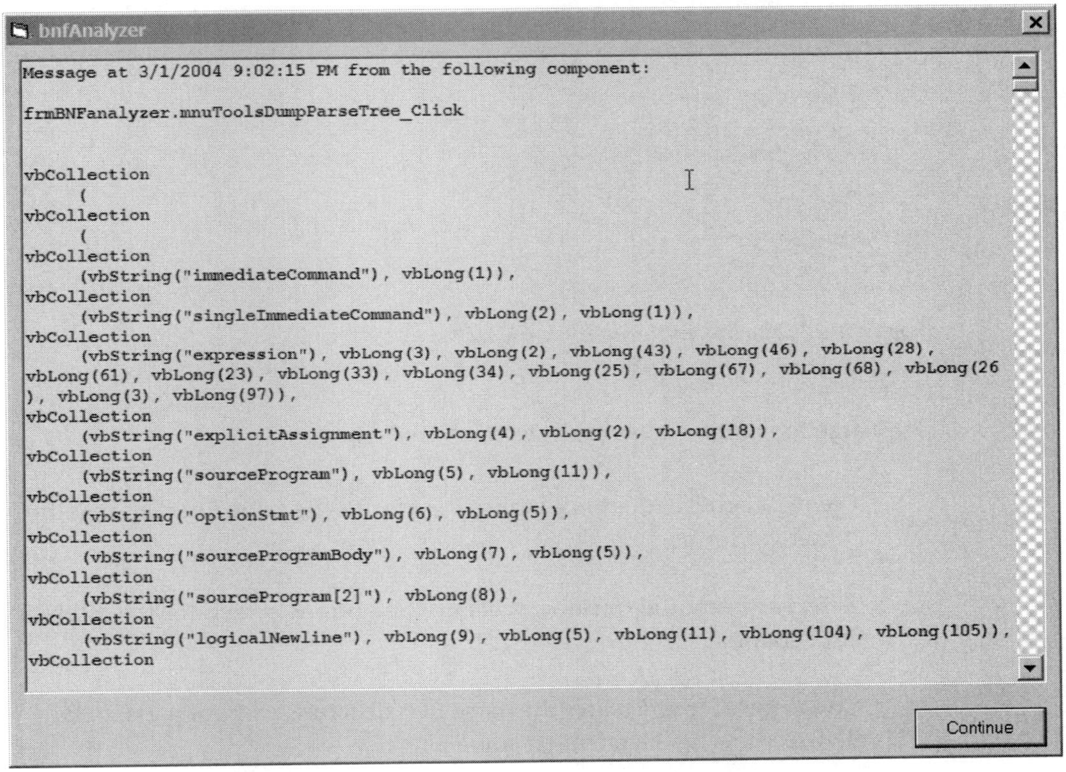

Figure 4-21. COLparseTree dump

This shows the collection and its members, which are subcollections using parentheses whenever a subcollection occurs. This is what I call the "decorated" approach to showing Visual Basic values in Visual Basic 6 and .NET. The decorated approach serializes variant types and values in Visual Basic 6, and object types and values in .NET. As you can see, it explicitly identifies not only the values of collection items, but also their types.

bnfAnalyzer Tools

There are a number of other options available in `bnfAnalyzer`, all accessible from the Tools menu, shown in Figure 4-22.

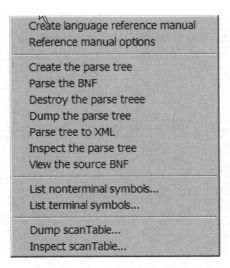

Figure 4-22. The bnfAnalyzer Tools menu

These functions are available from the Tools menu:

- **Create language reference manual:** Performs the same function that the button performs.

- **Reference manual options:** Calls up the options screen for the reference manual.

- **Create parse tree:** Creates the parse tree structure, without parsing the BNF or showing the reference manual.

- **Parse the BNF:** Creates the parse tree structure and parses whatever file is selected, without showing the reference manual.

- **Destroy the parse tree:** Destroys the parse tree, by freeing all subcollections and then setting the tree to nothing. Freeing all subcollections is important to avoid COM clutter.

- **Dump the parse tree:** Creates the collection dump of the parse tree (see Figure 4-21).

- **Parse tree to XML:** Converts the parse rules to an XML file, as shown in the previous sections of this chapter.

- **Inspect the parse tree:** Inspects the parse tree (see Figure 4-20).

- **View the source BNF:** Allows you to examine the source code, but not to change it. (You can use Notepad to change the source BNF.)

- **List nonterminal symbols:** Provides only the list of nonterminals, which is also embedded in the reference manual.

- **List terminal symbols:** Provides only the list of terminals, which is also embedded in the reference manual.

- **Dump scanTable:** Prints the scanned BNF in a readable form. This is the lexical analysis, as shown in Figure 4-23. The lexical analysis starts with several newlines because the input text file starts with several comment lines, and comments are ignored by the scanner. The scanner captures the token type, start index, length, and value of each token. The value is displayed using tools in `clsUtilities`, which serialize unprintable ASCII to a viewable form.

```
Message at 3/1/2004 9:06:18 PM from the following component:

frmBNFanalyzer.mnuToolsDumpScanTable_Click

SCAN DUMP AS OF 3/1/2004 9:06:03 PM

     Token Type           Start  Length                              Token Value
----------------------    -----  ------    ------------------------------------
newline                     40      2      "<newline>"
newline                     43      2      "<newline>"
newline                    117      2      "<newline>"
newline                    168      2      "<newline>"
newline                    242      2      "<newline>"
newline                    299      2      "<newline>"
newline                    302      2      "<newline>"
newline                    305      2      "<newline>"
newline                    331      2      "<newline>"
nonterminalIdentifier      333     16      "immediateCommand"
productionAssignment       350      2      ":="
nonterminalIdentifier      353     22      "singleImmediateCommand"
parenthesis                376      1      "("
stringToken                377      3      vbString(ChrW(34) & ":" & ChrW(34))
nonterminalIdentifier      381     22      "singleImmediateCommand"
parenthesis                403      1      ")"
mreOperator                404      1      "*"
newline                    405      2      "<newline>"
nonterminalIdentifier      407     22      "singleImmediateCommand"
productionAssignment       430      2      ":="
nonterminalIdentifier      433     10      "expression"
alternation                444      1      "|"
nonterminalIdentifier      446     18      "explicitAssignment"
newline                    464      2      "<newline>"
newline                    487      2      "<newline>"
nonterminalIdentifier      489     13      "sourceProgram"
productionAssignment       503      2      ":="
nonterminalIdentifier      506     10      "optionStmt"
newline                    518      2      "<newline>"
nonterminalIdentifier      520     13      "sourceProgram"
productionAssignment       534      2      ":="
```

Figure 4-23. Scanned BNF dump

- **Inspect scanTable:** Audits the scanned BNF for internal errors and produces the long and very boring inspection report shown in Figure 4-24.

> **NOTE** *My decision to use a user type for* USRscanned *instead of a collection means that I don't need to make certain checks. For example, the use of a type (or .NET structure) means that the compiler and the runtime enforce conformity to expected member types. However, the lack of an unsigned type means I do need to check members, in a full-dress inspection, for positive values. In addition, as I discuss in the next chapter, the tokens may not overlap, and this is checked in the inspection.*

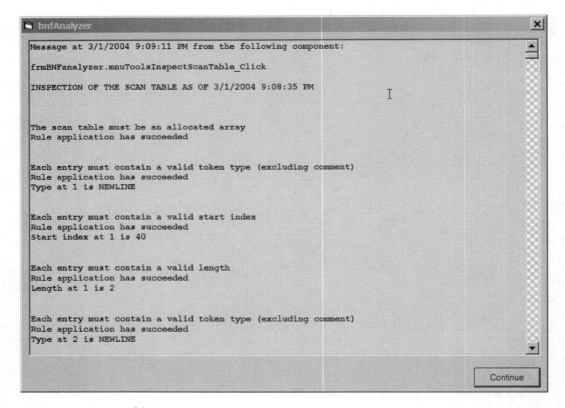

Figure 4-24. Scan table inspection report

The Status Report

You will have noticed that each time we create a reference manual, a Status box in the upper-right corner of the main form, and a progress bar under the Status box, go berserk and show status and progress. However, it's difficult to see what's being shown in the Status box.

You can select to see a detailed status report from the main bnfAnalyzer form. To see how this works, run bnfAnalyzer and, on the main form, select a small file, such as BNFanalyzer test 4, from the list in the lower-left corner of the screen. Notice that three levels of status report are available in a Parse Status group box on the main form. Select the highest level of detail: Complete report.

Click Create Reference Manual, and then cancel the options form to return to the main form. Click the Zoom box in the upper-right corner of the form. You'll see another pink dialog box, as shown in Figure 4-25. This one logs the status of scanning, parsing, and all other steps. Scroll through it to see how the BNF is compiled.

```
bnfAnalyzer                                                                   ×

        3/1/2004 9:14:53 PM Scanning BNF at character 152 of 205
        3/1/2004 9:14:53 PM Scanning BNF at character 154 of 205
        3/1/2004 9:14:53 PM Scanning BNF at character 166 of 205
        3/1/2004 9:14:53 PM Scanning BNF at character 169 of 205
        3/1/2004 9:14:53 PM Scanning BNF at character 179 of 205
3/1/2004 9:14:53 PM Scan complete
3/1/2004 9:14:53 PM Inspecting scan table
        3/1/2004 9:14:53 PM Inspecting scan table at token 1 of 13
        3/1/2004 9:14:53 PM Inspecting scan table at token 2 of 13
        3/1/2004 9:14:53 PM Inspecting scan table at token 3 of 13
        3/1/2004 9:14:53 PM Inspecting scan table at token 4 of 13
        3/1/2004 9:14:53 PM Inspecting scan table at token 5 of 13
        3/1/2004 9:14:53 PM Inspecting scan table at token 6 of 13
        3/1/2004 9:14:53 PM Inspecting scan table at token 7 of 13
        3/1/2004 9:14:53 PM Inspecting scan table at token 8 of 13
        3/1/2004 9:14:53 PM Inspecting scan table at token 9 of 13
        3/1/2004 9:14:53 PM Inspecting scan table at token 10 of 13
        3/1/2004 9:14:53 PM Inspecting scan table at token 11 of 13
        3/1/2004 9:14:53 PM Inspecting scan table at token 12 of 13
        3/1/2004 9:14:53 PM Inspecting scan table at token 13 of 13
3/1/2004 9:14:53 PM Inspection complete
3/1/2004 9:14:53 PM Parsing the scanned BNF
        3/1/2004 9:14:53 PM Checking for the nonterminal "bnfGrammar" using the
          production "bnfGrammar := production [ , production ]": the handle is
          "<newline>" at token 1 of 179
          3/1/2004 9:14:53 PM Checking for the nonterminal "production" using the
            production "production := [ nonTerminal := productionRHS ] NEWLINE": the
            handle is "<newline>" at token 1 of 179
            3/1/2004 9:14:53 PM Checking for the nonterminal
              "nonTerminal" using the production "nonTerminal :=

                                                              Continue
```

Figure 4-25. bnfAnalyzer parser, detailed status report

This progress report outlines the top-down recursive descent algorithm used in bnfAnalyzer. This same approach is used to parse QuickBasic, as explained in Chapter 7. A goal is set (parse the scanned BNF), then broken down into sub-goals, and then narrated in this level of detail.

In summary, bnfAnalyzer is itself a form of compiler, which compiles documentation rather than code. I did a lot of extra work in constructing it in the form of inspection and dump, so that I could rely on its output. Starting in Chapter 5, you'll see how these core methodologies allow you to create solid compiler objects.

Summary

You have seen that BNF can be specified using BNF, and, by processing the BNF file, you've seen how to use the bnfAnalyzer tool included in the sample code. We've examined how the large BNF for our QuickBasic was developed and pushed this file through the analyzer to make sure it is valid. And you've read eight rules for using BNF as a requirements definition language.

We can now write our compiler, which will consist initially of a lexical analyzer, a parser, and our own "Nutty Professor" interpreter.

Challenge Exercise

Develop the BNF for a simple language that uses letters as logical variables and the logical operators And, Or, and Not. Your language must support operator precedence such that Or has low precedence, And has medium precedence, and Not has high precedence. Your language must support parentheses.

Use bnfAnalyzer to make sure that your specification produces lists of non-terminals and terminals, as well as the reference outline, without error.

Remember how to support parentheses: define parenthesized groups at the same level as simple variables.

Resources

As noted in Chapter 3, a good reference for compiler theory is *Compilers: Principles, Techniques and Tools*, by Alfred Aho, Ravi Sethi, and Jeffery Ullman (Addison-Wesley, 1985). This book contains an excellent discussion of BNF.

CHAPTER 5

The Lexical Analyzer for the QuickBasic Compiler

*The question whether a computer can think is no more interesting than the
question of whether a submarine can swim.*
—Edsger Dijkstra

'What do you read, my lord?' 'Words, words, words.'
—William Shakespeare, Hamlet

YOUR BNF DEFINITION of the language, expanded into a reference manual perhaps
using the bnfAnalyzer software described in Chapter 4, is the detailed design, or
requirements document, for your compiler. It explains, in enough usable detail,
the semantic effect at runtime of user statements.

This chapter will enable you to get started with your own .NET compiler. It
describes the big picture, which starts with lexical analysis in support of parsing.
You'll learn some of the theory behind lexical analysis—just enough to help you
see how code implements theory (whether it wants to or not). You'll then see
how a scanner object (qbScanner) produces scanned tokens for lexical analysis.

The final section of the chapter describes object-oriented design principles
as they apply to the scanner object. These principles will be used consistently in
the rest of the QuickBasic compiler project.

The Compiler Big Picture

Our implementation of a classic compiler breaks down into three conceptual stages:

- The *lexical analyzer*, which reads the raw input text (almost always
  a stream of ASCII and Unicode characters) and synthesizes meaningful
  lexical units, passing them onward and upward to the parser

- The *parser*, which synthesizes the meaningful elements of the language (such as assignment statement, if statement, and so on)

- The *code generator*, which emits usable object code

Note that software tools for working with source code, other than compilers, might have this structure but replace the code generator with another form of generator. For example, the bnfAnalyzer tool used in Chapter 4 scans (lexically analyzes) BNF and parses it to create an internal representation of its structure. However, bnfAnalyzer generates documentation instead of object code. The yacc product generates C source code in place of object code, as do many preprocessors. This is, in fact, why this book stresses the front end of the compiler, as opposed to code generation for MSIL. The front end, consisting of the lexical analyzer and the parser, are utilities that allow you to craft, in any language, tools to make your job easier.

There are other conceptual units in commercial compilers. For example, popular units might be *optimizers*, which take either the source code or the object code and improve its performance by transformations that are known to be valid.

Our QuickBasic subset compiler, for example, notices *degenerate operations* in the source code, such as division by one or addition to zero. These operations are degenerate because their result is known: adding zero to a number always results in that number without change.[1] Our compiler can, as you will see in Chapter 6, remove these operations.

Our compiler also contains an *assembler* that resolves cross-references in the generated object code. The assembler will be discussed in Chapter 6.

Lexical Analysis Theory

As noted in Chapter 3, lexical analysis and parsing do the same general task. Literally or conceptually, they apply a formal grammar to the undifferentiated stream of characters and build a meaningful structure. They both apply a formal grammar, expressible using the BNF notation described in Chapter 4, to raw input.

For example, a Visual Basic identifier in .NET has a formal grammar. In ordinary training and in books, we state that a .NET identifier *must start* with a letter

---

1. Degenerate operations are not like staying out late in clubs and having fun. Mathematicians call operations like a+0 degenerate because, compared with useful operations like a+10, a+0 is a waste of my time and yours.

or an underscore, and it must contain one character.[2] A .NET identifier *may con-tain* letters, numbers, and underscores up to an arbitrary length, but keep it short for your sanity's sake.

The rule can be expressed in BNF:

```
VbIdentifier := ( LETTER | UNDERSCORE ) ( LETTER | UNDERSCORE | DIGIT ) *
```

However, notice that the right side of the informal BNF is actually using a notation, which you may already be familiar with: the regular expression as seen in .NET.

In Chapter 3, we briefly touched on the topic of regular expressions. Here, we will look at regular expressions and their relationship to formal automata, including Turing machines and a specialized, limited abstract machine called the *finite automaton*. This discussion should illuminate not only the tools for scanner generation, but also the manual writing of a scanner. It will show you how to think before you code the lexical analyzer for your language.

Regular expressions specify in a formal notation the rules for a class of strings. They originally appeared in Unix and are supported in Linux, as well as in objects shipped with COM and .NET. Regular expressions are a terse, if not gnomic, way of expressing the format of expected data. They are used to create good lexical analyzers, and thinking in terms of regular expressions is an important skill for the compiler developer. As you'll see, understanding a regular expression allows you to make predictions about what strings will satisfy it, and this is what makes a regular expression so very ... regular.[3]

Core Rules of Regular Expressions

Some core rules of regular expressions are seen in nearly all regular expression implementations. The rules for regular expressions can be expressed in BNF, as shown in Figure 5-1.

---

2. The ability of a .NET identifier to start with an underscore is a new, and somewhat useful, feature, added to Visual Basic as of .NET to bring Visual Basic in line with C++ practice. I use this ability in the code of this book. Shared variables in classes, which are not part of the object instance's state and which are, as their name implies, shared between objects, start in my code with an underscore. This reminds the reader that "we're not in COMsas anymore, Toto," and we are using a new .NET feature.

3. Mathematicians call regular expressions *regular* not because the regular expressions are regular; indeed, regular expressions appear rather irregular. However, the strings they specify have a regular and predictable structure once the regular expression is known.

```
regex := sequenceFactor [ regex ]
sequenceFactor := alternationFactor alternationRHS
alternationFactor := ( postfixFactor [ postfixOp ] ) | zeroOperandOp
alternationRHS := STROKE sequenceFactor
postfixFactor := string | charset | ( regex )
string := logicalChar [ string ]
postfixOp := ASTERISK | PLUS | repeater
repeater := LEFT_BRACE [ INTEGER ] [ COMMA ] [ INTEGER ] RIGHT_BRACE
zeroOperandOp := CARAT | DOLLAR_SIGN
charset := LEFT_BRACKET charsetExpression RIGHT_BRACKET
charsetExpression := charsetRange charsetExpression
charsetRange := logicalChar [ DASH logicalChar ]
logicalChar := ordinaryChar | hexSequence | escapeSequence
ordinaryChar := ORDINARYCHAR ' Where an ORDINARY CHAR is [^\*\+\^\$\\\-\(\)\[\]]
hexSequence := HEXSEQUENCE ' Where a hex sequence is \\x[0123456789ABCDEFabcdef]+
escapeSequence := ESCAPESEQUENCE ' Where an esc sequence is \\[\*\+\^\$\\\-\(\)\[\]]
```

Figure 5-1. Regular expressions in BNF (generic; may miss some features of actual processors)

We can use the `bnfAnalyzer` program to create a reference manual skeleton for a generic regular expression syntax, as shown in Figure 5-2.

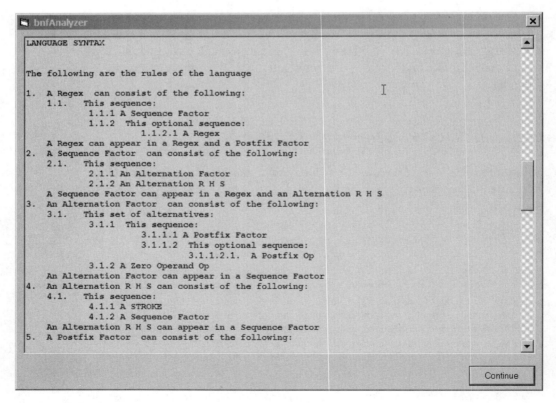

Figure 5-2. bnfAnalyzer output for regular expression syntax

> **NOTE** *For specifics on the* Regex *object available in Visual Basic .NET, see your Help system (you did install it, didn't you?). The lexical analyzer described here implements regular expressions without using a* Regex *object. Instead, it implements an* understanding, *in code, of the regular expression model of QuickBasic syntax, at the lexical level.*

Metacharacters

Any ordinary string can be a regular expression. For example, the regular expression A specifies only those strings consisting of the uppercase *A*. However, it's the use of special metacharacters that makes regular expressions so powerful. You saw a few examples of regular expression metacharacters in Chapter 3.

Asterisk

Any regular expression followed by an asterisk specifies all strings that meet the requirements of that regular expression, repeated zero, one, or more times (sometimes called *zero-trip*, because zero "trips" are allowed). Note that the asterisk allows null strings to satisfy its rule and that it allows a potential infinity of strings.[4] For example, A* is satisfied by a null string or any string consisting of uppercase *A*s only. Also note that this is a recursive definition, because it uses the concept in the definition ("a regular expression followed by an asterisk"). This is not cheating, since the inner regular expression is shorter and must meet all the rules of regular expressions.

Plus Sign

Any regular expression followed by a plus sign specifies all strings that meet its requirements repeated one or more times (called *one-trip*). For example, A+ is satisfied by the letter *A* and any string of *A*s.

Curly Braces

Another way of specifying iteration is to include a specific count of iterations in curly braces, as a multiple-character postfix operator to the right of the regular expression being repeated. For example, A{2} specifies only the string *AA*. Nearly all regular expression processors allow the digit in the braces to be a range, using

---

4. We say a regular expression is *satisfied* by a string; this means that the string conforms to the regular expression.

the comma to separate the minimum and maximum repetitions; therefore, A{1,2} specifies the strings *A* and *AA*.

Parentheses

Just as we have already used parentheses to group BNF elements, parentheses are metacharacters that can be used to group and clarify complex regular expressions, whether for the sanity of the reader or for correct execution. For example, A(BC)* is different from the regular expression (AB)C*. The first regular expression is satisfied only by strings that start with *A* followed by zero or more repetitions of *BC*. The second regular expression is satisfied by strings that start with *AB* followed by zero or more repetitions of *C*.

Vertical Stroke

The vertical stroke character (|) may be used to specify that, at the point where it occurs, the regular expression on its left is alternated or Or'd with the regular expression on its right. The regular expression (A*)|(B+) uses parentheses (which are actually unnecessary) to specify the valid "set of all strings," consisting of the null string (because the left side uses zero-trip iteration), a string of *A*s, **or** a string of at least one *B*.

Concatenation

To place a regular expression next to another regular expression is actually to use an invisible or implied operator, that of regular expression concatenation. This arrangement specifies that the regular expression on the left is followed by the regular expression on the right, and that correspondingly valid strings must satisfy the regular expression on the left and then that on the right, moving in that direction. This invisible operator is comparable to concatenation in BNF. For example, A*B+ specifies zero, one, or more occurrences of the letter *A*, followed by at least one or more *B*s.

Backslash

Because so many special characters are used in regular expressions to specify operations, any one of them may be preceded by the backslash character to specify that it appears as the occurrence *of that character*. In particular, the backslash character itself may be doubled to represent the literal appearance of the backslash character itself. For example, * can be used to represent a real asterisk. A* represents zero, one, or more occurrences of the letter *A*, and A* represents the letter *A* once, followed by an asterisk.

This is one of those marvelous Unix rules, an elegant feature in the sense that it gives the coder a lot of power. But the price is the gnomic character of regular expressions. * represents an asterisk. * represents a backslash repeated zero, one, or more times. * represents a backslash followed by an asterisk. * represents a backslash repeated one or more times (and it is equivalent to \\+).

In general, any odd number of backslashes followed by an asterisk represents a string of backslashes equal in length to the original number of backslashes, minus one, divided by two, and followed by the asterisk. Any even number of backslashes followed by an asterisk represents the set of strings consisting of *n* literal backslashes, where *n* is the backslash count minus two and divided by two, followed by zero, one, or more backslashes.

Like many structures invented by our friends, the gnomic developers of Unix, things tend to come together at the last minute in an elegant fashion.

Square Brackets and the Dash

Another important feature supported by all regular expression processors is the ability to identify a character set, and to thereby specify that "at this position, any character from this set is valid." The identification of the character set is performed in a regular expression by listing the members of the character set in the square bracket metacharacters. Metacharacters (including the square bracket) may be included in this list, as long as they are preceded by the backslash. In this list, the dash (-) metacharacter may be used to specify a range of adjacent characters in collating sequence. For example, [_A-Za-z] specifies the set of valid characters at the beginning of a Visual Basic .NET identifier: underscore, uppercase, and lowercase.

> **NOTE** *A set is not a string. A set is an unordered bag of objects, no two of which are the same (like my socks). A string is an ordered sequence of characters that can contain duplicates. All sets can be made into strings without loss of any information, and this is why we often represent a character set as a string. See the* verify *method in the utilities.vb code shipped with this book, for example. It accepts the character set to be verified in a string. However, because of order and the possibility of duplicates, not all strings can be converted to character sets.*

Regular Expression Processors

The core rules described here are supported by most regular expression processors. However, keep in mind that there are subtle, and sometimes dramatic, differences in the way specific processors work.

Also, it is easy to specify ambiguous regular expressions for the same reason it is simple to specify ambiguous BNF. The regular expression a*((aa){0,1}b)* is a simple example whose specific treatment may vary from one processor to another, with no error indication being typically provided, depending on the way the processor is implemented.

Consider each regular expression processor a new language, potentially different from the regular expression processor it replaces. This is very powerful stuff and confusing as hell. In the MIS world, as opposed to the more gnomic Unix world, you need to document regular expressions and avoid complexity for its own sake. Avoid ambiguous constructions.

In BNF, two adjacent grammar symbols should not share a right handle and a left handle, because this ambiguity can result in parse bugs. For example, the sequence "identifier identifier" is probably not valid, since an identifier may start with an alphabetic character or an underscore, and this set of characters overlaps the set of characters that may end an identifier (alpha, underscore, or digit). Likewise, it is usually not a good idea to concatenate two subexpressions in a regular expression such that the set of characters that ends the first subexpression overlaps the set of characters that start the second subexpression. For example, ([abc]d*)* ([def]g) may behave in unpredictable fashion, because the d might end the first part or start the second part.

And bear in mind that regular expressions can be used, not as a programming language driving a regular expression engine, but as a way of formally and in detail specifying a syntax for coding. Indeed, this is what has been done in quickBasicEngine.

The Relationship of Regular Expressions to Turing Machines and Finite Automata

Regular expressions can, with relative ease, be translated into an equivalent, abstract, mathematical machine, known in the math racket as an *automaton*. These formal, and often simplified, paper machines can prove important theses about the power and limits of computation, some of which are unfortunately ignored in the real world.

Turing Machines

The most famous abstract machine was also the earliest. Alan Turing described his 1936 Turing machine to show the limits of what is computable.

Now, what's a Turing machine? Is it a real computer in a museum, like the Commodore or Speak and Spell, from long ago? No, the Turing machine is a purely paper machine, the ultimate "Nutty Professor" computer— my affectionate term for computers that are described but never built.

As Alan Turing described the Turing machine in a famous paper written in 1936, it is conceptually (1) a state, (2) a read-write head of undetermined technology, and (3) a long paper tape upon which symbols can be read or erased.

The Turing machine, when fired up, is in a start state, usually state zero. It examines the symbol on its tape. It then consults a list of quintuples of the form *(oldState, oldSymbol, motion, newState, newSymbol)*. It locates the quintuple containing its current state (initially zero) and identifies the symbol it sees. Then it stamps the current square with a *newSymbol*, enters the *newState*, and goes left or right, depending on *motion*, which we can conceptualize as True for right or False for left.

Turing (who later became an early programmer) discovered using this formalization that, in general, a Turing machine cannot read the suitably encoded specification of another Turing machine and tell whether that Turing machine will halt. This formal limit to what is "computable" is why we get to debug our programs; why, indeed, the programming racket cannot be fully automated.

Turing machines are quite powerful, if you give them a lot of time. They don't use random access memory, and for this reason, would take, if actually built, an inordinate amount of time for the simplest problem. Windows 2000 on a Turing machine is too horrible to contemplate. But if you ignore the important question of time, and if the Turing machine has enough memory, it can make any calculation that a real computer can perform.

Turing machines are interesting to the programming language designer because, in most cases (not all), you would like your language to be *Turing-complete*, and as such, capable of expressing any calculation that a Turing machine can perform. The hard way to do this is to write, in your proposed programming language, a software simulation of a Turing machine. This is a great way to waste a lot of cycles on calculating sums of one-digit binary numbers, but it proves that your language can solve any problem that can be translated into a set of Turing machine quintuples.

Indeed, Turing's proof was that one application would be the acceptance of a set of quintuples that resulted in the Turing machine simulating any other Turing machine. All you need to do, after all, is decide on a way to encode the program, the quintuples, of the other Turing machine, and once you have done this, it is quite easy to write quintuples that examine the encoded program and do what it does.

This is really the fundamental theorem of computer science, because Turing proved that rule-following is, itself, following rules!

The easy way to prove that your language is at least as powerful as a Turing machine is to support, in your programming language, each of the structured control structures with which you're probably familiar: straight-line code including expression evaluation, If..Then..Else, and looping. This is because it's known that if a language supports these structures, it is Turing-complete.

Once Upon a Time, There Was This Machine...

The difference between programming and math annoys many programmers. I can wave my chalk around, not tell you implementation details such as *how* the Turing machine finds the right state, and symbol in the list of quintuples. But in the same way BNF as a *formal notation* and not a *programming language* allows us to assume shared knowledge and the shared willingness to suspend belief, Turing machines are a formal notation. The story could begin, "Once upon a time, there was this goofy machine..." It ends with a proof of what Turing machines *can* do (simulate any other Turing machine) and what Turing machines *cannot* do (detect in general whether another Turing machine will halt).

I'm not going to inflict the proofs on you, nor inflict on myself the need to write an amusing recount of the proofs. If you are interested, check out the numerous books on Turing written for the general reader. If you are really interested, write down some sets of Turing machine quintuples for solving some simple problems (such as binary addition). If you really want to dweeb out, write a visual simulation of the Turing machine in Visual Basic, but don't show it to your manager. This is one example of a *completely useless* program.

The ultimate geek movie, for the *Beautiful Mind* and *Lord of the Rings* crowd, would be about some aliens who use a Turing machine. Then we could see this gizmo on the silver screen, stamping and shuttling over a paper tape!

See www.turing.org for a discussion of Turing machines and simulators on real computers.

Finite Automata

Regular expressions can be transformed in a straightforward way to a simplified, limited abstract machine known as a *finite-state automaton*. Any Turing machine can simulate a finite automaton. This is a Turing machine, with a state and a memory tape, but it can travel only in one direction and cannot change the tape.

In a book with the formidable title *Programming Languages and Their Relation to Automata* (out of print, published by Addison-Wesley in 1969), Jeff Hopcroft and Jeff Ullman, of Princeton and Bell Labs, showed proofs that finite automatons and regular expressions parallel each other. Any regular expression and any finite automaton accept the same set of languages, in the sense that they will detect an error in the identical collection of languages. Both are incapable, in turn, of carrying out a larger set of tasks.

A regular expression (at least without extensions) cannot express all the syntax forms expressible by BNF, and regular expressions are less readable than BNF.

Regular expressions, as such, cannot (again, without extension) support structures with unlimited nesting, such as parenthesized groupings and the block structure of a typical programming language.

Another more real-world limitation of regular expressions is that they are less readable than BNF because they express syntax on a single line. For this reason, regular expressions (without extensions) such as those in .NET's `Regex` object, do not allow you to modularize and break down a complex parsing problem; BNF does.

Here is an example of a realistic regular expression for the syntax of the first line of a Visual Basic COM function or subroutine:

```
((\x0D\x0A)|\x0A)[ ]*((Public )|(Private )|(Friend)){0,1}((Sub )|(Function )|
(Property (Get|Set|Let) ))([A-Za-z_][A-Za-z0-9_]*)
```

I used regular expressions as a conceptual tool in developing the lexical analyzer for QuickBasic because mere code, in this complex case, did the work more efficiently and is easier to understand. I have nothing against regular expressions and have used them in application programming to save coding time. As an actual tool, and as a formal requirements notation for detailed geeky design, regular expressions are just as important as BNF. Therefore, I next present a regular expression laboratory.

A Regular Expression Laboratory

You were introduced to the regular expression laboratory application, `relab`, in Chapter 3. As I noted in that chapter, it helps you learn about regular expressions for common tasks. This application also allows you to test regular expressions using the standard .NET regular expression processor, and it converts regular expressions to their declaration in Visual Basic .NET. The code for `relab` is available from the Downloads section of the Apress Web site (`http://www.apress.com`), in the egnsf/relab/bin folder.

Regular Expression Testing

Run relab.exe from the code supplied with this book. Dismiss the initial Easter egg (after studying it, of course, to learn what the code is about). You will then see the form shown in Figure 5-3, which allows you to view, modify, and enter regular expressions.

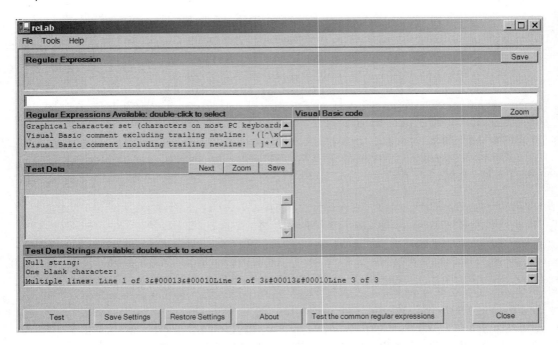

Figure 5-3. Use relab.exe to test, save, and document regular expressions.

Notice the list of regular expressions under the label Regular Expressions Available. Double-click the last visible entry, which starts with "Simple Visual Basic identifier (release 6 and before)." Now, drop down to the light-gray area under the label Test Data (the darker gray area under that label is for storage of your favorite test strings), and enter the string 12345 _a abce identifier1.

Before you do anything else, ask yourself, "What is the first (leftmost) identifier in the string?" Write down your answer.

Now click the Test button in the lower-left corner of the form. Since one of the purposes of the laboratory is to allow you to save your regular expressions and test cases, you will see a rather poisonously green screen, as shown in Figure 5-4.

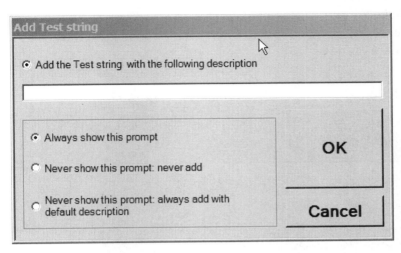

Figure 5-4. Trust me, this screen, which prompts you to identify your test data, is a yucky green.

The green screen also allows you to control the way in which you save test data. As you can see, you can tell relab to never either prompt or save test strings, or you can tell relab to always save, but not prompt for a description. The Tools menu of the main form will allow you to bring up this screen without adding test data.

When you are returned to the main form, be sure to click *to the left* of the test string and in the light-gray test string area, since the tester will always start at the location you specify. Click the Test button in the lower-left area of the form.

Oops, why was a in _a highlighted? This is because regular expressions *have no opinion about the strings that surround them,* and this is something to keep in mind. When used to find a string, they simply search for the handle of that string, consisting of any one of the set of characters that can start a string that satisfies the regular expression. For the regular expression we've selected, this set is [A-Za-z] (in regular expression set notation). Therefore, this is where the cursor has moved. Regular expressions, unlike BNF, do not care about context.

Press the right-arrow key, and then click the Test button to see the next regular expression, abce. Press the right-arrow key and click Test once more to see the last regular expression, identifier1.

Try a new regular expression. In the text box under Regular Expression at the top of the screen, enter the regular expression (^[ ]+[ ]+)*. Our goal is to find a series of blank delimited words.

> **NOTE** *This regular expression has a bug. What is it? If you know what it is, enter the buggy regular expression anyway, without fixing it, in order to follow the text.*

Press the Tab key to exit the text box. You'll see a blue screen that allows you to add a regular expression description. Enter the description **Parse words**, as shown in Figure 5-5, and click OK.

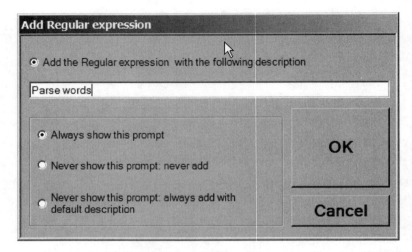

Figure 5-5. The blue screen (but not of death) allows you to describe the purpose of regular expressions.

Move back to the light-gray Test Data area and enter   **Moe Larry Curley,** with a few spaces before Moe, perhaps between the other Stooges,[5] but no spaces at the end! Click Test to see the green Add Test String screen (Figure 5-3), enter a description for the test string, and click OK.

Click all the way to the left of the test string in the light-gray box, and then click Test again.

Strange—only the blanks in front of *Moe* are highlighted. This makes no sense, since our goal was to find a sequence of blank separated words, and we entered "find a nonblank sequence, find some blanks, and repeat."

But we made a simple clerical error. We entered the caret *before* the square bracket. In this position, it *matches* "the start of the input."

Fix the problem in the black-on-white text box, and tab out to be prompted for a description of the new regular expression. (The Delete button above the Regular Expressions Available list box allows you to delete old regular expressions.) Click at the far left of the light-gray test data box and click Test. Oops, something is wrong.

---

5. The Three Stooges were three American comedians of the 1930s who lost title to their films. As a result, their films were repeatedly shown on American television during the 1950s. Their name became a byword for cluelessness. They may correspond in Russia to The Five Stupid Guys, or in India to The Junglee Fools from the Country.

The relab application allows us to "cudgel our brains" in isolation from code using our regular expressions and to focus on cleaning them up. It's no fun to debug a regular expression inside the business tier, in the server room, at 3:00 AM.

If you don't see why no match was found, ask yourself—cudgel thy brains—what is the handle of the leftmost unit. Since the leftmost meaningful unit is a nonblank, the regular expression doesn't start at the beginning of the string

Moe Larry Curley, with three blanks.

But shouldn't the search for the regular expression find, starting at the first blank, the regular expression that starts with *M*? It does not because we're starting inside characters that are valid inside the regular expression handle.

Furthermore, there is a bug inside the regular expression. It doesn't allow the input string to *start* with blanks. Many text strings will start with blanks. And it actually requires that the input string ends with a blank, which is not true of most input strings.

In other words, the regular expression is completely broken, showing the value of relab. It actually needs to be ([ ]*[^]+)*.

Strangely, the best way to express the fact that spaces occur between words is to start with zero-trip spaces, because the one-trip nonspaces required by [^]+ will always parse the word. Placing the zero-trip spaces first defines a word as "that which is preceded by zero or more spaces."

Enter the correct solution, and document it in the Add Regular Expression box (Figure 5-5) if you like (or press Cancel to skip this step; note that this will cause the solution not to be stored). Click again at the left side of the test string to see the correct answer finally highlighted.

Regular Expression Conversion to Visual Basic .NET

Next, examine the dark-gray text box on the right side of the relab form to see the regular expression converted to Visual Basic .NET code, which you can copy and paste. This means that once you've tested a regular expression (one you've typed into the text box at the top of the screen), you can grab this code (which is commented with the description you entered in the Add Regular Expression box) and paste it into your own code.

NOTE *The* relab *program doesn't actually convert the regular expression to code that doesn't use a regular expression. Instead, it produces the formatted definition of the regular expression commented with the definition. It is a more formidable task to convert the regular expression to code, although you can do that using the lexical analysis and parsing methods described in this book. However, you also need to know how the regular expression is translated to a nondeterministic finite automaton and from that to a deterministic finite automaton. If you're interested, refer to Aho, Sethi, and Ullman's "dragon book,"* Compilers: Principles, Techniques and Tools *(Addison-Wesley, 1985).*

When you leave the regular expression laboratory, it will save all of your test expressions and test strings in the Registry in a standard location. You will have your stash of tested and documented regular expression tools—your very own gnome factory.

TIP *To create a laboratory for a programming team, in which you can share regular expressions and test data, you can convert the source code for* relab *to save information in Microsoft Access or SQL Server. See the methods* form2Registry *and* registry2Form *for the code that should be modified.*

Regular Expressions for Common Tasks

The relab tool comes with the following common regular expressions:

- The regular expression that defines the characters available on standard PC keyboards in the US and displayable in most fonts (I call this the *graphical character set* in the documentation, but note that it has nothing to do with graphics)

- The regular expression for a Visual Basic comment that starts with an apostrophe, extends to the end of the line, and contains no tabs or other white space characters other than the blank

- The regular expression for a Visual Basic comment including end of line

- The regular expression for a block of contiguous Visual Basic comments

- Visual Basic identifiers (release 6 and before), excluding compound identifiers of the *form object.property*

- Visual basic identifiers (.NET), excluding compound identifiers

- Visual Basic identifiers (release 6 and before), including compound identifiers of the *form object.property*

- Visual Basic identifiers (.NET), including compound identifiers

- The newline for Windows (carriage return and linefeed) or the Web (linefeed only)

- The header of Visual Basic COM procedures (subroutines, functions, and Get/Set/Let properties), excluding their formal parameter list

- The header of Visual Basic .NET procedures outside event declarations (subroutines, functions, and properties), excluding their formal parameter list

- The Visual Basic COM formal parameter definition (a formal parameter is one that appears in a function, subroutine, or property header, as opposed to the actual parameter used to call the function, subroutine, or property) of the form *[ByVal\ByRef] identifier As Type*

- The Visual Basic .NET formal parameter definition of the form *[ByVal\ByRef] identifier As Type*

TIP *See the Visual Studio Help system for more application-oriented regular expressions, including regular expressions for phone numbers and ZIP codes.*

Most of the included regular expressions have to do with parsing source code. However, I don't recommend their use in a full compiler. This is because the common regular expressions do not take context into account and blindly accept the next string that meets their rules.

For example, a Visual Basic identifier by itself is a valid formal parameter declaration when Option Strict is not in effect in Visual Basic .NET, as in Private Sub A(B). The ByVal/ByRef clause is not required (it defaults to ByRef in COM and to ByVal in .NET), nor is the As clause, although omitting the As clause is always bad practice in COM and .NET. This means that if the common regular expression is used in the middle of arbitrary source code to find the next formal parameter, it will return a false positive when an identifier occurs to the left of the first formal parameter. In Private Sub A(B), the identifier A will be mistakenly recognized as a Visual Basic 6 formal parameter definition using the regular expression supplied in relab, as shown here.

```
(((ByVal )|(ByRef )){0,1}([A-Za-z]
[A-Za-z0-9_]*)(\([,]*\)){0,1}([ ]+As ([A-Za-z]
[A-Za-z0-9_]*)){0,1})
```

The regular expression can be used only after a procedure header has been located, along with an immediately following a left parenthesis.

The common regular expressions were developed for a variety of software tools that read and examine Visual Basic source as quick solutions to client problems, including the need to identify all procedures of a certain type. They use an ad-hoc or "lazy" approach to full-scale parsing of Visual Basic that is interested only in certain strings.

Full-scale parsing, almost of necessity, involves parsing not characters (as do these regular expressions) but of *scanned tokens*, such as those produced by an object like qbScanner, described in the next section.

The Dangers of Using Ad-Hoc Code to Examine Source

It is usually a mistake to sit down and write a software tool that reads Visual Basic source (or source in another language) and uses ad-hoc code, including ad-hoc regular expressions, to find structures that need to be examined or changed. That approach is full of nasty surprises, of which false positives, consisting of commented source code and quoted source code, are only the beginning. It gives tool-building a very bad name.

Essentially, to build self-reflexive Visual Basic tools (or tools in another language) that have source code as their input, you need to parse using the full-scale techniques of this chapter and Chapter 7, or you need to warn the users of the tool that it may fail, or you need to apply ad-hoc methods very carefully.

It would be great, for each Visual Basic dialect, to have a full-scale parser object that you could snap in to tool applications. In the add-in model, this object is available, in a sense, because it gives you access to the object model of the Microsoft parser. However, this is not something you can pick up and send, as part of a product, to a customer. Such a parser object may emerge from the Mono project to reverse-engineer an open-source .NET (visit http://www.go-mono.com). In fact, you can use the techniques of this chapter and Chapter 7 to develop such a tool, covering yourself with fame and glory.

The final feature of relab that I would like to show you is its regression test of the common regular expressions. Although the regular expressions are hard-coded and inside a Shared (static) class, utilities.dll, I was nervous about getting them right, so I included the regression test feature. Also, since you have the source, you might change them.

Click the button labeled Test the common regular expressions, on the bottom-right side of the form. You will see a success dialog box, followed by a Zoom box, which provides a text box view of a report, as shown in Figure 5-6. The report shows a series of test cases applied to the common regular expressions, such that the application is tested against expected results.

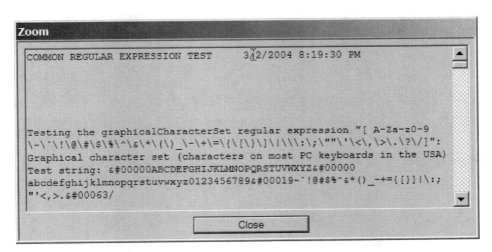

Figure 5-6. Regression testing the common regular expressions

We've revisited regular expressions. The next step is to see how we've wrapped the hand-coded lexical analysis into an object, which gives us a reusable tool for scanning QuickBasic and languages with related syntax.

The qbScanner Object

The lexical analysis of quickBasicEngine is implemented as a distinct object model and stateful object, named qbScanner. It is a stateful object because it contains variables that occupy memory, in its General Declarations section.

The .NET GUI application, qbScannerTest.exe, available from the Downloads section of the Apress Web site (http://www.apress.com), in the egnsf\Apress\QuickBasic\qbScanner\qbScannerTest directory, lets you examine how this object works. Figure 5-7 shows this program.

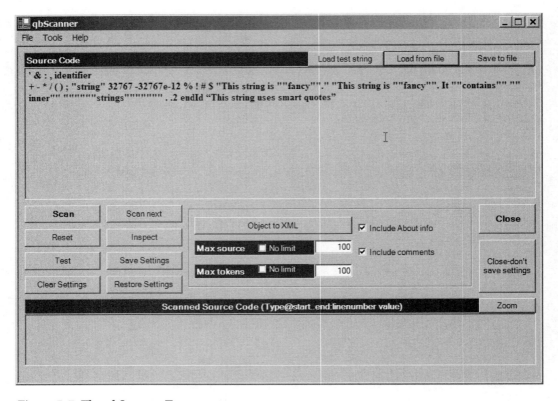

Figure 5-7. The qbScannerTest program

The purpose of a lexical analyzer is to get from an undifferentiated stream of input characters, including line breaks, to a series of tokens, where each token can be thought of as a word in our language. The set of tokens returned by an acceptable scanner partitions the input stream of characters into smaller sequences of characters.

As you will see, this is quite different from the situation in the parser. Even in a simple statement such as I = 1 + 1, the parser will need to recognize several different constructs. The entire statement is an assignment statement, which contains an LValue (I), followed by an operator, and so on. The LValue I to the left of the assignment is also an identifier.

Tokens as scanned by a scanner do not overlap in any way, but are instead a simpler partitioning of the input source code, which makes the parser's life easier. In our lexical analyzer, "meaningless" blanks (blanks outside comments and strings) are eliminated, also to make life easier for the parser.

NOTE *We could downsize the lexical analyzer out of existence, since what it actually does is a low-level parse. We could use the techniques described in Chapter 7 instead. But this would make the parser much too complex.*

Token Types

When you start up qbScannerTest.exe, it displays examples of each of the token types defined in the QuickBasic language:

- Apostrophe

- Ampersand

- Colon

- Comma

- QuickBasic identifier, which has the same syntax as Visual Basic identifiers prior to .NET

- Arithmetic and other operators (a single token type that excludes the ampersand)

- Left and right parentheses (a single token type)

- Semicolon

- String

- Unsigned numbers

- Pound sign

- Dollar sign

- Newline (carriage return, and line number)

Note that our scanner does not limit the length of identifiers, as did older QuickBasic and Visual Basic processors. This was necessary in older compilers, where tables had to be carefully allocated in C or even assembler to preserve scarce memory. In our implementation of quickBasicEngine, we have the nearly unlimited length String data type, so this limitation is not enforced.

> **NOTE**   *Several complex strings are provided in* qbScannerTest. *They test lexical analysis of strings and the Basic rule that doubled internal double quotes represent double quotes.*

Whether or not we use a regular expression to scan these tokens, any sensible code will be, in effect, an implementation of a regular expression. This raises a problem with token schemes, including any possible proposal to make signed numbers into tokens.

Ideally, each distinct token type should have a different handle—a different set of characters that may appear at the beginning of the token. In Chapter 4, the handle of a grammatical class was the symbol, or set of symbols, that could begin the grammatical class. For example, a Visual Basic expression starts with an identifier, a number, a plus sign, or a minus sign.

We would like to simply scan left to right for any one of the set of characters that can start a token, for each token, and take the first token we find left to right. There are, as I will show, dangers in this simple plan, but basically it's a good idea.

In fact, each token type in this data model has a different handle. The very simple token types for single characters (apostrophe, ampersand, colon, comma, semicolon, dollar sign, and pound sign) each has a unique handle: the character to which it corresponds, which does not appear anywhere else. Parentheses are restricted to the parenthesis token type. Identifiers start with letters and underscores, which appear nowhere else. Here are some examples:

- The apostrophe starts a comment.

- A letter starts an identifier, or, possibly, an operator like Mod, which has the form of an identifier.

- A plus sign starts and ends an operator.

- A decimal point or a digit starts a number, which in our tokenization is always unsigned; we treat the sign as a unary prefix operator. The next section explains why we use unsigned numbers.

> **NOTE**   *The ampersand is not included with the operators because it does double duty in QuickBasic as the string concatenation operator and a type suffix in an identifier. (QuickBasic has a legacy and ugly feature, which was preserved in Visual Basic through release 6: you can define the type of a variable using a special character at the end of its name.)*

The Consequences of Syntax Changes

At the 2001 Microsoft Author's event, we were sitting around discussing the new Visual Basic .NET capability of starting an identifier with an underscore. We agreed that it was a good idea because it gives the programmer the ability to isolate a class of "special" identifiers by prefixing them with the underscore.

Somebody asked why Microsoft did not go ahead and also allow digits at the beginning of identifiers, as this would be more "powerful." The problem, of course, is that then, the Visual Basic .NET token for an identifier would have an overlapping handle with the number, and the lexical analyzer would be very complex.

Failure to think through the consequences of "powerful" changes to the syntax can result in permanent and ineradicable compiler bugs (known as "issues" or even "features" when the user starts depending on them).

An old example happens to be the Fortran statement DOI=JTO3, which could be a valid Fortran assignment (of the value in JTO3 to the identifier DOI, or a Do statement (equivalent in Basic to a For statement) with no white space. The original designers, although they were heroes, wanted to allow programmers to leave out white space between the tokens of the language, but at the time they worked, language theory was in its infancy. They therefore wrote the rule out in English and did not spot the problem.

Software tools such as lexx, yacc, and Bison express in what I call a reified form (converted into a concrete thing) the accumulation of programmer wisdom, but this wisdom is a two-edged sword. Doing things in a more manual, less reified form, as we do them in this book, allows us to learn why lexx, yacc, and Bison enforce the rules they actually enforce.

Why Signs Are Not Included in Number Tokens

The number token defined in the QuickBasic language can contain an integer part, an optional decimal part, and an exponent (consisting of uppercase or lowercase *e*, an exponent sign, and the integer value of the exponent).[6] But why aren't signs included in numbers in tokens?

If we allowed signed numbers as tokens, then the number would share a handle with the plus and minus, because signs are also binary operators. There

---

6. The exponent represents shifting of the value by powers of ten. Exponents are used by nutty professors, mad scientists, and disturbed engineers to represent the very large and the very small.

are ways to code around the problem. The difficulty is that there are many ways to code this, and nearly all of them are wrong.

You could look for a number to the right of the operator or sign, but this means either one of two things: you have code for a token type of unsigned number anyway, which is useless to your user but that supports your actual number, or else you merely move to the right and look for a digit. Oops, remember, a valid unsigned number can start with a decimal point, and your code has to work for −.1, which is valid. Consider a- -1, which is ugly but valid. If we defined a signed number as a token, when we encountered the minus or plus sign, we would need to back up and examine context.

Another consideration is that your scanner would need to violate its commitment to basically act like a finite automaton, and move left to right. Where did this commitment come from? It came from the fact that our objective is to broadly define the scanner object's behavior in clear and understandable terms, as an implementation of a finite automaton, and a finite automaton moves left to right only. Also, if the scanner can move backward, and undo scanning, this makes scanner progress reporting all the more complex. As discussed in the "The Scanner Object Model" section later in this chapter, qbScanner exposes events to let user code manage progress reporting. If the scanner moves backwards, the user will be confused by progress reports that back up. More generally, any extra features of the scanner generate work as the scanner moves from left to right, and this work would need to be unperformed and undone on backup. Finally, if you want to use the scanner in multiple threads or as a scanner server that provides tokens on demand, a scanner that backs up will make the final product very complex.

Fortunately, there is a simpler solution, and this is to simplify the scanner. The scanner promises to give the parser unsigned real numbers only. It lets the parser worry about the difference between a plus sign and a unary positive sign, and between a minus sign and a unary negative sign. The result is that we can implement the scanner by scanning forward for the handle of each distinct token at any instant in scanning.

Scanner Implementation

Unfortunately, Visual Basic .NET does not provide an easy way (as do C and C++ with strspn and strcspn) to find any one of a set of tokens, other than by using the regular expression object (Regex), which is overkill for such a simple task. Instead, if you examine the qbScannerTest project in the source code, you will find a project and a stateless class (one with no variables that occupy storage at runtime in General Declarations) called the utilities class. This class exposes the verify utility, which scans for a set of alternative characters, or for the complement of this set: the set of all characters not in the specified set.

The proposed design looks simple in structured pseudocode:

```
Do until done
     Find the leftmost token
     Add It to the scanner's collection of tokens
End Do
```

However, there are two problems with this initial design. We will need to
have some sort of index to characters in source to keep track of position. This
initial design does not tell us how to manage the index, and this management
is tricky. Also, the pseudocode might result in slow real code, since Find the
leftmost token implies an inner loop.

Here is how we can manage the index:

```
Set Index to 1 (first character)
Do until Index > length(source code)
     Find the leftmost token starting at Index
     Add It to the scanner's collection of tokens
     Add the length of the leftmost token
End Do
```

This more refined design neglects the possibility of blanks between tokens.
This is a fairly simple issue to resolve—just place a simple loop, which won't
make the code much slower (because, generally speaking, one blank will appear
between tokens in source code) under the Do until and before the Find the
leftmost token.

```
Set Index to 1 (first character)
Do until Index > length(source code)
     For each possible token
          Find its leftmost location starting at Index
     End For
     Add It to the scanner's collection of tokens
     Add the length of the leftmost token
     Skip over blanks and other white space
End Do
```

However, the wasteful inner loop (or straight-line sequence of tests, which
has the same constant effect on runtime) remains. It is wasteful because, in the
case of tokens that overlap, it will return false positives. For example, if we are
scanning the string "Identifier" (a string containing quote, *Identifier*, quote),
the inner loop will find the *Identifier* one position beyond the start of the
string. It won't return this bogus Identifier as a real token, because when the
string is found to be the real token, Add the length of the leftmost token will
shift the index over the false Identifier. But in a more complex case, such as
the string "*/Identifier", the scanner will scan two bogus arithmetic operators
unnecessarily.

In the case of the string "*/Identifier", the programmer obviously means "a string containing an asterisk, a slash, and the word *Identifier*." However, the inner loop in the preliminary pseudocode will find a string at positions 1..14, an asterisk at position 2, a slash at 3, and the identifier *Identifier* at 4.

It would be better to create an "anticipatory" scan, and this was implemented in qbScanner. In this algorithm, each trip through the major scan loop goes through all or some tokens. For each token that hasn't already been found to the left of the index, the scanner locates this token. It doesn't do this in an inner loop. Instead, it uses Instr. Then it selects the leftmost and widest token. The next loop can simply ignore false positive tokens, which are inside the leftmost and widest token.

Consider the quoted string "*/Identifier". The first time through, the inner For loop will find all three token types: a string, an asterisk and a slash, and an identifier. But it can also note that the *string* is the *leftmost* and *widest* token. Therefore, the *string* will be selected as the next token.

Of course, the scanner could also find other tokens beyond the string. Suppose the string is followed by a number, one beyond the end of the string at position 15. Since the number is a different token type than the asterisk, slash, identifier, or string, it is also recorded in an array in the For loop. In fact, consider what happens when control returns to the For loop a second time: the main scan index will have been increased by 14 characters, since this is the length of the string. The second execution of the For loop will simply move beyond all preset tokens when they occur to the left of the main scan index, and scan for the next occurrence starting at the main scan index. Recall that its loop text is "find its leftmost token *starting at index*"!

> **NOTE** *Don't be overly concerned that "*/Identifier"123 is, in syntactical terms, complete garbage. Recall that it is the parser's job to worry about garbage at this level. As far as the scanner is concerned, this string is just fine, and it consists of two tokens: a string followed by an integer.*

The scanner implements an array for each token type—the anticipatory array—and each entry in this array has the following states: token unknown, token found, or token does not exist to the end of the string. Each time through the scanner's inner loop, when a token has unknown state, the scanner must locate that token.

```
Set Index to 1 (first character)
Set all tokens in an "anticipation" array of possible
"candidate" tokens to unknown
Do until Index > length(source code)
    Set the Index of the "candidate" past the end of the source code, because the
    "candidate" is the token that might be the next real token
```

```
    For each token In the array
        If It Is unknown
            Find It (If It doesn't exist then create an entry
                        pointing past the end of the source code)
        ElseIf It Is completely to the left of the leftmost token "candidate"
            Select It as the "candidate"
        End If
    End For
    If the "candidate" Is beyond the end of the source code, we're done
    Add the candidate to the scanner's collection of tokens
    Set the candidate to Unknown
    Add the length of the leftmost token to the scan Index
    Skip white space
End Do
```

Note that `completely to the left of the leftmost token` "candidate" means that it is not enough to compare the starting index of the candidate with the starting index of the anticipated token, because tokens can overlap. Instead, the start index plus the length of the candidate token must be less than the start index of the anticipated token.

All this seems fairly complex. In a nutshell, the algorithm does the following:

1. Finds the leftmost and widest token, while also finding a set of useless tokens inside the leftmost and widest tokens, and more usefully finds another set of tokens fully to the right of the leftmost and widest token

2. Adds the leftmost and widest token to the output list of tokens, sets the character index one past the end of the leftmost and widest token, and repeats until done

This algorithm is implemented in the `Private function scanner_` in `qbScanner.VB`, and it is probably the most complex feature of the scanner. Note that my coding standard within classes (but not within forms) is to end `Private` method names with an underscore.

A Scan Test

Let's try running the scanner for the test tokens. Click the Test button on the `qbScannerTest` GUI (Figure 5-7). You will get a Yes/No message box announcing success. Click Yes to see the output, as shown in Figure 5-8. As you can see, the output contains a test string, the expected results, and the actual results.

```
Zoom
Testing qbScanner qbScanner0001 3/2/2004 8:21:08 PM at 3/2/2004 8:33:32 PM

The test string is: ' & : , identifier &#00013&#00010+ - * / ( ) ; "string" 32767 -32767e-12 % ! # $ "This
string is ""fancy""." "This string is ""fancy"". It ""contains"" ""inner"" """""strings"""""""   . .2 endId
&#08220This string uses smart quotes&#08221

***** EXPECTED RESULTS ***********************************************************
* Apostrophe@1..1:1 '                                                            *
* Ampersand@3..3:1 &                                                             *
* Colon@5..5:1 :                                                                 *
* Comma@7..7:1 ,                                                                 *
* Identifier@9..18:1 identifier                                                  *
* Newline@20..21:2 &#00013&#00010                                                *
* Operator@22..22:2 +                                                            *
* Operator@24..24:2 -                                                            *
* Operator@26..26:2 *                                                            *
* Operator@28..28:2 /                                                            *
* Parenthesis@30..30:2 (                                                         *
* Parenthesis@32..32:2 )                                                         *
* Semicolon@34..34:2 ;                                                           *
* String@36..43:2 "string"                                                       *
* UnsignedInteger@45..49:2 32767                                                 *
* Operator@51..51:2 -                                                            *
* UnsignedRealNumber@52..60:2 32767e-12                                          *
* Percent@62..62:2 %                                                             *
* Exclamation@64..64:2 !                                                         *
* Pound@66..66:2 #                                                               *
* Currency@68..68:2 $                                                            *
* String@70..96:2 "This string is ""fancy""."                                    *
* String@98..170:2 "This string is ""fancy"". It ""contains"" ""inner"" """""strings"""""""  *
* Period@172..172:2 .                                                            *
* UnsignedRealNumber@174..175:2 .2                                               *

                              [ Close ]
```

Figure 5-8. Scan test output (zoomed)

The test string exercises qbScanner for each token type to regression test the scanner when its source code is changed. It also includes marginal tokens to make sure the scanner works for these cases. The test string uses XML notation for the nondisplayable characters in a newline.

The expected and the actual results list tokens in a serialized form, where to *serialize* an object is to convert it to printable characters. We have converted newline in the test string to a displayable form given our Windows internationalization locale (which, for us, is ASCII).

In the scanner data model, each token is an object of type qbToken, and its toString method creates the view of the token in the actual results.

For each token, the scanner has named its type, identified its starting and end index, shown its line number (to the left of the colon), and displayed its value in an expression of the following form:

tokenTypeName@startIndex..endIndex:lineNumber value

We really want the line number, by the way, since this will help display errors. Programmers can't find character indexes as readily as they can spot line numbers.

To ensure that nondisplayable ASCII and Unicode characters are displayed properly, a utility function (string2Object, available in utilities.dll and for which source code can be found in utilities.vb) converts nonprintable values to their

XML format, which is ampersand and pound, followed by the five digit decimal value of the ASCII or Unicode character. I developed the string2Object to support serialization because it drives me nuts when nonprintable characters such as newline sequences appear in output.

Scroll down to see the complete actual results and how numbers are handled, as shown in Figure 5-9.

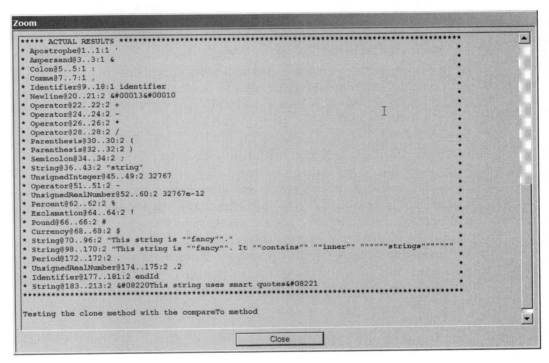

Figure 5-9. Complete results, including number scanning

The pure model of an unsigned number has actually been changed! It's true that the real number –32767e–12 has been divided into a unary minus followed by an unsigned real number. However, note that in the case of real numbers only, we've slightly violated the rule that two distinct token types must have two distinct sets of leading characters.

Unsigned integers may start with any digit; unsigned real numbers may start with a decimal point or any digit. The character set "any digit" is *shared* by two distinct token types.

The string 32767 was scanned as an unsigned integer, while –32767e–12 is scanned as an operator, followed by an unsigned real number. We've kept our promise not to include signs in numbers and let the compiler sort them out; however, we return two different, and apparently overlapping types, integer and real, which of course will have common handles. This is readily explained.

We could have simplified the scanner to just parse integers and let the parser synthesize real numbers. Real numbers have a sensible BNF syntax. But overall, it is the scanner's job to make life easy for the parser.

Instead, the token type Unsigned Real is a synthetic type that is based on Unsigned Integer. When it's time to find a real number in the inner, anticipatory scanner loop, the real number finder looks for an integer, followed optionally by a decimal point, followed optionally by another integer, e, exponent sign, and a third integer. The result is that in the anticipatory table described earlier in pseudocode, there will be overlapping entries. To select the correct entry, the scanner not only takes the leftmost token, but it also takes the widest token.

I have rather slyly postponed this discussion because I wanted to show how to stick to an ideal as long as possible, and then compromise. This issue could be a bug, but it isn't as long as the anticipatory loop selects the widest token. And it is an example of the kind of low-level and painful issues that arise in lexical analysis.

Scanner Object Design Considerations

This section discusses the scanner object model, certain core procedures found in this and other compiler objects, and the display of the scanner's internal data in XML. It will then address the scanner's event model. The goal is to introduce principles used in the compiler to achieve solid design and reliability.

I wanted to separate this book from an academic book about compilers, not by ignoring theory, but by a greater appreciation of the need, in the real world, to deliver software that works and is delivered on time.[7]

The Scanner Object Model

For the scanner and the other objects in the compiler, I have developed an object model, which is a statement of what is in the object's state.

The scanner's object model consists of the raw source code, which is preserved in the state as a string variable and a collection of zero, one, or more tokens, where each token is an object of the type qbToken. The object model of a qbToken consists of the following:

- The start index of the token in the source code

- The length in characters of the token

---

7. I find that while I am at times late with my software, especially when I have no say on the delivery date or am being passively aggressive, what I deliver is sound, as long as I have taken the time to use a structured approach. That way, I don't get any business as a "consultant" because the software works—oops. Seriously, the time-to-market statistic doesn't completely capture software quality.

- The end index of the token in the source code (which, as a property of the token, can be calculated from the start index and the length)

- The type of the token: identifier, operator, parenthesis, string, stand-alone special character, and so forth

Note that there is no need to store the actual value of the token—doing so is a waste of space. The source code is a part of the scanner state, as is the start and length of each token; for this reason, we can always get to the token by finding the Mid (substring) of the source code using the token's start index and length.

Core Object Design

The scanner implements a core object design approach that I find very useful. In this approach, we implement a core, favored set of properties and methods. This set has fuzzy boundaries (in the sense that some might not be present in some objects developed in the methodology) and thus cannot be implemented using an interface, but conceptually, it is like an interface.

Let's take a look at how the core object design classifies objects and uses the core procedures of qbScanner: Name, inspect, object2XML, and test. Then we will look at the simple event model of qbScanner.

Classification of Objects

The approach classifies objects into stateless and stateful objects. *Stateless objects* consist of pure code. These objects define static (shared) methods and properties, and never need to be created using New.

> **NOTE** *A good example of stateless objects in the code for this book is utilities.dll, a large collection of string handlers, math gizmos, and other methods I have found useful over the years.*

Stateful objects, on the other hand, have variables in their Common Declarations. To execute any property or method of a stateful object (that isn't declared as Shared), you must create an instance of the object. Many of the stateful objects that implement the compiler also expose as Shared procedures, which do not interact with the Common Declarations. These procedures are typically tools with a close association with the object. For example, qbVariableType represents, in its state, the facts about a variable's type, but it also exposes a set of shared methods for working with types in the abstract, including a shared method for telling whether two types enclose each other.

The Name Property

Tell me sweetie, what's my name?
—The Rolling Stones, "Sympathy for the Devil"

All stateful objects have a Name property so we can identify different objects in output. Name defaults to *className*nnnn date time, where *nnnn* is the sequence number of the object as created in the process.

Take a look at the New constructor for qbScanner in qbScanner.vb. Note that it references a Shared variable named _INTsequence. It starts with an underscore because it is shared. It then contains the Hungarian prefix for its type INT, and then contains a descriptive name, sequence. I uppercase the Hungarian prefixes of variables in the Common Declarations section.

We use the threading model to increment the sequence number for the default Name, since to add one to it would make the object unusable when running more than one instance of the object in multiple threads.

The inspect Method

An important method of stateful objects is the inspect method. This executes a series of assertions on the variables in the state of the object.

In most objects, the state is organized as a user data type of the type TYPstate and named USRstate. In some objects, the state is organized as a small object with its own state, containing variables instead of procedures. The latter technique is used when the object needs to be fully threadable.

The qbScannerTest program's GUI provides access to the inspect method. Click the Inspect button (see Figure 5-7) to see the message box informing you that the test scanner has succeeded.

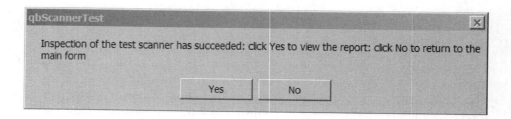

This message must appear. I mean it. This is because inspect, in qbScanner and the other stateful objects shipped, checks for errors that would be the result of serious internal problems.

Let's look at what it checks. Click Yes in the message box to see the inspection report, as shown in Figure 5-10.

```
Zoom
Inspection of "qbScanner0001 3/2/2004 8:21:08 PM" at 3/2/2004 8:31:33 PM
The object must be usable: OK
Each token in both the array of scanned tokens, and the array of pending tokens, must pass the inspect
procedure of qbToken. The tokens in the scanned array must be in ascending order with gaps OK but no
overlap. No token's end index (in either array) may point beyond the end of the source code in either the
scanned array, or the pending array: OK
The line number must be greater than or equal to 0: OK
The format of the line number index collection must be valid: this is a collection of three-item
subcollections. Item(1) must be a string containing the key of the index entry: item(2) and item(3) must
be positive integers: item(2) can't be zero: OK
If the nonnull code is fully scanned, the first token's start index should be the same as the position of
the first nonblank character in the source code. The last token's end index should be the same as the
position of the last nonblank character.
If the code is null and indicated as fully scanned the scan count must be zero.: OK
```

Figure 5-10. Inspection report

Four assertions have been tested against the state, the General Declarations variables of the qbScanner instance. Figure 5-11 is the declaration of the object state, as the TYPstate structure followed immediately by the state *instance*, USRstate. These assertions concern usability, the scanned tokens, line numbers, and the source code.

```
' ***** State *****
Private Structure TYPstate
    Dim strName As String               ' Object name
    Dim booUsable As Boolean            ' Object usability
    Dim strSourceCode As String         ' All source
    Dim intLast As Integer              ' Index of last token parsed
    Dim objQBtoken() As qbToken.qbToken ' Some or all tokens
    Dim objTokenNext() As qbToken.qbToken ' The pending tokens
    Dim intLineNumber As Integer        ' Current line number
    Dim colLineIndex As Collection      ' Line index:
                                        ' Key is _lineNumber
                                        ' Data is subcollection:
                                        ' Item(1): line number
                                        ' Item(2): start index
                                        ' Item(3): length
    Dim booScanned As Boolean           ' True: indicates a completed scan
End Structure
```

Figure 5-11. The state of qbScanner

> **NOTE** *These rules should not fail. If they do, this means one of two things. Either my ham-fisted original code has a bug (otherwise known as an issue or feature) or you have modified the code. If it is my bug, send me e-mail at* spinoza1111@yahoo.com. *If it is your bug, fix it.*

Usability

The first assertion is that the object must be usable. Usability is part of the core approach.

Object-oriented design with stateful objects raises an interesting problem. This problem existed before "objects," but only object-oriented design gives us a way of facing the problem squarely.

Old programs of the legacy sort often have thousands of variables and conditions. Often, only a few combinations of these variables and conditions are actually valid. Statistics, along with Murphy's Law, predict that these old programs might enter a state—a combination of values—which is unexpected, and of course, they do.

The mentality of a non-object-oriented programmer in a language like C is that "my program is special and will not enter a bad state—ever." This neglects the fact that, as hero computer scientist Dijkstra pointed out, any one program is best viewed as a *set* of related solutions that evolves over time. A payroll program is a member of related solutions, some of which the user wants, some of which the user would prefer, some of which the user will put up with, some of which the user will need next year, and so on—you get the picture.

This means that in a non-object-oriented language, it is just too easy to add variables over a life cycle in such a way that invalid combinations occur. Many of these combinations are benign tumors in the sense that they don't change results; others are malignant.

Using an inspect procedure, especially if it is executed automatically or at a regular interval, can tell the object if it is "sane" and has valid combinations of values (depending, of course, on how many conditions are actually tested). What is interesting is what the object can do if it does find a problematic state. The object, unlike legacy code, knows it is no longer in a state of grace. And, unlike legacy code, the object can do something with this knowledge. (Note that this discovery has nothing to do with compilers but everything to do with building good software.)

It can, as the objects in the compiler do, set a variable, in its state (called booUsable in the code) to False.

Whenever a Public procedure (property, method, or event handler) is executed subsequently, the object can raise an error and return a sensible default, instead of making life worse for itself and the rest of the world by returning bogus results, or, worse, doing damage to data outside itself. Therefore, at the conclusion of the New constructors for objects with state, we explicitly inspect the initial state, and, if it is valid, we set usability to True.

Many objects with state contain reference objects that occupy .NET's heap storage, and we consistently follow a .NET rule. This is to expose a Public procedure (called, consistently, dispose in our code), which the object user is urged, on pain of 20 lashes with a wet noodle, to use when the object is no longer needed. The original purpose of dispose was to ensure that reference objects did not clutter the CLR heap unnecessarily. However, in the QuickBasic compiler code, objects consistently self-inspect when dispose is executed as a sort of global sanity check.

Scanned Tokens

The next assertion is about the tokens that were scanned. Since each is a stateful object, each must pass its own qbToken.inspect procedure. Also, the tokens must always form an ascending series of nonoverlapping tokens. They don't need to be contiguous and won't be contiguous in general, because blanks may appear between them. If this rule is violated, the entire meaning of the scanner has been damaged.

Line Numbers

The third rule is trivial compared with the other rules. The line number starts at one. Therefore, it must start at one. It can't be zero or negative.

Collection Structure

We need a collection structure rule whenever we use the old standby Collection object to structure a tree or other data structure, by including collections as members in collections. Here, the collection is an index to map line numbers to character positions. The key of colLineIndex is the line number, prefixed with an underscore (because the legacy collection would otherwise treat the line number as a numeric index and not a key). Its data is the line number, the start index, and the length of the line. This is represented as a three-item, unkeyed subcollection.

In developing this collection with structure, we are performing object design without explicit stateful objects such as "line number index entry" and "collection of line number index entries." Logistically, it is unnecessary to go crazy and develop a full-dress *object* for each and every *potential* object. Logistically, it creates some source bloat because a project and a project's files exist for each possible object. Therefore, it makes sense for simple objects, such as an object that maps line numbers to character positions, to use a collection in a structured fashion. However, it does require inspect to check the structured collection for correct structure, since this is not enforced by an explicit object model.

Collections of Collections

You'll see more of these collections-on-steroids in the code; get used to them. Ordinarily, we think of the collection as a hash table or one-dimension array. However, the true power of the collection is obtained only when you realize that its entries can be objects, in particular, collections.

Because collections can contain collections, a collection can represent not only a simple array of basic data type but also an array of records, as has been shown here.

Recall the bnfAnalyzer tool introduced in Chapter 4. It stores the "parse tree" of the input BNF in a collection, which contains collections.

Of course, we can go overboard in using the collection in this way. I may have done so, in fact, in bnfAnalyzer. It might have been actually better to develop the parse tree as a separate COM object (recall that bnfAnalyzer uses COM). However, COM objects don't play as nice as .NET objects do, and I wanted to get the project done quickly.

Source Code

The final inspection rule tests the source code against the scanned tokens. The first scan token must coincide with the first nonblank character in the source code; the last scan token must coincide with the final nonblank characters in the source code.

The object2XML Method

Another core method, named object2XML, converts the USRstate of the object to XML. XML allows us to display clearly the current state of the object.

In the qbScannerTest program's GUI, click the button labeled Object to XML (see Figure 5-7). You will see the zoomed XML display, as shown in Figure 5-12.

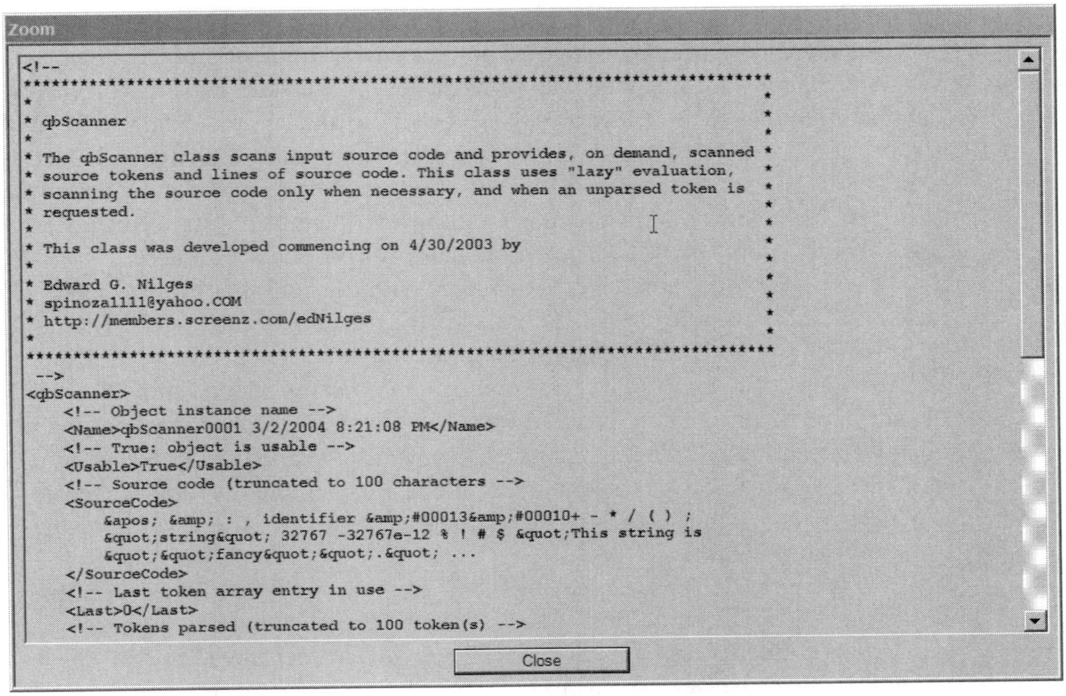

```
Zoom
<!--
******************************************************************************
*                                                                            *
* qbScanner                                                                  *
*                                                                            *
* The qbScanner class scans input source code and provides, on demand, scanned *
* source tokens and lines of source code. This class uses "lazy" evaluation,  *
* scanning the source code only when necessary, and when an unparsed token is *
* requested.                                                                 *
*                                                                            *
* This class was developed commencing on 4/30/2003 by                        *
*                                                                            *
* Edward G. Nilges                                                           *
* spinoza1111@yahoo.COM                                                      *
* http://members.screenz.com/edNilges                                        *
*                                                                            *
******************************************************************************
 -->
<qbScanner>
    <!-- Object instance name -->
    <Name>qbScanner0001 3/2/2004 8:21:08 PM</Name>
    <!-- True: object is usable -->
    <Usable>True</Usable>
    <!-- Source code (truncated to 100 characters -->
    <SourceCode>
        &apos; &amp; : , identifier &amp;#00013&amp;#00010+ - * / ( ) ;
        &quot;string&quot; 32767 -32767e-12 % ! # $ &quot;This string is
        &quot;&quot;fancy&quot;&quot;.&quot; ...
    </SourceCode>
    <!-- Last token array entry in use -->
    <Last>0</Last>
    <!-- Tokens parsed (truncated to 100 token(s) -->
Close
```

Figure 5-12. The output of the object2XML method

This XML has been formatted for easy readability, and it is heavily commented. In particular, the paragraph that describes the class is also available as the value of `qbScanner`'s read-only, shared About property (another core procedure, which in most objects, will supply information about the purpose of the class, as well as my name, e-mail address, and Web site).

Options of the XML object, corresponding to check boxes and text boxes on the scanner test form, allow you to suppress either the leading box comment or the line comments that describe each state variable.

The test method

Clicking the Test button in the `qbScannerTest` program's GUI executes the `test` method of the scanner, which presents a test instance with a string containing all possible tokens and some marginal difficult cases (see Figure 5-8, earlier in the chapter). It compares the serialized list of actual results with the serialized expected results. If they match, the object does not complain. If they do not match, the form will display an error message, and the object will mark itself as not usable.

Is this a bit much, or what?

An alternative, used in many MIS applications, is for a separate tester object to test the class. This is a good alternative; however, it creates logistical problems in that it doubles the count of overall projects. Also, this approach fails to parallel the inspect method, which is the static correspondent to the dynamic test. Additionally, it sends the object into the cold, cruel world without the ability to self-test. Therefore, when you are examining a suspicious object, in the cold, cruel server room at 3:00 AM, you don't have this particular resource.

For this reason, many objects delivered with the compiler expose a test method. The inspect and test methods lower error probabilities, in the same way my schoolmates and I lowered the probability of errors in Sister Mary Rose's arithmetic classes. Sister Mary Rose made us *subtract* the addend from the sum to see if the other operand of the addition was the result. Sister Mary Rose made us *add* the subtrahend to the difference to see if the second operand resulted. This was a pain, but it was a genuine error check. Given the frequency of errors in our business, it makes sense to add code such as inspect and test to provide the same sort of check.

Code checks don't guarantee bugs won't exist, of course. But Dijkstra reminds us (strangely for his reputation as an ivory tower theorist) that computer science is *applied* mathematics.[8] In building a bridge, we don't neglect additional checks merely because they are extra steps that might be wrong, because in the real world, they lower error probability. The same goes for programming!

The Event Model

I ain't evil, I'm just good lookin'
—Alice Cooper, "Feed My Frankenstein"

A concern in the scanner (and, as you will see in Chapters 7 and 8, also in the compiler and the interpreter) is the ability to accurately report progress in scanning, parsing, and interpreting large source programs. I wanted to avoid the irritating and vague progress reports we sometimes see in Windows.

At the same time, it is a bad mistake to make an object with code that builds forms, but whose mission is *not* to draw pretty forms on the screen. This is because this code must then import and reference System.Windows.Forms, which bloats it for no good reason, and worse, locks the code into the Windows client environment.

---

8. Dijkstra was less an ivory tower theorist than someone who actually believed that you cannot separate theory from practice, high-level design from mindless code, and so on. Perhaps for this reason, two of his results (structured programming and semaphores) are actually useful to ordinary slobs.

If, all of a sudden, you decide that the code in question would make a spiffy Web service, you are in a world of hurt when the object, like the scanner or the quickBasicEngine compiler itself, is large and complex. You must go through the object and find each and every line of code that has to do with presentation and make this code conditional on the mode of presentation.

You wind up with Frankencode, a dismal monster howling on the blasted heath for its author's ass, because it knows, as did Mary Shelley's famous monster, that its life has been destroyed by its very fabrication as "a thing of shreds and patches." Unlike Alice Cooper, singing "Feed My Frankenstein" in *Wayne's World*, your code might be good looking but will be evil.

Therefore, we need a way to separate presentation from logic and to have a way for the nonvisual object to display its progress. One way would be to have the presentation logic inherit the nonvisual object. This makes some sense in a language that allows multiple inheritance. However, Visual Basic doesn't allow multiple inheritance, meaning that the presentation logic can present only one object. Also, it doesn't make much sense to say that a mere progress report is-a compiler. This, in Shakespearean terms, dresses the progress report in "borrowed robes."

Instead, we use an event model in the scanner and elsewhere to transmit events, which can be ignored, used to display progress on a Windows form, or used to display progress in a Web service. Figure 5-13 shows the event model of the scanner. Note that to actually obtain these events, qbScanner must be declared using the WithEvents keyword and inside General Declarations.

```
' ***** Events *****
Public Event scanEvent(ByVal objQBtoken As QBToken.qbToken, _
                       ByVal intCharacterIndex As Integer, _
                       ByVal intLength As Integer, _
                       ByVal intTokenCount As Integer)
Public Event scanErrorEvent(ByVal strMsg As String, _
                            ByVal intIndex As Integer, _
                            ByVal intLineNumber As Integer, _
                            ByVal strHelp As String)
```

Figure 5-13. qbScanner event model

The scanEvent event fires each time a new token is found. It provides the token object, its start index, its length, and the total number of tokens found so far. The value and type of the token object is found using its properties. This allows the GUI to extend a progress bar, highlight the code being scanned, or both.

The scanErrorEvent event fires each time a user-related error such as unrecognizable characters occurs. It describes the error, identifies where it occurs by absolute character position and line number, and, in some cases, provides additional tips.

I have followed the object-oriented practice described in this section consistently in all stateful objects of the compiler. When I make additions to the core set, I will note them in the book. In particular, further objects will incorporate a `test` method, which will, inside an object instance, allocate a `test` instance as a local variable and then run a series of prepared tests. This will allow me to expose on object test forms, similar to the form of `qbScannerTest`, a Test button that runs portable regression tests, not inside the form (as is the case here), but inside the object.

Summary

This chapter described the development of the first major objects (`qbScanner`, which has `qbTokens`) of the compiler for its first task: lexical analysis. We have used modern techniques to support a legacy language because object-oriented development makes compiler development a much more visible and less arcane process.

Before object-oriented development, developing compilers involved a great number of tables interlinked in complex ways. They had a tendency to get into combinations of states that resulted in bugs, some of which were exploited by the compiler's user community and became features.

Object-oriented development does not dramatically increase the speed at which compilers are developed. In this case, I promised Dan Appleman (this book's editor) that I would refactor and make more intensively object-oriented the original compiler for QuickBasic that I had demonstrated to him at the Visual Studio rollout festival in 2002. I had decided to do so because it is very hard to explain a compiler in depth without showing that it is made up of distinct modules and without using the Windows form to exhibit internal behavior.

Refactoring each object demanded a heavy investment of time, not just in coding, but also in preparatory documentation. In the preparatory documentation, I defined the object model, the supporting object state, and the behavior of each Public procedure. I implemented the core procedures, including `inspect` and `object2XML`. I built a form to show off the object, which is a pain when you're born to code and not to be a glorified Etch-a-Sketcher.[9]

Too often, quality is mapped onto time to market. Dan told me he wanted a quality book, with quality software, and I hope that the use of the object-oriented paradigm here and in the rest of the book will ensure this. The flyover mini-compiler of Chapter 3 and the `bnfAnalyzer` COM object of Chapter 4 were merely small applications by comparison.

---

9. In particular, it made me crazy to have to select label colors. What is the color of a scanner? What is the color of a variable type? "Colorless green ideas sleep furiously" (Noam Chomsky). The overall goal is to have each form highlight its labels with a memorable primary or bright color, like a property card in the game of Monopoly. Thus, the scanner's color is dark blue.

Challenge Exercise

From the code of the scanner and/or the text of this book, reverse-engineer the regular expression that defines each token type supported: identifier, operator, number, string, and so on.

For example, a string is defined using the regular expression:

```
"([^"]*(""){0,1})*"
```

It defines a Visual Basic format string as a series of nonquotes, followed by an optional doubled double quote (where the bracketed 0,1 makes the parenthesized doubled double quotes optional), repeated zero or more times and enclosed in quotes.

Whenever you see a regular expression, treat it with suspicion based on what has been said in this chapter. Does the regular expression contain ambiguity, in the form of pairs of elements a,b, such that one or characters that can end a can appear at the start of b? It appears not, since if an element is informally understood to be any subexpression that is a regular expression in its own right, there are only two elements in the above regular expression:

```
[^"]* and (""){0,1}
```

These do not have the problem of ambiguity.

Try this expression out using relab.

Develop the remaining regular expressions for each one of our token types: apostrophe, ampersand, colon, comma, identifier, operator, parentheses, semicolon, string, unsigned integer, unsigned real number, pound sign, dollar sign, and newline.

Resources

For more information about regular expressions and compiler design, refer to the following:

Regular Expressions with .NET, by Dan Appleman, (electronic publication, available from http://www.amazon.com/exec/obidos/tg/detail/-/B0000632ZU). This publication provides the .NET rules for regular expressions.

Mastering Regular Expressions, Second Edition, by Jeffrey E. F. Friedl (O'Reilly, 2002). This book provides an in-depth look at regular expressions, primarily in the Unix world.

Advanced Compiler Design and Implementation, by Steven S. Muchnick (Morgan Kaufmann, 1997). This book gives a comprehensive, in-depth discussion of high-intensity source and object code optimization for (I fear) yesterday's high-performance Unix servers (which are being pressured from one direction by Linux servers and from Redmond by Windows 2003 server). These servers are often RISC (Reduced Instruction Set) machines. Compilers for these systems are fascinating, not only because they often need to do more work in object code generation for RISC, but also because for high-performance applications, they need to do a variety of optimizations.

CHAPTER 6

QuickBasic Object Modeling

The law wishes to have a formal existence.
— *Stanley Fish*

In whatsoever mode, or by whatsoever means, our knowledge may relate to objects, it is at least quite clear, that the only matter it relates to them is by means of an intuition.
— *Kant, Critique of Pure Reason*

Under the paving stones lies the beach!
— *Assorted, if not motley, French students of 1968*

IN THE PREVIOUS CHAPTER, you saw how the lexical analyzer, or scanner, transforms the raw characters of source code into a stream of token objects, where each token object has a start index and a length. In the next chapter, you'll see how this stream of token objects is converted to a nested structure of BNF grammar categories, as described in Chapter 4, while also emitting output code for a "machine," which exists purely as a software simulation of the Nutty Professor machine.

But before we get to the flagship object quickBasicEngine in the next chapter, we need to build two .NET objects, qbVariableType and qbVariable, to represent data types and their values. And to do that, we need to model the data, since it's always a bad idea to develop a language— whether for the .NET CLR or any other platform—without a clear idea of how to represent the values and types of values of the target language. We did not need to concern ourselves with these issues in the flyover compiler of Chapter 3, because all the values in that example are numbers that were easily mapped to the double-precision number type (which is able to handle integers as well as real numbers). However, in scaling up to our QuickBasic compiler, we need to do some hard work. We want to make sure that no variable is instantiated in our compiler without complete, strong typing. The payoff is that all parts of the quickBasicEngine speak the same language about variables.

In this chapter, we will go through the same cycle of design, code, and test as in previous chapters. The GUIs for testing the implementations of the QuickBasic variable type model will give you a hands-on demonstration of what is, honestly, rather dry (but necessary!) material.

The Abstract QuickBasic Variable Type Model

QuickBasic variables have a structure that is unique to Basic, because of the variant data type and the user data type. The variant data type is not unique to Visual Basic; prior to .NET. Variants appeared in QuickBasic and other Basic compilers during the 1980s and the 1970s. The user data type, a collection of subordinate data types organized into a structure (now known as the .NET structure) also appeared in Basic compilers, including QuickBasic and True Basic (a version of Basic from the original developers of the language).

Variants, user data types, and arrays can contain each other in complex ways. Therefore, how support is provided for variable types and values is a nice case study in object design, demonstrating once again the utility of the core properties and methods.

The abstract model we must use for QuickBasic variable types can be represented by a little language for identifying data types. This includes the names of simple types (known as scalars), such as integer and double, as well as structured expressions for complex types, such as `Variant,Integer` (a variant known to contain an integer) and `Array,Integer,1,10` (a one-dimensional array of integers with a lower bound of 1 and an upper bound of 10).

Here, I present a "requirements analysis," which identifies the features our representation of QuickBasic variables *must* support. For us, QuickBasic variable types come in six different categories: scalars, variants, arrays, user data types (UDTs), null, and unknown. We'll look at the requirements for each type in the following sections.

Scalars

Scalars are simple Basic values that can be any one of the following types:

- Boolean—`True` or `False`

- Byte—Integers in the range 0..255

- Integer—Math integers in the range –32768..32767 represented as two's complement values in a 16-bit word

- Long—Two's complement values in a 32-bit word, in the range $-2^{31}..2^{31}-1$

- Single—Single-precision numbers in floating-point notation

- Double—Floating-point values with a wider exponent and/or a wider mantissa

- String—Strings of characters

> **NOTE**   *Older Visual Basic developers may remember that strings in Visual Basic through release 3 were limited to 64KB, in all probability because the C-language runtime represented string length in an unsigned 16-bit C integer, which can range from 0 to 2^16–1 (64KB). QuickBasic shared this limit before release 4, which produced interesting bugs and fascinating hacks for longer strings. For example, in those pre-object days, I wrote a procedure in a classic Visual Basic module that stored 64KB chunks in an array. Visual Basic 4 made it possible to rewrite this as a "long string" object much more elegantly and without exposing the array, but it also removed any need for the object, since Visual Basic 4 increased the string limit to about 2^32.*

Some scalars involve *two's complement* or *floating-point* notation. The integer value range from a negative, even number to a positive, odd number looks wrong, since it appears to be one less than it should be. The oddity of the range results from the fact that most modern computers use two's complement to represent integers. This notation represents positive numbers, in binary, as you might expect, padded to whatever the word length happens to be. In this notation, using a 16-bit word,[1] the number 4 is 0000000000000010. Negative numbers, however, are represented by inverting each bit, placing a 0 where you expect 1 and 1 where 0 is expected. For example, –4 in a 16-bit word becomes 1111111111111101. It all works out, in a Rube Goldberg fashion, as long as you remember that the range of values, for a 16-bit word, is between –2^15 and 2^15–1. The most attractive feature of this notation is that it avoids the possibility of negative zero, which in a straight, non-two's-complement notation would be one followed by zeros. That would complicate both hardware and software operations.

Floating point is the notation used by mad scientists and disturbed engineers to represent that-which-is-large and that-which-is-small, such as the size of the universe, Donald Trump's bank balance, the mass of an electron, or my bank balance. A floating-point number such as –1.2e-3 consists of a sign, a mantissa, and an exponent (consisting of the sign and value of the exponent). The sign in the example is negative. The mantissa consists of just the numbers and not the decimal point to the left of the *e* divider; in the example, the mantissa is 12. We sort of drop the decimal point, because the exponent takes over the function of the decimal point. The end of the floating-point number consists of the letter *E* (or *e*), another optional sign, and an integer number. This is the exponent, and it usually takes over the function of the decimal point (although the decimal point can be used, as in the example, in combination with the exponent). Mathematically, the exponent specifies a power of ten as applied to the mantissa to arrive at a final value. The value is $M(10^e)$, where M represents the mantissa with the sign and

---

1. QuickBasic shared this surprisingly narrow integer range with Visual Basic releases 1 through 6. Its narrowness results from the fact that in QuickBasic's salad days, microcomputers still often worked in words (units) of memory that were only 16 bits long.

decimal point left in, or (when the decimal point is unspecified) implied to the left of the mantissa. Here is an example: -1.2e-3 = -1.2 * 10^-3 = -.0012.

Variants

You are probably familiar with the variant, which is a variable no longer supported by .NET. Considered strictly as a type, the QuickBasic or old Visual Basic variant is a container for another type. The contained type can be a scalar, a null, an unknown, or even an array or UDT, but it cannot be another variant type. Variants cannot nest within each other.

> **NOTE** *If a variant could contain a variant, this would raise the hard-to-model possibility of multiple-level variants. Code using such variants would be hard to debug, and in the absence of object-oriented design, complex vectors and tables would be needed. However, this situation is easy to model in object-oriented design. The variant-containing variant would simply contain an object: a distinct variant. One problem would be avoiding loops, presumably in object inspection, where the same object appears more than once and the variant directly or indirectly refers to itself.*

We need to model two types of variants for different uses:

- **Concrete variant types:** These contain a known contained type such as "is a variant integer" or "is a variant string."

- **Abstract variant types:** These contain an unknown type, which we can represent because of our unknown variable type (described shortly in the "Null and Unknown Types" section).

We need the abstract variant for arrays of variants because, in the model, we cannot declare that an array type is "array of variant integer." In QuickBasic, a variant array is declared simply as a variant, and it's not possible to declare that "my array is of variants that must contain integers."

Laying to Rest Urban Legends About Variants

There is an urban legend concerning the variant: it is said to be slow. Of course, "the variant is slow" isn't even a grammatical statement. What the sayer means is code that uses variants is slow, because it uses variants, of course.

In the pre-.NET runtime, each variant had to carry type information, familiar to coders of APIs, and each variant was a vector of storage. As such, some extra code had to be executed to get to the value of the variant, or to "unbox" the value. And, of course, the extra bits took space.

But note that experts on software performance, including Steven Skiena in his 1997 book *The Algorithm Design Manual*, urge programmers to avoid penny-wise, pound-foolishness. The major determinant of efficiency is, as Skiena shows, the overall form of the module's execution time formula. For example, if it multiplies the number of input records by itself in an MIS program, the program will run fine for small sets of test data, but it will crash when it goes live.

Many MIS programs still have a classic loop form, which means that their execution time formula is the multiplication of the constant time for processing a record times N, where N is the number of records. Skiena's lesson is that you don't want this to be multiplied by N itself. For example, it's obvious that when sequentially processing a large table, you should not search the entire table or a table of nearly equivalent size for each record in the table.

The straightforward formula $N*K$ for the efficiency of a program (number of records times a constant time) will not be substantially changed by replacing a scalar with a variant, especially when there is a good reason for doing so. The replacement does not alter the overall execution time formula; it changes only the time for processing a record by a small, fixed amount.

In COM, there was often a good reason for using variants: they provided a limited object-oriented capability. They were useful for a primitive, and admittedly unsafe, form of polymorphism when the COM programmer needed to represent fuzzy data. For example, a real-world application might exist with an `orderQty` (order quantity) in which the user needs to represent a fixed and known number, a completely unknown value, or a range of values. An example is that some customers might like a minimum quantity in cases where the order cannot be fulfilled from the warehouse in full and on time. If the variant effectively and in context represents this situation—as an integer, a null for the completely unknown scenario, a string representing a minimum quantity, or even a complex formula (translatable by the compiler itself as a business rule, as I will show in Chapter 9)—then the variant is a technique for representing an object in a rather lightweight fashion.

It is also said that variants take too much space. However, depending on the type, they take a small, constant amount of space. Variants take too much space only when their additional bytes are repeated in large arrays.

Urban legends about variants can therefore be laid to rest.

However, there are many stressed-out programmers trying to maintain code in which the overuse of the variant has created a toxic smog. In this toxic smog, you cannot tell when you look at `vntFoobar` what it might contain! If you have experience with older Active Server Pages (ASP) or Visual Basic for Applications (VBA), you know what I mean—in VBA for ASP, everything was a variant, and it drives you nuts.

I use polymorphously perverse variants in my remaining COM efforts only after I've exhausted alternatives and slain a goat. In many cases, I've implemented an `inspect` method, which actually checks the variants to make sure they have only the expected types. For example, the `inspect` method will run when the object is terminated and check the example, `orderQty`, for a number or properly formatted string. Of course, this is the cure that might kill, since the `inspect` method is *more code*. It was motivated by my rage to use an object-oriented approach, which commenced in 1990 when I saw that the UDT of C would not be equal to the challenges of the coming decade.

Arrays

Arrays should have the following properties:

- **Dimensionality:** This is unlimited in the model but is usually in the range 1..3. In our model, all nonarray data types should return a dimensionality of 0 as a quick test to see if the object represents an array.

- **Lower bound:** Although the lower bound can default to 0, in QuickBasic the lower bound of an array can be any integer, negative or positive. This is the same rule found in Visual Basic COM.[2]

- **Upper bound:** This denotes the variable type of each array entry, as a contained `qbVariableType` (each `qbVariableType` has a `qbVariableType` delegate).

User Data Types (UDTs)

UDTs should be modeled as a set of one or more members. Each member should consist of a member name and its associated `qbVariableType`.
UDTs can contain the following types:

- Scalars

- Variants

- Arrays

- UDTs

---

2. This feature has been largely found to be useless, or not useful enough to warrant modifying the architecture of .NET. .NET architecture is based on the runtime semantics of C, and C did not include this dubious feature.

Unlike variants, UDTs are recursive and can contain UDTs. Within a QuickBasic UDT, a COM Visual Basic UDT, or a .NET structure, the As clause can be itself a UDT, with one exception: it cannot be the same UDT as is being defined.

UDTs cannot contain unknown or null data types.

Null and Unknown Types

The null and unknown types are unique in that their value and type are the same. Null is used only as the default value of a variant, and it corresponds to Nothing in .NET.

I added the unknown type, since I am developing a method for interpreting both full-scale programs and business rules using partially unknown values, in order to be able to manage the effect of using legacy code and complex business rules. Unknown represents the fact that the variable's type is not known. It's useful as the contained object of the variant that is contained in an array, where we do not know the type of all of the array's elements.

Type Containment and Convertibility

In Table 6-1, you can see which types can contain which types, or the valid containment of types in the model.

Table 6-1. Containment of Types

Type	Can Contain					
	Scalar	Variant	Array	UDT	Null	Unknown
Scalar	No	No	No	No	No	No
Variant	Yes	No	Yes	Yes	Yes	Yes
Array	Yes	Yes	No	Yes	No	Yes
UDT	Yes	Yes	Yes	Yes	No	No
Null	No	No	No	No	No	No
Unknown	No	No	No	No	No	No

A separate issue is the convertibility of types. The difference between containment and convertibility is that type *a* is **contained** in type *b* when an instance of type *a* can contain a reference to an instance of type *b*. Type *a* is **convertible** to type *b* when all possible values of type *a* can, without loss of information or error, be assigned to a variable of type *b*. Table 6-2 shows the convertibility of types in the model.

Table 6-2. Convertibility of Types

| Type | | | | | Can Convert To | | | | | |
	Boolean	Byte	Integer	Long	Single	Double	String	Variant	Null	Unknown
Boolean	Yes	Yes	Yes	Yes	Yes	Yes	Yes	Yes	No	No
Byte	No	Yes	Yes	Yes	Yes	Yes	Yes	Yes	No	No
Integer	No	No	Yes	Yes	Yes	Yes	Yes	Yes	No	No
Long	No	No	No	Yes	Yes	Yes	Yes	Yes	No	No
Single	No	No	No	No	Yes	Yes	Yes	Yes	No	No
Double	No	No	No	No	No	Yes	Yes	Yes	No	No
String	No	No	No	No	No	No	Yes	Yes	No	No
Variant	No	No	No	No	No	No	No	Yes	No	No
Null	No	No	No	No	No	No	No	Yes	Yes	No
Unknown	No	No	No	No	No	No	No	Yes	No	Yes

Note that two arrays cannot be converted to each other in this sense, because the assignment of an entire array is not supported, and because changing any attribute of an array makes a distinct type. While the assignment of UDTs is supported, this is only possible when their list of members is identical, thus no conversion is involved.

Figure 6-1 shows some examples of how the object should behave. In the figure, boxes with a heavy border represent full-scale `qbVariableType` objects, with state; boxes with a light border denote the "lightweight" enumerator (`ENUvarType`) that represents the variable categories as one of unknown, null, Boolean, byte, integer, long, single, double, string, variant, array, or UDT.

Figure 6-1 illustrates four scenarios:

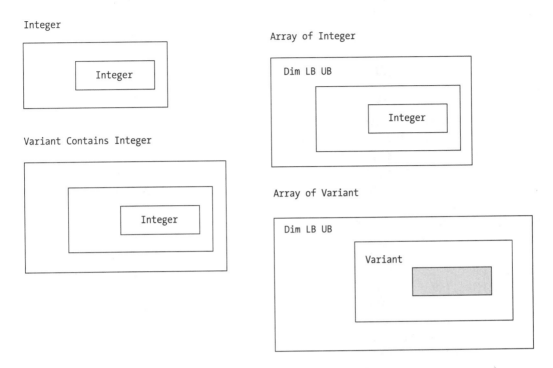

Figure 6-1. Type object scenarios

- An integer will be represented by a stateful `qbVariableType` containing the value of the integer.

- A concrete variant that contains an integer will be represented by a stateful `qbVariantType` with a reference to a stateful `qbVariantType` for the integer.

- An array of integers will be represented by a `qbVariantType` that includes dimension as well as a list of lower and upper bounds. This `qbVariantType` will reference an ordinary integer box.

> **NOTE** *The list of lower and upper bounds for an array is sometimes referred to as a dope vector. This has nothing to do with the Three Stooges or Five Stupid Guys. It merely provides the "dope" about the area: the information.*

- An array of variants will also be represented by a qbVariantType that includes dimension and bounds. This qbVariantType will reference an abstract variant that contains the unknown type.

Type and Value Serialization

Both the qbTypeVariable object and qbVariable object (which contains the type, value, and name of a QuickBasic variable) will allow full and reversible serialization of both variable types and variables. *Serializing* an object refers to creating an image of the object in the form of ASCII text. Ideally, the ASCII text should be totally restricted to printable characters (characters available on common keyboards and displayed in common fonts such as Times New Roman and Courier New).

Both objects will expose a toString method, which will return the serialized state, and a fromString method, which compiles the toString expression back to the object state. This compilation will use a recursive-descent algorithm for parsing the serialized state, as described in the next chapter. For variables and their types, but not for all objects in general, the serialization should be palindromic,[3] such that the fromString of the object state yields a string, from which the object state can be fully constructed.

As noted in Chapter 5, in the serialization provided by the core method object2XML in qbScanner, newlines are allowed, and the serialization is a multiple-line list. On the other hand, from any method named toString, developers will probably expect a string without newlines or XML.

Ideally, the serialization should be completely reversible with no loss of information. The object exposes an xml2Object method or a fromString method that accepts XML or a serialized string to re-create the state with no loss of information. This ideal is not always useful. For example, the qbScanner has no foreseeable need to dump its state and then restore it. However, this need is quite foreseeable in both a qbVariableType and a qbVariable.

The compiler will need to assemble and communicate both types and values to the object code, and at runtime, it will be important to provide a complete image for debugging of QuickBasic types and values. Therefore, both qbVariableType and qbVariable will need to expose toString and fromString in such a palindromic manner that it will always be true that object2.fromString(object1.toString) creates a clone of object1 in object2.

This also implies that both objects need to be cloneable and comparable. *Cloneable* .NET objects are objects implementing the ICloneable interface of .NET, and therefore can return a copy of themselves. *Comparable* .NET objects are

---

3. What I mean is that it's based on the palindrome—a string like "aha," which reads the same forward and backward.

those that implement the ICompareable interface, and therefore return 1 or 0, depending on whether objects are duplicates, and in this context, clones.

Let's examine the serialization requirements for the type and value objects.

qbVariableType Serialization

We need a language for describing types, since only the simple scalar types can be identified by enumeration. There are, strictly speaking, an infinite number of different array types, because each change in dimension or bounds makes a new array type.

There are also an infinite number of different UDTs. Variants, which can contain arrays, only complicate the issue. Therefore, the toString method of qbVariableType and qbVariable should return an expression that, in all cases, is acceptable to the fromString method and re-creates a clone of the original object.

For a simple scalar, null, and unknown type, this may be the name of the type and one of null, unknown, Boolean, byte, integer, long, single, double, or string. For a concrete variant known to contain a scalar, unknown, or null type, this can be an expression of the form Variant,*type*, where *type* is the name of the simple type. For example, a variant that contains an integer is represented as Variant,Integer.

The fun starts when we deal with arrays. We need to identify the fact that we have an array, identify the type of its entry, identify its number of dimensions (one dimension is probably used in 90% of all MIS programs, but you never know), and in QuickBasic (as for Visual Basic COM), we need to support nonzero lower bounds. Therefore, for an array, the type expression should be Array,*type*,*boundList*. The *type* is the type of each entry. The *boundList* specifies both dimensionality and bounds, since it will be a list of 2*n entries, where n is the number of dimensions. Each list entry will be of the form *lowerBound*,*upperBound*. For example, a two-dimensional array of integers might be Array,Integer,1,10,0,5 if it contains ten rows (numbered 1..10) and six columns (numbered 0..5).

The need for the abstract variant arises at this point. As noted earlier in the chapter, in specifying a Visual Basic COM or QuickBasic array, you cannot say "this array is restricted to variant integers." Therefore, the toString/fromString language for arrays cannot allow the syntax in Array,(Variant,Integer),1,10,0,5. Instead, the syntax must be Array,Variant,1,10,0,5, and the type should be an abstract variant that contains the unknown type.[4]

A UDT is represented as UDT,*typelist*, where *typelist* is a comma-separated series of parenthesized type expressions. Each parenthesized type expression should be in the form *name*,*type*. In this form, *name* is the member name, and *type*

---

4. I created the unknown type because of an ultimate goal to write a compiler and an interpreter for full symbolic evaluation of business rules and source programs with partially or fully unknown values, but I was delighted to find a use in this context for this feature.

is another type expression in the toString/fromString language. Each parenthesized type expression must be a scalar, a variant, an array, or a UDT. Consider this UDT:

```
Public Type TYPexample
    intInteger As Integer
    strArray(1 To 10) As String
End Type
```

This UDT will have the following expression:
UDT,(intInteger,Integer),(strArray,Array,String,1,10).

Objects vs. Tables

UDT expressions, unlike variant and array expressions, can go on forever. A UDT can contain another UDT, which can contain another, ad infinitum (and perhaps ad nauseum). Here's another indicator of the benefits of taking an object-oriented approach to compiler writing: we do not need to manage a stack or a table of nested UDTs.

Management of tables was a glory and misery of non-object-oriented compilers. An important skill was (and remains, although not necessarily in compiler writing) being able to write a hash table algorithm for mapping a large set of keys onto limited space.

Object-oriented development actually replaces much of the need for complex tables because the relationship between what were table entries, and what are now stateful objects, becomes delegation and inheritance, and the efficient management of the data structures becomes the runtime's problem.

This is why it saddens me to see the continued popularity of pure C, because it preserves the necessity of linked lists and tables in applications where these techniques are not needed. The claim is that the centralized object management is less efficient. The insinuation is the centralized Framework is some sort of government bureaucracy and is slow code written by dull fellows. This does not seem to be the case; quite the opposite, I would say.

Figure 6-2 shows the BNF definition of the qbVariableType toString/fromString language. After you have read Chapter 7, check the code and its procedures that start with fromString to see the recursive-descent parsing of this BNF. It is lexically analyzed by the qbScanner object described in Chapter 5, which means that the details of lexical syntax are identical to those of the QuickBasic language, as

implemented in our compiler. Note that this syntax allows a variant to contain
an array, as in Variant,(Array,Integer,1,10).

```
typeSpecification := baseType | udt
baseType := simpleType | variantType | arrayType
simpleType := [VT] typeName
typeName := BOOLEAN|BYTE|INTEGER|LONG|SINGLE|DOUBLE|STRING|
            UNKNOWN|NULL
variantType := abstractVariantType COMMA varType
varType := simpleType|(arrayType)
arrayType := [VT] ARRAY,arrType,boundList
arrType := simpleType | abstractVariantType | parUDT
parUDT := LEFTPARENTHESIS udt RIGHTPARENTHESIS
udt := [VT] UDT,typeList
typeList := parMemberType [ COMMA typeList ]
parMemberType := LEFTPAR MEMBERNAME,baseType RIGHTPAR
abstractVariantType := [VT] VARIANT
boundList := boundListEntry | boundListEntry COMMA boundList
boundListEntry := BOUNDINTEGER,BOUNDINTEGER
```

Figure 6-2. qbVariableType's toString/fromString language BNF

qbVariable Serialization

The goal of the qbVariable object is to *represent* the value and *reference* the type.
Therefore, the overall syntax of the fromString/toString language exposed by
qbVariable should be *type:value*. The *type* should be an expression in qbVariableType's
language. The colon is a safe delimiter, because if you examine the qbVariableType
BNF shown in Figure 6-2, you will see that the colon cannot occur anywhere in
a qbVariableType expression. Colons can appear in values (for example, inside
quoted strings), but what matters is that the leftmost colon must appear if a type
and value are specified.

> **NOTE** *One primary reason for using BNF as described in Chapter 4 is the
> ability to examine the BNF, by hand or automatically with a tool similar to
> bnfAnalyzer, and make sweeping generalizations about the language, such
> as that a colon cannot appear in a serialized qbVariableType.*

For example, the qbVariable expression Integer:10 represents an integer with
a value of 10; the expression Variant,String:"ABC" represents a variant with a string
value of ABC. The string follows the rules of QuickBasic and Visual Basic: it must
use double quotes, and internal double quotes represent singly occurring double
quotes.

A complete notation is supported for arrays. One-dimensional arrays are supported as comma-separated lists of scalar values, where each scalar value can be a number or a string. For example, Array,Variant,1,2:1,True represents the array containing the byte value 1 and the Boolean value True.

Note that the scalar value is always fitted to the narrowest QuickBasic type. Therefore, we support an additional notation, useful for variants but applicable to values. This is the decorated notation *type(value)*, where *type* names a QuickBasic type and *value* is a value. To accurately show a variant array containing an integer and a Boolean, the expression may be Array,Variant,1,2:Integer(1),Boolean(True). The use of decoration overrides the selection of the narrower type.

The asterisk may be used to specify a default value. For example, Boolean:* specifies a Boolean type and the value False. When an asterisk is used as the value part of an array, this fills all entries with the default for the entry type. For example, Array,String,1,10:* creates a string array with null strings in each entry.

Any expression for an array can follow individual values with a parenthesized number, to repeat the entry *n* times. The expression Array,Integer,1,1014(10) creates an array with the letter *A* in ten entries. In fact, an asterisk may replace the parenthesized number, and this will repeat the default array value to the end of a one-dimensional array.

Arrays with higher dimensions are represented as lists of parenthesized *slices*, where a slice is the entry at the lower dimension. Array,Integer,1,2,1,2:(1,2),(3,4) represents the type and value of a two-dimensional array. Array,Integer,1,2,1,2,1,2: ((1,2),(3,4)),((5,6),(7,8)) represents the type and value of a three-dimensional array.

> **NOTE** qbVariable *and* qbVariableType *expressions aren't very user-friendly. They are intended for internal production and consumption between objects of the compiler. They do not form any part of the QuickBasic language.*

Although the usual syntax of these qbVariable expressions is *type:value,* either the type or the value may be omitted. When the type is omitted, it is determined empirically from the value alone, as follows:

- If the value is a single number, it is converted to the narrowest QuickBasic type. For example, the number 1 as an expression will convert to a byte; the number 32767 converts to an integer.

- If the value is a single string in quotes and using Visual Basic rules, it is converted to a string.

- If the value is a list of scalars (strings and numbers), it is converted to a one-dimensional array with a lower bound of zero. If the variables all convert to the same type, this will be an array of that type; if the variables all convert to different types, this will be a variant array.

- If the value is a list of decorated scalars in the *form type(value)*, it is converted to an array. If they are all the same type, the array will be of that type; otherwise, it will be an array of variants.

- If the value uses parentheses to specify subcollections in such a way that it represents an orthogonal collection, so that all subcollections contain the same number of members at all levels, it is converted to an array with dimension equal to the depth of parentheses nesting, with a lower bound of 0 for each dimension and an upper bound at each dimension that is the number of listed elements, or slices. Again, if the entry types are the same, the array has the scalar entry type; otherwise, it is a variant. For example, (1,2),(1,2) specifies a two-dimensional byte array containing two rows and two columns. Entries can be decorated.

- If the value is a list of valid parenthesized members in the form *(name,type)*, the type is UDT.

- If the value is the keyword UNKNOWN or NULL, the type is the corresponding type.

Figure 6-3 shows the BNF of the qbVariable toString/fromString language.

```
fromString := fromStringType
fromString := fromStringValue
fromString := fromStringWithValue
fromString := fromStringType COLON fromStringValue
fromString := COLON fromStringValue
fromStringType := baseType | udt
baseType := simpleType | variantType | arrayType
simpleType := [VT] typeName
typeName := BOOLEAN|BYTE|INTEGER|LONG|SINGLE|DOUBLE|STRING|
            UNKNOWN|NULL
variantType := abstractVariantType COMMA varType
varType := simpleType|(arrayType)
arrayType := [VT] ARRAY,arrType,boundList
arrType := simpleType | abstractVariantType | parUDT
parUDT := LEFTPARENTHESIS udt RIGHTPARENTHESIS
udt := [VT] UDT,typeList
typeList := parMemberType [ COMMA typeList ]
parMemberType := LEFTPAR MEMBERNAME,baseType RIGHTPAR
abstractVariantType := [VT] VARIANT
boundList := boundListEntry | boundListEntry COMMA boundList
boundListEntry := BOUNDINTEGER,BOUNDINTEGER
simpleType := [VT] typeName
typeName := BOOLEAN|BYTE|INTEGER|LONG|SINGLE|DOUBLE|STRING|
            UNKNOWN|NULL
variantType := abstractVariantType,varType
varType := simpleType|(arrayType)
arrayType := [VT] ARRAY,arrType,boundList
arrType := simpleType|abstractVariantType
abstractVariantType := [VT] VARIANT
boundList := boundListEntry | boundListEntry, boundList
boundListEntry := BOUNDINTEGER,BOUNDINTEGER
fromStringValue := ASTERISK | fromStringNondefault
fromStringNondefault := arraySlice [ COMMA fromStringValue ]
arraySlice := elementExpression | ( fromStringNondefault )
elementExpression := element [ repeater ]
element := scalar | decoValue
scalar := NUMBER | VBQUOTEDSTRING | ASTERISK | TRUE | FALSE
decoValue := quickBasicDecoValue | netDecoValue
quickBasicDecoValue := QUICKBASICTYPE ( scalar )
netDecoValue := netDecoValue := [ SYSTEM PERIOD ] IDENTIFIER
                LEFTPARENTHESIS ANYTHING RIGHTPARENTHESIS
repeater := LEFTPAR ( INTEGER | ASTERISK ) RIGHTPAR
```

Figure 6-3. qbVariable's toString/fromString language BNF

QuickBasic Variables Mapped to .NET Objects

This section addresses the way in which we map a QuickBasic variable to the
.NET object. The .NET object is capable of accurately representing any possible
QuickBasic variable (with two exceptions in our implementation only, as described
in this section). But what's the best way to do this?

The easier, softer way might be to just use the broadest and most general
type: the .NET Object. But we know that we would need to pay for the apparent
simplicity. Payment will be extracted when the Nutty Professor interpreter tries

to do arithmetic or other operations on pure Objects, because the types of the results will be determined by .NET rules and not QuickBasic rules. Life will be less difficult when we use the CLR, but it will still be difficult, because the CLR won't have QuickBasic type information.

Therefore, I propose the mapping shown in Table 6-3.

Table 6-3. Basic Mapping of QuickBasic Variables to .NET Objects

QuickBasic Variable	.NET Object
Boolean	Boolean
Byte	Byte
Integer	Short integer
Long integer	Integer
Single-precision real	Single
Double-precision real	Double-precision real
String	String
Array	Collection
UDT	A collection of members, each of which is a qbVariable object
Null	Nothing in the .NET object value and the associated type
Unknown	Nothing in the .NET object value and the associated types

Of course, this isn't as straightforward as it looks. Let's see how the mapping works.

Scalar Mapping

We start off easily, with Booleans represented by .NET Booleans and bytes represented by .NET bytes. QuickBasic integers are represented accurately in .NET by short integers. However, .NET integers are 32-bit and cannot accurately represent QuickBasic integers.

> **NOTE** *Of course, all QuickBasic integers in the 16-bit word can indeed be represented by .NET integers in the 32-bit word. However, code that depends on the word size for accuracy won't work the same. You may think that code should not depend on the word size, and it shouldn't in most cases; nonetheless, the compiler and runtime must account for this fact.*

QuickBasic long integers, which are 32 bits, are represented by .NET integers. Now things get a bit messier. QuickBasic single-precision reals are represented *inaccurately* by .NET singles. The representation is inaccurate because no .NET floating-point tool, out of the box, provides support for QuickBasic floating-point values precisely. To represent QuickBasic single-precision reals, we would need to write a software simulation for this type of floating-point representation (and we won't do this).

QuickBasic double-precision reals are represented, again *inaccurately*, by .NET double-precision reals. .NET is more mathematically accurate, but the older inaccuracy isn't *accurately* simulated (whew).

QuickBasic strings are represented accurately by strings in the compiler because a limit of 64KB characters is actually enforced, both to be accurate and also as a sort of trip down memory lane, back to when strings, outside the C language, were severely restricted in length. This retro feature can be suppressed by a compiler option, but you need to go to the code for details.

Array Mapping

Arrays are represented by a collection with the following constraints, which will be checked by the core `inspect` method of `qbVariable`:

- Each collection member that is not a collection containing a slice of the array, as described next, is the .NET representation of the QuickBasic scalar entry value. For example, a one-dimensional byte array would be a collection of three bytes.

- Subcollections as items represent slices of the array, containing the contents of a lower dimension. This means that a two-dimensional array is represented as a collection of collections.

It would be a bad mistake to map QuickBasic arrays onto .NET arrays. Each .NET array has a fixed dimensionality, even when it is dynamically allocated using `ReDim`. We would go crazy trying to represent a QuickBasic array using a .NET array, creating and re-creating arrays.

It would be a simpler matter to just represent any QuickBasic array using a single .NET array of objects with one dimension, and convert multidimensional subscripts to a single .NET subscript. The math is easy. However, the overriding advantage of the collection approach is that much of the access can be pushed down into an independent object that is outside the compiler. This object is named `collectionUtilities`, which provides several tools for working with the classic collection, including tools for serialization and deserialization, and accessing recursive collections that contain subcollections. The `collectionUtilities` tool is available from the Downloads section of the Apress Web site (http://www.apress.com), in the egnsf/collectionUtilities/bin folder.

Since we have represented arrays as collections and higher-dimension arrays as collections that contain collections, accessing an element is straightforward. For example, suppose you have the array that is represented in `fromString` notation as `Array,Integer,1,3,1,2:((1,2),(3,4),(5,6))`. This is a two-dimensional array, and it is represented as one collection with three items. Each item is a subcollection with two items. To access this (or any) array, given a list of subscripts, access the top-level collection and go to the subscripted item. It is either a collection or, at the highest dimension, it is not. If it is not a collection, you're finished, and the value can be returned through all recursion levels. If the item is a collection, reapply the same probe recursively to the next level down, using the subcollection. At each level of recursion, you examine one collection—either the main collection or some subcollection.

This recursion has a hidden loop to get to the appropriate depth. There would be no looping in the use of a single .NET one-dimensional array, just calculation. However, the looping depends on what is almost always a very small number of dimensions. Roughly 90% of arrays are one-dimensional, 9% are two-dimensional, and perhaps 1% will have three or more dimensions (perhaps in rocket science applications, voyages to the fourth dimension, and high finance).

UDTs, Null, and Unknown Mapping

UDTs can be represented by a collection of members, each of which is a `qbVariable` object.

Finally, null and unknown types are represented by placing Nothing in the .NET object value and their associated types, because these types are identical with their value.

Delegation vs. Inheritance

The `qbVariable` model provides some opportunities for its state to become invalid, because it stores the value and the type. The type may be scalar, but the value may be a collection, or the collection may not have the expected structure of entries, and so forth. Murphy's law dictates that because this possibility exists, it will happen, and it requires that the core `inspect` method of `qbVariable` check the correspondence of type and value. The problem seems unavoidable, simply because there is no one-to-one mapping of QuickBasic types to .NET types.

One design decision I made was to make separate objects to represent just the type (`qbVariableType`) and the type and value (`qbVariable`). An alternative would be to have `qbVariable` inherit `qbVariableType`, such that a variable would not have a type; it would instead be a sort of type-with-more-stuff. If a design decision is hard to put into clear words, sometimes this is a danger sign. The fact that it sounds basically more sensible to say that a variable "has a" type means that it is probably the better decision. A variable with a type and value is not a subspecies of a type at all. Furthermore, inheritance would not solve the problem that the .NET representation of the type might be at odds with the inherited type attributes. Therefore, I decided to use delegation rather than inheritance. The next sections describe the details of the qbVariableType and qbVariable implementations.

The qbVariableType Object

The qbVariableType class represents the *type* of a variable according to the abstract model described in the preceding sections. As such, this class contains no value information and does not identify the variable by name, with one exception: when it defines a UDT, it identifies member names only. The source code of qbVariableType is available from the Downloads section of the Apress Web site (http://www.apress.com), in egnsf/Apress/quickBasic/ qbVariableType/qbVariableType.vb.

qbVariableType State

In terms of object taxonomy, it's obvious that qbVariableType will have a state. Figure 6-4 shows the State section of the code.

```
' ***** State *****
Friend Structure TYPstate
    Dim booUsable As Boolean        ' Object usability
    Dim strName As String           ' Instance name
    Dim enuVariableType As ENUvarType ' Main type
    Dim objVarType As Object        ' Contained type(s):
                                    ' Nothing (for a scalar, Unknown or null)
                                    ' Contained type for Variant
                                    ' Entry type for Array
                                    ' Collection for UDT:
                                    ' key is member name:
                                    ' data is 3-member subcollection:
                                    ' Item(1) is member index:
                                    ' Item(2) is member name:
                                    ' Item(3) is member as a qbVariableType
    Dim colBounds As Collection     ' No key: data is 2-element collection:
                                    ' item(1): lowerBound
                                    ' item(2): upperBound
    Dim colTypeOrdering As Collection ' Type ordering
    Dim booContained(,) As Boolean  ' Type containment
    Dim objTag As Object            ' User object
End Structure
Private USRstate As TYPstate
```

Figure 6-4. qbVariableType state

Most fields in the state are self-explanatory, but the objTag is a bit of a mystery. It supports the core Tag property shared with a number of the compiler objects, including qbVariable. This allows us to use code to add objects and data to a variable type instance in a spontaneous manner to meet extra needs in the compiler, or in any program that uses qbVariableType as a stand-alone object. The Tag property is not visible to the user of the QuickBasic system; rather, it is a convenience for using the object.

The additional fact that the qbVariable object must, in many cases, delegate when a variant, an array, or a UDT contains one or more types means that a full-fledged stateful object, using the core methodology introduced in Chapter 5, is needed. Therefore, qbVariableType informally implements the core methodology as a stateful object.

At all times, a qbVariableType instance is either usable or not usable. The instance becomes usable at the end of a successful new constructor call, and it remains usable until the object is disposed of or a serious internal error occurs.

qbVariableType also has a Name property, which defaults to qbVariableType*nnnn date time* to identify the type in XML output and other messages. This doesn't name the type; it names the object instance.

The object2XML Method

Like qbScanner, qbVariableType exposes a core object2XML method: the start of its output is shown in Figure 6-5.

```
<!--
*********************************************************************************
*                                                                              *
* variableType                                                                 *
*                                                                              *
*                                                                              *
*                                                                              *
* This class represents the type of a quickBasicEngine variable, including support *
* for an unknown type and Shared methods for relating .Net types to Quick Basic *
* types.                                                                       *
*                                                                              *
* This class was developed commencing on 4/5/2003 by                           *
*                                                                              *
* Edward G. Nilges                                                             *
* spinoza1111@yahoo.COM                                                        *
* http://members.screenz.com/edNilges                                          *
*                                                                              *
*                                                                              *
*                                                                              *
* This instance represents the following variable type:                        *
*                                                                              *
* Type:                                                                        *
* Member1: Variant containing 32-bit Long integer in the range -2**31..2**31-1 *
* Member2: Variant containing 32-bit Long integer in the range -2**31..2**31-1 *
* Member3: Variant containing Boolean                                          *
* End Type: total size is 3                                                    *
*                                                                              *
*                                                                              *
*                                                                              *
* CACHE INFO                                                                   *
*                                                                              *
* A cache of recently parsed variable types is maintained to save time: here is *
* the state of the cache.                                                      *
*                                                                              *
* Cache status: available                                                      *
* Cache maximum size: 100                                                      *
* Cache current size: 7                                                        *
* Cache contains: "Unknown", "Variant,Long", "Long", "Variant,Boolean"...      *
*                                                                              *
*********************************************************************************
-->
<qbVariableType>
    <!-- Indicates the usability of the object -->
    <booUsable>True</booUsable>
    <!-- Identifies the object instance -->
    <strName>qbVariableType0001 3/4/2004 6:25:56 AM</strName>
    <!-- Identifies the variable's type -->
    <enuVariableType>vtUDT</enuVariableType>
    <!-- Identifies the type of a contained variable -->
    <objVarType>
        (1
        &quot;Member1&quot;
        Variant,Long)
        (2
```

Figure 6-5. qbVariableType.object2XML output (beginning)

As shown in Figure 6-6, this XML includes type information when the instance contains a type as part of the objVarType tag. In all cases, this can be just the toString method output (with commas changed to newline for readability) because it contains all the information about the embedded type, rather than the complete XML for the embedded type. In the example, a UDT is shown with three members as seen in the comment block.

```
<qbVariableType>
    <!-- Indicates the usability of the object -->
    <booUsable>True</booUsable>
    <!-- Identifies the object instance -->
    <strName>qbVariableType0001 3/4/2004 6:51:17 AM</strName>
    <!-- Identifies the variable's type -->
    <enuVariableType>vtUDT</enuVariableType>
    <!-- Identifies the type of a contained variable -->
    <objVarType>
        (1
        &quot;Member1&quot;
        Variant,Long)
        (2
        &quot;Member2&quot;
        Variant,Long)
        (3
        &quot;Member3&quot;
        Variant,Boolean)
    </objVarType>
    <!-- Identifies the bounds of an array type -->
    <colBounds>emptyCollection</colBounds>
    <!-- Identifies type ordering -->
    <colTypeOrdering>noCollection</colTypeOrdering>
    <!-- Identifies type containment -->
    <booContained>Unallocated</booContained>
    <!-- User's tag -->
    <objTag>&quot;&quot;</objTag>
</qbVariableType>
```

Figure 6-6. More qbVariableType.object2XML output

The inspect Method

The inspection rules applied by the core qbVariableType.inspect method are shown in Figure 6-7.

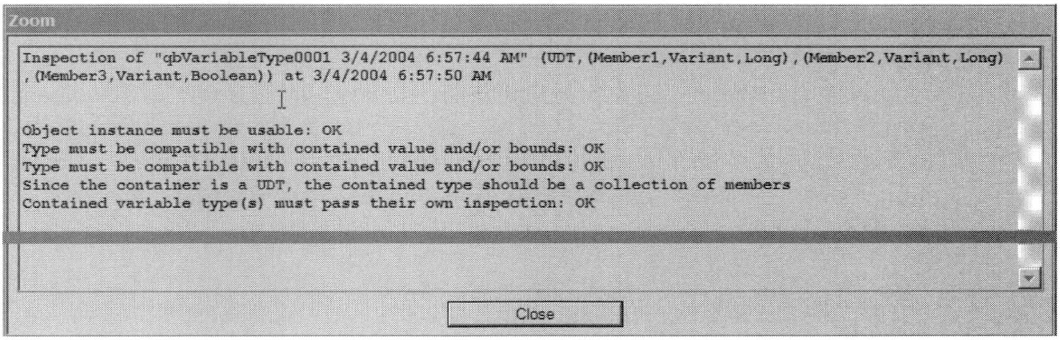

```
Zoom
Inspection of "qbVariableType0001 3/4/2004 6:57:44 AM" (UDT,(Member1,Variant,Long),(Member2,Variant,Long)
,(Member3,Variant,Boolean)) at 3/4/2004 6:57:50 AM
                              I

Object instance must be usable: OK
Type must be compatible with contained value and/or bounds: OK
Type must be compatible with contained value and/or bounds: OK
Since the container is a UDT, the contained type should be a collection of members
Contained variable type(s) must pass their own inspection: OK



                              [ Close ]
```

Figure 6-7. qbVariableType inspection

Note that inspection is two layers deep, because a UDT containing three scalars as seen in Figure 6-5 is two object levels, and `qbVariableType` always inspects its constituent objects. For each object, the instance must be usable. The type must be compatible with the contained value and bounds. For example, a user type must have a nonempty collection of members.

Inspection also clones the object to make sure the clone returns a `toString` that matches the original `toString`. For all objects, `object2.fromstring(object1.tostring)` must create the clone of `object1` in `object2`, and the `compare` method for the two objects must return `True`. Both assertions are checked in the inspection.

A Note on Inspection

Multilevel inspection is time-consuming, and objects that may have multiple levels are inspected when they are disposed. This may turn out to be excessively time-consuming in a production compiler. In a lab compiler, however, it is a benefit.

As I scale up, I may need to eliminate, or make optional, the inspection that now occurs in `qbVariableType` (and most stateful objects) when the object is disposed. For a large object, it will clone the object and its constituents, and this could be too time-consuming even in the lab.

But I would rather preserve the `inspect` routine and just limit its scope when it "notices" that the object is "large," because software objects should be reliable. Unreliable objects give object-oriented programming a bad reputation.

Hardware is built with all sorts of self-checks. I do not understand why any form of checking in production is suspicious in the real world. But perhaps in reaction, I sometimes overdo it.

---

qbVariableType Testing

The .NET application qbVariableTypeTester.exe is available from the Downloads section of the Apress Web site (`http://www.apress.com`), in egnsf\apress\qbVariable\ qbVariableTester\bin. You can use this application to test the `qbVariableType` object. Run it to see the screen shown in Figure 6-8 (after an introductory and one-time screen).

Figure 6-8. The qbVariableTypeTester program

Creating Test Objects

Enter **Variant,Integer:** in the text box at the top of the window, and then click
the button labeled Create Variable Type. The object is created and inspected for
validity. Click the Describe button to see an explanation of the type.

qbVariableTypeTester

The variableType Form1 has this description:

Variant containing 16-bit Integer in the range -32768..32767

OK

Click the Inspect button to see the internal inspection report, as shown in
Figure 6-9. This applies a series of assertions about the state of the object to the

state, as we've seen. Here, the contained type is a full-scale type in its own right and cannot (as in Figure 6-7) be represented as a toString.

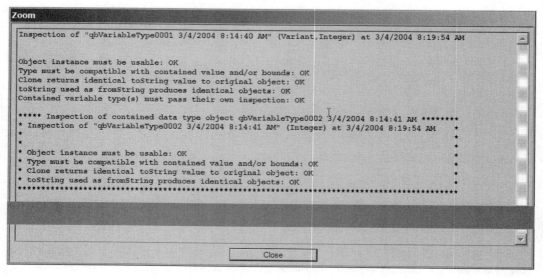

Figure 6-9. A qbVariableTypeTester inspection report

Dispose of the object by using the Dispose button.

Next, enter **Array,Integer,1,10,1,10:** and click Create Variable Type. Then click Describe to get a description of the array data type.

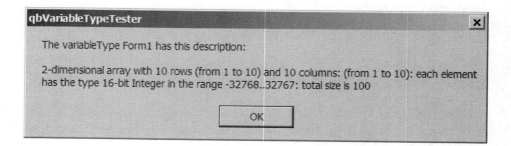

Note that each time you create a test object using this interface, the object will be inspected. If an internal error is found, a report will appear. These reports won't appear for syntax errors. For syntax errors, a simple dialog box will appear, and the object will not be created.

Converting to XML

Click the object2XML button to convert the object state to XML. Figures 6-10 and Figure 6-11 show the results.

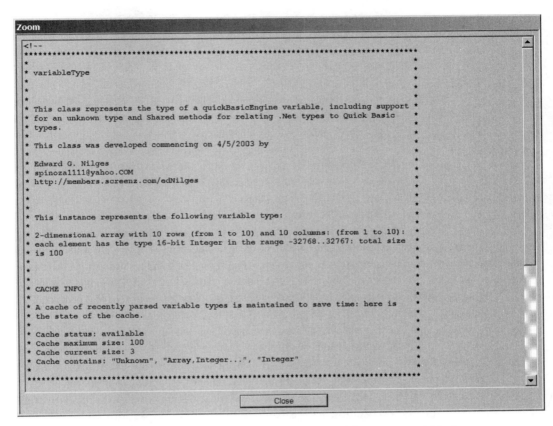

Figure 6-10. The XML description of the data type starts with a comment block.

```
<qbVariableType>
    <!-- Indicates the usability of the object -->
    <booUsable>True</booUsable>
    <!-- Identifies the object instance -->
    <strName>qbVariableType0001 3/4/2004 1:02:57 PM</strName>
    <!-- Identifies the variable's type -->
    <enuVariableType>vtArray</enuVariableType>
    <!-- Identifies the type of a contained variable -->
    <objVarType>Integer</objVarType>
    <!-- Identifies the bounds of an array type -->
    <colBounds>(1,10),(1,10)</colBounds>
    <!-- Identifies type ordering -->
    <colTypeOrdering>noCollection</colTypeOrdering>
    <!-- Identifies type containment -->
    <booContained>Unallocated</booContained>
    <!-- User's tag -->
    <objTag>&quot;&quot;</objTag>
</qbVariableType>
```

Figure 6-11. The XML description of the data type contains the object state.

Note that the object2XML output of Figure 6-10 shows a cache. The cache is used to avoid unnecessary parsing of fromString expressions. Each time a new fromString expression is presented to the object, the object parses the expression and saves it in a keyed Collection, such that the key is the fromString expression. The object is saved by forming its comprehensive, or "deep," clone. Later on, when a fromString is presented, the object can check the cache quickly for a copy of the required object.

The XML comment describes the state of the cache. In the example, four fromString expressions have been parsed and cached. Up to 100 fromString expressions can be saved in this way. Caching saves time. For example, running the nFactorial QuickBasic program using the Nutty Professor interpreter introduced in Chapter 8 takes about 60 seconds on a contemporary system from start to finish when no caching is performed; it takes about 40 seconds with caching.

Stress Testing

You can conduct a comprehensive stress test of most of the functionality of the object. Click the Stress Test button to see a progress report, as the object executes about 50 self-tests. On completion, click Yes to see the test report shown in Figure 6-12.

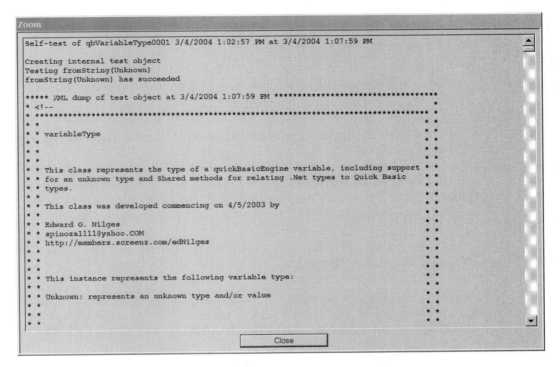

The window shows:

```
Zoom

Self-test of qbVariableType0001 3/4/2004 1:02:57 PM at 3/4/2004 1:07:59 PM

Creating internal test object
Testing fromString(Unknown)
fromString(Unknown) has succeeded

***** XML dump of test object at 3/4/2004 1:07:59 PM ********************************
* <!--                                                                         *
* ***********************************************************************  *
* *                                                                    * *
* * variableType                                                       * *
* *                                                                    * *
* *                                                                    * *
* * This class represents the type of a quickBasicEngine variable, including support * *
* * for an unknown type and Shared methods for relating .Net types to Quick Basic * *
* * types.                                                             * *
* *                                                                    * *
* * This class was developed commencing on 4/5/2003 by                 * *
* *                                                                    * *
* * Edward G. Nilges                                                   * *
* * spinoza1111@yahoo.COM                                              * *
* * http://members.screenz.com/edNilges                                * *
* *                                                                    * *
* *                                                                    * *
* *                                                                    * *
* * This instance represents the following variable type:              * *
* *                                                                    * *
* * Unknown: represents an unknown type and/or value                   * *
* *                                                                    * *
* *                                                                    * *
* *                                                                    * *

                              Close
```

Figure 6-12. qbVariableType test report

Scroll down through the test report to see a series of random (but repeatable) tests that exercise the functionality of the object and the syntax of its fromString expressions. You can also click the Randomize button for nonrepeatable tests. The object is continually self-inspecting during these tests.[5]

qbVariableType Shared Methods

The qbVariableType object is an appropriate place for several Shared methods for working with variable types. These methods can be used without creating an instance of an object. They include the following:

- containedType(type1,type2) tells whether the qbVariableType in type1 is "contained" in type2 (as specified in Table 6-1, earlier in the chapter).

---

5. While passing these tests proves nothing, in the sense that nothing proves software correct, the tests have been invaluable to me in regression testing while changing the source code. They will be of equal value to you if you change the source code.

- `defaultValue(type)` provides the default .NET value for a type. For example, it will return 0 for an integer type and a null string for the string type.

- `mkRandomType` constructs a random but valid `toString`/`fromString` expression for a type, in the event you want to play around. Its serious purpose was to supply test cases to the `test` method.

- `netValue2QBdomain` supplies the QuickBasic type that will be used to represent a .NET value.

All of these shared methods and all the unshared properties, methods, and events of `qbVariableType` are fully documented in the `qbVariableType` reference manual (see Appendix B).

The `qbVariable` Object

The `qbVariable` object contains the type, value, and name of a QuickBasic variable. Again, the source code is available from the Downloads section of the Apress Web site (`http://www.apress.com`), in egnsf/apress/quickBasic/qbVariable/qbVariable.vb.

All variables (including constants) are "boxed" inside `qbVariable` objects. About 75% of the work of `qbVariable` is accomplished inside its `qbVariableType` delegate. The remaining tasks are as follows:

- Record, modify, and return the value

- Record the variable name (different from the object instance name in the `Name` property)

- Expose core object procedures, including `toString`/`fromString` expression translation

qbVariable State

The value of `qbVariable` is recorded in the generic .NET object, `objValue`, as part of the object state, as shown in Figure 6-13.

> **NOTE** *The* `objTag` *is the same as in the* `qbVariableType` *state, described earlier in the chapter. It supports the core* `Tag` *property shared with a number of the compiler objects, including* `qbVariableType`. *This allows using code to add objects and data to a variable instance in a spontaneous manner to meet extra, unforeseen needs. For example, the compiler stores the variable's index in its collection of variables in the variable* `Tag`.

```
' ***** State *****
Private Structure TYPstate
    Dim booUsable As Boolean                          ' Object usability
    Dim strName As String                             ' Instance name
    Dim strVariableName As String                     ' Variable name
    Dim booVariableNameDefaults As Boolean            ' True: variable name has default value
                                                      ' False: variable name has been changed
    Dim objDope As qbVariableType.qbVariableType      ' Variable type
    Dim objValue As Object                            ' Variable value: .Net scalar or collection
    Dim objTag As Object                              ' User object
End Structure
Private USRstate As TYPstate
```

Figure 6-13. qbVariable state

The `objValue` object has the following values, which are checked for consistency with the `qbVariableType` delegate, which is in `objDope` (so-called because the variable type gives us the "dope" about the variable). This check is performed by the `qbVariable.inspect` method.

- If the type is unknown or nothing, `objValue` is Nothing.

- If the type is QuickBasic scalar, `objValue` contains its corresponding mapped .NET type.

- If the type is variant, `objValue` is a distinct `qbVariable` delegate, which is never a variant. It can be a scalar `qbVariant`, null (this is the default), unknown, or an array.

- If the type is one-dimensional array, `objValue` is a collection containing .NET values for the array elements.

- If the type is *n*-dimensional array, `objValue` is a collection. This collection must be orthogonal—either a collection of noncollection items or of collections. In the latter case, each collection must have the same number of items as all the other collections at its level, and each collection must be recursively orthogonal.

- If the type is UDT, `objValue` is a nonorthogonal collection of `qbVariable` objects, one for each UDT member.

It would be very glamorous in the academic sense to make the scalar entries of arrays `qbVariable` values instead of .NET values. This would appear to reduce multiple objects to one object. But if a large array collection consists of a massive collection of stateful `qbVariable` values, each will burden the CLR heap, and each will take time to allocate, create, and access. To avoid this overhead, array elements are .NET scalars. They are protected against outside tampering by the array `qbVariable`.

Variable Modification and Value Return

To modify any variable, including subscripted array entries, qbVariable exposes the valueSet method. valueSet(value) can set any nonarray/non-UDT to a .NET value object.

For one-dimensional arrays, valueSet(value,index) modifies the value at the index. valueSet(value,index1,index2) does the same in a two-dimensional array. For any array, valueSet(value,indexes) sets the entry, where indexes provides all subscripts as a comma-separated list.

For UDTs, valueSet(value,member) identifies the member and sets it to the value. Note that a UDT member can be a UDT. Therefore, member can be in the form name1.name2..., a sequence of period-separated names down to the last member to access nested UDTs. If the UDT member is an array, valueSet(value,member,indexes) can access the UDT member.

valueSet cannot change the preexisting type of the qbVariable. Only fromString(e) can set the type and value, if e is an expression, as described in the "qbVariable Serialization" section earlier in this chapter.

The value method of qbVariable returns values of qbVariables. It has the same syntax as valueSet, without the value parameter. For example, objQBvariable.value returns a scalar value. objQBvariable.value("member01.member02") retrieves member02, in the UDT that is member01, inside the variable.

qbVariable also exposes most of the core procedures that are exposed by qbVariableType, including inspect, test, Name, and object2XML. For a comprehensive reference manual, see Appendix B.

qbVariable Testing

The qbVariableTest.exe application, available from the Downloads section of the Apress Web site (http://www.apress.com), in egnsf/apress/quickBasic/qbVariable/qbVariableTest/bin, will test the qbVariable object and allow you to enter expressions in qbVariable's toString/fromString language that specify value and type. Figure 6-14 shows the program's interface.

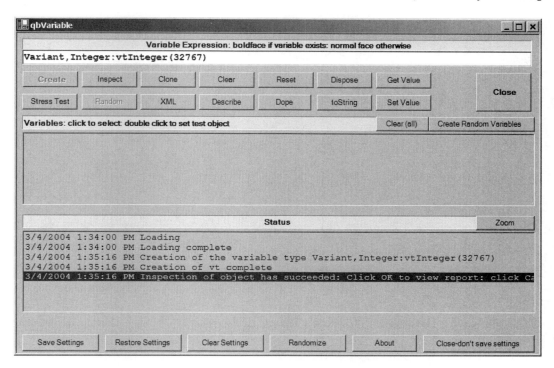

Figure 6-14. The qbVariableTest.exe program

In the text box at the top of the window, enter **Variant,Integer:vtInteger (32767)**, as shown in Figure 6-14, and click the Create button. Then click the XML button to see how the object, along with the type delegate, appears in XML, as shown in Figure 6-15.

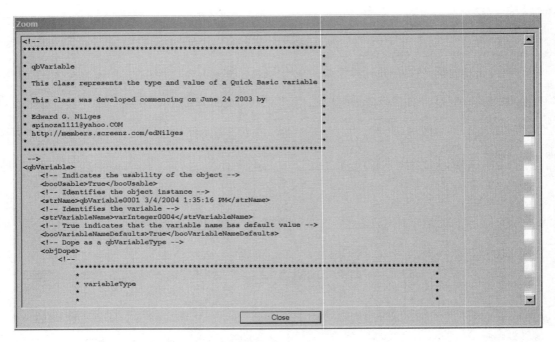

Figure 6-15. XML representation of the qbVariable

Note that in both `qbVariable` and `qbVariableType`, the `toString` serialization is almost as comprehensive as the XML and more compact (should you decide to use these objects, as free software, in any project where you need to represent QuickBasic values and their types).

Using XML to Capture Types and Values

I've used XML as a notation primarily to show the documentation of variable types and their values in a readable fashion. For example, this application of XML might be useful if you're working with a legacy Basic program that creates output for database consumption, and you need to accurately record, in addition to data values, the types of data. In comparing data from multiple source databases, the values may mean more in comparison to the limits expressed in their types—a 16-bit integer can mean something different when it is converted to 32 bits. The selection of a 16-bit representation might be a pure accident, and the user may want values outside the range –32768 through 32767, or it may mean that the value is limited to the range, and a value outside the range is an error. For example, "number of employees reporting to a manager" is definitely a small integer (unless your company manages by horde).

In effect, a data type is, in many cases, a *business rule.* Whether the CEO wills it or not, restricting gross pay values to a 16-bit integer representation means (1) all employees must be paid in whole dollars and (2) no employee will earn more than $32,767.00 per pay period.

qbVariable and qbVariableType allow you to obtain one-dimensional serialization in the form of toString/fromString expressions, or more self-descriptive and two-dimensional XML tags. Either can be stored in a database field without loss of fidelity. However, these objects do not support an xml2Object method.

I have never found a fully satisfactory XML parser (commercial parsers tend to enforce goals I don't necessarily share). XML is easy to parse using recursive descent, but the issues are very complex when you consider the size to which XML can grow and the resulting need for incremental parsing of part of an XML file.

This book could, I suppose, include a chapter on "XML parsing for fun and profit," because an XML parser, like a classic compiler, can consist of a lexical analyzer and parser. The problem is that there may be no profit in getting involved in XML wars. It's also no fun to fight with the boss over which parser to select.

Under the CLR Lies the Beach!

I'm ambivalent. I love and scorn these object-oriented digressions, for in them, "the law wishes to have a formal existence," as our academic friend Stanley Fish (a literary critic, turned administrator at the University of Illinois) says. In object-oriented design, the absolute need for an object has a tendency to haunt designers, especially if they neglect to implement the object, and does so with pure code in procedures.

My ambivalent love and scorn is based on the sheer amount of work it takes to create a halfway decent object-oriented program that meets the promises of its detailed design. I love to code, but at the same time, I sometimes would rather read Kant, play basketball, or go to the beach. Object-oriented design doesn't really free you to go to the beach, but it does let you do more work, because it makes new objects possible. In fact, sometimes these objects seem to force you to create them, because they have a cruel beauty. You love them, but they don't love you back (this is great preparation for your real love life, if you're a total masochist and assuming you have one).

The original QuickBasic compiler I designed simply mapped all values to a .NET object. This worked easily for simple scalar values including integers and strings. As you've seen in this chapter, it took some more effort to make it work for arrays. I could have just told you, "to represent the array, I stick a .NET collection in the value object at such and such a place, and you are now free to go to look at my wonderful code, and good luck." But that wouldn't be very helpful. Instead, I needed to describe the data architecture of the compiler.

Managers may tear their hair when programmers break a problem down into unforeseen components; the user wanted X, not X.Y.Z. But one lesson that can be derived from any number of disasters is that objects, and before them reusable procedures, want very much to have a formal existence.

In actual programming, it is common for a programmer to see needs beyond the formal requirements written by nonprogrammers, and it is important to be able to communicate these needs. For example, the programmer may understand that a problem is best solved by a language that describes instances of the problem and write a compiler for that same language.

No tedious recitation of individual procedures and what they do can replace the broad understanding afforded by describing what an object is. "This object represents all possible QuickBasic variables" summarizes an intuition and is, for this reason, better than a list of procedures, all of which must run in harmony to provide the unmentioned variable object.

In this chapter, you've seen the design, development, and testing of the qbVariableType and qbVariable objects. Like the qbScanner object introduced in Chapter 5, creating these objects involves a disciplined methodology for requirements analysis, detail design before coding, and developing the core procedures (including Name, inspect, and object2XML). This takes time.

I have found the payoff for this object-oriented approach to be large, and one that fulfills the unmet promise of the structured methods of old. Structured programming promised, but did not (for the most part) deliver, chunks of code that would snap together with a satisfying "thunk," "ka-chunk," or "bada-bing." The modular and structured methods often failed to obtain the desired productivity gains, because they only seemed to make bad designs worse through incorrect problem analysis. Object-oriented design, done right, seems indeed to deliver the hoped-for "ka-chunk" sound. Because the prerequisite for delivering the object is so much analysis, it has a tendency to concentrate the mind (kind of like the prospect of a hanging).

But both structured programming and object-oriented development require a big time investment. Because of this, management put the structured methods on a very back burner in the 1970s and now gives object-oriented development low priority. For this reason, it is best to practice the arts described here, and earlier in Chapter 5, in secret. In particular, it is just wrong to describe this art as "better," when at your office, *better* means faster.

Summary

This chapter has been a real forced march, and I do hope you are as tired as I am, but not tired of me.

We have done a requirements analysis as mere programmers of what it means to fully support a classic variable, whether in QuickBasic or old Visual

Basic, as a value or as a container for another simple value, an array of values, or a collection of disparate values.

In this analysis, we designed two little languages, produced by `qbVariableType.toString` and `qbVariable.toString`, and consumed by `qbVariableType.fromString` and `qbVariable.fromString`. The `toString`/`fromString` language of `qbVariableType` specifies all possible types, and it is a subset of the language of `qbVariable`. In the code, lexical analysis uses the scanner described in Chapter 5 and coded-by-hand, recursive, top-down descent to set type and value objects to the specified values. This approach to the tactical use of parsing is fully described in the next chapter. As in Chapters 4 and 5, we then ran a test GUI for the objects to see how they run and self-test.

The object-oriented approach shows how to factor the very large problem of building the front end of a compiler. The tables for this model would be very complex, whether implemented as linked lists or tables in a relational database. Linked lists are an excellent technique in pure C, and it might be a very good idea to create compiler tables as an Access, SQL Server, or Oracle database, thereby using SQL to retrieve data that would automatically persist between invocations of your compiler.

Objects, however, increase the ratio of nouns to verbs, since they tend to change a description of the code from the description of actions (such as "search the identifier table" to a description of data (such as "the variable object, which has a variable type"). This may make the discussion more understandable, because instead of listing tables and verbs (procedures), the object becomes a storyboard.[6]

But we need to cut to the chase. In the next chapter, we'll get to the `quickBasicEngine` itself. This object uses all the objects of Chapters 5 and 6—`qbScanner`, `qbVariableType`, and `qbVariable`—to scan, parse, and interpret (using an onboard Nutty Professor interpreter) QuickBasic code.

Challenge Exercise

Translate the following variable types and variables to the `fromString`/`toString` notation of `qbVariableType` and `qbVariable`. Make sure you can create and inspect the variable types using `qbVariableTypeTester`. Make sure you can create and inspect the variables using `qbVariableTest`.

- As a type: an integer

- As a value: an integer that contains 10

- As a type: a variant that contains a long integer

---

6. Of course, you may have other ideas. Please e-mail me your thoughts at `spinoza1111@yahoo.com`.

- As a value: a variant that contains the long integer 32768

- As a value: a string that contains a single double quote (hint: remember that our strings follow Visual Basic rules)

- As a type: the two-dimensional integer array with rows numbered 1..10 and columns number 0..3

- As a value: the array in the previous item with zeros in all entries, represented using the shortest possible `fromString`

- As a type: the UDT consisting of an integer and a string

Resources

For more information about data modeling for compilers, refer to the following:

Compiler Construction for Digital Computers, by David Gries (John Wiley, 1971). This book is out of print, but of historical interest. It is about writing compilers principally for IBM mainframes and spends a good deal of time on table management.

The Algorithm Design Manual, by Steven S. Skiena (Telos Press, 1997). This book is an excellent reference for the theory of "complexity," which in computer science, means efficiency metrics.

CHAPTER 7

The Parser and Code Generator for the QuickBasic Compiler

Cut to the chase.
—Old Hollywood saying

IN HOLLYWOOD'S TERMS, this is the chapter where the widow in arrears is tied to the railroad track by the heinous landlord, young Jack overtakes the onrushing locomotive to rescue the distressed widow, gets the widow a second mortgage on the Web, sends the villainous landlord to rehab, and organizes a men's retreat for the boys back at the ranch.

Or, if you prefer, this is where Luke Skywalker defeats the Dark Side of the Force and finds that dad is Darth Vader, which just goes to show you.

After much object development at the mother ship, we have arrived at the flagship, and indeed the largest object in our compiler object fleet, quickBasicEngine. A brilliant editor of mine has said, in so many words, that programmers are homeys who be chillin' when they see code. What I think he meant was that I need to supplement a theoretical discussion with at least a mad dash through the overall solution architecture of quickBasicEngine and its roughly 10,000 lines of code. I will postpone discussion of the onboard Nutty Professor interpreter that is included in quickBasicEngine until the next chapter. Here, I will cover the parser algorithms as generated from the BNF definition of the language described in Chapter 4.

This chapter will show how the parsing procedures can be manually, but rapidly, cranked out as multiple-algorithm implementations using a simple set of rules. You will see how the compiler generates individual instructions as objects and how this allows us to associate as much data as is appropriate to each instruction, including data that ties the instruction to the source code to aid in debugging. Just because we're implementing a legacy language, there is no reason for using retrograde methods from the dawn of man.

I will also introduce the fascinating topic of compiler optimization, demonstrating how constant expressions are evaluated by default during parsing and how the compiler eliminates unnecessary operations in a safe manner. Finally,

I will present an end-to-end example of the compilation and execution of a very simple program ('Hello world,' everyone's favorite).

The Recursive-Descent Algorithms

The word *Algorithms* is plural in this section's title because a different algorithm is needed for each production in the BNF. A separate algorithm must be constructed for each production in the BNF grammar. Each parser method in our compiler needs to pass a series of parameters expressing state or reference state in Common Declarations, and the most important single fact in the state is the position of the next token.

Before we look at the "meta" algorithm for actually coding individual recursive-descent procedures for the grammar symbols in your BNF, let's review recursive-descent algorithms in general.

Recursive-Descent Approaches

Recursive descent is one of the oldest parsing algorithms. It is not a compiling algorithm, per se, because it has little to do with scanning or code generation. It has to do with recognizing the language.

Hero computer scientist Niklaus Wirth, the creator of the Pascal language,[1] said that recursive descent must be used for block-structured languages such as Pascal. This is extreme, but as a manual parsing method, it is the most understandable.

Two general approaches to parsing exist: top-down and bottom-up. In the top-down, or goal-oriented, method of recursive descent, you decide on an overall goal or task and break it down into smaller tasks. In bottom-up algorithms, you instead run through the series of scanned tokens with auxiliary data structures, and enter a variety of higher states as these symbols are seen to build higher structures. Basically, in top-down algorithms, you start with *program* and go down to *token*; in bottom-up algorithms, you start with *token* and go up to *program*.

Both approaches can be automated by parser generators, but on the whole, bottom-up is better automated because of its complex data structures. Top-down recursive descent is easier to understand, and, as a tactical solution to quick parsing, it is nonpareil. So, top-down is the method used for our compiler's parsing procedures.

---

1. Niklaus Wirth was an early proponent of safe, as opposed to merely efficient, computing.

Cain's Amulet—A Recursive Descent Story

One of the oldest discussions of recursive descent was in terms of fathers and sons.

The first man (Adam, if you like) is told, "Compile a program," and as you'll recall from Chapter 4, program:= sourceProgram | immediateCommand. In other words, a program is a source program or an immediate command.

The first man has two sons (Cain and Abel, if you like). Since Cain only knows how to compile source programs, Adam tells Cain to try to compile a source program. (All of this predates the messier business between Cain and Abel.)

Cain goes off, and he and his descendants compile the source, or not, depending not on their ability, but on whether the source is valid. Cain and his descendants pass among themselves a magic amulet, which at all times tells them the *next* source token to be examined.

Cain knows that a source program is one or more option statements (that must appear at the start of the code and nowhere else), followed by a list of newline-separated statements. He passes the amulet to his eldest son, OptionParser, who checks for either no option statements or a small list. If OptionParser finds option statements with errors, he has to report failure to Cain and also give Cain back the amulet. Cain then goes back to Adam and reports failure. Adam can then hand the amulet to Abel to see if an expression exists.

The goal at the end happens to be that the amulet points one past the end of the source code as presented to Adam. Success, but an incomplete parse, is actually failure, because it means (as in the case of the simple program I=0###) that there are invalid sequences beyond the end.

My Cain and Abel exposition ignores some important details, the most important being the fact that Cain and Abel will need to use the same "descendants" in many cases. Think of these as laborers on their farm, and not as physical descendants, who move between the two farms as journeymen. The most important journeyman is the expression parser, which is needed to compile both source programs and expressions.

Recursive-Descent Procedures

If you know how to code individual recursive-descent procedures as methods in Visual Basic .NET or another language, then using a generator may be overkill for small to medium parsing tasks, including parsing common languages.

The simplest case occurs when the production is of the form a := b, where b as the right-hand side (RHS) may be complex but does not contain any direct or indirect recursive reference back to a; that is, a does not occur in b, nor does any part of b break down into an RHS that includes a. This simple case can be handled by a series of checks for terminals and grammar symbols. In quickBasicEngine, for example, each grammar symbol method is a Boolean function that returns True or False. On success, each advances the token index one symbol beyond the end of the context parsed.

In quickBasicEngine, each terminal is checked by calling the procedure compiler__checkToken_. This procedure checks for either a literal terminal value (such as a comma when expected) or a class of terminal values (such as an identifier).

> **NOTE** *As part of the coding convention for the compiler, all* Private *methods are terminated with an underscore. All members that are called exclusively by a higher procedure, including all procedures called exclusively by the* Private *method* compiler_, *are prefixed by the name of the caller. For example, the name of the procedure responsible for checking both expected token values and expected types is* compiler__checkToken_, *with two underscores after* compiler. *The first underscore shows that* compiler_ *is private; the second separates its name from its suffix.*

Basically, in b, which can be a complex sequence as long as it does not refer to a directly or indirectly, operators can be separated by spaces (which indicate implicitly that they must follow each other left to right) or by alternated sequences. Operators that are separated by spaces must each appear. Operators that are separated by the alternation operator (the vertical bar) are alternate possibilities, of which one or the other should appear. Consider the production a:=b | (c d), where the grammar symbol a consists of either a b or a c that is followed by a d. The code for this would be as follows:

```
If b Then Return(True)
If Not c Then Return(False)
If Not d Then Return(False)
Return(True)
```

This simplified code ignores "Cain's amulet"—the index of the next token that is known by all compiler procedures and available for modification by all compiler procedures. In the actual code of quickBasicEngine, the index is passed by reference to the compiler procedures as intIndex. Nearly all modifications of intIndex (the "amulet") take place at the lowest possible level, when compiler__checkToken_ is called to check for a token.

In quickBasicEngine, nearly all procedures can assume that a successful parse of a grammar category has advanced intIndex exactly one token beyond the end of the code that corresponds to the grammar category, and that an unsuccessful parse will leave the index unchanged. For this reason, many of the more complex procedures start with the declaration and saving of `intIndex`, so that they can reset it cleanly on a `False` exit.

Revisiting the BNF Design

As you learned in Chapter 4, dangers arise when the grammar construct can appear directly or indirectly on the RHS of its own production. For example, there is a problem when a binary expression such as a `Or` b can be replaced by one that contains recursive instances of the same grammar category, as in a `Or` b `Or` c.

The key is to design the BNF to avoid the infinite looping of left recursion seen in `orExpression := orExpression Or orExpression`, or the more tricky problem of associativity seen in `orExpression := orFactor Or orExpression`. Changing the first production directly into code will loop when it tries to parse the first `orExpression`. The second production will work for `Or` operations but will evaluate the RHS first. If converted to subtraction or division, as in `addFactor := mulFactor multiplyOrDivide addFactor`, this will create wrong answers at high speed.

The general form of any expression factor of a binary operator is seen in the production for `addFactor` (a factor of an addition or subtraction operation): `addFactor := mulFactor [addFactorRHS]`. We know that any `mulFactor` (any expression valid as the factor of a multiplication or division operation) can also be an `addFactor`, although the reverse is not true (1+1 must be parenthesized to work as the factor in (1+1)*2). We also know that it can be followed by any multiplicative operator. Therefore, the production `addFactorRHS` expands to `addFactorRHS := mulOp mulFactor [addFactorRHS]`. And, from Chapter 4, we know the right sort of recursion here is one that will not loop. By the time we parse `mulOp` and `mulFactor`, we know that we have increased the index, and this is because we know that neither `mulOp` nor `mulFactor` can ever be satisfied with null strings. As predicted in Chapter 4, this is how we can produce the code for a solid BNF.

Examining a Parser Procedure

Basically, all the compiler parsing procedures have the same general structure. Here, we'll examine the `addFactorRHS` procedure as an example of how these procedures work. Figure 7-1 shows the procedure header for `addFactorRHS`.

```
'  --------------------------------------------------------------
'  addFactorRHS := mulOp mulFactor [addFactorRHS]
'
'
Private Function compiler__addFactorRHS_(ByRef intIndex As Integer, _
                              ByVal objScanned As qbScanner.qbScanner, _
                              ByRef colPolish As Collection, _
                              ByVal intEndIndex As Integer, _
                              ByVal strSourceCode As String, _
                              ByRef objConstantValue As qbVariable.qbVariable, _
                              ByRef colVariables As Collection, _
                              ByVal intCountPrevious As Integer, _
                              ByRef booSideEffects As Boolean, _
                              ByVal intLevel As Integer) As Boolean
```

Figure 7-1. addFactorRHS procedure header

Note that the methods in a subset of the Private methods of quickBasicEngine have a common form starting with compiler__addFactor. They all start with compiler__, and in place of a sentence or phrase describing purpose, their comment header is a BNF production. These procedures are recognizers for productions. They are passed the same set of parameters, including intIndex (the next token) and the scanned code in objScanner. They attempt to recognize the production in their header comment, returning True on success and False on failure. On success, they solemnly guarantee that intIndex (which is passed ByRef) will point one beyond the end of the successfully recognized context. On failure, they make an equally solemn covenant that intIndex will have its value on entry.

These procedures could have been generated by an automated tool (with minor changes to the generated code), but were instead generated by an ordinary slob (me), using the very good editor in Visual Studio in a few hours. One flaw is that making systematic changes to these procedures is tedious and error-prone.

Another possible flaw happens to be the pile of parameters you see in the procedure, commencing with the ByRef token index intIndex. It exists because the original version of the code was written in a non-object-oriented style: one single object not factored into objects for scanning and for variables. This object did not have a single state in Common Declarations containing all changeable object-level variables. For this reason, information about the compiler state, including the token position, was passed as a combination of reference and value parameters.

In the current version of the compiler, the complete state of the compiler is in one place (the OBJstate object in the Common Declarations section of the quickBasicEngine class), and all parser procedures could access this one place. However, I decided to keep the older standard of passing items as parameters and not referring to the state in most compiler procedures, because it shows clearly what each procedure is interested in evaluating and changing. Having said this, however, in my next language engine, I will refer instead to a common state, or a state passed as a reference parameter.

Figure 7-2 shows the beginning of the procedure body. The first step raises an event that indicates to the GUI that a parse is starting. Note that the parse is tracked using three events: `parseStartEvent`, `parseEvent`, and `parseFailEvent`. In the "The Dynamic Big Picture" section later in this chapter, you will see how the GUI uses these events for progress reports.

```
raiseEvent_("parseStartEvent", "addFactorRHS")
If intIndex > intEndIndex Then Return compiler__parseFail_("addFactorRHS")
Dim intIndex1 As Integer = intIndex
Dim strMulOp As String
If Not compiler__mulOp_(objScanned, _
                        intIndex, _
                        strSourceCode, _
                        strMulOp, _
                        intLevel + 1) Then Return compiler__parseFail_("addFactorRHS")
Dim objConstantValueRHS As qbVariable.qbVariable
Dim booSideEffectsLHS As Boolean = booSideEffects
```

Figure 7-2. addFactorRHS start

The next step is to check whether the token index is beyond the end of the code, and the end of the code is passed by value as `intEndIndex`. It is not equivalent to the end of the source program or immediate expression, because when compiling inside a parenthesized subexpression, the end index for the expression parser, of which `addFactorRHS` is a part, is the position of the closing parenthesis. The expression parser calls itself recursively when it finds a parenthesized subexpression. This step is not needed in recognizers that can assume when called that the main index is not beyond the end of the context. But here, `addFactorRHS` is called in a recursive loop when it finds a multiplicative operator and a multiply factor (see the BNF in Figure 7-1). On entry, it needs to know whether it is past the end. If this index is past the end, failure is indicated by calling the `compiler__parseFail_` procedure, which calls `parseFailEvent` and returns `False`.

Then `compiler__mulOp_` is called to check for a multiplication operator (asterisk, forward slash for normal division, backward slash for integer divide, or Mod). Note that we have, in terms of American baseball, struck out if a multiplicative operator is not found and must call the parse failure routine in this case. This is because the BNF requires that the `addFactorRHS` start with a multiplicative operator.

The next two `Dim` statements exploit an elegant new feature of .NET: its allocation of local (`Dim`) variables just in time. The first `Dim` both declares a save area for the token index and initializes it to `intIndex`. The next `Dim` just declares a string work area.

> **NOTE** *Previous editions of Visual Basic 6 allocated all local variables on entry and deallocated them on exit, and their name scope was the complete procedure. In Visual Basic .NET, variables are assigned storage and their default value (or the value assigned in the* Dim *statement) when the* Dim *statement is encountered. If the* Dim *statement is encountered in an* If..Then..Else..End If *structure, or inside a loop, the variable may be referred to inside that structure. However, if the variable is "Dim'd" between* If *and* Then, *it may not be referred to after the* Else *and before the* End If. *The variable loses its place after control leaves the structure. For practical coding, this means that variables can be placed near the point of use, which makes code more readable. The only execution penalty occurs when the variable is defined in a* Do *or* For *loop, and for this reason, variables should be allocated outside* Do *and* For *loops.*

As shown in Figure 7-3, the next step checks for a multiply factor to match the multiplicative operator. If this isn't found, the compile fails. Otherwise, we can emit code in compiler__binaryOpGen_, which will emit the interpreter's Multiply opcode.

```
If Not compiler__mulFactor_(intIndex, _
                            objScanned, _
                            colPolish, _
                            intEndIndex, _
                            strSourceCode, _
                            objConstantValueRHS, _
                            colVariables, _
                            booSideEffects, _
                            intLevel + 1) Then
    Return compiler__parseFail_("addFactorRHS")
End If
objConstantValue = compiler__binaryOpGen_(strMulOp, _
                                          booSideEffectsLHS, _
                                          objConstantValue, _
                                          booSideEffects, _
                                          objConstantValueRHS, _
                                          colPolish, _
                                          intIndex)
```

Figure 7-3. Next step in addFactorRHS

Because of the optimization features of constant evaluation (folding) and lazy evaluation (discussed in the "Code Optimization" section later in this chapter), we need to call the code generator through a wrapper for all binary operators. This wrapper will not only generate code, but it will also test for the opportunity to combine constants, as in the expression a+1+2. This will take care of associative operators, including addition, subtraction, multiplication, and division, where all operators to the left must be evaluated first.

> **NOTE** *It's true that addition and multiplication are "symmetrical" such that they can be evaluated either way. But quite apart from the issue of Mod, it is bad practice for compiler writers to depart from the language specification, which typically will tell them how to evaluate and in what order. This is because of the finite precision of computer numbers, which will give different answers if the evaluation order is changed.*

Then we can proceed to the rest of the RHS, shown in Figure 7-4, for the case where there are several operators of multiplication precedence, such as a*b/c Mod d. We note the current position and recursively call ourselves. If this returns False, and the noted index is the same as intIndex, this means that we have gone past the end of the RHS and are finished. Whatever lies to the right (probably a newline) is the concern of another grammar symbol (probably the statementBody).

```
Dim intIndex2 As Integer = intIndex
If Not compiler__addFactorRHS_(intIndex, _
                               objScanned, _
                               colPolish, _
                               intEndIndex, _
                               strSourceCode, _
                               objConstantValue, _
                               colVariables, _
                               intCountPrevious + 1, _
                               booSideEffects, _
                               intLevel + 1) _
    AndAlso _
    intIndex2 <> intIndex Then Return compiler__parseFail_("addFactorRHS")
compiler__parseEvent_("addFactorRHS", _
                      False, _
                      intIndex1, _
                      intIndex - intIndex1, _
                      intCountPrevious, _
                      colPolish.Count - intCountPrevious, _
                      "", _
                      intLevel)
Return (True)
```

Figure 7-4. End of addFactorRHS

For unusually long expressions, such as a*b/c/d/e*f, the compiler__addFactorRHS calling itself for each RHS will load the stack proportionally. However, deep stack programming is no crime,[2] as long as the underlying runtime efficiently pushes and pops the stack.

If at any time the recursive call yields False but the index changes, this is an error, and the procedure returns False, which is the value of the parseFail procedure.

The final step fires the "parse event," which is emitted by parser procedures when a grammar symbol has been successfully parsed. quickBasicEngine uses events for reporting its progress (as does qbScanner, described in Chapter 5). The compiler produces a progress report that identifies the grammar category and the start and end of the corresponding source code during parsing.

The initial compiler referenced the Windows Forms object and had extra code to display forms it built on the fly with progress information. However, after I converted this edition of the compiler to a Web service for a potential client, I realized that it was quite wasteful to have an engine that referenced both Web GUI tools and Windows forms, not only in terms of total size, but also in terms of software maintenance. Therefore, this version avoids any references to GUI namespaces. Instead, it produces events to show its progress, and these events can be used to show progress on Windows or the Web, or ignored in a server.

The final step is to return True, showing success.

Why Not Use an Automated Tool Instead of Manual Recursive Descent?

I cranked out all of the compiler parsing procedures manually in a day or so, using the excellent GUI of Visual Studio.

An automatic code generator using top-down recursive descent can be built; I wrote one in the Rexx language. However, I think that if the programmer has a good editor, developing a parser generator doesn't save enough time to be worthwhile. Indeed, commercial compiler developers have, in place of simple parser generators, more comprehensive compiler kits, which handle a variety of tasks, including lexical analysis, parsing, and code generation.

---

2. Saul Rosen's 1968 anthology of compiler papers, *Programming Systems and Languages*, showed it was clearly the Europeans who liked the stack, while Americans like John Backus were optimizing small sets of registers, swapping data in and out. Later on, Calvin Moore's Forth language showed that in terms of expressivity, deep stack languages were better than register-oriented languages, including Fortran, for complex languages. In 1979, I implemented a compiler and interpreter in 1KB on a programmable calculator for the stack language Mouse, a simplified Forth. This language had the semantic power of Visual Basic, including recursion, but used single characters for operations to save space.

Manual recursive descent is no more efficient than an automated tool, since these tools use best practice. Therefore, I do not justify the manual method as more efficient. Instead, it demonstrates in code how a parser works. The best reason for learning to write a manual recursive descent parser quickly is that quick parsers for small languages can be developed rapidly, as you've seen in the toString/fromString languages of qbVariable and qbVariableType, described in Chapter 6.

Visual Basic programmers of the world unite, for I think I have shown you that you can write the most critical parts of a compiler simply. This shows that language snobbery in computer science is almost as bad as any illusion that any human language is better than another.

If you desire to write compilers for a living, you must learn C++, yacc, Bison, and other tools of the trade. This is because so many existing compilers are written in C++. But you can obtain an understanding of what goes into building a compiler, which is critical to your success as a compiler writer, in Visual Basic or C#. To see what I mean, convert the entire compiler to C++ and C#, or any language you do not know, in order to learn the language and the structure of quickBasicEngine at one time.

The qbPolish Object

As you'll see in the next chapter, the virtual machine for executing compiler code is included in quickBasicEngine as the Nutty Professor interpreter. In the code, it comprises all methods that start with interpreter. Like the simple virtual machine for arithmetic expressions presented in Chapter 3, this machine obeys Polish instructions (so-called because the operators follow the operands in Polish logic) that interact with an interpreter stack to produce results. Recall that in Chapter 3, we compiled expressions into simple Polish tokens to calculate expression values.

Here, we will examine the qbPolish object for representing operation codes usable by the Nutty Professor interpreter. The qbPolish object consists of data and is only a carrier of this data. Other than logic to support its core methods, the qbPolish object doesn't do anything to its data. For this reason, a test interface (as seen in Chapter 6 for qbVariable and qbVariableType) hasn't been provided for qbPolish.

The core object2XML method shows the state of all Polish objects emitted for the simple program Print 'Hello world,' as shown in Figure 7-5. (This XML is generated by the quickBasicEngine.object2XML method, available on the extended GUI, discussed in the "The Dynamic Big Picture" section later in this chapter.)

```
<!-- Polish collection -->
<colPolish>
    <qbPolish01><qbPolish>
        <!-- Indicates usability of object -->
        <booUsable>True</booUsable>
        <!-- Names the object instance -->
        <strName>qbPolish0002</strName>
        <!-- Identifies the op code -->
        <enuOpCode>opPushLiteral</enuOpCode>
        <!-- Identifies the first token responsible for this op code -->
        <intStartIndex>2</intStartIndex>
        <!-- Identifies how many tokens are responsible for this op code -->
        <intLength>1</intLength>
        <!-- Identifies the operand (if any) -->
        <objOperand>&quot;Hello world&quot;</objOperand>
        <!-- Comments the opcode -->
        <strComment></strComment>
    </qbPolish></qbPolish01>
    <qbPolish02><qbPolish>
        <booUsable>True</booUsable>
        <strName>qbPolish0003</strName>
        <enuOpCode>opPushLiteral</enuOpCode>
        <intStartIndex>3</intStartIndex>
        <intLength>1</intLength>
        <objOperand>String:vtString(ChrW(13) &amp; ChrW(10))</objOperand>
        <strComment></strComment>
    </qbPolish></qbPolish02>
    <qbPolish03><qbPolish>
        <booUsable>True</booUsable>
        <strName>qbPolish0004</strName>
        <enuOpCode>opConcat</enuOpCode>
        <intStartIndex>3</intStartIndex>
        <intLength>1</intLength>
        <objOperand>&quot;&quot;</objOperand>
        <strComment></strComment>
    </qbPolish></qbPolish03>
    <qbPolish04><qbPolish>
        <booUsable>True</booUsable>
        <strName>qbPolish0005</strName>
        <enuOpCode>opPrint</enuOpCode>
        <intStartIndex>3</intStartIndex>
        <intLength>1</intLength>
        <objOperand>&quot;&quot;</objOperand>
        <strComment></strComment>
    </qbPolish></qbPolish04>
    <qbPolish05><qbPolish>
        <booUsable>True</booUsable>
        <strName>qbPolish0006</strName>
        <enuOpCode>opEnd</enuOpCode>
        <intStartIndex>3</intStartIndex>
        <intLength>1</intLength>
        <objOperand>&quot;&quot;</objOperand>
        <strComment></strComment>
    </qbPolish></qbPolish05>
</colPolish>
```

Figure 7-5. qbPolish XML

Each opcode is a stateful object, rather than a mere opcode enumerator value as in the example in Chapter 3. Each opcode exposes the operation defined as an enumerator, an operand in some cases, a comment, and its source as the start and the end of the source code responsible for the opcode.

Figure 7-5 shows the following for each of the five opcodes generated for the Print 'Hello world' program:

- Each instance is usable (it better be), and its name is qbPolish*nnnn*, where *nnnn* is the sequence number of the object, as generated within one compiler invocation.

- The opcode is specified next. The first opcode is pushLiteral, which causes the Nutty Professor interpreter to push its operand (the string "Hello world") on the interpreter's stack.

- It is important for debugging tools that the qbPolish object model support linkage of the object code back to source. Therefore, the next two tags specify the first scanned token responsible for generating this opcode and the total number of scan tokens responsible. Only one scan token— the quoted string "Hello world"—is literally responsible for emitting pushLiteral.

- The next XML tag provides the literal operand for pushLiteral.

- The last XML token for each Polish opcode is a comment that can be associated with the opcode.

> **NOTE** *To keep the display of the Polish code in XML to a manageable size, I used the GUI to set an option in the compiler (on the GUI's Tools ➤ Options menu). It suppresses the generation of Polish opcodes for* Rem *statements and the addition of comments to Polish opcodes. However, by default, the compiler generates Polish opcodes for* Rem *statements and comments opcodes to allow the Polish code to self-document at some cost to its speed. When the option to suppress this material is not in effect, the last XML token's value will be* push string constant.

As you can see, a collection of Polish opcodes is created by the compiler, and it can be converted, along with the rest of the compiler's state, to XML.

Code Optimization

Ever since the first compilers, compiler developers have noticed that compilers can assist the programmer in generating efficient code. In this section, I'll demonstrate two entry-level techniques for code optimization. In MSIL code generation, more advanced techniques, such as the global analysis of blocks and their structure, are not important in the front end of a compiler, since JIT parsers do a lot of optimization behind the scenes.

`quickBasicEngine` does simple optimization in the form of constant folding and lazy evaluation.

Constant Folding

A surprisingly large number of programs contain expressions like 32767-2, where a piece of the expression or the entire expression consists of constants, and it's pretty obvious that this expression is mathematically and computationally equivalent to 32765. The reason can be clarity of expression, the use of symbolic constants, or the generation of code automatically.

> **NOTE** *A common example is found in the* `quickBasicEngine` *code itself, which contains concatenated strings segmented for readability on different lines.* "A" & _ <newline> "B" *is reduced in scanning to the obvious constant expression* "A" & "B", *and the compiler reduces this, by the method described in this section, to one string.*

I suppose you could write a preprocessor to *simplify* the source code. However, this would *complicate* your life. That's because a decent preprocessor would need to parse the complete source program. Even if you could cleverly factor the job and reuse the same parser in both your preprocessor and the compiler, there still would be two passes in the old style, and the optimization pass would be a waste of time for most programs not containing constant expressions. Instead, it's relatively easy to perform such calculations during parsing.

Take a look at Figure 7-1 again. One of its numerous parameters (which, as I mentioned earlier, could be part of state) is `objConstantValue`, a `qbVariable` described in Chapter 6.

In the example of 32767-2, on entry to `addFactorRHS`, `objConstantValue` will actually be 32767. This is because `addFactorRHS` is called exclusively from `addFactor`, and `addFactor`'s first BNF step (in its BNF `addFactor := mulFactor [addFactorRHS]`) is to check for a `mulFactor`.

The check for a `mulFactor` will descend to `compiler__term_`, whose job it is to check for the basic term of any expression. This can be a number; a string; a subscripted or unsubscripted identifier; a function call; or a complete, inner, parenthesized expression.

In the scenario, however, `compiler__term_` will find the scanner token corresponding to the number 32767. Because it has found a constant, `compiler__term_` will set its by reference `objConstantValue` parameter to a `qbVariable` of the most appropriate type (QuickBasic integer) for the token value, which in this case, just fits into a QuickBasic integer, represented by a .NET short integer.

When `addFactorRHS` moves on past the multiplicative operator to find another constant, it then has constant values other than Nothing in `objConstantValue` (the left-hand side value `32767`) and `objConstantValueRHS` (the right-hand side value 2). The procedure `compiler__binaryOpGen_` is responsible for emitting code for binary operators—including multiply, divide, and Mod—and it finds that the operation can be performed on the values.

But there's a tricky aspect to this. The `compiler__binaryOpGen_` method cannot use .NET arithmetic to perform the evaluation, since this will give different results from QuickBasic in some cases. Instead, it must use the Nutty Professor interpreter to perform the evaluation, or the compilation with constant folding might give different answers than compilation without this optimization. Furthermore, the binary operator generator must use the settings of `quickBasicEngine`. Suppose that you were to add a setting that affected the way in which arithmetic was performed (not likely, but possible). The compile-time evaluation must perform exactly as the engine has been set. Fortunately, a nifty method of `quickBasicEngine` is available: the `evaluate` method, described in the next section.

> **NOTE** *You can turn off constant folding by using the* `ConstantFolding` *property of the* `quickBasicEngine` *object.*

The Evaluate Methods

`quickBasicEngine` supports three functions along with corresponding methods: evaluate, eval, and run. You can include the functions in source code, and you can execute the methods from .NET programs.

- The `evaluate` method evaluates an expression using all the options and data of the engine running `evaluate`. The expression may be a single expression or a series of assignment statements, each prefixed by the keyword `Let`, followed by an expression using the assigned variables.

- The `eval` method is "lightweight." It creates a new instance of `quickBasicEngine` to ensure that the expression is evaluated using the default values of all object properties. `eval` is lightweight because it is Shared. While `quickBasicEngine.evaluate(string)` must be run on a `New` object, `quickBasicEngineval(string)` may be run on a code-only object that has not been created.

- The `run` method runs complete programs consisting of one or more executable statements.

The evaluate, eval, and run functions are not available in their full glory in Visual Basic and other commercial products, for a very good reason. If a product with the power of Visual Basic exposed the general ability to interpret the code of the language submitted as strings, developers could rather easily license copies of Visual Basic to others, by using Visual Basic to build a GUI.

Of course, corporate developers are allowed to extend the power of the VBA language engine to users with no fees for internal applications, but shrink-wrap vendors cannot do this. One of the joys of developing software for open release is the fact that you don't need to worry about giving away the store, since you have already done so.

Evaluation

The evaluate method takes a string consisting of a QuickBasic expression, compiles the string, and returns its value as a qbVariable. In fact, an evaluate function is provided as part of the language— evaluate(string) will return its value as a QuickBasic type. This function has been used in several Basic compilers, and it was supported in the Rexx language. It is very useful because it allows the developer to extend to the user the ability to specify logic as data and business rules.

Here, compiler__binaryOpGen_ can call compiler__constantEval_ to do the evaluation using the current settings of quickBasicEngine, using an internal evaluate method. compiler__binaryOpGen_ also implements the second form of optimization, known as *lazy evaluation*.

Lazy evaluation is the elimination of mathematical, logical, and string operations known to be unnecessary. Examples include A+0 (always the same as A), B And False (always False), and C & "" (always the same as C).

Lazy evaluation is related to math arcana in the form of the theory of groups. In math, a *group* is a set of elements (such as numbers, Boolean values, or strings) and a set of operations defined over those elements, usually an additive operation and a multiplicative operation. Also, groups have a *unity* element and a *zero* element. The unity element of a group is characterized by the fact that whenever it is applied to another element using the multiplicative operator, the value of the second element is unchanged. The zero element has the same effect when it is applied using the additive operator. The unity element of the group is one. The zero element is, of course, zero. The unity element in the group that consists of the Boolean values (True and False) and their operators (Or and And) represent truth, whereas its zero element is falsehood.

The group consisting of strings has, strictly speaking, no multiplicative operator, but it has addition cognate to string concatenation. Therefore, although strings have no unity, their zero is the null string.

This means that `compiler__binaryOpGen_` can apply the same logic to the binary operator when one of its parameters `objConstantValueLHS` or `objConstantValueRHS` is the unity, or zero, element of their group. Here are some examples:

- When either is zero and both are numeric, the code for stacking the alternate element can be generated instead of addition.

- When either is one and both are numeric, the same code can be generated instead of multiplication. In fact, this code replaces division when the RHS is one.

- When either is `False` and both are Boolean, the code for `False` can be generated instead of `And`.

- When either is `True` and both are Boolean, `True` can be generated instead of `Or`.

- When either are zero-length and both are strings, the non-null string can be stacked instead of using a concatenation.

Optimization in the form of constant folding and lazy evaluation can be applied by the recursive-descent parser inline in place of a separate pass over either the source code or the object code, and this may be one benefit of developing the recursive-descent parser by hand.[3]

The Architecture of the Compiler

The overall architecture of the compiler as a Visual Basic .NET object solution is illustrated in Figure 7-6. You can see the delegated relationship of the compiler objects. Notice how it shows that an object "has a" collection of delegates with a double line. There is only one scanner, for example, which has a collection of tokens.

---

3. Of course, there is no reason why in `yacc` the optimizations could not be inserted in tags, but overall, the manual method provides a little more insight into what's going on under the hood.

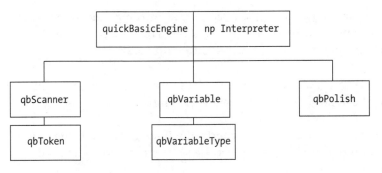

Figure 7-6. quickBasicEngine object overview

The Nutty Professor interpreter is embedded in the code, and therefore more closely bound, or bolted on, the engine. This is mostly an artifact of scheduling pressures; ideally, the Nutty Professor interpreter would be a separate object.

Figure 7-7 shows the solution architecture of the testing GUI, qbGUI. Most of the projects in the solution should be either familiar or understandable. qbGUI is the startup project and the only form-based project. You will recognize old friends described in previous chapters, including qbScanner, qbVariable, and qbVariableType. Also notice that documentation can be attached to a .NET project. Here, each project has a readme.txt file, which describes the project goals, changes, and open issues. The solution as a whole has a solutionReadMe.txt project with the solution goals, changes, and open issues.

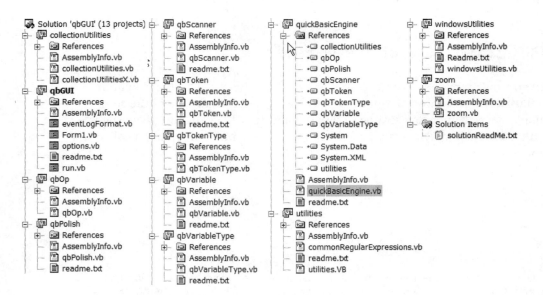

Figure 7-7. qbGUI solution architecture

The following projects in the qbGUI architecture may not be familiar:

- collectionUtilities is a project for the collectionUtilities.dll. This object, which is stateful but lightweight, consists of a set of utilities for dealing with collections, including converting them to and from strings. It is useful with collections containing subcollections, and the compiler uses this type of structure to represent trees.

- utilities generates utilities.dll, a stateless collection of utilities for math and string handling. It is independent of any presentation environment such as Windows or the Web.

- windowsUtilities generates windowsUtilities.dll, a stateless collection of utilities for Windows presentation.

- zoom generates a visual object for "zooming" in on Windows controls and expanding their contents to a read-only text box, from which they can be copied to the Clipboard.[4]

In the next section, we'll run the compiler, which includes the ability to examine its operations. This will give you the "dynamic" big picture.

The Dynamic Big Picture

As noted in the previous section, qbGUI is the testing GUI for quickBasicEngine. Obtain the code for this book from the Downloads section of the Apress site (www.apress.com), if you haven't already done so. Run qbGUI.exe, which will be in the bin file of the folder labeled qbGUI. The first screen that you see (the Easter egg) appears only the first time you start the program, as shown in Figure 7-8.[5]

---

4. In general, I try to stay away from developing a lot of my "own" visual controls, so forms don't become too "welcome-to-my-world." However, the zoom project seemed to fulfill a genuine need.

5. You'll notice the quotations on the qbGUI Easter egg. I first saw quotations in Bill McKeeman's excellent, now out of print, book, on how to write a parser generator in PL/I, *A Compiler Generator*. In introducing the need for a formal BNF notation, he quoted American poet Emily Dickinson: "After great pain, a formal feeling comes." It was a reminder that the ultimate guarantor of software correctness and efficiency is the person behind the machine.

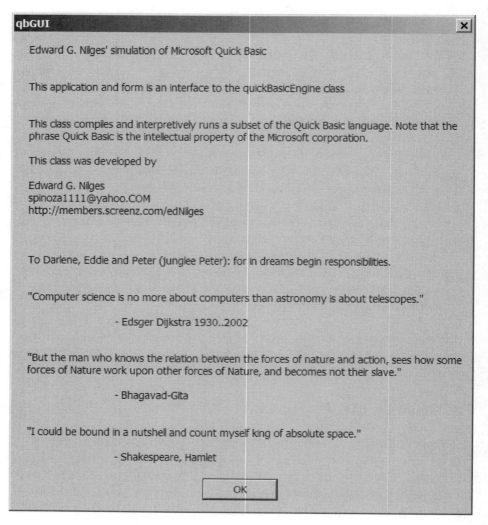

Figure 7-8. Easter egg from qbGUI

NOTE qbGUI *will use your registry with sensitivity. It will create one folder in the proper place (VB and VBA Program Settings) labeled qbGUI. At any time, you can reset the product simply by deleting qbGUI.*

Click OK to see the simple qbGUI window shown in Figure 7-9. This screen is meant for the public. Since you've come this far with me on the arcana of the compiler, you might as well click the More button to see the full monty.[6]

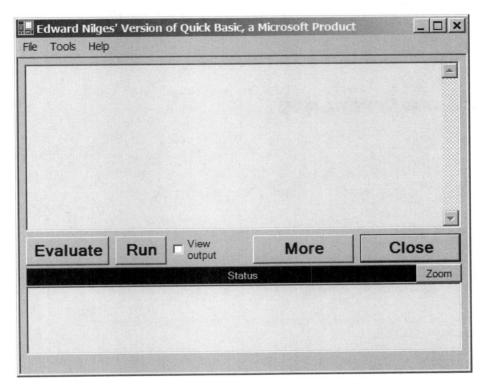

Figure 7-9. Simple interface

Once you have the expanded display, click the Replay check box in the lower-left corner of the window. Then select File ➤ Load Source ➤ Code, navigate to egnsf/Apress/QuickBasic, and obtain the file helloWorld.bas, to see the display shown in Figure 7-10. This will allow you to examine a simple compile operation step by step.

---

6. *Full monty* is British slang for "the whole thing." The term became more well-known after the release of the film called *The Full Monty*, in 1997.

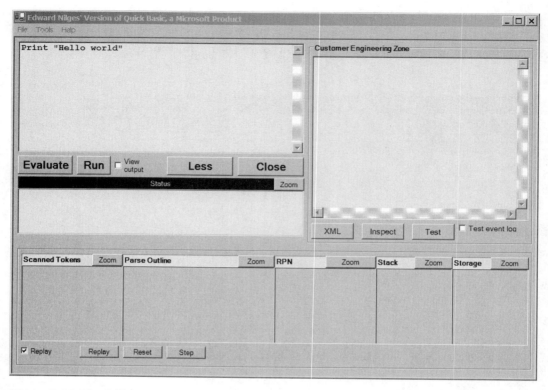

Figure 7-10. The full monty, obtained by checking the Replay box in the lower-left corner and loading helloWorld.bas

The full display contains the code for the famous 'Hello world' program. Click Run to see the screen shown in Figure 7-11. The most obvious effect is the "green screen" output of running 'Hello world,' but more interesting is the history at the bottom (obtained by checking Replay).

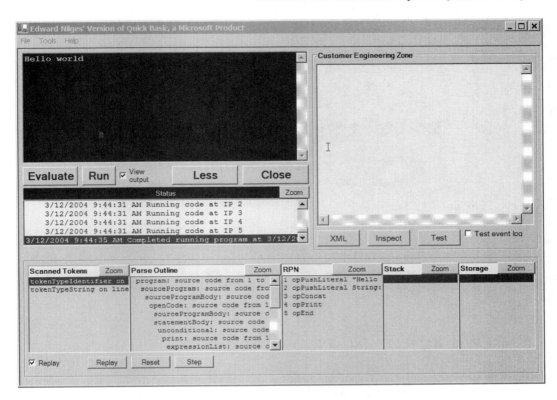

Figure 7-11. Effect of running the 'Hello world' program

Let's review this history to get an overview of how a very simple program is handled by the QuickBasic compiler.

Scanning the Tokens

Click the Reset button at the bottom of the form. Then click the Step button twice. This will scan the two tokens in the program using qbScanner, the Print identifier, and the "Hello world" string, as shown in Figure 7-12. qbGUI handles scanner progress events with displays in its list box. Click the Zoom button at the top right of the Scanned Tokens list box to see the full scan.

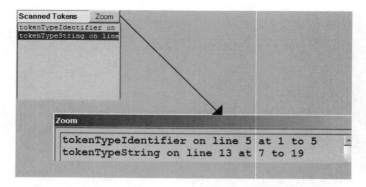

Figure 7-12. Scan result

Essentially, two qbTokens exist in a collection in the state of the quickBasicEngine. Confirm that their start and end indexes, as serialized, correspond to the start and end in the code.

Viewing Parsing and Code Generation

Click the Step button several times and watch the parsing and code generation. The first change to the screen will be the emission of code, because the compiler generates a leading comment to the object code. Then the compiler will outline the parse as it finds higher and higher level constructs, to arrive at the parse and RPN code display shown in Figure 7-13.

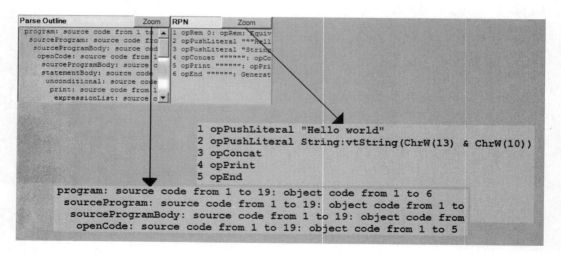

Figure 7-13. Complete parse and code

The parse outline may look intriguing. Click the Zoom buttons. From the Zoom box, copy the parse outline to a Notepad or Word file (with Courier New as a monospace font) to see the outline, as shown in Figure 7-14.

```
program: source code from 1 to 19: object code from 1 to 6
  sourceProgram: source code from 1 to 19: object code from 1 to 5: Expression
  sourceProgramBody: source code from 1 to 19: object code from 0 to 4
    openCode: source code from 1 to 19: object code from 1 to 5
      sourceProgramBody: source code from 1 to 19: object code from 1 to 4
        statementBody: source code from 1 to 19: object code from 2 to 5
        unconditional: source code from 1 to 19: object code from 2 to 5
          print: source code from 1 to 19: object code from 1 to 5: Print ...
            expressionList: source code from 7 to 19: object code from 2 to 2
              expression: source code from 7 to 19: object code from 1 to 2: No Or occurs
                orFactor: source code from 7 to 19: object code from 2 to 2
                  andFactor: source code from 7 to 19: object code from 2 to 2
                    notFactor: source code from 7 to 19: object code from 2 to 2
                      likeFactor: source code from 7 to 19: object code from 2 to 2
                        concatFactor: source code from 7 to 19: object code from 2 to 2: No RHS
                          relFactor: source code from 7 to 19: object code from 2 to 2: No RHS
                            addFactor: source code from 7 to 19: object code from 1 to 1
                              mulFactor: source code from 7 to 19: object code from 2 to 2
                                powFactor: source code from 7 to 19: object code from 2 to 2
                                  term: source code from 7 to 19: object code from 2 to 2
        "PRINT": source code from 1 to 5: object code from 0 to -1
        "PRINT": source code from 1 to 5: object code from 0 to -1
```

Figure 7-14. Parse outline

Now the outline just looks strange. What's going on here?

Notice that this resembles an outline for a paper, written by a graduate student a hair from the edge, who forgot to number the lines, but who is, in general, too conscientious. An outline happens to be mathematically equivalent to a tree, and this is the complete parse tree for the 'Hello world' program.

The compiler per se does not produce this output. Instead, as explained earlier in the chapter, it fires nonvisual events, which can then be displayed by the GUI.

You may have noticed while watching this display being built that it actually appears in reverse, with the lowest element (term) appearing first. This seems to contradict our description of the algorithm as top-down. But, in fact, it did operate top-down. It set itself the goal of *program* and kept calling procedures, down to *term*. However, the lowest procedure (compiler_term_) was the first procedure to find anything when parsing the expected material (an expression) to the right of the Print keyword, so it was the first to fire an event. Therefore, the productions were added to the list box bottom-up. Also, Print, as a separate parse tree element, is after the information to its right in the parse tree. This is because it was parsed before the expression.

The outline shows how even a simple program has a somewhat complex structure. It is a program, which can be a sourceProgram. A sourceProgram consists of one or more Option statements, followed by a sourceProgramBody. A sourceProgramBody consists of an open source (source code that isn't contained in a function or subroutine),[7] mixed with functions and subroutines. Each statement is an optional numeric or symbolic label, followed by a statementBody. A Print statement is an example of an unconditionalStatement.

You get the picture. This is a "descent" right down to the term, which is the string parsed for us by qbScanner, "Hello world."

The algorithm seems inefficient, but do not confuse *efficiency* with the fact that you have to think. In fact, the time taken is in a linear relationship with the nesting depth of the program—its If..Then nesting, its loop nesting, and the complexity of its expressions. As this overall complexity increases, the algorithm takes more time, but in steady and nonexponential correspondence with the growth of complexity. Therefore, even a silly statement with excess parentheses, such as A = (((((5))))), won't generate an explosively increasing number of steps, just a silly parse tree.

Note that this particular compiler never actually constructs parse trees, although many compilers do. Many compilers will construct the parse tree in memory, and this can be both time-consuming and space-consuming as programs get large. But our parse tree is lightweight because it literally exists only as events fired by quickBasicEngine. The GUI can reconstruct the parse tree for presentation completely from parseStartEvent, parseFailEvent, and parseEvent, which you saw in the code for addFactorRHS earlier in the chapter. Using an idea from MIS programming, this demonstrates separating the business logic (parsing) from the presentation tier, because the business of a parser is parsing.

The reason for the linear relationship between source program size and time is that there is little backup or lookahead in recursive descent. The only place lookahead occurs is in compiler__term_. When this method finds a left parenthesis at the start of the candidate term, it must use a simple parenthesis balancing loop to find the right parenthesis.

A Note on Tactical Parsing

"Tactical" parsing is the design and parsing of a little language for data and business rules. Tactical parsing is useful in many hard problems such as this one, where a large or infinite number of cases occur.

Many MIS projects have come to grief when the designers or programmers discover that the user did not want to handle a small number of cases but a large number of combined cases. The usual strategy is more work, as the programmers chase their tails to code Case statements for the possibilities, until they realize that they are engaged in a voyage measured in parsecs rather than yards.

---

7. A major difference between QuickBasic and Visual Basic is that in QuickBasic, executable statements, as opposed to module-level declarations, can exist outside functions and subroutines and form part of an implicit main procedure. I call this "open" source (not to be confused with either free software or free beer).

Everyone then piles on the user to convince her that she was wrong in wanting too much. I would ask her, like Leonard Cohen in *Bird on a Wire*, "Why do you ask for so much? Why not ask for more?" That's because a user with many elements that combine may want, without being able to express it, not a set of cases, but a language for describing cases, and programmers who can design a language.

Of course, giving people a new language is a venture fraught with hazards. My experience is that they are never grateful, and like Shakespeare's Caliban (in *The Tempest*) are likely instead to say, "Thou taught'st me language, and my profit on't, is I know how to curse." To avoid this, you can actually hide the language in a GUI, or as we have done, make it strictly an internal language for production and consumption by objects. The beauty of this gesture is that it typically generates a more powerful system that is easier to debug and maintain.

For example, I worked at one firm that was trying to debug a program that analyzed phone records for billing purposes. The problem was that conference-calling and other features interacted to produce an unlimited number of cases. I developed a language that specified the state transitions of the underlying switch and an interpreter that simulated the switch in Cobol by reading the state transitions. I got the engineers to approve the state transitions, and then produced bills by essentially simulating the calls. Case closed.

Examining the Generated Code

Next, zoom the RPN box to examine the generated code, as shown in Figure 7-15.

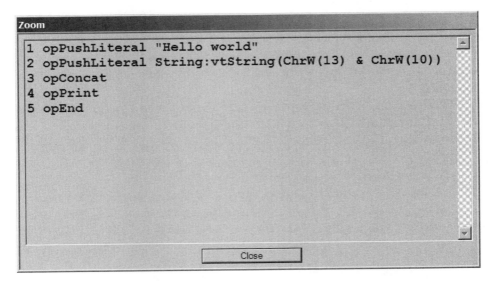

Figure 7-15. Generated RPN code for 'Hello world'

The following instructions are generated:

1. The first instruction is the opPushLiteral, which pushes its operand as a qbVariable onto a stack found in the interpreter_ method.

2. Since the Print statement was not followed by a semicolon, by the arcane (but perfectly formalizable, as we have seen in Chapter 4) rules of QuickBasic, we must insert a hard Windows newline. Therefore, the next statement pushes a qbVariable with the nonprintable value displayed, qbVariable.toString having converted the value to a display.

3. The next statement simply concatenates the string and the newline.

4. The string is then printed. Of course, for quickBasicEngine, which doesn't know anything about either Windows or the Web, this is a can of worms. It has no place, as a pure server, to place the string! Therefore, just as in the case of progress, the engine fires an event with the print string, letting the GUI worry about whether to display the text in a control (as we have, in fact, done), format it using HTML, or even print it to a daisywheel printer.

Finally, click the Step button a few more times to see the execution of the program and its effect on the stack. There will be more about actual interpretation in the next chapter.

Converting the State to XML

Next, move to the Customer Engineering Zone area, which allows you to convert quickBasicEngine's state to XML and inspect the state for internal errors, since quickBasicEngine implements the core object methodology described in Chapter 5.

Click XML, and select and copy the results. Paste them in a maximized Notepad file. The start of the XML will look like Figure 7-16.

```
<!--
*****************************************************************
*                                                             *
* quickbasicEngine                                            *
*                                                             *
* This class compiles and interpretively runs a subset of the *
* Quick Basic language. Note that the phrase Quick Basic is   *
* the intellectual property of the Microsoft corporation.     *
*                                                             *
* This class was developed by                                 *
*                                                             *
* Edward G. Nilges                                            *
* spinoza1111@yahoo.COM                                       *
* http://members.screenz.com/edNilges                         *
*                                                             *
*****************************************************************
 -->
<quickbasicEngine>
    <!-- Indicates object usability -->
    <booUsable>True</booUsable>
    <!-- Object instance's name -->
    <strName>quickbasicEngine0001 3/12/2004 9:58:29 AM</strName>
```

Figure 7-16. Start of quickBasicEngine's XML

In Notepad, scroll down to see the XML of the scanner delegate and the collection of qbPolish instructions. The end of the XML will show a variety of properties, as you can see in Figure 7-17. Of course, for a simple program, most of these values are default.

```
<!-- Collection utilities -->
<objCollectionUtilities>collectionUti...</objCollectionUtilities>
<!-- Indicates compiled status -->
<booCompiled>True</booCompiled>
<!-- Indicates assembler status -->
<booAssembled>True</booAssembled>
<!-- Source code type -->
<enuSourceCodeType>program</enuSourceCodeType>
<!-- Constant folding -->
<booConstantFolding>False</booConstantFolding>
<!-- Removal of "degenerate" operations -->
<booDegenerateOpRemoval>False</booDegenerateOpRemoval>
<!-- Value of recent immediate expression -->
<objImmediateResult>&quot;&quot;</objImmediateResult>
<!-- Indicates whether Option Explicit is in effect -->
<booExplicit>False</booExplicit>
<!-- Subroutine/function table -->
<usrSubFunction><subFunctionTable></subFunctionTable></usrSubFunction>
<!-- Subroutine/function table index -->
<colSubFunctionIndex>emptyCollection</colSubFunctionIndex>
```

Figure 7-17. Part of the XML of quickBasicEngine

The XML for the 'Hello world' program will consist of the usability and name of the object, followed by the XML of the scanner state, as described in Chapter 5. It will contain a null collection of variables (with the XML name colVariables), because the 'Hello world' program doesn't contain any variables. It will contain a Polish collection of opcodes identical to the one shown in Figure 7-5, and it will end with a miscellaneous set of values for the engine, such as its queue of information for the legacy Read Data statement.

XML allows us to capture not only a set of business rules as a QuickBasic expression, but it also can capture execution properties that will change, subtly or in the extreme, their evaluation. Using XML, we have a shot at capturing some logic, including its execution environment, and placing it in a file.

The Non-Mercator Projection

What I am trying to master here is the non-Mercator, or nondistorting, "projection" of logic to data—its serialization. As you know, a Mercator projection map distorts information, whereas a globe doesn't distort it.

Recently I had to fly from Chicago to Hong Kong. At first, my fellow travelers and I were rather confused, because we went due north, and the route map projected on the video screen showed us going a roundabout way. Of course, we were going the shortest polar route in almost a straight line due north and then due south. The trip featured spectacular polar views and the north coast of Siberia, far more interesting than the movies on tap.

When we left the Canadian Arctic islands, the Mercator projection of the world map made it appear that we needed to hang a left to get to Siberia, but a globe makes it clear that you need to go straight.

Similarly, when a database that contains numbers that are in 16-bit integer format *for a reason* is converted to a database with 32-bit integers (because the numbers were converted from 16-bit to text, and then by a C program to C 32-bit integers), a business rule associated with the data *for a reason* (this field must range between –32768 and 32767) has been *lost*.

The concern began when I realized that in popular databases, including SQL Server, the insertion of a trigger or stored procedure could change the meaning of a field. This means that statically comparing two editions of a database would yield *wrong* results.

Inspecting the State

Next, click the Inspect button on the full monty display to carry out a rather comprehensive inspection of quickBasicEngine's state, as shown in Figure 7-18.

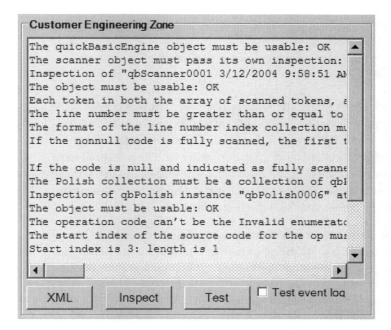

```
Customer Engineering Zone
The quickBasicEngine object must be usable: OK
The scanner object must pass its own inspection:
Inspection of "qbScanner0001 3/12/2004 9:58:51 AM
The object must be usable: OK
Each token in both the array of scanned tokens, a
The line number must be greater than or equal to
The format of the line number index collection mu
If the nonnull code is fully scanned, the first t

If the code is null and indicated as fully scanne
The Polish collection must be a collection of qbP
Inspection of qbPolish instance "qbPolish0006" at
The object must be usable: OK
The operation code can't be the Invalid enumerato
The start index of the source code for the op mus
Start index is 3: length is 1
```

    XML   Inspect   Test   □ Test event log

Figure 7-18. Inspection of quickBasicEngine*'s state*

The inspection is a monster, without apology. Some of its complexity is caused by the inclusion of the results of inspection of delegates. For example, as you can see in Figure 7-18, inspection first checks the scanner delegate after making sure that quickBasicEngine hasn't marked itself unusable. In conformance to our core methodology, the inspection checks for *internal* errors. These are errors caused by my boneheaded coding or your own ham-fisted changes to the source code.

We have, as your manager would say, "drilled-down" through the levels of quickBasicEngine. But what's amazing is that this engine is, in turn, supported by the giants at Microsoft who developed the .NET framework. The fact is that the engine can run code with reasonable efficiency, while producing an amusing display of progress and monitoring its own health. What this means is that the .NET Framework is very efficient, and there is no excuse for not adding quality.

Error Taxonomy

Three types of potential errors are recognized and handled by the quickBasicEngine object:

> **Errors in logic of the code:** There are two subtypes of this type of error: bugs in the code I have developed and any errors you may add while modifying the compiler. Errors in the logic of the code detected by this code itself (such as in the inspect method) will result in calls to the low-level errorHandler utility exposed by the utilities object, which typically displays a message box. These errors will usually mark the instance object as not usable, so it does not damage your data.

> **Errors in using the object interface:** This type of error could be in a GUI or an object using the QuickBasic engine as a Web service. Mistakes in calling the object also result in calls to utilities.errorHandler, but do not mark the object as unusable.

> **Errors in QuickBasic coding and logic:** Errors in coding QuickBasic and errors in logic are handled by a userErrorEvent for GUI display.

Summary

We have, I trust, cut to the chase. You have learned how to generate recursive-descent parsers for a sizable language, as well as how to generate code, including optimized code that eliminates unnecessary runtime computation.

We then ran the qbGUI program to step through an exceedingly simple program and see how it is parsed. The same overall approach was used as in Chapter 3's fly-over compiler, but here, the object model means that the elements handled are themselves reference objects on the .NET heap, rather than simple values on the .NET stack.

I hope I have shown that writing a compiler is a nontrivial task, but one that is doable; for the dialogue in programming is always between simplicity and complexity. In order to give the user a simple experience, we have to wrestle with complexity.

The methods are not unique to Basic and can transfer to your own language development. You may want to develop a language for the disabled and "parse" their gestures. You may want to develop a language for dancers and "parse" their leaps. You may want to teach language to gorillas in the wild. You may want to develop a language to dodge responsibility and spin events to your best advantage. You may have some killer ideas for a programming language, as did the developers of Ruby and Python. Or you may wish to help a user who needs to compile very old source code, for which the compiler has disappeared ("retro" computing, or computing for old guys).

If a sequence of gestures has a logic, it has a grammar. And if the grammar can be formalized in BNF, a nonvisual language engine may do your altruistic job.

In the next two chapters, I will complete the picture by showing in more detail how the compiled code can be assembled and executed. Chapter 8 will describe how to develop an assembler and a software interpreter that uses .NET to simulate an appropriate target machine.

Challenge Exercise

Run the qbGUI program. What happens when you click the Test button in the Customer Engineering Zone of the full monty display?

Try testing some simple expressions. If you enter a math expression and click the Evaluate button, the "green screen" will show its value. Try entering a real program and clicking the Run button.

Resources

See *Compilers: Principles, Techniques and Tools*, by Alfred Aho, Ravi Sethi, and Jeffery Ullman (Addison-Wesley, 1985) for much more information about parsing and compiler optimization. This is the famous "dragon" book referenced in earlier chapters.

CHAPTER 8

Developing Assemblers and Interpreters

No, I'm not interested in developing a powerful brain. All I'm after is just a mediocre brain, something like the President of the American Telephone and Telegraph Company.
—Alan Turing

TURING'S HOPE has not been realized; the CEO of AT&T was a pretty smart cookie. Furthermore, if Dijkstra is right, the nature of computer intelligence is constituted in the ability to manipulate symbols and not conscious choice and awareness.

However, Turing made a discovery in 1936 all the same. Obeying an algorithm is itself obeying an algorithm...which manages to be obvious, or profound, or stupid, or all three: "To follow the rules, follow the rules for following the rules."

In the last chapter, you learned how the quickBasicEngine generates code. In this chapter, I will discuss the details of assembling code with jumps and with Go To instructions and related issues having to do with assemblers.

The compiler generates qbToken objects and stores them in a collection. These qbToken objects reference each other using labels, and in a rather clerical (but rather tricky) operation, these labels must be translated to numeric addresses.

A more exciting operation, discussed in the second half of this chapter, is the simulation of a computer by an interpreter. Rather surprisingly, even a complex computer architecture can be completely imitated by another computer architecture (even one less powerful or less complex) using software. In most cases, the simulation will be slower than a native implementation, but this is not necessarily the case when the computer doing the imitation is several orders of magnitude faster.

This chapter will discuss assembly in the context of the simple assembler embedded in the QuickBasic compiler. I will then discuss the design of the onboard Nutty Professor interpreter, a software machine for executing the qbPolish objects emitted by the compiler.

Assemblers

Let's take a look at assemblers in general and in their historical context, and then examine the simple assembler embedded in the quickBasicEngine.

Assemblers, in General

Assemblers have been around since the earliest days of computers, although paradoxically, assemblers may postdate compilers. This is because the earliest computer scientists, including Charles Babbage, John von Neumann, and Konrad Zuse, did not work as lowly programmers. Instead, they prepared equations for the earliest programmers to enter by keying or setting switches.

Of the three pioneers I have mentioned, Konrad Zuse also developed in the early 1940s the PlanCalcul, which was a prototype of a high-level "compiled" language, and this predates the first assemblers: the first compilers predated the first assemblers (cf. *A History of Modern Computing, Second Edition* by Paul E. Ceruzzi [MIT Press, 2003]).

Later in the 1940s, Grace Murray Hopper (an early ENIAC programmer and an officer in the United States Navy) started to "reuse" the code for common equations by borrowing tapes containing ENIAC codes and lending her own code in return. This activity related more to the early compilers than to assemblers, but Hopper's team was, as noted in Chapter 1, the first to see the economic value of saving programmer time.

The first assemblers were developed by working programmers to avoid having to code in straight binary machine language. In fact, John von Neumann (the Hungarian émigré mathematician who, at Princeton's Institute for Advanced Study, is credited with the stored program concept) did not think that an expensive and rare computer should be used at all to make its programmer's life easier.

Nonetheless, the earliest commercial mainframes of the 1950s were shipped with assemblers after managers discovered that programming was much more time-consuming than originally thought, and because compilers were harder to develop at the time than assemblers (modern compiler theory not yet having been developed).

These early assemblers required the early programmer to specify actual machine operations, but allowed him or her to identify storage locations with mnemonic names. Such assemblers took over the job of assigning numeric locations to the names.

From Machine Language to Assembler Language

In January 1970, I took one of the first computer classes offered for academic credit at Roosevelt University, Chicago, which was taught by the great Max Plager, still on the math faculty at Roosevelt. As I mention in Chapter 1, this class was conducted during a lot of university upset and chaos.

Max had us students code our first program in actual machine language so we would appreciate assemblers and Fortran more.

I sat down in Northwestern University's then new library on a cold January day and coded my first program, a program to make change for a ten dollar bill, in machine language. Fortunately, the target machine was the decimal IBM 1401, whose architecture allowed addresses to be specified as three-digit decimal numbers.

These digits were in fact 6-bit characters in the 1401 64 character set. A rather strange, but logical, system was used to "address" memory past location 1000 that was, over the lifetime of the 1401, expanded to several kilobyte models.

When writing in machine language, I had to create a careful flowchart and keep track of the position of all variables, writing the code on a sheet of graph paper.

A philosophy major, engaged in an elaborate draft-dodging scheme, I was impressed by the parallels between machine language and symbolic logic, and math.

After coding, I then brought the program to the lab. Max showed us how to punch it on cards and place the resulting deck behind a two-card loader. Max and I watched as my program proceeded to load itself on top of the loader, for I had forgotten that I wasn't supposed to use the memory used by Max's loader between 333 and 400.

I fixed the problem and the program worked, but I certainly learned the joys, and the miseries, of machine language programming. My lesson came in handy a year or so later when I debugged the Fortran compiler, as described in Chapter 1.

Later on, as a 1401 programmer for the university, I would occasionally build quick, one-time utilities by toggling in machine language from the auxiliary 1401 console. This was an era when many universities and corporations placed their mainframe computers on display; Roosevelt's 1401 was behind plate glass windows on street level at Michigan and Congress, and one block north a Burroughs system was on display.

However, although the Burroughs programmers were men in gray flannel suits, I killed the serious image Roosevelt wanted to project with a scruffy appearance and shoulder-length hair. In a way, that has become standard; the administration put up with me to get results (including Fortran support as I've described) as a one-man skunk works.

The writing of a basic assembler is easily mastered (if you ignore efficiency) in any language that supports keyed collections.

The assembler must scan each line of assembler source code for constituent parts: usually including an instruction label, a mnemonic op code, one or more operands, and comments describing the operation. Older assemblers (including the IBM 1401 "Symbolic Programming System") that I used forced the programmer to put these fields in fixed columns, usually on an IBM punch card.

Paper tape and newer assemblers (commencing with IBM 1401 Autocoder and IBM 360 BAL) gave programmers more freedom because they allowed fields to be separated with blanks or commas and used a primitive form of lexical analysis as described in Chapter 5 to separate the individual tokens.

Operators were typically looked up in a fixed table of operators and their numeric codes, typically using the well-known algorithm called a *binary search*.

The data labels were slightly more complex to find because a fixed table could not be used. Instead, the best programmers of assemblers built tables of the operands used and employed a hash method to access these tables.

In a hash method, a large number of names has to be mapped onto a limited space for fast retrieval. Of course, if efficiency does not matter, you can simply build (for example, using Redim in Visual Basic) a table that grows as more and more distinct names are found and use a linear search.

However, the execution time formula grows rapidly as the number of variables increases. Each time a variable is used, it must be looked up with, on average, n/2 probes of the list of variables. The execution time as a factor, not only of the number of variables, but also of the number of *occurences* of all variables, is m*n/2. As m or n grow, the execution time slows dramatically.

Early assembler programmers therefore developed variants of hash tables, and this technology was used by Microsoft to build the collection with a key.

The best hash algorithm will consider an identifier as a number and take some part of this number, which is bounded by the space available for the hash table (like Hamlet, quoted in the qbGUI Easter egg of Chapter 7, the hash table can be bound in a nutshell but counts itself king of infinite space). For example, if 256 table entries are allocated, a fairly good (by no means optimal) hash algorithm might take the **last** byte of the operand name as the hashed index; the last byte is probably better than the first byte for most input programs to the assembler, as the first byte might have distinctly nonrandom prefixes (many identifiers, for example, might start with the letter *I*, and the use of systematic prefixes for identifiers, sometimes known as Hungarian notation, will tend to create many identifies with the same first letter).

However, because more than one operand can have the same last byte and thus the same index in the table, the algorithm needs a plan for a "collision." It turns out the most effective plan is simply to proceed to the next empty entry of the table (wrapping back to the start of the table as needed) and use this as the entry.

At worst, a small linear search, usually restricted to one or two entries, results. One further complication occurs when entries have to be deleted in an assembler or compiler that allows symbols of limited scope, which have to be thrown away when their context is compiled; for example, a compiler that supports variables local to procedures like the Visual Basic compiler must throw away local variables. The Visual Basic 6 compiler had to throw away all local variables at the end of the procedure; the Visual Basic .NET compiler must throw away variables at the end of each block as well as at the end of the procedure, because Visual Basic .Net supports the declaration of variables inside For loops, Do loops, With clauses, and other blocks.

The deleted symbol's hash table entry must be located and tagged as free; but it is not quite the same as it was before it was used. This is because when searching for a symbol that hashes to a location between the hash for the deleted symbol and the deleted symbol, the freed entry doesn't stop the search.

Ordinarily, in searching a hash table just to find a symbol, the first unused entry encountered shows that the search is complete, and has failed, because if the symbol hashing initially to entry n was in the table, it would be in the first available entry to the right of n, wrapping around to the beginning. But if a deleted entry is found, it may have hashed to another initial starting location; therefore, the search must continue.

The solution is to mark deleted entries specially so that they are distinct from empty entries. For example, a .NET solution might be to set deleted entries to a blank while making sure empty entries are Nothing. Many of these techniques were discovered by early writers of assemblers.

But keep in mind you may never need to create a hash table for your parsers and language tools because the classic collection of VB and other languages and the .NET Framework collections solve the problem.

You can write a better-performing collection than those provided in the .NET Framework by taking advantage of recent research in hash algorithms, or by encapsulating knowledge of the keys to be hashed. But my experience in doing this produced at best only a marginal speed advantage of about 15%.

One problem with the collection, whether used in Visual Basic 6 or in Visual Basic .NET, is that it is a collection of untyped objects. This means in practice that code that uses collections (of any type) might be altered, erroneously, to contain objects of the wrong type. Also, retrieval is slowed because the pure objects used by the collection need to be converted to the right type.

There are, however, many solutions for this problem.

The collection can be an object that inherits the collection member as a base type. Or, you can wait for the next edition of Visual Basic .NET, which will allow you to use "generic types." Or, you can bite the bullet and implement a strongly typed hash table as an array with a strong type. Or, you can use the solution of the quickBasicEngine, which is to use collections and to inspect them for correct types.

Assemblers often have features to make programmers' lives easier. For example, it was a chore to have to use a literal, such as the number one, by naming it and defining its position as a labeled instruction. Therefore, early common assemblers allowed the programmer to use literal values, usually numbers, and the assembler took over their assignment to storage.

A significant development was the macro assembler, which allowed the programmer to define sequences of defined opcodes as a new opcode. And it was then a short step to the conditional macro assembler.

Conditional macro assemblers select sequences of code for assembly based on conditions and the values of symbols. In fact, the Visual Basic preprocessor statements that commence with the pound sign (such as #If, #Then, #EndIf) represent a conditional compiler version of this facility.

Conditional macro assembly was used mostly by manufacturers to ship customizable and modifiable source code. For example, the IBM mainframe system of the 1970s and 1980s, Virtual Machine, Conversational Monitor System (VM/CMS), was shipped to large clients in the form of source code.

The client would set symbols in a special area or through a primitive GUI, and the assembler would then use these values to select the actual source code for that client's installation.

The modern C and C++ preprocessor is an almost complete conditional macro "compiler" that supports the definition, assignment, and computation of compile-time values in addition to traditional if..then..else statements.

Some conditional macro assemblers include the ability to branch to labels, which meant that the engine underlying the conditional macro assembler was in fact a general-purpose, simulated computer available at assembly or compiler time that could engage in complex calculations to determine the final source code presented to the assembler.

In fact, some of these products were not even used to generate code to the assembler at all. Instead, they generated code for other environments or even, in some cases, documents.

> **NOTE** *Working on an early cellular system, I used the conditional macro assembler on the IBM mainframe to generate Z-80 assembly code for this early microprocessor. It wasn't my idea, but it worked.*

The nearly extinct language PL/I, developed for IBM mainframe programming, extended all computational power to the macro writer with all the power, and obfuscatory potential, that this implied. Basically, proprietary software vendors don't deliver source code to their customers any more; therefore, there is no reason to deliver, as before, highly and generally customizable source to customers. But this may change. There is increasing interest in obtaining source code instead of object code because of the greater quality and safety of the former, whether as "open" source or as a commercial product. This may cause a return to the shipment of source that can be customized, using a preprocessor.

Also, writing a full preprocessor would be a useful exercise and would create a product unlinked to any one programming language, because there is no reason why the macro processor has to care about the language it processes. It would provide the ability to have a single source image of a large software system rather than multiple copies with changed code, with one limitation: it might have trouble with the fact that today, source code is created not as flat files but as project "trees."

For example, a large Visual Basic source could be used with a preprocessor to generate either Visual Basic 6 or VB .NET source code.

Here is an example. The following code uses a C preprocessor to conditionally generate a debugging statement:

```
#if (debugMode)
    #define DEBUG(proc,msg) MsgBox("Debug message from...
#else
    #define DEBUG(proc,msg) ' No debugging
#endif
```

The DEBUG symbol is a macro symbol. When debugging is in effect, the DEBUG symbol is replaced here by a MsgBox that includes the parameter names proc and msg: when debugging isn't in effect, the DEBUG symbol is replaced by a comment.

The preceding example is not usable inside the Visual Studio GUI (because the C preprocessor is not called for VB .NET programs), but you could create an external build system that would work if you needed to.

The advantage of the approach is that one source representation can support debugging after the system is placed into production, with no runtime cost.

Macro assembly and preprocessors, especially the C++ preprocessor, however, have a terrible reputation, and programmers who use the C and C++ preprocessor have been known to be punished by 20 lashes with a wet noodle.

There are two reasons for this. One was pointed out to me by my son several years ago when he taught me about object design. Many of the jobs that were formerly performed by macro processing are now accomplished in a cleaner and safer way using OO concepts such as overloading and encapsulation. If (for example) some customers want version A of a method, which exposes an extra parameter, and others don't want this parameter to be exposed, it might make more sense to use overloading to provide both versions rather than using a preprocessor to generate the desired signature.

Another reason for the unpopularity of the preprocessor is the way in which extensive use of macro processing creates unnecessary complexity.

However, I happen to disagree with the many writers on this topic (such as the very droll Bill Blunden, who has written *Software Exorcism: A Handbook for Debugging and Optimizing Legacy Code* [Apress, 2003], a guide to maintaining code and pronouncing curses upon the original authors) who feel that using extended definitional facilities is always and everywhere the sign of a flawed character. That's because the whole point of this book is that at times it makes sense to develop a language for a problem solution. In fact, important solutions have been developed using the C and C++ preprocessor, including Bjarne Stroustrup's first C++ compiler, which was written using C preprocessor statements.

Although the era of macro processing in programming languages may be over, the technique is still important in areas including text processing, and may represent for you a problem solution when you have to process text with substitution.

Assembly in the quickBasicEngine

This chapter will use a simple nFactorial program in Figure 8-1 to demonstrate assembly and interpretation concepts. This program calculates the value of any integer times all of its predecessor integers down to 2.

```
' ***** CALCULATION OF N FACTORIAL *****
DIM N
DIM F
PRINT "ENTER N"
INPUT N
IF N<>INT(N) THEN
    PRINT "N VALUE " & N & " IS NOT AN INTEGER"
    END
END IF
IF N<=0 THEN
    PRINT "N VALUE " & N & " IS NOT A POSITIVE NUMBER"
    END
END IF
F = 1
DIM N2
FOR N2 = N TO 2 STEP -1
    F = F * N2
NEXT N2
PRINT "THE FACTORIAL OF " & N & " IS " & F
```

Figure 8-1. The nFactorial program

A simple onboard assembler named `assembler_` is included in quickBasicEngine.vb to translate the code generated by the compiler to code acceptable code for the Nutty Professor interpreter. The assembler is needed for two reasons:

1. The `quickBasicEngine` generates forward-jumping Go To instructions with symbol labels. The NP interpreter actually needs the index of the `qbPolish` object in the collection in order to perform the jump.

2. The compiler "decorates" the output code with remarks to show what instructions are generated from which lines of source code, as shown in Figure 8-2: this decoration needs to be removed when a user option (available on an options form in the GUI as I will describe) is set.

```
1 opRem 0: ***** ' ***** CALCULATION OF N FACTORIAL *****
2 opRem 0: ***** DIM N
3 opRem 0: ***** DIM F
4 opRem 0: ***** PRINT "ENTER N"
5 opPushLiteral "ENTER N": Push string constant
6 opPushLiteral String:vtString(ChrW(13) & ChrW(10)): Terminate print line
7 opConcat : opConcat(s,s): Replaces stack(top) and stack(top-1) with stack(top-
1)&stack(top)
8 opPrint : opPrint(x): Prints (and removes) value at top of the stack
9 opRem 0: ***** INPUT N
10 opInput : Read from standard input to stack(top)
11 opPop 1: Pop the stack to N
12 opRem 0: ***** IF N<>INT(N) THEN
13 opNop 0: Push lValue N  contents of memory location
14 opPushLiteral 1: Push indirect address
15 opPushIndirect : Push contents of memory location
16 opNop 0: Push lValue N  contents of memory location
17 opPushLiteral 1: Push indirect address
18 opPushIndirect : Push contents of memory location
19 opInt : Round to integer function
20 opPushNE : Replace stack(top) by opPushNE(stack(top-1), stack(top))
21 opJumpZ LBL1: Jump to False code
22 opRem 0: ***** PRINT "N VALUE " & N & " IS NOT AN INTEGER"
23 opPushLiteral "N VALUE ": Push string constant
24 opNop 0: Push lValue N  contents of memory location
25 opPushLiteral 1: Push indirect address
26 opPushIndirect : Push contents of memory location
27 opConcat : Replace stack(top) by opConcat(stack(top-1), stack(top))
28 opPushLiteral " IS NOT AN INTEGER": Push string constant
29 opConcat : Replace stack(top) by opConcat(stack(top-1), stack(top))
```

Figure 8-2. Assembler code list, prior to assembly, of part of the nFactorial program

For now, ignore the details of the individual instructions. As you can see from the "decoration" consisting of opRem instructions and opNop instructions (neither of which have any effect on execution and both of which can be removed by the assembler), the compiler has generated many instructions for each line of source code. I'll discuss what these instructions do in the next section of this chapter.

The listing in Figure 8-2 for the nFactorial QuickBasic program starts with four remarks, the first of which repeats the header comment, the second and third of which include declarations, and the fourth of which heads the generated assembler code to print the prompt for the value of N. The assembler should remove these lines.

Take a look at line 21 in Figure 8-2. opJumpZ examines the top of the "stack" maintained by the interpreter (a LIFO stack similar to that seen in Chapter 3) for zero, and goes to LBL1 when the top of the stack is zero.

> **NOTE** *You may wonder why we use Go To: is not Go To a thing of darkness? The answer is that although Go To is not absolutely necessary in machine language, I use it here because so many languages at the machine level do so.*
> *At the end of Shakespeare's Tempest, Prospero says, "This thing of darkness I acknowledge mine."*

It is the assembler's job to track down all pseudo opcodes of the type opLabel, record their position in a keyed collection (where the key is the label and the data is the position), and replace each occurrence of each label by its position. This job is complicated, of course, by the fact that when you remove labels (and sometimes the comment decoration), the position of the label changes and has to be adjusted; this is the "tedium" of the assembler's clerical task I mentioned in the previous section.

The compiler's assembler code is found in the quickBasicEngine Private method assemble_. The assembler makes two complete passes over the input source, which is in the collection of qbPolish tokens named colPolish.

> **NOTE** *I will discuss the* qbPolish *object in more detail in the next section. Here, understand that it is an object with state that represents one instruction to the Nutty Professor interpreter and which is called a Polish token in honor of the Polish logicians mentioned in Chapter 3.*

The first pass is the most difficult because it must remove labels, opRems and opNops from the code while tracking the effect of removal on the value of labels; opRems are instructions that do nothing but contain compiler comments, and opNops are instructions that do nothing, period.

The first pass therefore has the form of a Do while loop that proceeds through the code, and inside this loop you find a For loop. The For loop's job is to advance from the current point to the next "real" instruction that is not a label. If this For loop finds labels, it must record their position and value in a temporary labels collection.

Each time the For loop finds a real instruction, a separate For loop, also inside the Do loop, backs up to the previous instruction; deletes the labels, remarks, and no operations; and deletes each one. The deletion process consists of executing the dispose method of the qbPolish object and removing it from the colPolish collection.

Then all new labels found inside the first inner For loop are added to the real label table. It is very possible that during the pass through the first loop, you did not know the position of a label. However, because you moved the labels to a temporary area during the first For loop, all the labels found now have a known address.

This is the surprising tedium of assembly I mentioned. Assembly, and code generation inside a compiler, rather resembles DLL hell both in the tedium and because you are close to the goal when the tedium occurs.

The quickBasicEngine also allows you to assemble without removing any labels, remarks, or no operations. The qbGUI application gives you access to this option as shown in Figure 8-3. Assembly is, of course, simpler when the option to keep labels is retained.

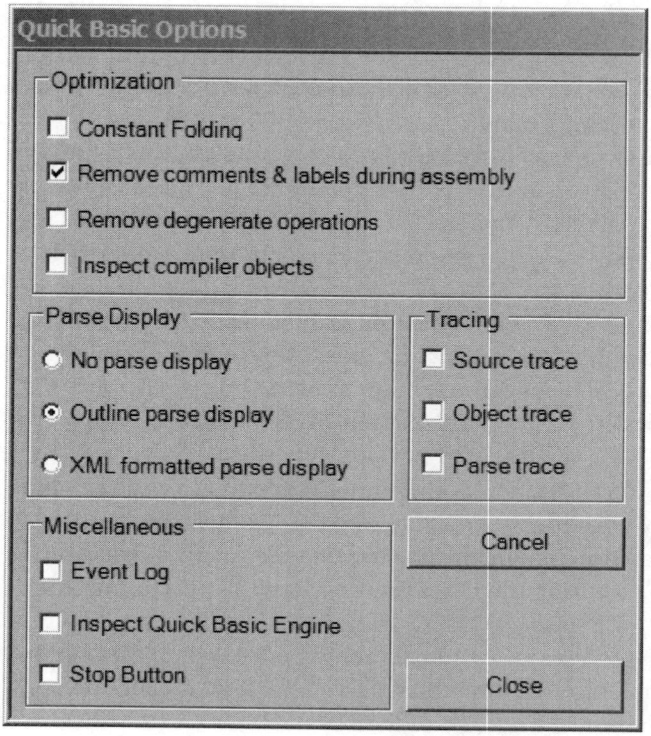

Figure 8-3. Use Tools ➤ Options on the main menu of qbGUI to see this form.

Pass two is straightforward by comparison. It does not remove code and instead only replaces the Operand property of each qbPolish instruction when it recognizes that the qbPolish instruction is a jump style operation. It looks up the Operand in the label table by key and replaces the Operand with the value of the key.

Figure 8-4 shows the result of assembling the code in Figure 8-1 (with removal of comments and labels enabled).

```
 1 opPushLiteral "ENTER N"                                    40 opPop 2
 2 opPushLiteral String:vtString(ChrW(13) & ChrW(10))         41 opPushLiteral 3
 3 opConcat                                                    42 opPushLiteral 1
 4 opPrint                                                     43 opPushIndirect
 5 opInput                                                     44 opPopIndirect
 6 opPop 1                                                     45 opPushLiteral 2
 7 opPushLiteral 1                                             46 opRotate 1
 8 opPushIndirect                                              47 opPushLiteral 0
 9 opPushLiteral 1                                             48 opPushLiteral 1
10 opPushIndirect                                              49 opSubtract
11 opInt                                                       50 opRotate 1
12 opPushNE                                                    51 opForTest 60
13 opJumpZ 24                                                  52 opPushLiteral 2
14 opPushLiteral "N VALUE "                                    53 opPushIndirect
15 opPushLiteral 1                                             54 opPushLiteral 3
16 opPushIndirect                                              55 opPushIndirect
17 opConcat                                                    56 opMultiply
18 opPushLiteral " IS NOT AN INTEGER"                          57 opPop 2
19 opConcat                                                    58 opForIncrement
20 opPushLiteral String:vtString(ChrW(13) & ChrW(10))         59 opJump 51
21 opConcat                                                    60 opPopOff
22 opPrint                                                     61 opPopOff
23 opEnd 0                                                     62 opPopOff
24 opPushLiteral 1                                             63 opPushLiteral "THE FACTORIAL OF "
25 opPushIndirect                                              64 opPushLiteral 1
26 opPushLiteral 0                                             65 opPushIndirect
27 opPushLE                                                    66 opConcat
28 opJumpZ 39                                                  67 opPushLiteral " IS "
29 opPushLiteral "N VALUE "                                    68 opConcat
30 opPushLiteral 1                                             69 opPushLiteral 2
31 opPushIndirect                                              70 opPushIndirect
32 opConcat                                                    71 opConcat
33 opPushLiteral " IS NOT A POSITIVE NUMBER"                   72 opPushLiteral String:vtString(ChrW(13) & ChrW(10))
34 opConcat                                                    73 opConcat
35 opPushLiteral String:vtString(ChrW(13) & ChrW(10))         74 opPrint
36 opConcat                                                    75 opEnd
37 opPrint
38 opEnd 0
39 opPushLiteral 1
```

Figure 8-4. Assembly results without comments or labels

Take a look at line 13 (the JumpZ, jump on zero, instruction). Ignoring until later its meaning in context, just note that it now jumps not to LBL1, but to instruction 25, which is the first real instruction after LBL1.

The compiler's graphical user interface, qbGUI, available at the Apress Web site (http://www.apress.com) as an executable, allows you to run to the end of assembly using menu commands to see the result. Bring up qbGUI and, using the File menu, navigate to egnsf\apress\quickBasic and load the file nFactorial.BAS to see the window shown in Figure 8-5. (Because you've already run the compiler, it should expand to the More info screen; but if it does not, click the More button.)

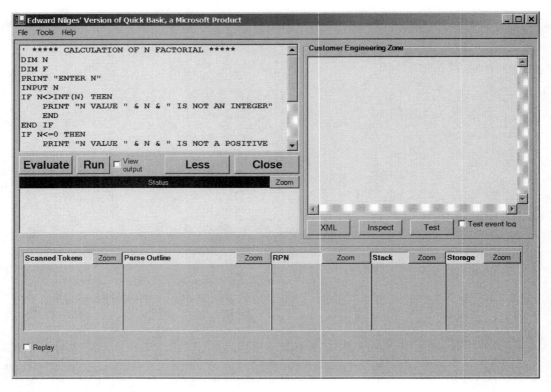

Figure 8-5. nFactorial example

Using the Tools menu, click Compile to get a compiled version of the RPN object code, and if you use the Zoom button on the RPN label after compiling, you will see the assembly code in Figure 8-1. Again, using the Tools menu, click Assemble to get the assembly with labels, remarks, and no operations removed.

This section has explained how assembly basically creates an efficient machine language representation of code. The next step is to see how it is possible to "build your own computer" without soldering computer parts together, starting fires, or chipping your nails on top of a real computer by crafting an interpreter.

Interpreters

In this section, I'll cover interpreters in general and historical context, and then examine the Nutty Professor interpreter embedded in the quickBasicEngine.

Interpreters, in General

Interpreters may have been invented in Alan Turing's 1936 paper "On Computable Numbers with Applications to the Eintscheidungsproblem." The formidable insertion of a monster German word in the title of Turing's paper is reflective of the fact that prior to WWII, German was like English is today: a lingua franca of science owing to the prestige of German science and mathematics. The "Eintscheidungsproblem" was the problem of the decidability of mathematics, and whether or not all mathematical statements could be proved and/or whether mathematics was even consistent.

Turing's concern in the paper was to formalize the notion of following a rule, that is, executing an algorithm. He developed the ultimate paper computer, the ultimate Nutty Professor computer, and the ultimate Reduced Instruction Set Computing (RISC) machine because of its simplicity. This computer is called a *Turing machine,* and you read about it in Chapter 4. Turing machines were an important discovery in the history of software, for without them, we would not be nearly as free to represent logic as data.

Back in the real world, interpreters came into commercial use when early models of new computers were being designed and programmed before the hardware was fully available.

When IBM introduced the IBM System/360 in 1964, a large number of business customers had invested quite a lot of effort in coding programs for older IBM 7094 and IBM 1401 architectures. A form of interpretation came to their rescue courtesy of hardware-assisted interpretation...also known as emulation.

Firmware in the 360 caused the operation codes and operands of older machines to be unpacked and simulated in native 360 instructions, often at a faster rate than the original computer executed its native instruction set. This allowed 1401 developers to migrate to the 360 without losing their existing investment in software.

There is, in other words, a range of interpreters, commencing with slow and simple interpreters, more complex interpreters such as the Nutty Professor interpreter for the `quickBasicEngine`, and virtual machines.

Slow and simple interpreters have a well-deserved reputation as being inefficient, and, in fact, the Nutty Professor interpreter belongs in this class.

The Onboard Nutty Professor Interpreter

The Nutty Professor interpreter simulates a stack-oriented machine with an architecture designed for QuickBasic.

I call it the Nutty Professor interpreter because one way of academically exploring computer architecture happens to be designing machines and writing software interpreters for those machines, and doing this is an excellent way to learn low-level machine language programming (not, of course, in the sense of a job skill, but conceptually).

This interpreter is based on objects of type qbPolish. Each instance of a qbPolish object represents a single instruction to the interpreter, and each instance contains an opcode, the associated operand (or Nothing), an optional comment, and the token start index and length of the source code that generated the opcode. The opcodes listed in Table 8-1 are available. The operators supported are defined by the stateless class qbOp. Table 8-1 identifies each operator supported.

Table 8-1. qbPolish Op Codes

Op	Op Description
opAdd	Replaces stack(top) and stack(top-1) with stack(top-1)+stack(top).
opAnd	Replaces stack(top) and stack(top-1) with stack(top-1) And stack(top). Note that the And operator is not short circuited: the operator expects two values at the top of the stack.
opAndAlso	Replaces stack(top) and stack(top-1) with stack(top-1) AndAlso stack(top). Note that the AndAlso operator is short circuited. If the value at the top of the stack is False, the second value isn't created or stacked. Instead, the code that develops this value is skipped.
opAsc	Replaces stack(top) by its ASCII value.
opCeil	Replaces stack(top) with first integer n > stack(top).
opChr	Replaces stack(top) with its ASCII character value.
opCircle	Draws a circle on the graphic screen; stack(top-) is the *x* coordinate, stack(top-1) is the *y* coordinate, and stack(top) is the radius.
opCls	Clears the simulated QuickBasic screen.
opCoGo	Computed GoTo/GoSub.
opConcat	Concatenates stack(top) and stack(top-1).
opCos	Replaces stack(top) with its cosine; expects numeric.
opDivide	Replaces stack(top) and stack(top-1) with stack(top-1)/ stack(top).
opDuplicate	Duplicates the value at the top of the stack.
opEnd	Stops processing immediately; expects nothing on the stack.
opEval	Evaluates stack(top) as a QuickBasic expression using lightweight evaluation. A new quickBasicEngine with default options is used to evaluate stack(top).

Table 8-1. qbPolish Op Codes (continued)

Op	Op Description
opEvaluate	Evaluates stack(top) as a QuickBasic expression using heavy-weight evaluation. A new quickBasicEngine with the same options as the current engine is used to evaluate stack(top).
opFloor	Replaces stack(top) with first integer n < stack(top).
opForIncrement	Increments or decrements the For control value in a For loop.
opForTest	Jumps to the for exit when contents of control variable location are greater than final value (when step value is positive); jumps to the for exit when contents of control variable location are less.
opIif	Replaces stack(top-2)..stack(top) with stack(top-1) when stack(top-2) is True, with stack(top) otherwise.
opInput	Reads a number or a string to stack(top) by generating the compiler input event.
opInt	Replaces stack(top) with integer part.
opInvalid	Invalid marker op intended in certain contexts to flag the opcodes with a deliberate error; not used in the current compiler.
opIsNumeric	Replaces stack(top) with True when stack(top) is a number, False otherwise.
opJump	Jumps to location in operand; expects integer.
opJumpIndirect	Jumps to location identified at the top of the stack.
opJumpNZ	Jumps to location when stack(top) <> 0 (pops the stack top).
opJumpZ	Jumps to location when stack(top) = 0 (pops the stack top).
opLabel	Identifies position of a code label or statement number; inserted by the compiler and removed by the assembler.
opLCase	Replaces the string at stack(top) with its lowercase translation.
opLen	Replace stack(top) by its length as a string.
opLike	Compares two strings at the stack top for a pattern match, replacing them by True or False.
opLog	Replaces stack(top) by its natural logarithm.
opMax	Replaces stack(top) and stack(top-1) with the maximum value found.
opMid	Replaces stack(top-2)..stack(top) with the substring of stack(top-2) starting at stack(top-1) using the length at stack(top).

Table 8-1. qbPolish Op Codes (continued)

Op	Op Description
opMin	Replaces stack(top) and stack(top-1) with the minimum value found.
opMod	Replaces stack(top) and stack(top-1) with the integer division remainder from stack(top-1) \ stack(top).
opMultiply	Replaces stack(top) and stack(top-1) with stack(top-1)*stack(top)
opNegate	Reverses the sign of the value at the top of stack.
opNop	Does nothing.
opNot	Replaces stack(top) with Not stack(top).
opOr	Replaces stack(top) and stack(top-1) with stack(top-1) Or stack(top) (Or is not short circuited).
opPop	Sends stack(top) to a memory location.
opPopIndirect	Sends stack(top) to a memory location at stack(top-1); removes stack(top), leaves stack(top-1) alone.
opPopOff	Removes stack(top) without sending it to a memory location.
opPower	Replaces stack(top) and stack(top-1) with stack(top-1)^stack(top).
opPrint	Prints (and removes) value at top of the stack, strictly by raising the PrintEvent (does not display).
opPush	Pushes the contents of a memory location specified in its operand.
opPushArrayElement	Replaces elements at the top of the stack by an array element: expects n+1 entries at the top of the stack. The entry at top-n is the high-order array subscript down to the low-order subscript at top-1, and the top of the stack should be the qbVariableType to which the new element needs to be converted before it is pushed. For example, a reference to the first row, second column of the intArray integer array (intArray(1, 2)) that needs to be converted to a Long will compile to the stack frame 1,2,Long.
opPushEQ	Replaces stack(top) and stack(top-1) by -1 when stack(top-1)=stack(top), 0 otherwise.
opPushGE	Replaces stack(top) and stack(top-1) by -1 when stack(top-1)>=stack(top), 0 otherwise.

Table 8-1. qbPolish Op Codes (continued)

Op	Op Description
opPushGT	Replaces stack(top) and stack(top-1) by -1 when stack(top-1)>stack(top), 0 otherwise.
opPushIndirect	Pushes the contents of a memory location indexed at stack(top), replacing the index.
opPushLE	Replaces stack(top) and stack(top-1) by -1 when stack(top-1)<=stack(top), 0 otherwise.
opPushLiteral	Pushes a literal string or number.
opPushLT	Replaces stack(top) and stack(top-1) by -1 when stack(top-1)<stack(top), 0 otherwise.
opPushNE	Replaces stack(top) and stack(top-1) by -1 when stack(top-1)<>stack(top), 0 otherwise.
opPushReturn	Pushes the subroutine's return address.
opRand	Seeds the random number generator to unpredictable values.
opRead	Reads from the data statements to stack(top).
opRem	Equivalent to a NOP.
opReplace	Replaces all occurrences of the string at stack(top-1) by the string at stack(top) in the string at stack(top-2). Replaces all entries by the translated string.
opRnd	Pushes an unseeded random number on the stack.
opRndSeed	Pushes a seeded random number on the stack (seed is stack(top), and is replaced).
opRotate	Exchanges stack(top) with stack(top-n); when n=0 this is a NOP.
opRound	Rounds stack(top-1) to stack(top) digits.
opSgn	Replaces stack(top) with its signum (0 for 0, 1 for positive, -1 for negative).
opSin	Replaces stack(top) with its sine.
opSqr	Replaces stack(top) with its square root.
opString	Replaces stack(top) and stack(top-1) with n copies of the character at stack top, where n is at stack(top-1).
opSubtract	Replaces stack(top) and stack(top-1) with stack(top-1)-stack(top).
opTrace	Changes trace settings.

Table 8-1. qbPolish Op Codes (continued)

Op	Op Description
opTracePop	Restores trace settings from a LIFO stack.
opTracePush	Saves trace settings in a LIFO stack.
opTrim	Replaces stack(top) with trimmed string (leading and trailing blanks removed).
opUCase	Replaces the string at stack(top) with its uppercase translation.

The interpreter in the method interpreter_ is a very large case statement that moves through the Polish collection and jumps to individual support routines. A stack collection keeps the working elements in the form of qbVariable objects.

The interpreter is rather slow because it imposes a "strongly typed" frame on top of the stack. For each operation as defined with its description in qbOp, the stack frame expected is specified in a string form that lists the expected types of the operation: for example, the expected types of the Add operation are "number, number". A pop routine obtains the expected stack as an array, and returns it to the caller.

About the only advantage of its slow rate of execution is that you can sit back and watch how it works in the GUI, or go to the fridge for a beer, or read *Motor Trend*. Also, as in the case of the flyover compiler in Chapter 3, you can replay the interpretation, as well as the scanning and compilation, in the GUI.

To see how the interpreter executes the nFactorial program, call up the qbGUI application, and load the nFactorial.BAS program. Being sure that the More screen is shown, go to Tools ➤ Options to set up the options shown in Figure 8-6. In this form, enable the Object trace option in the Tracing box.

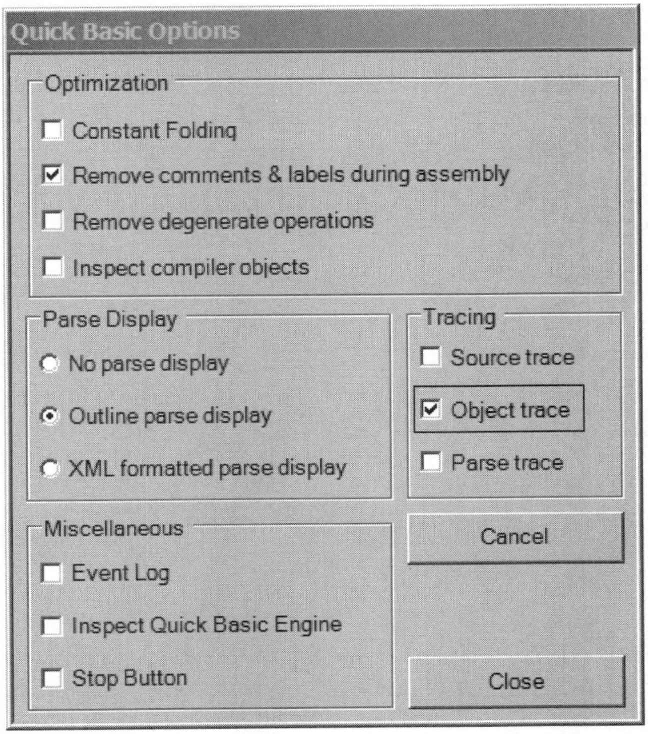

Quick Basic Options

Optimization

☐ Constant Folding

☑ Remove comments & labels during assembly

☐ Remove degenerate operations

☐ Inspect compiler objects

Parse Display

○ No parse display

◉ Outline parse display

○ XML formatted parse display

Tracing

☐ Source trace

☑ Object trace

☐ Parse trace

Miscellaneous

☐ Event Log

☐ Inspect Quick Basic Engine

☐ Stop Button

Cancel

Close

Figure 8-6. Options for testing the nFactorial.BAS application

Click the Run button to watch the nFactorial program execute. It will prompt you for input when the interpreter sends the GUI an input event: try 5. You should see the screen in Figure 8-7.

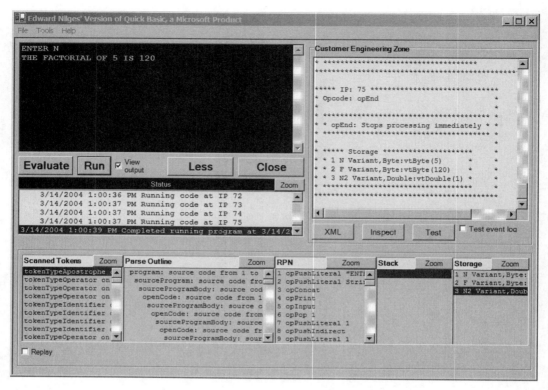

Figure 8-7. qbGUI screen after execution of the nFactorial program with Object trace enabled

Check the result, which should be 120. Then, click the Zoom button on the Storage list box to see the strongly typed storage of the quickBasicEngine, which is contained in the colVariables collection of the quickBasicEngine state (see Figure 8-8).

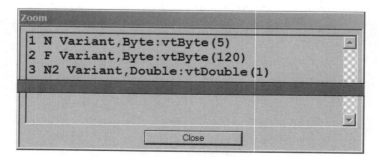

Figure 8-8. Storage after execution of the nFactorial program

Because the Dim statements for N, F, and N2 (the input number, the factorial, and the "work" copy of N used in the For loop) are untyped, N, F, and N2 are each variants. Note that the displays of each storage item are the output of the toString method for qbVariable as described in Chapter 6.

Because you selected the Object trace as shown in Figure 8-6, the upper-right hand of the screen will contain trace blocks like those in Figure 8-9. Figure 8-9 shows the trace block for the concatenate instruction that finishes the display of the result.

```
***** IP: 73 ***********************************
* Opcode: opConcat                            *
*                                             *
* ******************************************** *
* * opConcat(s,s): Replaces stack(top) and  * *
* * stack(top-1) with stack(top-1)&stack(top) * *
* ******************************************** *
*                                             *
* ***** Storage ********************          *
* * 1 N Variant,Byte:vtByte(5)       *        *
* * 2 F Variant,Byte:vtByte(120)     *        *
* * 3 N2 Variant,Double:vtDouble(1)  *        *
* *********************************            *
*                                             *
* ***** Stack **********************          *
* * String:vtString(ChrW(13) & Ch... *        *
* * String:vtString("THE FACTORIA... *        *
* ********************************             *
***********************************************
```

Figure 8-9. Trace information

Figure 8-9 shows the interpreter's situation just prior to the execution of the opConcat opcode to join two strings; the strings being joined are "THE FACTORIAL OF 5 IS 120" and the newline that terminates the Print operation. The trace block shows the opcode, and it documents the function of the opcode.

As in the case of the flyover compiler of Chapter 3, you can click the Replay check box at the bottom of the screen to save and store each scan, parse, and execution step, and replay the complete process in detail.

I'd like to show you one final feature of the compiler at this point: its test method, which tests the complete compiler after options or source code is changed. It exercises most of the functions of the compiler.

Recall from the discussion of core methodology in Chapter 4 that I prefer to write complex objects with their own test method so that they can be rapidly tested after a change or in installing the software.

Click the Test button in the customer engineering zone. You may get slightly different results than the ones you see in Figure 8-10 if I add more tests between this writing and installation of the compiler software on the Apress Web site, but you should see the number of test cases actually run, the total time for the tests, and the important message "The test succeeded".

```
9 test cases took 4 second(s)


The test succeeded


Testing the expression "1+1"

expected result: "2": actual result: "2"



Testing the expression """Ooga"" & ""Chukka"""

expected result: "OogaChukka": actual result: "OogaChukka"



Testing the expression "5478/3+21-((4+1)*8) + .1"

expected result: "1807.10000000149": actual result: "1807.10000000149"
```

Figure 8-10. Test report

The report will start with three expressions, and it will contain several programs including Hello World and nFactorial. Note that the Print statements don't affect the screen of the qbGUI because the test method creates a quickBasicEngine and intercepts its Print events to test them against expected results.

Thus like qbScanner, qbVariableTypeTester, and qbVariableTest, qbGUI can test the underlying object if you alter the source code.

Summary

In this chapter, you've seen how to "assemble" the code by translating symbolic labels inserted by the compiler to numeric indexes and optionally removing labels, source code information, and comments. You've then run the Nutty Professor interpreter to simulate the quickBasicEngine on your system, and you've seen (depending on your hardware's capabilities) why the interpretation process is slow.

You also learned how to continually test the quickBasicEngine.

Therefore, let's see if you can generate more efficient code by using the Common Language Runtime, which I'll discuss in the next chapter.

CHAPTER 9

Code Generation to the Common Language Runtime

We all live in a virtual machine, a virtual machine, a virtual machine.
—Sung at IBM Share conferences in the era of
Conversational Monitor System/Virtual Machine

What's worth doing well is worth doing slowly.
—Gypsy Rose Lee

I FEAR THIS CHAPTER may be a bit of an anticlimax, and this is because in this book I have deliberately focused primarily on the front end of a compiler, including language design, language specification using Backus-Naur Form, lexical analysis, and parsing.

In order to avoid the distracting issues of the Common Language Runtime and Ilasm, I even defined the onboard Nutty Professor interpreter—a stack-based virtual machine tuned towards the needs of QuickBasic—with machine language that directly supports QuickBasic needs.

It was also important to develop data types as objects because I wanted to avoid a common pitfall of the tyro language designer—defining a language that encourages the use of untyped variables including the .NET object or the COM variant.

There are many sources of valuable content for using the Common Language Runtime and its associated tools. At the entry level, *Visual Basic .NET and the .NET Platform: An Advanced Guide,* by Andrew Troelsen (Apress, 2001) is still solid on basic interaction through the Reflection types with the CLR.

At a more advanced level, Serge Lidin, the actual developer of Microsoft's Ilasm (which assembles CLR code into machine language), has written *Inside Microsoft .NET IL Assembler* (Microsoft Press, 2002); this book describes not only how to get started writing assembler code, but also how to write real code, since the author gives comprehensive reference information on the opcodes and the important issue of the loader, which combines multiple assemblies and links them into a run unit.

In this chapter, I will simply describe how the quickBasicEngine is able in a prototype sense to generate CLR code ... which runs much faster than Nutty Professor code, though without the benefit of allowing you to see its inner workings.

What I've implemented transforms a subset of possible QuickBasic expressions, the part that does math with constants, into CLR instructions for fast execution.

For the rest, I shall have to use the sleazy academic practice of leaving the fun part of coding full code generation to you, the reader. I do expect that because you have fully documented source code through the Apress Web site (http://www.apress.com), this will be a relatively easy task, and I've dedicated the final part of this chapter to showing how this can be done.

CLR Generation in the quickBasicEngine

Unlike the full-featured compiler, I've kept the CLR generator very simple.

Try it out. Run the qbGUI executable (make sure the More display is in effect), and type in a math expression using addition, subtraction, multiplication, and division, exclusively.

Compile the code (click the Compile item of the Tools menu) and then zoom the RPN box to see the window shown in Figure 9-1.

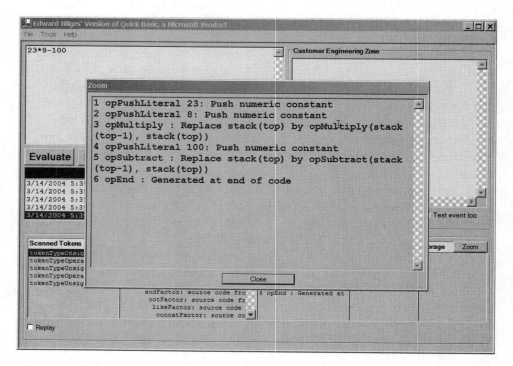

Figure 9-1. Expression compiles to the indicated Nutty Professor code

As you see, the expression compiles to the following stack operations: push 23, push 8, multiply the two numbers at the top of the stack, push 100, and subtract.

Close the Zoom display and click the Run button to run the code. You need to look for the result in the Stack box because no code is generated to print the result, and unlike the Evaluate button (which will display the result on a green-on-black output screen), the Run button leaves the expression value on top of the stack, as shown in Figure 9-2.

Figure 9-2. Result of running the expression code

Even for this small amount of code, the interpreter took a noticeable amount of time. Let's up the ante and use MSIL!

Go to the Tools menu and select the menu item named Run the MSIL Code, and in a flash you should see the results shown in Figure 9-3.

Figure 9-3. Result of running Microsoft Intermediate Language in the CLR

OK, I hope this is reasonably cool. Here is how it works.

The MSILrun method of the quickBasicEngine takes existing Nutty Professor code, whether assembled or not, and attempts to create a CLR program. I say "attempts" because at this writing this method only translates a small subset of operations for demonstration purposes.

> **NOTE** *As a side benefit, I will show you how the compiler implements full thread capability simply so that multiple instances of the compiler can run simultaneously, the compiler can be running while the user interacts with a form, and multiple procedures in one instance of the compiler can run simultaneously. The compiler is fully threadable.*

Here is the code of the `MSILrun` method:

```
Public Function msilRun() As Object
    Return dispatch_("msilRun", True, Nothing, "Returning Nothing")
End Function
```

All the actual functionality of the `msilRun` method is contained in the `Private` `msilRun_` method because in general you should try to keep `Public` routines simple shells around `Private` code. But note that you call `msilRun` by way of a private dispatcher routine.

The purpose of this dispatcher routine is to make the `quickBasicEngine` multithreaded by placing the needed threading logic in one place. You must lock the state on entry to the dispatcher and release the lock on exit.

This is because at any time in the dispatcher itself or in a `Private` procedure called by the dispatcher, you may need to reference the variables concentrated in the user data type `usrState` (of type `TYPstate`) in the `General Declarations` section of the `quickBasicEngine`.

If two procedures running in separate threads reference and change these variables simultaneously, the execution of the program will be unpredictable and buggy.

This strategy is rather primitive and broad. By the time any thread is executing code inside the dispatcher, other threads trying to run procedures will simply queue up and pound, as it were, on the door of the SyncLock ... waiting their turn, like the kids in the house with one bathroom. A more fine-grained approach would be to identify specific zones of the dispatcher that specifically interact with the state and lock only these zones.

Several different procedures come to the dispatcher and identify the specific functionality they need. The problem that you create in this design is that every time a new `Public` property or method is created, the dispatcher center must be upgraded with new execution cases. Their advantage is that they allow you to concentrate logic, here locking, in one place and to wrap it around the transaction center.

Here is the dispatcher code, somewhat shortened:

```vb
Private Overloads Function dispatch_(ByVal strProcedure As String, _
                                     ByVal booFlag As Boolean, _
                                     ByVal objDefault As Object, _
                                     ByVal strDefaultHelp As String, _
                                     ByVal ParamArray objParameters() _
                                                         As Object) _
         As Object
    Dim strDummy As String
    Select Case UBound(objParameters)
        Case -1
            Return (dispatch_(strProcedure, _
                              strDummy, _
                              objDefault, _
                              strDefaultHelp))
        Case 0
            Return (dispatch_(strProcedure, _
                              strDummy, _
                              objDefault, _
                              strDefaultHelp, _
                              objParameters(0)))
        Case 1
            Return (dispatch_(strProcedure, _
                              strDummy, _
                              objDefault, _
                              strDefaultHelp, _
                              objParameters(0), _
                              objParameters(1)))

        .
        .
        .

        Case Else
            errorHandler_("Internal programming error: " & _
                          "too many parameters", _
                          "dispatch_", _
                          "Making object unusable and returning Nothing", _
                          Nothing)
            OBJstate.usrState.booUsable = False
            Return (Nothing)
    End Select
End Function
' --- Returns the reference value
Private Overloads Function dispatch_(ByVal strProcedure As String, _
                                     ByRef strOutstring As String, _
                                     ByVal objDefault As Object, _
```

```
                                        ByVal strDefaultHelp As String, _
                                        ByVal ParamArray objParameters() _
                                                    As Object) _
            As Object
      SyncLock OBJthreadStatus
          If Not checkAvailability_(strProcedure, strDefaultHelp) Then
              Return (objDefault)
          End If
          OBJthreadStatus.startThread()
      End SyncLock
      Dim objReturn As Object = objDefault
      SyncLock OBJstate
          If checkUsable_(strProcedure, strDefaultHelp) Then
              With OBJstate.usrState
                  Select Case UCase(strProcedure)
                  .
                  .
                  .

                      Case "MSILRUN"
                          objReturn = msilRun_
                  .
                  .
                  .

                      Case Else
                          errorHandler_("Invalid dispatch method " & _
                                    _OBJutilities.enquote(strProcedure), _
                                        "dispatch_", _
                                        "Marking object unusable and " & _
                                        "returning default", _
                                        Nothing)
                          .booUsable = False
                  End Select
              End With
          End If
      End SyncLock
      SyncLock OBJthreadStatus
          OBJthreadStatus.stopThread()
      End SyncLock
      Return (objReturn)
  End Function
```

Note that the dispatcher not only locks and frees a lock on the usrState but
also on a minor player, OBJthreadStatus, which keeps track of running threads so
that you can monitor them in the qbGui form: to see this, run the qbGUI executable

and bring up the Options form used in the last chapter. Click the check box labeled "Stop button", return to the main form, and load the nFactorial.bas demonstration program used in Chapter 8. Run this to see a new form that will allow you to stop a runaway compile or run (see Figure 9-4).

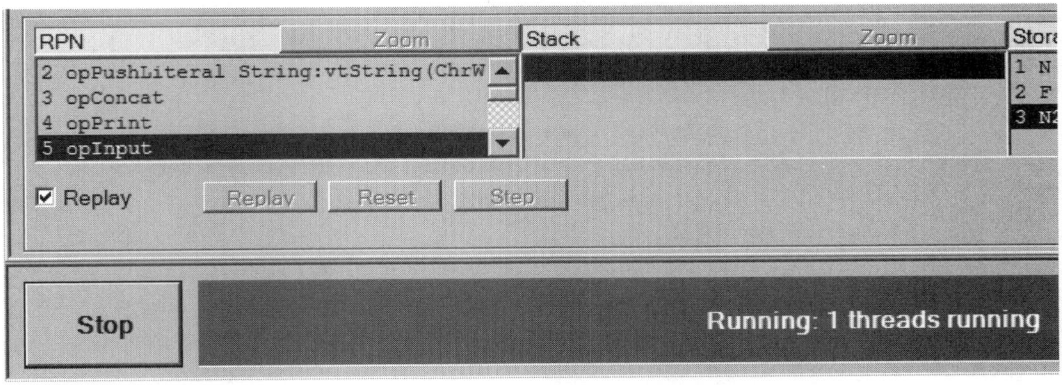

Figure 9-4. Stop button

As you can see in the dispatcher code, there is a case for the msilRun method that sets an object to the value returned from msilRun_ that does all the work of translating into CLR code using Reflection.

The code in msilRun_ requires the following imported namespaces identified at the beginning of the quickBasicEngine:

```
Imports System.Reflection
Imports System.Reflection.Emit
Imports DotNetAssembly = System.Reflection.Assembly
```

System.Reflection provides the basic tools that allow you to discover the properties of your types, methods, and fields. System.Reflection.Emit provides you with the ability to create code in the CLR. DotNetAssembly is what you need to create and load a single dynamic assembly that will execute the compiled functions.

Here is the code of msilRun_ itself:

```
Private Function msilRun_() As Object
        With OBJstate.usrState
            If (.colPolish Is Nothing) Then
                errorHandler_("Cannot run MSIL code: " & _
                                "no Polish code is available", _
                        "msilRun_", _
                        "Returning Nothing", _
                        Nothing)
```

```
            Return Nothing
        End If
        Dim objAsmName As AssemblyName
        Dim objAsm As AssemblyBuilder
        Dim objClass As TypeBuilder
        Dim objILgenerator As ILGenerator
        Dim objMethod As MethodBuilder
        Dim objModule As ModuleBuilder
        Try
            objAsmName = New AssemblyName
            objAsmName.Name = "msilRun"
            objAsmName.Version = New Version("1.0.0.0")
            objAsm = _
            AppDomain.CurrentDomain.DefineDynamicAssembly _
            (objAsmName, AssemblyBuilderAccess.Run)
            objModule = objAsm.DefineDynamicModule(objAsmName.Name)
            objClass = objModule.DefineType(objAsmName.Name, _
                                            TypeAttributes.Public)
            objMethod = objClass.DefineMethod(objAsmName.Name & "_", _
                                            MethodAttributes.Public, _
                                            Type.GetType("System.Double"), _
                                            Nothing)
            objILgenerator = objMethod.GetILGenerator
        Catch objException As Exception
            errorHandler_("Not able to initialize MSIL generation: " & _
                        Err.Number & " " & Err.Description, _
                        "msilRun_", _
                        "Returning nothing", _
                        objException)
        End Try
        Dim intIndex1 As Integer
        Dim objArgument As Object
        Dim objNextOpcode As OpCode
        Dim objNextValue As Object
        With .colPolish
            For intIndex1 = 1 To .Count
                loopEventInterface_("Generating MSIL code", _
                                    "collection item", _
                                    intIndex1, _
                                    .Count, _
                                    0, _
                                    "")
                With CType(.Item(intIndex1), qbPolish.qbPolish)
                    If msilRun__qbOpcode2MSIL_(.Opcode, objNextOpcode) Then
                        objILgenerator.Emit(objNextOpcode)
```

```
            Else
                If .Opcode = ENUop.opPushLiteral Then
                    If UCase(.Operand.GetType.ToString) _
                        = _
                        "QBVARIABLE.QBVARIABLE" Then
                        objNextValue = _
                        CType(.Operand, qbVariable.qbVariable).value
                    Else
                        objNextValue = .Operand
                    End If
Try
                    objILgenerator.Emit(OpCodes.Ldc_R8,
                                            CDbl(objNextValue))
Catch
    Exit For
End Try
                End If
            End If
        End With
    Next intIndex1
    If intIndex1 <= .Count Then
        errorHandler_("Not able to convert Polish code to MSIL", _
                    "msilRun_", _
                    "Returning Nothing", _
                    Nothing)
        Return Nothing
    End If
    objILgenerator.Emit(OpCodes.Ret)
    Dim objReturn As Object
    Try
        objClass.CreateType()
        Dim objType As Type = objAsm.GetType(objClass.Name)
        Dim objInstance As Object = Activator.CreateInstance(objType)
        Dim objMethodInfo As MethodInfo = _
objType.GetMethod(objMethod.Name)
        objReturn = objMethodInfo.Invoke(objInstance, Nothing)
    Catch objException As Exception
        errorHandler_("Not able to run MSIL: " & _
                    Err.Number & " " & Err.Description, _
                    "msilRun_", _
                    "Returning Nothing", _
                    Objexception)
        Return Nothing
    End Try
```

```
                    Return (objReturn)
             End With
        End With
    End Function
    Private Function msilRun__qbOpcode2MSIL_ _
                        (ByVal enuPolishOpcode As qbOp.qbOp.ENUop, _
                         ByRef enuMSILopcode As OpCode) As Boolean
        Select Case enuPolishOpcode
            Case ENUop.opAdd : enuMSILopcode = OpCodes.Add
            Case ENUop.opAnd : enuMSILopcode = OpCodes.And
            Case ENUop.opDivide : enuMSILopcode = OpCodes.Div
            Case ENUop.opEnd : enuMSILopcode = OpCodes.Nop
            Case ENUop.opMultiply : enuMSILopcode = OpCodes.Mul
            Case ENUop.opNegate : enuMSILopcode = OpCodes.Neg
            Case ENUop.opNot : enuMSILopcode = OpCodes.Not
            Case ENUop.opOr : enuMSILopcode = OpCodes.Or
            Case ENUop.opSubtract : enuMSILopcode = OpCodes.Sub
            Case Else
                Return False
        End Select
        Return (True)
    End Function
```

msilRun_ is a function with no parameters because it gets all its input from the colPolish collection in usrState, which contains all the Polish operations. msilRun_ will iterate through colPolish and compile what operations it can. If it finds an operation it cannot convert, it will give up, report failure through an error handler that throws an error, and return Nothing to the caller.

However, the first and rather formidable job of msilRun_ is to create the objects needed to build a dynamic assembly in the first place. The job is formidable because the objects need to tie together in one and only one way.

```
        Dim objAsmName As AssemblyName
        Dim objAsm As AssemblyBuilder
        Dim objClass As TypeBuilder
        Dim objILgenerator As ILGenerator
        Dim objMethod As MethodBuilder
        Dim objModule As ModuleBuilder
        Dim objObject As Object
        Try
            objAsmName = New AssemblyName
            objAsmName.Name = "msilRun"
            objAsmName.Version = New Version("1.0.0.0")
```

```
        objAsm = AppDomain.CurrentDomain.DefineDynamicAssembly _
                        (objAsmName, AssemblyBuilderAccess.Run)
        objModule = objAsm.DefineDynamicModule(objAsmName.Name)
        objClass = objModule.DefineType _
                        (objAsmName.Name, TypeAttributes.Public)
        objMethod = objClass.DefineMethod(objAsmName.Name & "_", _
                                MethodAttributes.Public, _
                                Type.GetType("System.Double"), _
                                Nothing)
        objILgenerator = objMethod.GetILGenerator
    Catch objException As Exception
        errorHandler_("Not able to initialize MSIL generation: " & _
                    Err.Number & " " & Err.Description, _
                    "msilRun_", _
                    "Returning nothing", _
                    objException)
    End Try
```

This code first defines several objects:

- objAsmName: The name of the assembly to contain the compiled code. Note that this is an object and not a string, because the CLR requires (primarily for security and interoperation) a structured name that includes the string name, the version, and the locale information.

- objAsm: The assembly itself, a container for the type and the method. Many assemblies contain multiple classes (also referred to as types), but this assembly will contain one class.

- objClass: The class is a type builder because you need to not only use it, but also assign its properties.

- objILgenerator: This is the object that will enable you to emit code to the method itself.

- objMethod: Again, the method is a builder for the same reason the class is a type builder.

- objModule: You might need multiple classes and namespaces in more advanced projects, so the module is a container for the class.

The next step, in the Try..Catch block, is to create the objects.

```
objAsmName = New AssemblyName
objAsmName.Name = "msilRun"
objAsmName.Version = New Version("1.0.0.0")
objAsm = AppDomain.CurrentDomain.DefineDynamicAssembly _
                    (objAsmName, AssemblyBuilderAccess.Run)
objModule = objAsm.DefineDynamicModule(objAsmName.Name)
objClass = objModule.DefineType _
                    (objAsmName.Name ,
                     TypeAttributes.Public)
objMethod = objClass.DefineMethod(objAsmName.Name & "_", _
                              MethodAttributes.Public, _
                              Type.GetType("System.Double"), _
                              Nothing)
objILgenerator = objMethod.GetILGenerator
```

You first create the assembly "name" as an object that contains the string name and the version: in this simple application, you don't need to identify the locale.

The next step is to define a new, "dynamic" assembly with the structured name and a type. The type you select is Run, because all you want to do is run the code. You can also choose Save if all you needed to do was save the code to disk or RunAndSave to do both.

Inside the new assembly, you create the single module and then the one-and-only class (also known as type).

For the one-and-only method, you need to specify its name (msilRun_), its scope as Public, and its return type; the return type is Double because all you can compile are arithmetic operations. The rest of the DefineMethod would specify the parameters expected by the method if it had any.

Finally, you need to assign an IL generator to the method as the hose that will transmit specific CLR instructions.

The next segment of code is pretty straightforward, so I won't reproduce it here: instead see the complete listing. It loops through the colPolish collection, converting each entry to a qbPolish.

Note how in more than one place the compiler needs to convert collection entries to specific types. This is because as of Visual Studio .NET 2003 a "generic" facility is absent. This would allow you to specify that the colPolish collection always contains objects of type qbPolish. This feature will be available in the 2004 release of Visual Studio for Visual Basic and C#.

Then the code calls msilRun__qbOpcode_ to see if the colPolish opcode can be "transliterated" one for one to a CLR opcode. msilRun__qbOpcode_ returns the IL opcode or Nothing on failure. If the opcode cannot be translated, it might be any one of the large number of opcodes not supported by your prototype.

In Nutty Professor machine and assembler code, the pushLiteral opcode has an operand that is a constant represented either as a .NET value or as a qbVariable. You determine what type it is and try to emit an instruction for the CLR Ldc_R8 opcode.

Note that `Ldc_R8` loads a constant in the CLR operand that is a Double precision value represented in 8 bytes. What we call a push in the Nutty Professor interpreter is a load in the CLR. Furthermore, note that the Nutty Professor interpreter has one instruction that obtains the type of the operand from an object or the `GetType` of a .NET value, whereas the CLR is more strict: it uses distinct opcodes for distinct data types, which makes the CLR more reliable and efficient at the same time.

If the generation of the IL for the value fails, then the operand in the interpreter's code cannot be converted to double, and the expression deals with strings that the demo object code generator cannot handle.

The "piece of resistance," of course, is where the code is actually run.

```
objILgenerator.Emit(OpCodes.Ret)
Dim objReturn As Object
Try
    objClass.CreateType()
    Dim objType As Type = objAsm.GetType(objClass.Name)
    Dim objInstance As Object = Activator.CreateInstance(objType)
    Dim objMethodInfo As MethodInfo =
      objType.GetMethod(objMethod.Name)
    objReturn = objMethodInfo.Invoke(objInstance, Nothing)
Catch objException As Exception
    errorHandler_("Not able to run MSIL: " & _
                  Err.Number & " " & Err.Description, _
                  "msilRun_", _
                  "Returning Nothing", _
                  Objexception)
    Return Nothing
End Try
Return (objReturn)
```

To complete the method, you must emit the `Ret` opcode to return to the caller. The `Try` block then uses `objClass` (which, you'll recall, is a class builder) to "bake" the ingredients into an executable pie. You then have to obtain as a Type the created type, and make an instance of that type.

Note that having to create an instance is somewhat of an unnecessary requirement because the very simple method you create is stateless and could be, in terms of both C# and C++, a static method; in Visual Basic, it could be a method with shared procedures and no variables in general declarations.

Using the `instance` object, you invoke, or run, the method without any parameters. Because it leaves one value on the stack, the CLR returns this as the function value. This is returned by the code.

Towards a Complete Object Code Generator

The simple prototype could itself form a basis for a complete object code generator, but you'd have to expand the `Select Case` statement in `msilRun__qbOpcode2MSIL_` to handle all "zero address" opcodes as well as add logic to the main `msilRun_` routine to handle strings, functions, and IO.

Two better ways would be to either change the `compiler__genCode_` procedure or else develop a macro processor to do the translation from Nutty Professor opcodes to the CLR.

`compiler__genCode_` could use a compile-time switch to translate its input, including the opcode and the operand to CLR.

The macro processing approach would define each possible Nutty Professor opcode as one or more CLR opcodes and then expand the former to the latter.

You'd need to retain the Nutty Professor level to be able to watch code execute, or simulate this functionality in CLR to trigger the `interpretEvent` of the main compiler. This event sends information to an event handler (which in `qbGUI` places the updated stack on the screen and refreshes the highlight of the RPN code), and it would have to be changed to carry CLR information.

Challenge Exercise

Develop the MSIL object code generator for the `quickBasicEngine`.

Summary

Both the Nutty Professor interpreter and the CLR are stack machines that execute opcodes that interact with the stack. In Chapter 8, you saw how a simulator for the CLR itself could be written in a similar manner to the `interpret_` method of the `quickBasicEngine`.

Unlike many Microsoft products, .NET and the CLR were developed in an open spirit. Officially, we don't know how the Visual Basic interpreter for VB 6 programs worked apart from the fact that it was a C++ program that at times imposed some strange performance penalties. But the operation of any valid interpreter for the CLR is well defined, even if you don't have its code, by the governing standard.

The open standards create an aftermarket of opportunities for unemployed compiler writers, not only for .NET compilers for traditional languages, but also for business rule compilers for expressing the rules of the organization in a highly maintainable, and reasonably efficient, form.

Beyond the books by Andrew Troelsen and Serge Lidin on basic and advanced use of the Common Language Runtime and ILASM, a considerable amount of content is shipped with Visual Studio on the CLR and ILASM.

CHAPTER 10

Implementing Business Rules

It's not simple unless it's complete.
—*Larry Ellison, CEO of Oracle*

MANY ENTERPRISE SYSTEMS require the implementation of a large set of so-called business rules, which interact in complex ways and tend to be hard to change and hard to document. Junior programmers often think that as a program gets more complex, it will be necessarily larger and have more interactions, but Edsger Dijkstra's 1968 discovery of structured programming shows that this isn't necessarily the case. When a program gets to a certain level of complexity, its actual text can become radically simpler by thinking of logic as input data, and translating the input data to interpreted code.

This chapter describes how you can use the QuickBasic engine in particular, and compiler design theory in general, to handle complex business rules, a source of some difficulty in large enterprise systems. But first, we'll look at some real-world problems with business rules and how they were solved.

Business Rule Solutions

Problems with handling business rules are common in the real world. Here, we'll look at two examples of what can happen. The first is an example from a book, and the other is a "war story" from my own personal experience.

Step-by-Step Engineering Instructions

Gerald Weinberg, in his book, *The Psychology of Computer Programming,* described a large auto manufacturer's system that was failing repeatedly. It was supposed to transform a customer's requirements for his built-to-order auto into a set of step-by-step engineering instructions. The system was creating specifications for autos with ridiculous configurations, such as without any doors. The step-by-step assembly procedures were impossible for the lads to follow at the shop floor. It appears from Weinberg's story that the requirements were being translated into sequential assembly steps with many dependencies.

The code was, according to Weinberg, a rather confusing mess, and a programmer was assigned to rescue the project in a way that will be completely familiar to modern programmers (the story happened long ago).[1] After examining the code, the programmer realized that he could rewrite the buggy program faster than he could fix it, by creating a program that read tables, looked up the configuration requests in the table, and found the specific sequence of steps.

Weinberg doesn't go into any detail about specifics about what the programmer went through, but it is clear that he recognized *logic as data*, and that the existing, buggy solution did not make manifest the *business rules*. The business rules were hidden in the complex code, and for this reason weren't being correctly implemented. Weinberg's hero seems to have rethought his problem as less a question of implementing a specific set of business rules and more as an exercise in implementing a second level of logic, in the form of a system that read, "compiled," and processed the actual engineering requirements.

Digital Switch Usage

A program to bill users for complex usage of a digital switch was failing in a manner that reminded me, at the time, of Weinberg's story of the auto assembly program. It was failing to handle conference calls and other calls with complexity over and above a simple two-person call.

This program was written in Cobol using the latest structured techniques, but all that meant was that the program was a structured mess of exceedingly small routines. These routines called each other in such a complex way that nobody was able to predict what the program would do for any particular telephone call above a certain level of complexity.

In projects like these, you spend a few rather disheartening days, gazing at the code and making notes, learning what it's about. A danger is that you will get obsessed prematurely with one solution. Any one flash of intuition must be critically examined, lest its attractiveness lie in merely giving you something to do.

One particular brain flash turned out to be the solution. I realized that what the program needed to do was re-create a call when all it had was a call event,

---

1. In these programmer-to-the-rescue situations, the company retaining your services is told by your "broker" or direct boss that you leap tall buildings in a single bound and walk on water. This sort of oversell used to be more the norm, but it still happens. You waltz or foxtrot in, and in many cases you do solve a problem. In other cases you don't, because you can't or the problem isn't solvable.

such as "caller removed the phone from the hook."[2] Therefore, I needed to get from an event to a call. How could I do this?

I realized that the mere Cobol program *had to act as if it were a digital switch, and thereby create calls from events.* I knew in general how the Cobol program had to act to simulate a Private Branch Exchange (PBX), which is a limited but general-purpose (in Turing's sense) digital computer, since these switches are commonly state machines.

Starting in a "start" state, they wait for symbols that consist of atomic user events, such as user picks up the phone, user dials digit x, user hangs up, and user throws phone across room (sorry, just making sure you're awake).

Characteristic of this type of state machine is the fact that a state and symbol fully determine a new state and perhaps a list of actions. I demonstrated to the client that the simple transitions could be obtained from the original designers of the switch and placed into a fixed table defined using the Cobol occurs clause. Then, as the program read the file of events, it would actually retrace the sequence of events the original switch had encountered. The billing people were then able to identify at which points an actual call completed and how to apportion the bill, for example, by dividing the cost of the call by the number of conference callers. The solution worked (lucky me), and the client was happy.

The Dilbert Factor

Younger developers need to be cautious. Even a brilliant solution, if it involves any new code, represents a financial risk to management. This means that you need to do due diligence to make sure that a solution to the problem does not already exist.

Another problem younger developers will encounter is the "Dilbert factor." Scott Adam's popular comic strip seems to be on the side of the ordinary developer because it mocks (sometimes cruelly) low-level managers. In recent years, it has mocked offshore and immigrant developers.

A very interesting deconstruction of the Dilbert phenomenon by Norman Solomon, *The Trouble with Dilbert: How Corporate Culture Gets the Last Laugh* (Common Courage Press, 1997) describes how the real Scott Adams hated his job and uses irony to essentially exploit the ordinary working folks he left behind.

---

2. As a recovering philosophy major, I call these moments ontological moments. *Ontology* isn't the study of how to get onto the bus. It's the theory of the fundamental constituents of reality. This was an ontological moment because I realized that the entity analysis of just what a phone call might be had never been carried out, and as a result, the programmer had no clear pathway from event to call. Business rules must be based on a clear business ontology in this sense, which ordinary users know without having to study philosophy.

The Dilbert factor is the belief, subtly fostered by the strip, that (1) everything interesting and worthwhile has been done in computing, and that for this reason work should be the boring installation and cleanup of existing solutions; and (2) even if there's room for innovation, we here at XYZ company are probably going to be laid off, we don't have a clue, and it's best not to take any risks.

Because of the Dilbert factor, you need to present your idea carefully, you need to do your homework, and above all, you need to be sensitive to the feelings of the designers of the bad solution if one exists. (But since I'm an insensitive clod who treads on other people's feelings when I am not otherwise engaged in walking on water or shooting myself in the foot, my advice in this area is somewhat limited.)

Logic As Data

As you know, client server and Web systems should be organized into two or more tiers. The simplest design separates the GUI from the logic/data side. This allows the GUI to be developed in Visual Basic when it runs on Windows and in HTML, ASP, JavaScript, and other technologies when it runs on the Web.

The next step is to divide the logic from the data, and when this is done, the logic consists of business rules. Normally, business rules are code in Visual Basic, C#, and other compiled languages. In some cases, business rules linked directly to data appear in Transact/SQL procedures. There is nothing wrong with this, as long as the business rules are completely specified by the end user and are reasonably static.

When the rules change, problems arise. This is because changes to the rules, caused either by users changing their minds or by changes in business needs, cause a lot of work in the typical Windows development environment. Programmers must obtain the current version from the source code library. They must then determine where to change the code and, of course, make the changes. The changes must then be tested, and a new version built and installed.

The code changes are simple in many scenarios and might involve tweaking a few operators or changing the value of a constant, but the interactions with the source code library and the installation process constitute a large, fixed investment of programmer time. That's why it makes sense to represent much of the logic in such a way that authorized users can change the logic without bothering the programmers. It makes sense because the programmers are freed to concentrate on new problems and to work on the data and presentation tiers, where their skills are best leveraged. It also makes sense because end users can understand rules presented as data.

Logic as data also means less exposure to multiple versions of source code with different business rules, a source of bugs. Of course, if the logic consists of text business rules stored as SQL or Oracle fields, there can be multiple copies of the database. But security procedures normally protect the end user from using the wrong version of a database, whereas no such protection exists against using multiple versions of compiled code, except internal programming procedures. In some environments, these procedures may be more than adequate. In many other situations, the user will prefer to see a layer of business rules in the data.

In his book, *What Not How: The Business Rules Approach to Application Development* (Addison-Wesley, 2000), C. J. Date (a relational database pioneer) makes the case for the use of pure predicate logic for the control of the business organization. Here, complex expressions—including but not restricted to mathematical, logical, and relational expressions as seen in ordinary programming languages—would be used to implement the mission, goals, and constraints of the business such as a formalized version of "For all customers, their satisfaction level must never be less than 5; if it is, call the customer to find out what's wrong."

Although this level of control is what many users want, they also find that it locks them into a dependence on a vendor. Therefore, my humbler and tactical (as opposed to strategic) approach has the ordinary programmer using the logic as data approach in specific situations, rather than across the board, and from the view of the executive suite. Furthermore, this book is about what it takes to develop a processor for business rules, while management texts typically assume they are already available.

Case Study: Credit Granting

This is a song to celebrate banks,
Because they are full of money and you go into them and all
*   you hear is clinks and clanks,*
Or maybe a sound like the wind in the trees on the hills,
Which is the rustling of the thousand dollar bills.
Most bankers dwell in marble halls,
Which they get to dwell in because they encourage deposits
*   and discourage withdrawals,*
And particularly because they all observe one rule which woe
*   betides the banker who fails to heed it,*
Which is you must never lend any money to anybody unless
*   they don't need it.*
—Ogden Nash, "Bankers Are Just Like Anybody Else, Except Richer"

There are many areas in which representing logic as data makes sense. I've mentioned a customer engineering application and a combined business and engineering application earlier in this chapter. Legal applications and "expert" diagnostic/strategic systems also generate rule sets of a complexity and rapidity of change that strain the typical software change cycle.

The case study we'll look at in this section is taken from the credit industry, presenting a part of a credit-rating solution.

Credit Assessment Systems

Many grantors of credit, whether consumer credit or home equity, use complex models to assess the ability and willingness of people to repay their loans. This is because if you restrict your loans to blue-chip citizens, who pay their bills on time and floss daily, you will have no market, for the very good reason that these good people don't need to borrow money. They are your competition, because they are buying equities and mutual funds with their spare cash. Therefore, credit grantors have been forced to expand their markets repeatedly over the years. In the 1950s, only solid citizens like James Bond had the early credit cards issued by Diner's Club and American Express.

But then, the early credit grantors discovered a very interesting fact: people actually are very willing to repay their debts and on time. This was first noticed when the returning GIs of World War II faithfully repaid their home and school loans. The civil rights movement also sent a message to these companies: Americans of all races can be deadbeats or good risks, completely independent of race. Companies were forced by 1960s legislation to ignore race on credit applications, and found, much to their delight, that the market was bigger and nearly all the new credit users were solid risks.

The credit grantors realized that even their primitive systems were a resource that they could study to find out ideal risks. Behavioral studies of the era discovered that men as debtors will do almost anything to repay automobile loans, and would go hungry rather than lose their moped, Honda, TransAm, or GTO. Later on, studies conducted internationally by the Grameen Bank discovered that poor women worldwide are very conscientious about repaying loans that allow them to set up their own businesses and talk back to their husbands.[3]

However, the companies were obviously unwilling to use a random-number generator—a lottery—to take a chance on applicants. Instead, they have, over time, developed two approaches:

- The somewhat older approach is to apply a series of rules, or questions, such as does the borrower own or rent, is the borrower employed and for how long, and what about the borrower's credit record. These rules are documented and explained to the borrower. I call this the "open system."

- A more recent approach, employed by a company in the US, uses a complex metric (a proprietary trade secret) to give a single number that represents the borrower's credit worthiness. This saves thinking time, since the only business rule is whether the score is above a number set by the lender. I call this the "closed system."

---

3. Cultural and religious factors play a role in credit; for example, Islamic law forbids high interest rates and advises the credit grantor that he is taking just as much a risk of nonpayment as is the debtor and is therefore bound by sha'aria to investigate the borrower's ability to repay and his own risk aversion.

The advantages of the open system are twofold: the company can do a detailed analysis, and the open system is more easily internationalized. For example, a detailed analysis may find, by a complex application of the rules to existing payment records, that people who rent in a particular Louisiana parish and whose income is less than $15,000 a year always pay their debts on time, but people in the same parish with incomes higher than $15,000 never pay their debts on time. The single number may or may not reflect this research. And, of course, the open system is more easily used in international markets where there is no preexisting credit scoring database.

A disadvantage of the open system is that borrowers can circumvent the rules if they know the rules. This isn't true with the closed system, since you cannot question the finality of the single number.

Many companies combine the new single-number, closed system with their own rules.

In our example, we want loan officers to have a "calculator" to evaluate the credit-worthiness of applicants for consumer credit, first-time home loans, home equity loans, and so on. But in addition, the calculator should be itself change-able—programmable when the loan supervisor wants to change the rules. Our tool will use the open system, in that it will make clear the rules, indeed in such a way that the calculator itself will explain the rules.

Credit Evaluation Considerations

In credit evaluation, annual income is probably the most important data point. Undischarged bankruptcy is also important as a strong negative, although many lenders will lend to people who have declared bankruptcy during the statutory period of seven years. As a matter of public records maintained by credit-reporting companies, the company can obtain the number of bills the customer has paid, after 30 and after 60 days.

Housing is a consideration for many lenders. They tend to like homeowners, although they seldom inquire whether the home is paid for. Renters are far more numerous and less loved by lenders, except insofar that they are willing to pay higher interest rates. Additionally, our application will have an "other category," for those who do not rent or own. Consider, for example, social critic Barbara Ehrenreich's identification, in her book *Nickel and Dimed* (Owl Books, 2002), of large numbers of honest, working people who pay their debts but live in motels.

Our system will not output a yes/no decision. Rather, it will generate an annual percentage rate because we've decided (1) to offer a favored demographic of middle income people a promotional rate and (2) to charge a higher rate to people with high incomes.[4]

---

4. Note that the latter varies somewhat from common practice, but I would like to show how the flexibility of logic as data makes it possible to recognize either a reality we've discovered or the populist tendency of the boss.

This solution can use the QuickBasic engine as a nonvisual object to compile and run a set of rules transliterated by us from a user-oriented notation into strict Basic. The transliteration can be done with the `qbScanner` object that was used to construct the QuickBasic engine to translate rules in the user's notation to Basic.

The user's format is *condition, action: comments*. When the condition is true, the action is taken. The condition can use the same operators as are used in QuickBasic, since they will be familiar as simple math to the end user. It can use the data names `annualIncome`, `bankrupt`, `thirtyDayPastDue`, `sixtyDayPastDue`, `owns`, `rents`, `other`, and `otherDescription`. The only annoyance is the fact that the user cannot put spaces between word breaks in data names. This can be overcome by careful language design, but it's probably not important enough to warrant the effort.

The action will be either `decline` or an integer interpreted as the loan's annual percentage rate. Note that the action is an object represented as a weak type .NET object, because it is either a single-precision annual percentage rate or the string "`decline`".[5]

The Credit Evaluation Calculator Application

Run the sample application creditEvaluation.exe, available from the Downloads section of the Apress Web site (`http://www.apress.com`). After an introductory message box, you will be asked if you want a set of example rules. Click Yes to see the `creditEvaluation` main form with an example, as shown in Figure 10-1.

---

5. The word *decline* is used by credit grantors to remind the borrower that a loan in our society is a contract into which both parties freely enter.

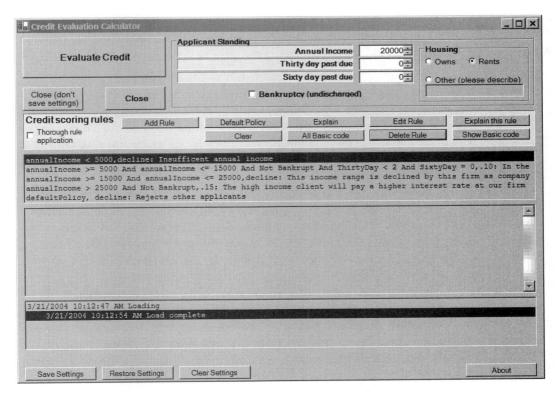

Figure 10-1. Credit Evaluation Calculator with an example

The calculator has been set up to enforce these rules:

- If the applicant's annual income is less than $5,000.00, decline. We keep income levels low in this example for clarity.

- Our favorite demographic group is people with a very moderate income between $5,000 and $15,000, who have a good history, including no bankruptcy within the past 7 years, not more than one bill paid past 30 days in the statutory period, and no bills paid past 60 days.

- We have discovered that people in the target demographic area with incomes between $15,000 and $25,000 don't pay their bills; therefore, we decline to do business with them. In order to avoid the appearance of discrimination, we need to give a bona fide business reason for doing so, and it is because they don't pay their bills.

- Our company would like to concentrate its business among people of moderate income, but if high-income, good risks apply, we accept them at a higher rate. (If they are foolish enough to apply to us, when our mission statement is "loans for the honest poor," let's soak them for spare change.)

These rules in particular, and any set of rules in general, may or may not be logically *sealed*, or airtight, in the sense that one or more rules exist for each logical possibility. The set of rules used by the calculator is not logically sealed. Consider, for example, what happens when the applicant makes $25,000 or more but has an undeclared bankruptcy. Since this set of rules is not logically sealed, we need a default decision, which is decline here. The Default Policy button in the Credit scoring rules section allows you to define the default policy. Later in this chapter, in the "Handling Contradictory and Redundant Rules" section, I will discuss an application of compiler and symbolic interpretation technology that can analyze complex sets of rules to see whether they are sealed, and if multiple rules apply to one case.

A requirement is that we explain the rules to the credit analyst and the applicant in an understandable way. This is why the rules contain a comment field.

Also, code inside creditEvaluation uses an instance of the qbScanner object to transliterate the rules from source form to lengthier explanations. To see a specific example, click the third rule in the list box, which excludes the income range from 15000 to 25000. Then click the button labeled Explain this rule, on the right side of the form, to see an explanation of the rule:

```
If annual income is greater than or equal to 15000 and annual income is less than or equal to 25000, the
application will be declined (This income range is declined by this firm as company policy)
```

Since we want to make sure the user knows that coding < (less than) versus >= (greater than or equal to) has a different result, we use words to clearly state the effect of the rule. Since we're using the QuickBasic engine to compile rules, this transliteration can be applied to any changes in the rules.

You can document any set of rules completely. Try clicking the button labeled Explain (in the Credit scoring rules section). You should see the report illustrated in Figure 10-2. You can copy and paste this report into documentation.

```
1. If annual income is less than 5000, the application will be declined
(Insufficent annual income)

2. If annual income is greater than or equal to 5000 and annual income is less
than or equal to 15000 and not undischarged bankruptcy and 30-day overdue
reports is less than 2 and 60-day overdue reports equals 0, the application will
be accepted with an Annual Percentage Rate of 0.1 (In the midrange group we
accept most applicants at a very favorable rate)

3. If annual income is greater than or equal to 15000 and annual income is less
than or equal to 25000, the application will be declined (This income range is
declined by this firm as company policy)

4. If annual income is greater than 25000 and not undischarged bankruptcy, the
application will be accepted with an Annual Percentage Rate of 0.15 (The high
income client will pay a higher interest rate at our firm)

5. If no other rules apply, the application will be declined (Rejects other
applicants)
```

Figure 10-2. Explaining the rules

Applying Rules

Let's try applying the rules to the starter applicant standing. Take a look at the applicant information, which provides the applicant's credit history.

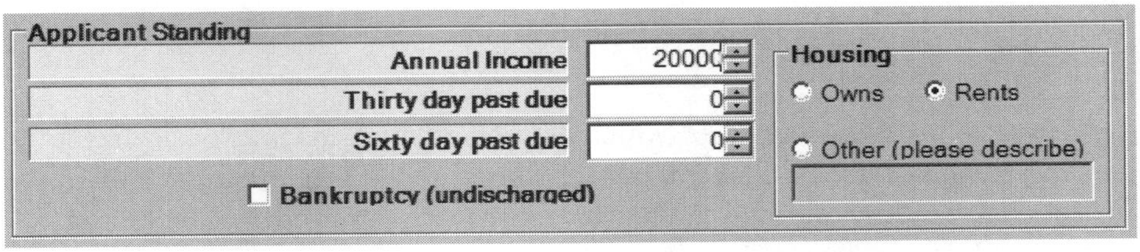

The applicant has an income of $20,000, pays her bills on time, has no undischarged bankruptcy, and rents her home.

Click the large Evaluate Credit button in the upper-left corner of the screen, and then wait. This prototype software is fully scanning, parsing, and interpreting the code, and its progress appears at the bottom of the screen. It takes about 30 seconds on my Pentium 4 (much of this time is spent in making the progress report). Later in this chapter, in the "Improving the Credit Evaluation Calculator" section, I will suggest some ways to make this prototype faster.

Since a system requirement is that we explain the result to the applicant, the screen in Figure 10-3 should appear. This screen provides a statement, similar to the preliminary explanations shown in Figure 10-2, which can be provided to the user.

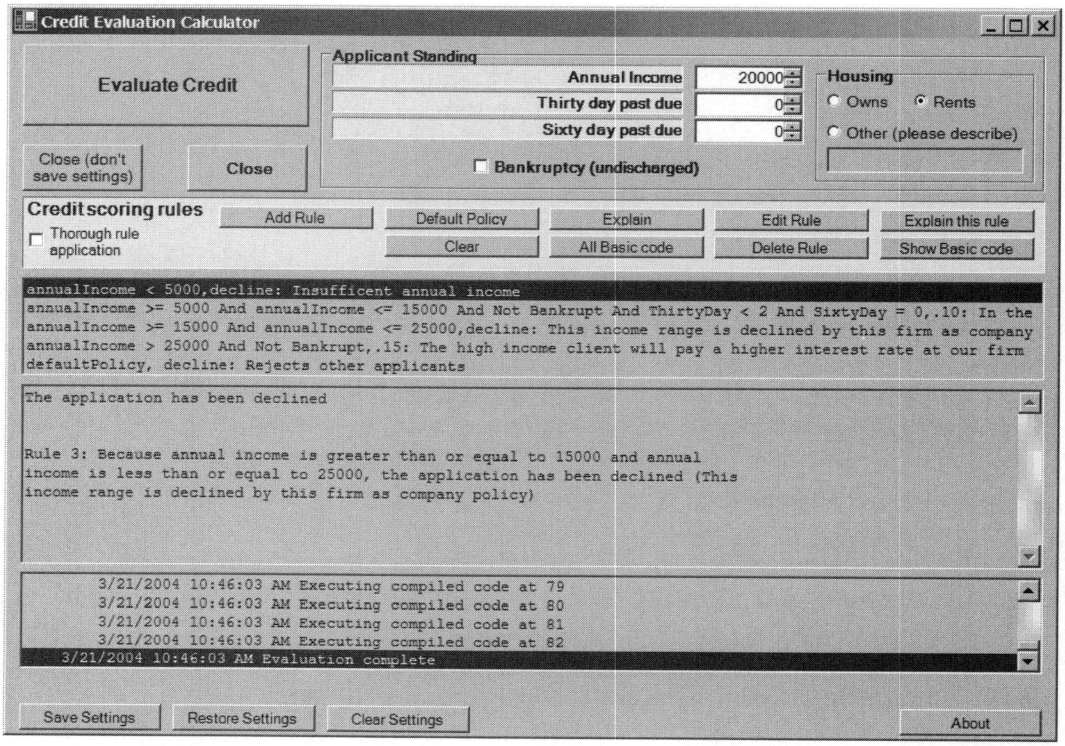

Figure 10-3. Credit evaluation

Let's examine how the rules (which are not, after all, in QuickBasic on the screen) are transliterated into QuickBasic source code using the independent lexical analyzer. Any one rule can be viewed as its corresponding QuickBasic code. Highlight the third rule (the rule that was used in the previous example) and click the button labeled Show Basic code to see the basic form of the business rule:

```
If annualIncome >= 15000 And annualIncome <= 25000 Then
    Print "decline" & " " & 3
    End
End If
```

Note how the Basic code communicates results.

quickBasicEngine and the Nutty Professor interpreter do not do any printing. Needless to say, they don't search for and activate your printer. Nor do they display on the screen, because quickBasicEngine needs to be completely independent of any graphical environment to move from the Windows environment of qbGUI to a Web service.

Instead, the `Print` command raises the `interpreterPrintEvent` event, which is intercepted and parsed by the credit evaluation software, which then displays the decision and the applicable rule number. This is what you see when you click the Show Basic code button.

Viewing the Code in the QuickBasic GUI

You can see how the code is executed in the QuickBasic GUI. The button labeled All Basic code displays the complete program transliterated from the rules. Click this button and copy and paste the code into the code section of the qbGUI program. Then click Run in qbGUI to see the results, as shown in Figure 10-4. If the More screen is displayed, you will see the detailed, step-by-step execution of the business rules.

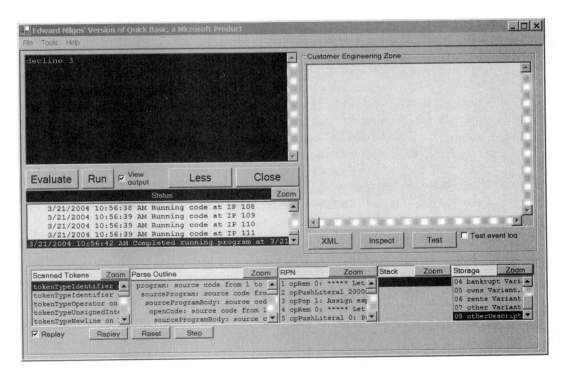

Figure 10-4. Running the business rule code in the qbGUI application

In qbGUI, click the Storage Zoom button to see the business rule data storage, as shown in Figure 10-5. Note that each data point has been compiled as a `Variant`, with the narrowest type for its current value; therefore, `annualIncome` and `rents` have the `Integer` type and the value 20000 and –1, while other data points are zero bytes. The `rents` variable is –1, not Boolean and `True`, owing to the way in

which the value of the Rents radio button is converted to the value of the `rents`
`qbVariable`.

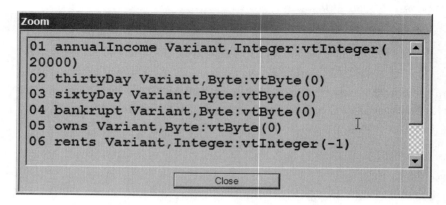

Figure 10-5. Business rule data storage

When the Rents radio button's `Checked` status is passed to the `valueSet` method
of `qbVariable` (discussed in Chapter 6), it is a .NET object, and `valueSet` tries to
assign it to a series of widening QuickBasic data types, starting with the byte. If it
started with Boolean, the integer value –1 would be converted to Boolean, and in
many cases, this would be wrong.

The .NET representation of `True` is –1, and this fails to convert to a byte but
can be converted to a QuickBasic Integer (represented by a .NET `Short Integer`).
Therefore, the selected type is `Integer`. Since `quickBasicEngine` is not as fussy as
is .NET Visual Basic with `Option Strict`, the `Integer` value –1 can still be used in
Boolean rules such as "rents or owns."

In `qbGUI`, click the RPN Zoom button to see the generated Nutty Professor
code. Figure 10-6 shows what this code looks like when it contains comments.

When you selected a rule and clicked the Show Basic code button in the
`creditEvaluation` application, you saw an `End` statement in the generated code,
which brings us to another feature of that application. Scroll to the bottom of
the RPN list box in the main form of `qbGUI` to see it at location 155.

```
45 opRem 0: ***** If annualIncome >= 5000 And
annualIncome <= 15000 And Not Bankrupt And ThirtyDay <
2 And SixtyDay = 0 Then
46 opNop 0: Push lValue annualIncome  contents of
memory location
47 opPushLiteral 1: Push indirect address
48 opPushIndirect : Push contents of memory location
49 opPushLiteral 5000: Push numeric constant
50 opPushGE : Replace stack(top) by opPushGE(stack(
top-1), stack(top))
51 opNop 0: Push lValue annualIncome  contents of
memory location
52 opPushLiteral 1: Push indirect address
53 opPushIndirect : Push contents of memory location
54 opPushLiteral 15000: Push numeric constant
55 opPushLE : Replace stack(top) by opPushLE(stack(
top-1), stack(top))
56 opAnd : Replace stack(top) by opAnd(stack(top-1),
stack(top))
57 opNop 0: Push lValue Bankrupt  contents of memory
location
58 opPushLiteral 4: Push indirect address
```

Figure 10-6. Assembly code for a business rule

Handling Contradictory and Redundant Rules

By default, when the check box on the calculator's main form labeled Thorough rule application is not selected, each successful rule causes the rule evaluation to be terminated. We need to allow the user to thoroughly apply all rules to detect contradictory and redundant rules. This is not because "users aren't programmers" (in fact, many are). It's needed because programmers and users make mistakes when managing large sets of rules.

Three types of contradictory situations may exist in this application:

- A benign contradiction (from our point of view and not that of the customer) occurs when more than one rule indicates that the customer should be declined. A benign contradiction is resolved by declining the user and providing him all the reasons, so that he can recover his creditworthiness with us.

- An APR contradiction occurs when two or more rules indicate that the customer should be accepted at different annual percentage rates. An APR contradiction is resolved by giving the customer the lowest interest rate; otherwise, she will complain if another customer in a similar situation receives a better rate.

- A fatal contradiction exists when one or more rules indicate that the customer should be accepted and other rules indicate a decline. Here, the rule set is broken, and a decision cannot be made based on our system; the analyst needs to fix the erroneous collection of rules.

Let's see how each type of contradiction is handled. This will also let you see how rules can be added and edited.

Benign Contradictions

First, let's add a benign contradiction. Make sure that the Thorough rule application check box on the main calculator form is checked, indicating that you want all of the rules to be applied. Click the Add Rule button above the rule list to see the ruleEntry form. Double-click bankrupt in the Data Names list to get a condition of `bankrupt`, and enter the explanation **Cannot lend when there is an undischarged bankruptcy**, as shown in Figure 10-7. Make sure the Decline radio button is selected in the Policy section, and then close the form.

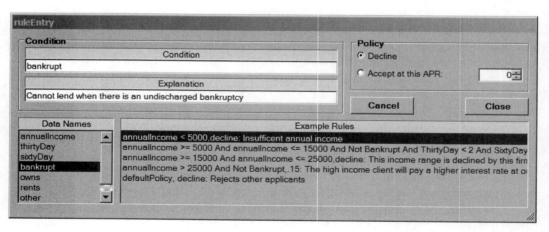

Figure 10-7. Adding the bankruptcy rule

   Click the Bankruptcy (undischarged) check box in the Applicant Standing
area of the main form to indicate that the applicant has a bankruptcy. Then click
Evaluate Credit to see the rejection and its explanation, as shown in Figure 10-8.
In the explanation, two rules are explained in the benign case, where the applicant has been declined for two reasons.

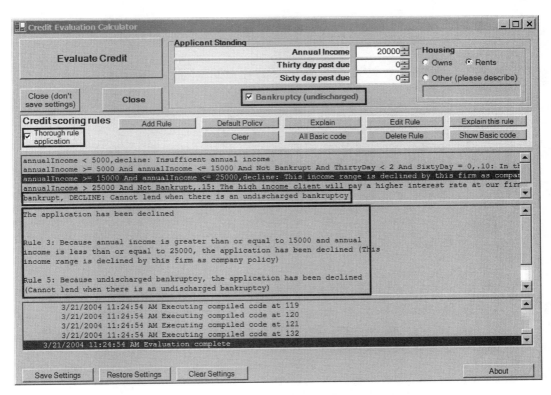

Figure 10-8. Multiple declines explained in thorough rule application

   Click the button labeled All Basic code to see the code that is generated
when the rule application is thorough, as shown in Figure 10-9.

```
Let annualIncome = 20000
Let thirtyDay = 0
Let sixtyDay = 0
Let bankrupt = True
Let owns = False
Let rents = True
Let other = False
Let otherDescription = ""
If annualIncome < 5000 Then
    Print "decline" & " " & 1
    decisionMade = True
End If
If annualIncome >= 5000 And annualIncome <= 15000 And Not Bankrupt And ThirtyDay < 2 And SixtyDay = 0 Then
    Print 0.1 & " " & 2
    decisionMade = True
End If
If annualIncome >= 15000 And annualIncome <= 25000 Then
    Print "decline" & " " & 3
    decisionMade = True
End If
If annualIncome > 25000 And Not Bankrupt Then
    Print 0.15 & " " & 4
    decisionMade = True
End If
If bankrupt Then
    Print "DECLINE" & " " & 5
    decisionMade = True
End If
If Not decisionMade Then
    Print "decline" & " " & 6
    decisionMade = True
End If
```

Figure 10-9. Basic code for thorough application of rules

The thorough code moves the default action to the bottom and uses the decisionMade flag to indicate whether the default rule needs to fire.

The interpreterPrintEvent handler in creditEvaluation in this scenario intercepts two events. The first is the detection that the applicant's annualIncome is between the excluded range of 15000 to 25000, and here the event handler receives a decision of decline and a rule number of 3. The second is the detection of an undischarged bankruptcy, with a decision of decline and a rule number of 5.

Each time the event handler code receives a new decision, it executes the following logic:

1. If the evaluation is unassigned in the module global OBJevaluation, OBJevaluation is assigned to the new evaluation.

2. If the evaluation is a string (which will be "decline") and a new evaluation is also "decline", this is a benign contradiction.

3. If the evaluation is a number (which is the APR for an acceptance) and a new evaluation is another acceptance, we continue to accept, using whichever APR is more favorable.

4. If the evaluation is a number and the new evaluation is decline, or vice versa, the rules are invalid.

APR Contradictions

Now, let's try an APR contradiction, where multiple APRs are specified. Delete the rule you just added by clicking the rule bankrupt,DECLINE, and then clicking the Delete Rule button. Add the rule shown in Figure 10-10. Here, we've decided to accept people at the high end of the favored range (whose annual income is between $14,000 and $15,000) with a promotional APR of 5%.

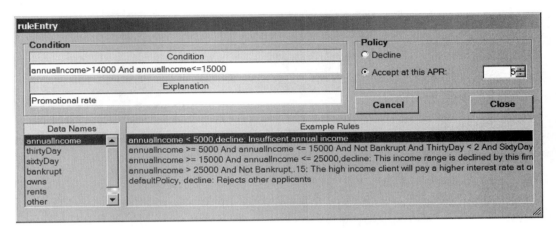

Figure 10-10. Adding the promotional rule

Return to the main form, and then set the applicant's income to **14500**. Turn off the Bankruptcy indicator. Click Evaluate Credit to see the screen in Figure 10-11.

```
The application has been accepted: the annual percentage rate shall be 0.05


Rule 2: Because annual income is greater than or equal to 5000 and annual income
is less than or equal to 15000 and not undischarged bankruptcy and 30-day
overdue reports is less than 2 and 60-day overdue reports equals 0, the
application has been accepted with an Annual Percentage Rate of 0.1 (In the
midrange group we accept most applicants at a very favorable rate)

Rule 5: Because annual income is greater than 14000 and annual income is less
than or equal to 15000, the application has been accepted with an Annual
Percentage Rate of 0.05 (Promotional rate)


Note that rule 5 confirms a preceding acceptance: selecting lowest applicable APR
```

Figure 10-11. Results of an APR contradiction

The customer is given the best APR in a clear and documented fashion, because we've treated logic as data.

Fatal Contradictions

Now, let's see what happens when we insert a "fatal" contradiction. We'll try to decline any applicant who is a renter.

Go to the ruleEntry form and enter the rule shown in Figure 10-12. (In general, creditEvaluation requires that each rule be rather verbose and specify all the conditions that apply, which for many applications, is a good thing.)

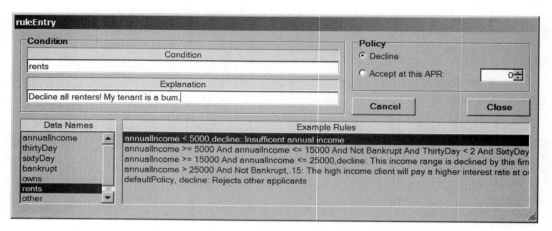

Figure 10-12. Frivolous rule

Close the ruleEntry form and click Evaluate Credit again, to see the report shown in Figure 10-13.

```
The decision cannot be performed because the rules are not consistent


Rule 2: Because annual income is greater than or equal to 5000 and annual income
is less than or equal to 15000 and not undischarged bankruptcy and 30-day
overdue reports is less than 2 and 60-day overdue reports equals 0, the
application has been accepted with an Annual Percentage Rate of 0.1 (In the
midrange group we accept most applicants at a very favorable rate)

Rule 5: Because annual income is greater than 14000 and annual income is less
than or equal to 15000, the application has been accepted with an Annual
Percentage Rate of 0.05 (Promotional rate)

Rule 7: Because rents home, the application has been declined (Decline all
renters! My tenant is a bum.)


Note that rule 5 confirms a preceding acceptance: selecting lowest applicable APR

Note that rule 7 contradicts a preceding rule
```

Figure 10-13. Frivolous rule causes this report

The rule was a bad rule, since it logically contradicts two other rules. When business rules of this or greater complexity are encoded in a programming language, the bad rule would be at best dead code (where the renter test follows the other tests); at worst, it would be live code that prevents code that contradicts its effect from executing.

Improving the Credit Evaluation Calculator

Considerable improvements can be made to the approach shown in creditEvaluation. For example, the Basic code for the benign case, shown earlier in Figure 10-9, could be optimized by the creditEvaluation form code, and this would be a worthwhile exercise. Consider that the calculator assigns and then uses several variables that reflect the applicant's standing. We've noted how they are variants and the Nutty Professor interpreter imposes a "tax" on their retrieval.

Instead of this technique, it would be a simple matter to replace the names by Applicant Standing values. This may be combined with the constant evaluation optimizing feature of the quickBasicEngine's compiler (described in Chapter 7) to speed up evaluation considerably by reducing the Nutty Professor code. If you add complete MSIL generation, the speed of evaluation will approach, and in some cases exceed, that of hard-coded business rules.

Or, the code seen in Figure 10-9 can be copied and modified if the user decides the rules won't change, and the code can be transferred to a business object. For example, you can add declaration statements for each data point and easily convert the code to a Visual Basic .NET validation rule.

Another enhancement would be static evaluation of the rules, added to the dynamic evaluation we obtain when the check box labeled Thorough rule application is checked. The problem with dynamic application is that it reports only contradictions—whether benign, APR, or fatal—for a specific case in which the contradictions arise. A more intensive analysis of the static semantics of the rules would reveal flaws for the user at a deeper level. For example, note that the credit evaluation rules specify a series of contiguous income bands. A trivial but dangerous error would be to leave gaps inadvertently, so that certain people receive the default treatment.

Note that the first rule shown in Figure 10-3 specifies that annualIncome must be less than 5000, and the second rule states that annualIncome must be greater than or equal to, since the opposite of less than is not greater than; it is greater than or equal to. (This isn't "programming" knowledge; it's high school math.) Suppose the user mistakenly uses the greater than in the second rule. People with incomes of $5,000 won't be treated correctly.

Since logic is represented as data, there are two approaches that can be used to prevent these problems:

- A stress test button could be added to the creditEvaluation form to provide random applicant information, and the output can be examined by the user.

- A more advanced method would be to create a set object and make each rule the defining rule of each set. Then set operations—including intersection, union, and complement—could determine the existence of error sets, including, in the example, the set of all people making exactly 5000, which are wrongly declined.

For the more advanced set solution, you would need the ability, probably inside the Nutty Professor interpreter, to do symbolic calculation with unknown variables. This would be a version of the interpreter that when given (let's say) the And operation, a stack value of False, and another stack value of unknown, would push False, transforming the unknown value back into a known value.

The symbolic version of the Nutty Professor interpreter would need to use fairly advanced math in cases where it had to compute with values known as ranges of values. For example, to symbolically "add" 5 to a value known to be in the range 10..20 is to get the range 15..25. The object-oriented approach empowers this type of development since it can define sets, ranges, and unknown values as objects and value types.

Summary

This chapter has shown you that, with a performance penalty, treating logic as data provides a new level of flexibility and control for real applications. And note that as long as you have an effective tokenizing tool for transforming the external representation of business rules on a form or in a database and a compiler/interpreter, it's not necessary to write lexical analyzers and compilers to get to this level of flexibility.

Consider applying the techniques in the preceding chapters to get any user with a business rule problem to a level that genuinely eliminates "programming." The elimination of programming has long been a Philosopher's Stone. Many programmers claim it is not possible. However, this chapter shows that if pure, declarative, nonprocedural logic isn't programming, it is indeed possible to eliminate, for classes of applications, traditional procedural programming, and that it has benefits even in the area of mere documentation, as our automated explanations show.

In the next and final chapter, we need to address the issue of language design as it occurs in crafting a notation for an end user, as in our simple *condition,action:comment* notation, or in creating a traditional language.

Challenge Exercise

Refine the rules in this chapter, by taking into account a new fact: homeowners in the 5000..15000 band are better risks than renters and other housing categories. Give the homeowners a better rate, and test the new rules.

For a real challenge, find a new industry with which you are familiar and define a set of business rules. Using Visual Basic .NET, design a calculator using `creditEvaluation` as a model and the `quickBasicEngine` DLL. For example, if you are selling life insurance to put yourself through school and your sales calls involve pricing life insurance based on the age of the applicant, his financial standing, and whether he smokes, you can design a simple GUI, using `quickBasicEngine` to evaluate the rules (using `quickBasicEngine`'s `eval` method) to come up with a yes/no accept/decline decision, or a rate versus decline. Your code will gather the input data from the screen and assemble a valid QuickBasic expression, which will then be passed to `quickBasicEngine`.

Resources

The following are some resources for more information about handling business rules:

The Psychology of Computer Programming: Silver Anniversary Edition, by Gerald M. Weinberg (Dorset House, 1998). This book is a well-known classic, first printed in 1972. Weinberg, a former IBM "wild duck" employee, concluded from his experience in Big Blue that programmers and their managers systematically disregarded human factors and psychology, and related the story from auto manufacture that I passed along in the "Step-by-Step Engineering Instructions" section of this chapter.

Softwar: An Intimate Portrait of Larry Ellison and Oracle, by Matthew Symonds (Simon & Schuster, 2003). Larry Ellison is an interesting guy who matured from just wanting to have fun to a real commitment to his company.

The Trouble with Dilbert: How Corporate Culture Gets the Last Laugh, by Norman Solomon (Common Courage Press, 1997). Dilbert communicates hopelessness and lack of initiative as a positive virtue that masquerades as cool. As such, he reminds me of Herman Melville's Bartelby the Scrivener, who was so burned out that he preferred not to do much of anything. Norman Solomon shows how this is passive/aggressive, and while it may manufacture consent to corporate policies, it is a recipe for nonproductive organizations that serve, at best, only an inner ring of top-level people. Norman Solomon also observes that the comic strip never mocks or disrespects top-level executives, only middle managers.

What Not How: The Business Rules Approach to Application Development, by C. J. Date (Addison-Wesley, 2000). C. J. Date's original vision was that we would be able to write the rules once for the organization in a non-procedural language. The reality is that not only are the rules hard to discover, but also that different stakeholders want different rules. That's why my example stays at a low level—that of "loans for the honest poor." The boss is easy to identify, and while he occasionally makes mistakes ("deny all renters!"), he is able to admit his mistakes.

CHAPTER 11

Language Design: Some Notes

Confucius, hearing this, said, "Don't bother explaining that which has already been done; don't bother criticizing that which is already gone; don't bother blaming that which is already past."
— *Confucius, The Analects*

MASTER KONG FU (Confucius' real name) might have thought that in this book I have "explained that which has already been done," "criticized that which has gone," and perhaps even "blamed that which is past." But, like most great ones, Kong contradicted himself, for even he was concerned with transmitting the past and scorned originality for its own sake. I do believe that as so much knowledge is increasingly encapsulated in products, we forget how much work the basics represent.

You have learned techniques for specifying a language precisely in Chapter 4, and for building a lexical analyzer in Chapter 5. You learned how to parse and interpret this language in Chapters 6 through 9, and saw how to apply this tool to a practical, real-world problem in Chapter 10.

This chapter addresses, broadly and generally, how to design a language. This in itself warrants an entire book and a thorough knowledge of software history, in order to avoid repeating mistakes. Here, I will simply talk about four important issues:

- Determining the goals of your language design

- Deciding on the semantics of your language

- Deciding on the syntax of your language

- Documenting your language

Determining Your Goals

Your first step in language design should be goals definition. This is primarily identifying the audience of users who will use your language. You may wish to design a language for yourself, purely for fun; or you may have a genuine problem to solve for a client, such as how to represent a set of logic statements as data, as demonstrated in the preceding chapter.

It is unlikely but possible that you may have some ideas for more productive general programming of .NET applications. In this case, you need to keep your audience in mind. It's not enough for you to be more productive with a unique language; you need to convince your prospective audience that they, too, will be more productive with your solution. This is an almost impossible task. Managers call it a "people" task. I call it social engineering.

How Hard Is It to Overcome Network Externality?

The Dvorak typewriter keyboard was invented during World War II by an inventor who recognized correctly that the existing arrangement, which persists today on computer keyboards, makes the most common letters easily accessible to most of us who have two hands, but also makes typing slower. The original keyboard was arranged to avoid jams, so that fast operators of the machines of the 1890s would not cause two typefaces to arrive at the paper at the same time.

But by the time the Dvorak keyboard was introduced, a more than critical mass of typists had jobs only because they tested out at high rates of speed on the existing equipment, and they were not about to retrain on the Dvorak typewriter! Typing was brutally difficult to learn well (Tennessee Williams' play *The Glass Menagerie* shows the misery of a poor Southern gentlewoman being forced to learn it in business school), and the typists did not want to go through the pain all over again.

As a consultant, Charles Moore, the author of the Forth language (which is based on RPN) insisted that his prospective clients allow him to write applications and all tools in this language. If they said no, he was willing to reject the work. Few programmers have Moore's combination of willingness to part with opportunities and willingness to maintain, in effect, his own infrastructure.

In fact, during the 1950s and 1960s, a critical mass of programmers did notice the applicability of Polish logic to programming, and many modern procedural languages, including C, rely on the stack, of Polish logic, to run. However, they cover up this fact by using infix, "normal" syntax at the level of source code.

Of course, if we lived in a World State, in which children at a young age were ripped from their mother's arms and taught the Dvorak typewriter and Polish logic, then both the Dvorak typewriter and Forth would be universally used. Fortunately, this is not the case.

Because we are different, there is no one solution for general programming—not even the C language, which is showing its age and is unsafe for the general programming of simple applications.

However, you may well discover that you are more productive using your own notation in general, procedural programming. For example, highly skilled but dyslexic programmers have been known to secretly use system facilities to create a comfortable environment, without desiring to make their different abilities the norm.[1]

The non-Dvorak keyboard, and the prevalence of operating systems like Windows (which cause purists to shudder and gag) are both examples of the network externality, in which success is reinforced as long as your product fits into an existing technical infrastructure. As far as the "ideal computer system" is concerned, be well advised that your typical user might be a poor Southern gentlewoman in reduced circumstances forced to put up not only with your ideal but also with you. The acceptance of something new in any one case is going to take into account far more than the bits and the bytes. It will also be based on the way in which the new paradigm fits in the existing network.

The #define capability of the C language can be used to create a completely different language at the lexical level. But no standard way exists to restore the program to a standard C without the #define. This means there is no way of lexically changing the style back to the norm. The problem was the same in PL/I's large redefinition capability. In general, any compiler writer who provides a macro facility needs to make one that can be used to change a nonstandard program back to the norm or to a different, nonstandard style.

A tool like qbScanner (described in Chapter 5)—as long as it conforms to the language definition at the lexical level of individual operators, identifiers, and so forth—can be used to make these transformations. If lexical transformation were indeed flexible, this would reduce the volume of debates over a maintainable style.[2]

---

1. Microsoft provides comprehensive facilities for the differently abled (just as the blind "see" that which is hidden from the view of the sighted, the handicapped are differently abled in that their difference should be added to the sum total of their insight) to use computers, but not as many to program computers. The SIGCAPH (Special Interest Group for Computers and the Physically Handicapped) of the American Association for Computing Machinery, and similar organizations worldwide, address programming for the deaf and other groups, but mostly when the different ability makes the candidate attractive as a programmer of existing systems.

2. Program maintainability is another issue that needs to be addressed in relation to differently abled programmers, because we want to maintain the code written by the differently abled. But in terms of corporate needs, maintainability is often exaggerated by programmers in search of job security.

But on the whole, it is unlikely that your goal will be to save the world with a new programming language. Typically, your goal will be humbler, like my goal to adequately bill switch users for complex calls, described in Chapter 10.

Far from creating a general-purpose language, you may wish to create, for a user, a language that is deliberately limited, so the user doesn't get into trouble. The `creditEvaluation` software described in Chapter 10 is an example of a program designed to meet this goal. The user doesn't need to think step-by-step or procedurally. The system orders the default rule so it appears last, and it watches for collisions of the benign form (where an applicant is declined because of multiple rules), the APR form (where multiple annual percentage rates are entailed by multiple rules and we select the highest), and the fatal form (where the rules are contradictory).

Such languages have a tendency to disappear into the woodwork; that is, the business rules are stored as data. An example would be where you discover that a SQL column's value is sent to a transaction center and parsed, and used to drive a `SELECT` statement strangely akin to the `interpreter` method of `quickBasicEngine`. In fact, logic as data may be said to occur when a data field *drives a process*. A customer name field does not drive a process—it's just data. On the other hand, a customer request code field used to select from a large number of options does drive a process.

Deciding on the Semantics of Your Language

The syntax of a language (both programming and human) consists of the rules for forming valid constructs. In human language, *semantics* is the study of meaning; in programming languages, semantics is the study of the meaning of the program— for the most part, the program's effect at runtime.

It is necessary to "put the cart before the horse" and make the semantics decisions first, since these will influence the syntactical decisions.

Here are five major issues involved in making semantic decisions:

- Object-oriented or traditional

- Interpreted, compiled, or both

- Backdoor problems

- Data typing

- Mathematical and logical details

Let's take a look at each of these issues.

Object-Oriented or Traditional

Your first instinct, in all probability, will be to keep it simple for the end user and not implement object orientation, because the end user wouldn't understand it. Well, you need to look deep within yourself, for many times we say the end user won't understand it, when the truth is that we don't understand it.

In fact, the experience of the early designer (the late Ole-Johan Dahl) of the prototype object-oriented language, Simula, was that end users found the object-oriented paradigm far more understandable than the procedural paradigms of Fortran and Algol, because code was tightly coupled to objects familiar in the industrial shop floors where the end users worked. Dahl did not babble on in computerese about new processes and new files, but instead about Simula proto-objects with a clear relationship to the daily work of the shop floor.

One problem, which I haven't addressed in this book, is the question of how to develop a compiler and/or interpreter for object-oriented code. In fact, the object-oriented paradigm itself comes to the rescue. An investigation into the System namespace of CLR will make it clear that object-oriented approaches are closed in the benign sense; a closed system is one whose objects combine to form new members of the same system. An Object is an Object is an object, and in particular, within an object-oriented compiler within an object-oriented language, an Object can be represented by an object. Contrast this with traditional development, whether of complex MIS programs or compilers.

Entities multiply within MIS and compiler development. For each user object, a table or file is typically created, and the designers focus on its care and feeding—often in excess of what the user wants. On the other hand, object-oriented development tries to ensure a one-to-one mapping between the nouns that the user wants and what we are working on.

Within traditional compilers, there was often a one-to-many, or even many-to-many, relationship between what the user (here, the application programmer) wanted and the entities of the compiler. For example, the IBM Fortran compiler I encountered in 1972 (described in Chapter 1) was divided into 99 phases. These phases had nothing to do with Fortran per se and instead were necessitated by the small storage of the machine. The designers had to write special code to manage the transition between phases.

In an implementation of an object-oriented system like .NET, whether the proprietary implementation created by Microsoft or the open implementation created by the Mono organization (see http://www.go-mono.org), many, many objects need to be created. Using tables would create many more relationships between the target and the implementation; therefore, the only sensible way to develop an object-oriented system seems to be with an object-oriented approach.

Interpreted or Compiled

Traditional procedural languages fell into two broad categories: interpreted or compiled. Languages like Fortran, Algol, and C were meant to be compiled to efficient object code. But soon after the introduction of these tools, a need was seen for fast compile times, even at the expense of efficiency, especially in one-time prototyping in industrial settings and student coding in universities.

An early effort was PUFFT, described in Chapter 1, which compiled to a sort of bytecode in order to provide Purdue students the ability to get their assignments done on time in a mainframe environment. Another early effort was Basic, whose first compilers compiled to generally undocumented bytecodes.

> **NOTE** *An old joke: How do you debug a C program? Answer: Change your major. The attraction of CompSci 101 for Boneheads is that if your programs work, you get an A, while in Literarily Theorizing Jane Austen and Relating It to Women and Their Lives in the Post-Colonial Era, you need to behave yourself. The attraction is also the downside—if your code doesn't work, you get an F. Therefore, students demand good turnaround, which PUFFT was the first to provide.*

If you want, through your language, to provide fast turnaround and comprehensive debugging, the language should be designed with this goal in mind. Often, but not universally, such languages use a single, weak type to represent all data. This way, the debug messages can present data easily. A popular weak type is the string, which is the least narrow value object in .NET. But if you desire efficiency, the language will need strong data types, as described in the "Data Typing" section coming up soon, because you need to avoid runtime conversions.

However, the issue of security, if it is one of your issues, complicates this distinction. Interpreted, weakly typed languages like VBA have been found to host crude viruses. These aren't anything like the very vicious, industrial-strength viruses (like SoBig in the summer of 2003), which are coded by extremely knowledgeable, if evil, people. Rather, they are like the Outlook viruses, which used an innocent and helpful feature to run macros. The Outlook viruses were run by unsuspecting users in the late 1990s when they opened certain e-mail. These viruses executed in a pesky and self-replicating fashion. This is why the CLR for .NET is strongly typed: so that remote platforms can determine what a remote executable will do, as far as possible.

If your language is interpreted and weakly typed, you need to determine whether its use will create exposure in the form of crude Trojans, viruses, and worms, and whether, in its intended environment, this risk is acceptable.

Backdoor Problems

This section describes some business exposures that can be unintentionally created by overeager compiler developers. I call these "backdoor" problems.

One little-known problem can be described as unintentionally (or intentionally) giving away the store. Consider the eval, evaluate, and run methods of quickBasicEngine (described in Chapter 7). The eval method evaluates an expression in source form and returns its value. The evaluate method does the same job using the current settings of quickBasicEngine. The run method acts as if a string contained a QuickBasic program, and it compiles and interprets the string.

If you plan to sell a language for money, you need to know that providing this level of functionality will mean that for common use, your users don't need extra copies of the compiler. Instead, because the compiler runs at interpretation time, the user simply can build a GUI around your compiler to get a new copy.

In open source, university, and older large-corporate environments, this anxiety about giving away the code doesn't exist. For example, the Rexx language for running interpreted code contained a function that executed Rexx source code. However, at the time I encountered Rexx, its use was restricted to universities and large companies running the Conversational Monitor System on IBM mainframes.

Backdoor problems exist whenever language facilities are of one class such that any object can be explicitly processed (as in Reflection) by another object. They can have unpredictable effects when programmers discover unintended uses for the facility, and you should assess their impact if you want to make money. If, on the other hand, you don't want to make money, this is not a concern.

Data Typing

quickBasicEngine provides a selection of data types current when QuickBasic was in vogue: Boolean, Byte, Integer, Long, Single, Double, String, Variant, and Array.

The native types supported in the CLR are Boolean, Byte, (16-bit) Short, (32-bit) Integer, (64-bit) Long, Single, Double, String, and Object. A strongly typed language designed for .NET should probably support these data types. The CLR also supports, on behalf of C# and C++, the unsigned integer types Unsigned Short, Unsigned Integer, and Unsigned Long (which will also be supported natively in the next version of Visual Basic .NET).

Beyond this starter set, you may decide that the user's needs demand a new primitive type. For example, the hash table Collection of traditional Visual Basic genuinely replaces the need to create special-purpose code for fast access to tables.

However, one lesson from the PL/I language is still germane: A language can become bloated with a variety of cool primitive types to the point where there are so many features that the programmer doesn't know which ones are optimum. So, the programmer finds a suboptimum subset and cultivates her own personal style based on the subset, making her code hard to understand and debug.

The Power of Keeping Things Simple and Focused

A parallel problem of feature-bloat occurred in machine design. As more and more mainframes came onstream in the 1950s, 1960s, and 1970s, manufacturers naturally added more and more features in the form of complex instructions. For example, the IBM 360 came with `Translate` and `Translate and Test` opcodes, which appeared to allow the programmer to scan and modify strings quickly. But, in many cases, the speed advantage was illusory. On simpler, smaller machines, the advanced instructions took many cycles because they were implemented in firmware—as hard-coded instructions that carried out tasks dictated by the regular opcodes. Furthermore, when IBM introduced virtual memory in the early 1970s, it found that the `Translate` and `Translate and Test` instructions could induce page faults when the translated string lay across the boundary between two pages.

The furthest evolution of the tendency was probably Digital Equipment Corporation's (DEC's) VAX line of minicomputers and mainframes, which provided an elegant and comprehensive line of instructions. However, it was discovered here that, as in the case of PL/I, assembler programmers had a hard time utilizing this embarrassment of riches. It was also discovered that compiler writers had a hard time writing code generators that could utilize these large instruction sets.

The reaction, in the 1980s, was the Reduced Instruction Set (RISC) movement, in which entrepreneurial companies, including MIPS and Sun, discovered that a simpler instruction code (one that, in some cases, even excluded multiply and divide) allowed compilers to generate fast programs by finding the right combination of simple opcodes. They also used optimization techniques, including the simple constant evaluation and degenerate opcode elimination methods described in Chapter 7.

The discovery was similar to the discovery made by the initial designers of the C language, who did not have the time or the manpower to add, as part of the language, all sorts of cool features. Instead, they decided that libraries of code, either brought in using the `call` mechanism or included using the preprocessor's `#include` command, could, in effect, provide the extended facilities. What's more, they could be removed and replaced by better code, in a more modular fashion.

In fact, one of the charges in the anti-Linux lawsuit filed by SCO, a company that owns a commercial Unix, is that Linux's runtime libraries for C programs were not scaled up to industrial strength until an abortive partnership between IBM and SCO in 2000. At that time, IBM was able to look at C libraries that had benefited from 15 years of testing and improvement within AT&T, Bell Labs, and Lucent. SCO maintains that a C-written system can be very different, depending on the libraries.

The situation in kernel operating system design is parallel. This design focuses on the basic job of any operating system, which is apportioning resources, such as computing time and I/O facilities. We ordinarily think of an operating system as something like Windows 2000, a vast empire of device drivers, DLLs, APIs, and fun games. However, in kernel design of the operating system, developers focus, like the hedgehog of the proverb and not the fox, on one thing. A *kernel* doesn't drive devices or expose tools for programmers; instead, it gives processes time slices and access to resources. Around the kernel, various drivers and GUIs (also known as *skins*) provide the final computing experience to the end user. But all of these extras must go through the kernel to get work done. The kernel approach thus restricts the operating system to the basics and allows itself to be retrofit with different layers of functionality.

RISC design, the C language's use of libraries, and kernel operating systems demonstrate the power of keeping things simple and focused, and argue strongly for a language that provides users with definitional capabilities in place of facilities (like the Collection) that they could code, copy, or buy from others.

Mathematical and Logical Details

Over the years, language designers have found that our pre-computer notions about math have failed to anticipate how a mathematical or logical expression is actually evaluated. This refers to the labor process of evaluation, which the traditional mathematicians (before Turing) regarded as simple and clerical. A well-known example, to which I have referred in previous chapters, is the semantics of the Boolean operators And and Or.

Lazy vs. Busy And and Or

In C, logical And is represented by two ampersands, and it has always been "lazy." If a in a&&b (a And b) is True, then b is not evaluated. If you think about it, since And requires that a and b be True, evaluating b is a *waste of time* when a has been found to be False, in a left-to-right evaluation.

Also in C, logical Or is represented by two strokes, and it is also lazy. When a in a||b (a Or b) is True, then b is not evaluated.

In Visual Basic, the semantics, or runtime effect, of And and Or is different, and the evaluation is "busy." In a And b, when a is False, b is always evaluated. In a Or b, when a is True, b is still examined. This may not be consistent in all of the many versions of Basic, but it was the case in Visual Basic as well as QuickBasic, and it remains so in Visual Basic .NET (despite the fact that the Visual Basic .NET team follows the Tao, or way, of C).

In fact, prior to March 2001, Microsoft attempted a change to the runtime effect of And and of Or from lazy to busy, only to be subject to a hue and cry from users who thought this would make programs hard to convert. Here, the user community was wrong and the Microsoft team was right, but Microsoft caved in and changed the semantics of And and Or back to the old way. Fortunately, Microsoft also had its clever devils on the compiler team implement two very slick operators: AndAlso and OrElse, which I've talked about in Chapters 3 and 4.

AndAlso and OrElse are lazy and work exactly the same as C's && and ||, and, as I've said in earlier chapters, they should replace all use of And and Or. But, by now you may ask, "Why is this issue important?"

It's important because, while it's true that for simple variables a and b, both the lazy and the busy ways of evaluation are equivalent in effect, suppose b is a function with side effects, such as opening a needed database. If the code containing the Boolean logic is mindlessly converted (let's say) from Visual Basic to C, the worst type of bug in the world might occur: a bug unnoticed until it is too late.

Prior to Pascal, for which the busy And and busy Or were consciously selected, this issue was rather invisible, and at times, it was left to the discretion of the compiler developers—a bad idea. Today, lazy evaluation pretty much rules the world; it is standard in C, Perl, JavaScript, and Java.

Because I am such a total dweeb on this issue, I could not resist implementing AndAlso and OrElse operators in quickBasicEngine.[3] To see the compiler effect of lazy and busy evaluation, run qbGUI.exe (the testing GUI for quickBasicEngine, introduced in Chapter 7) and enter the following code:

```
Print False And eval(False)
```

Recall that the eval function evaluates QuickBasic expressions by creating a new quickBasicEngine, and observe that this code will take a long time, relatively, to evaluate both sides of the And operator. Run the code to see, of course, a 0, which is how unformatted False appears in a normal Print statement. In a More view, click the Zoom button of the RPN box to see the Nutty Professor assembler language that appears in Figure 11-1.

---

3. This departs from an exact implementation of QuickBasic, but at this writing, the compiler isn't standard in all respects, anyway.

```
1 opRem 0: ***** Print False And eval(False)
2 opPushLiteral 0: Push the False
3 opPushLiteral String:vtString("False"): Function
parameter 1
4 opEval 0: Evaluate the Quickbasic expression (
lightweight) "False"
5 opAnd : Replace stack(top) by opAnd(stack(top-1),
stack(top))
6 opPushLiteral String:vtString(ChrW(13) & ChrW(10)):
Terminate print line
7 opConcat : opConcat(s,s): Replaces stack(top) and
stack(top-1) with stack(top-1)&stack(top)
8 opPrint : opPrint(x): Prints (and removes) value at
top of the stack
9 opEnd : Generated at end of code
```

Figure 11-1. Assembly language for a busy And

Notice that line 2 pushes False, and line 3 pushes the string "False" for evaluation by the opEval opcode in line 4, despite the fact that the eval is always unnecessary. Of course, the False value that is pushed in line 2 could be a variable, a function, or a subexpression. Likewise, the eval could be far more complex and time-consuming; however, it is always evaluated.

Next, change the And operator to AndAlso, and compile and/or run the code. Then click the Zoom button of the RPN box to see the Nutty Professor assembler language that appears in Figure 11-2.

```
1 opRem 0: ***** Print False AndAlso eval(True)
2 opPushLiteral 0: Push the False
3 opDuplicate : AndAlso: duplicate stack and skip RHS
when LHS is False
4 opJumpZ 7: opJumpZ(n): Jumps to location when stack
(top) = 0 (pop the stack top)
5 opPushLiteral String:vtString("True"): Function
parameter 1
6 opEval 0: Evaluate the Quickbasic expression (
lightweight) "True"
7 opLabel "LBL1": AndAlso jump target for False
8 opPushLiteral String:vtString(ChrW(13) & ChrW(10)):
Terminate print line
9 opConcat : opConcat(s,s): Replaces stack(top) and
stack(top-1) with stack(top-1)&stack(top)
10 opPrint : opPrint(x): Prints (and removes) value at
top of the stack
11 opEnd : Generated at end of code
```

Figure 11-2. Assembly language for a lazy AndAlso

In this example, line 2 still pushes False because constant folding—the replacement of constant expressions described in Chapter 7—is not in effect. Then line 3 uses the opDuplicate opcode to make a copy of the value at the top of the stack, and executes opJumpZ to both test and remove the value at the top of the stack. The opJumpZ operation transfers control to the label at line 7 if the top of the stack is zero or False, and thereby avoids the evaluation when it is unnecessary.

In the challenge exercise for this chapter, you will repeat this experiment for busy Or and lazy OrElse.

Floating-Point Math

Another issue can be floating-point mathematics. My recommendation in this area is that you implement an open standard such as that of the Institute of Electrical and Electronics Engineers (IEEE), if you expect mad scientists, disturbed engineers, or Nutty Professors to use your language (see http://www.research.microsoft.com/~hollasch/cgindex/coding/ieeefloat.html). Of course, if your platform already implements this important standard, you don't need to worry about it. However, if you are writing any sort of retargetable compiler, this can be an issue.

> **NOTE** *Early compilers forced many users to become numerical analysts in spite of themselves in order to predict how their code would evaluate expressions, and mere humility would probably declare that it's unlikely that your implementation will be more useful than an open standard.*

String Handling

Another form of complexity is in string handling. You should probably decide how long strings may be. Basically, if you use a "sentinel" character, as does the C language to delimit strings (standard C strings are delimited by the ASCII null character, which has the value zero), you've decided that the sentinel character cannot be a member of the string. This may hurt the character's feelings. Far more important, it means that a large number of strings (strictly speaking, an infinite number of distinct strings) cannot be represented in your language.

However, the alternative also is a limitation, and, interestingly, it means that a very large but finite set of strings is representable by your language. This approach allocates a separate number to hold the string length. In the case of Visual Basic, this number is a 4-byte unsigned integer and capable of representing strings up to $2^{32}-1$ characters long.

Another mistake in string handling is being ASCII-centric. C originally made provisions for only the ASCII character set, which in fully extended form supports only 256 characters and is inadequate for many world languages. Note that XML did not make this mistake and allows full Unicode representation. Visual Basic has been repaired in this regard; its older Asc and Chr functions (which return the numeric value of a character and the character value of a number in the range 0..255, respectively) have been replaced by AscW and ChrW, which work for double-byte characters.

Deciding on the Syntax of Your Language

Syntax decisions generally follow semantic decisions. If, for example, you have decided on a procedural language, there are strong arguments in favor of making it look like C. The developers of Java, Perl, and many other languages have used C as their basis. An alternative is to use the less "friendly" syntax found in the Ada and Eiffel languages, which are marginally "harder" to code because their designers were concerned with correct mission-critical code.[4]

C's syntax and semantics have numerous flaws. C encourages overly terse coding styles, and it uses delimiters and opcodes in ways that, at least in the past, were unique to C. An example is the C operator that consists of the question mark and colon in two different places, as in a?b:c, which returns b when a is True (that is, evaluates to a number other than 0) or returns c when a is False. This operator is like the IIf of Visual Basic, with the important difference that ?: does not evaluate c unnecessarily when a is True, or b unnecessarily when a is False. IIf evaluates both sides and is easier to read.[5]

Some combined semantic and syntactical constructs of C should have been drowned in the bathtub at birth, including C's overly general for statement. Starting out as the promise of a straightforward For as seen in Visual Basic's For and the Fortran Do, the for in C (as in for (intIndex1 = 0; intIndex1 < intLimit; intIndex1++)) suddenly and without warning allows you to code a Do. That is, the second semicolon-separated clause can be *anything*. If it returns anything but zero, the loop starts, and to terminate the loop, the second clause must return zero. This is asking for trouble because of the weak typing of C, in which numbers can change, unpredictably, into truth values. But strengthening the type system can correct this problem.

---

4. I use quotes because it's news to me that programs should be always easy to write. What's worth doing well is worth doing slowly, and Ada and Eiffel impose constraints that have been shown to create better software with less programmer self-abuse.

5. Although I will admit that the ?: operator has its own gnomic charm once you start dweebing out with it.

To see an illustration of the real difference, bring up qbGUI.exe (the QuickBasic engine's GUI) and key in the code in Figure 11-3. What will print?

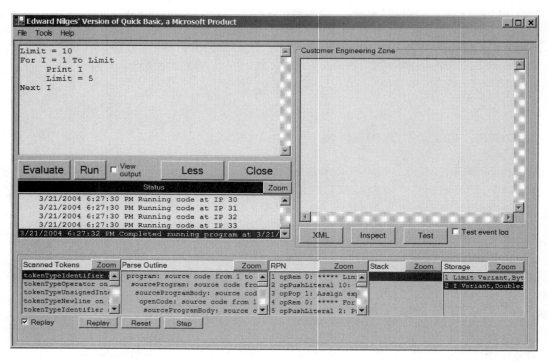

Figure 11-3. Testing For in qbGUI

The equivalent for loop in C is this:

```
for ( i = 1; i <= limit; i++ ) limit = 5 ...
```

It will print 1 through 5, because the limit can be changed in the loop (which is nearly universally unsafe practice), and because the second expression in the semicolon-separated list of expressions in the for loop header is evaluated by reference in such a way that it reads refreshed values of its operators.

But, if you run the preceding code in qbGUI, Visual Basic 6, or Visual Basic .NET, the For will print a list of numbers from 1 to 10. It will ignore the change to the limit.

C's approach is flawed because the Do construct of C already provides this capability, and missing is the ability to provide a checkable for loop header.

The qbGUI implementation of the rule that for is by value is shown by zooming and examining the commented assembly language code for the preceding example, as shown in Figure 11-4.

```
1 opRem 0: ***** Limit = 10
2 opPushLiteral 10: Push numeric constant
3 opPop 1: Assign expression 10 to Limit
4 opRem 0: ***** For I = 1 To Limit
5 opPushLiteral 2: Push the control variable I
6 opPushLiteral 1: ctlVariable-
>ctlVariable,initialValue
7 opPopIndirect : ctlVariable,initialValue-
>ctlVariable
8 opNop 0: ctlVariable->ctlVariable,finalValue
9 opPushLiteral 1: Push indirect address
10 opPushIndirect : Push contents of memory location
11 opRotate 1: ctlVariable,finalValue-
>finalValue,ctlVariable
12 opPushLiteral Byte:vtByte(1):
finalValue,ctlVariable-
>finalValue,ctlVariable,stepValue
13 opRotate 1: finalValue,ctlVariable,stepValue-
>finalValue,stepValue,ctlVariable
14 opLabel "LBL1": For loop starts here
15 opForTest 29: Test For condition using the stack
frame
16 opRem 0: ***** Print I
17 opNop 0: Push lValue I  contents of memory location
18 opPushLiteral 2: Push indirect address
19 opPushIndirect : Push contents of memory location
20 opPushLiteral String:vtString(ChrW(13) & ChrW(10)):
Terminate print line
21 opConcat : opConcat(s,s): Replaces stack(top) and
stack(top-1) with stack(top-1)&stack(top)
22 opPrint : opPrint(x): Prints (and removes) value at
top of the stack
23 opRem 0: ***** Limit = 5
24 opPushLiteral 5: Push numeric constant
25 opPop 1: Assign expression 5 to Limit
26 opRem 0: ***** Next I
27 opForIncrement : For loop increment or decrement
28 opJump 14: Jump back to start of For loop
29 opLabel "LBL2": For loop exit target
30 opPopOff : Remove the For stack frame
31 opPopOff : opPopOff(x): Removes stack(top) without
sending it to a memory location
32 opPopOff : opPopOff(x): Removes stack(top) without
sending it to a memory location
33 opEnd : Generated at end of code
```

Figure 11-4. Compiling the For statement

Notice in line 13 that, with some pain, we create a stack frame for the For, as illustrated in Figure 11-5.

Figure 11-5. Stack frame for the For statement

Take a look at `finalValue`. Its value is pushed on the stack in steps 5 and 10, and this is why the loop will execute ten, not five, times.

Notice that `ctlVariable` (`I`) is pushed on the stack in step 5. Note that it is 2, which is not `I`'s value but its location. This is because most dialects of Basic (including our `quickBasicEngine`, Visual Basic .NET, and Visual Basic 6) allow change to the control variable, although this is terrible practice.[6]

Change the code in Figure 11-3 as shown here:

```
Limit = 10
For I = 1 To Limit
    Print I
    I = 10
Next I
```

In `qbGUI`, as well as in Visual Basic 6, Visual Basic .NET, and most versions of Basic, this code will print `I` and stop. This is because, as Figure 11-3 shows, the control variable will be referenced on the stack, not placed on the stack. Of course, this is what we want if we need to use the variable in the loop, although to change it is poor practice.

From the standpoint of syntax, we should, as this example shows, stay as close as possible to the user's natural expectations of the semantics.

A final syntax consideration, seen in the credit evaluation application in Chapter 10, is whether syntax is important if the users have a GUI that enters rules. Generally speaking, it remains a good idea to have a documented "serialization" standard for the business rules, to allow both power users and support personnel to modify the rules in XML or as straight text files.

---

6. Unlike MIS programmers, compiler writers cannot be dissing code; we need to compile pathological, if not psycho, programs.

Documenting Your Language

If your language is actually for procedural programming, it's a good idea to write at least two documents: a tutorial and a reference manual.

The tutorial should walk the new user through the creation of a set of simple programs, starting perhaps with the infamous Hello World program, and then some simple tasks germane to what the beginner wants to do. The tutorial needs to be thorough enough so that as the tyro reads your article or book, he or she can be simultaneously running code successfully as a powerful way to reinforce your lessons and stay awake.

The job of the reference manual is very different and often neglected. Experienced programmers tend to get through just enough of a "for dummies" tutorial (just the Hello World), and then think they "grok" enough to start doing what they really need to do to complete a job. These aren't folks in week-long or semester-long computer classes. Rather, they have maybe a day to get up to speed, and they often want to do their own projects in your language. They need a comprehensive reference manual, rather than a partial tutorial.

The reference manual should include the formal, BNF, definition of the language, as described in Chapter 4. Surprisingly, this was never done for Visual Basic before .NET. If it's possible that some of your audience won't understand pure BNF, you can use the `bnfAnalyzer` program to transform the BNF into a list of the language nonterminals, a list of the terminals, and a list of the BNF rules in an outline form, again as shown in Chapter 4.

Summary

This chapter addressed four important issues regarding language design: the goals, the semantics, the syntax, and the documentation. The bottom line of all these considerations is that you need to write the language reference manual before writing the compiler. If you have a specific target audience in mind, host a tea party, bun fight, or conference to get them to buy into your goals. Or, more sensibly, you can just create the new language, unleash it on the Internet, and be damned; in fact, this is how many useful new languages were created.

The lesson of the failure of Esperanto, an attempt to design a global language, is applicable. In practice, programming languages behave like real languages, with dialects, extensions, and pidgins proliferating. The Algol team attempted to do it right according to the Eurocentric and social-engineering notions popular in Europe and in American universities in the 1950s. They hosted any number of international bun fights and meetings, only to discover (as have social reformers throughout history) that actually getting people to "do it my way" is hard, if not impossible.

The founder of modern Columbia and Venezuela, Simon Bolivar, compared revolution to plowing the sea. Many programming managers find that managing programmers is like herding bobcats. Programming language design is difficult for the same reason.

Indeed, the best way to be successful in this venture is Taoist in the sense that you, like water, just follow your instincts with no expectation of riches or fame. It isn't true that the best languages were designed in this way. C has deficiencies directly related to the humility of its designers, and the development of Algol was aborted by the marketplace, but might have worked. However, if we follow the rule that we are happiest when we do what we want, then no one in his right mind would ever want to create another Algol—another massive social-engineering effort to get programmers to code one way.

Challenge Exercise

Repeat the experiment we did in the "Lazy vs. Busy And and Or" section of this chapter with lazy and busy Or. Compile a Or eval("b") to determine what will happen when a is True and confirm that this will evaluate the eval. Then compile a OrElse eval("b") to confirm that this will not unnecessarily evaluate the eval.

Conclusion

I never blame myself when I'm not hitting. I just blame the bat, and if it keeps up, I change bats. After all, if I know it isn't my fault that I'm not hitting, how can I get mad at myself?
—Yogi Berra

Many programmers, having learned on the job, are curious about computer "science." This book, I hope, has motivated you to use .NET to investigate an area of computer science unexplored by many programmers.

On September 11, I was appalled by the unprecedented loss of life. I was also saddened a few months later when one of the FBI field agents assigned to tracking the highjackers reported in Congressional testimony that she had no way to enter simple Boolean queries of the form terroristAssociation AndAlso attendsFlightSchool. The separate queries were possible, but their Boolean combination was not, according to the FBI whistleblower, Colleen Rowley.

Had the system been any one of a large number of mainframe or network-based systems, it would be, as far as I can tell, simple for a programmer to develop such queries by defining the BNF of the additional queries using the techniques in Chapter 4, developing a scanner for identifiers and operators using the techniques in Chapter 5, and developing a recursive-descent parser as described in Chapter 7.

However, the attitude that such techniques are rocket science seems to have been a minor contributing factor in a tragedy, and if at a minimum, I can show a proactive approach, I am more than satisfied.

On a more positive note, I feel confident that your new knowledge of the DNA of computer science, indeed, the way it propagates, gives you a better sense of how your source code actually runs and illuminates some of the darker corners of the CLR.

If you decide to write a production .NET compiler, I urge you to get your hands on a copy of Aho, Sethi, and Ullman's "dragon book" (*Compilers: Principles, Techniques and Tools*), to which I have referred more than once in this book. That's because I've only scratched the surface and got you started, in the way we programmers get started: hands-on examples.

When I started out, developing compilers was rocket science. In 1970, compiler developers were not in all cases fully aware of how choices made by the coders of compilers (such as how to evaluate a Boolean operator) were not mere crotchets and conveniences, but became part of the reality of the compiler. But many years of intense development in the Unix world under the long-gone corporate sponsorship of the former AT&T monopoly taught a generation of programmers how compilers work and are best constructed. I have meant little disrespect by characterizing these characters as gnomes of Unix (I meant some disrespect, because that is healthy).

.NET developers have, in their own quiet way, absorbed the lessons learned, most especially the value of open standards in particular and *glasnost* in general. You can find, for example, a large amount of useful source code in the .NET releases, including a full C compiler. Partly due to the surprising success of Linux, more and more products are available as source code, and this trend will make compiler and parser development a growth field in the future.

In this book, I've shown you an extremely Basic approach towards compiler design theory. I do not want to give the impression that this is all you need to know. However, I have seen the power of a low-level, grassroots parser in simplifying a genuine user problem, and this motivated me to write this book.

The technology we use every day should not be a sort of mystery accessible only to a temple priesthood; this has always tended to retard and even reverse progress. Although we need to use each other's production, it is nevertheless good to know how things work. I demur from the Dilbert philosophy, that we should not worry our pretty, little heads about what goes on under the hood of society or its technology, and instead take our anger out on hard-working middle managers for doing their rather thankless job (of herding polecats and losing golf games with the CEO). In fact (and as Krishna admonishes Arjuna in the qbGUI Easter egg), knowledge is freedom, for the man or woman who knows the relations between the forces of nature is no longer their slave. A compiler, although a mathematical artifact, is part of nature. The rest is television.

quickBasicEngine Language Manual

Then anyone who leaves behind him a written manual, and likewise anyone who receives it, in the belief that such writing will be clear and certain, must be exceedingly simple-minded.
—Plato

Plato was wrong. The attitude expressed has caused a lot of mystification and a lot of damage. French philosopher Jacques Derrida has shown how Plato's preference for speech over writing (which includes as a subcase the automatic preference for tutorials "for dummies" over reference manuals) runs through our culture as a presumption that results in prejudice against a well-meaning reference manual.

But because real programmers (who Plato might consider Sophists) prefer reference manuals for many purposes, this appendix forms the comprehensive reference manual for the programming language that is actually supported by quickBasicEngine. This appendix describes the low-level lexical syntax supported by quickBasicEngine, the keywords and system functions of this language, and the parser syntax in Backus-Naur Form (BNF). It then identifies each of the built-in functions supported by quickBasicEngine.

> **NOTE** *The language of* quickBasicEngine *supports only a subset of the QuickBasic language, with extensions including the* AndOr *and* OrElse *operators. Also,* QuickBasic *remains, as a name and as a product, the intellectual property of Microsoft. QuickBasic, in other words, refers to the language that was supported by Microsoft's QuickBASIC for MS-DOS and Windows.* quickBasicEngine *(expressed in camelCase) refers to the .NET object that supports a dialect of QuickBasic, where a dialect of a language is a language that overlaps it, containing most of its features (but not necessarily all) and extensions.*

Lexical Syntax

Input for quickBasicEngine consists of the string containing either an executable program or expression. This string may contain blanks, tabs, and tokens. Outside strings and comments, blanks and tabs are ignored. This string may consist of multiple lines, and line breaks (see the newline token in Table A-1) are significant. There is no limit on the length of a line.

Table A-1 lists the supported token types.

Table A-1. Token Types Supported by quickBasicEngine

Token	Notes
Identifiers	Identifiers must start with a letter but may contain digits, the underscore, and letters. There is no limit on the length of identifiers. Some tokens, including Mod (division remainder), have the form of identifiers but are recognized later by the parser as operators.
Operators	The operators supported are +, -, *, /, \ (integer division). Note that the Mod operator is, from the point of view of lexical syntax, an identifier.
Apostrophe	The single quote is recognized as a separate token.
Ampersand	The ampersand is recognized as a separate token.
Numbers	Numbers may be integers with or without a leading plus or sign, or floating-point numbers in the form *<sign> <mantissaInteger>* . *<mantissaDecimal>* (e|E) *<exponentSign> exponent*.
Strings	Strings must be surrounded by double quotes. If they contain double quotes, the inner double quotes must be repeated once. Note that in addition to straight double quotes, Word "smart quotes" may also be used.
Newline	A logical newline separates distinct statements. This is either a colon (allowing multiple statements to occur on the same line) or a carriage return and linefeed (or a linefeed by itself) *not* preceded by a space and an underscore.
Parentheses	The left and right round parentheses characters.
Semicolon	
Percent sign	
Exclamation point	
Pound sign	
Dollar sign	
Period	

Keywords and System Functions

Table A-2 lists the names that cannot be used in source code to identify data because their meaning is predetermined. Note the following:

- You may actually be able to get away with using these names in certain contexts because these names are checked in certain contexts and not others.

- Some names might be problematic even though they do not appear in this list. This applies to names not listed, but, like Option, perform a syntax role.

> **TIP** *The best policy is to use Hungarian names that start with an abbreviation (normally three characters long) for all data. Languages, including Basic, that rely on keywords with identifier syntax have a slight inherent ambiguity because the identifier syntax overlaps that of the keyword.*

Table A-2. quickBasicEngine Keywords and System Functions

Abs	And	AndAlso	Apostrophe	As	Asc
Boolean	ByRef	ByVal	Byte	Ceil	Chr
Circle	Colon	Comma	Cos	Data	Dim
Do	Double	Else	End	EndIf	Eval
Exit	False	Floor	For	Function	GoSub
GoTo	If	Iif	Input	Int	Integer
Isnumeric	Lbound	Lcase	Left	Len	Let
Like	Log	Long	Loop	Max	Mid
Min	Next	Not	Or	OrElse	Print
Randomize	Read	Rem	Replace	Return	Right
Rnd	Screen	Sgn	Sin	Single	Step
Stop	String	Sub	Tab	Then	To
Trace	Trim	True	Until	Ubound	Ucase
Until	Variant	While	Wend		

Parser Syntax (Backus-Naur Form)

The following shows the BNF of the quickBasicEngine.

> **NOTE** *Over and above the standard disclaimer of warranty concerning my compiler as a whole, which is pretty sleazy but necessary in the time available, I should also mention that a downside of the manual method of production of parsers is that I may have made mistakes such that the following syntax fails to correspond to the parser. Therefore, the following reference material may contain errors. Please let me know if you find errors, and I will fix them and make the corrections available from the Downloads section of the Apress Web site (http://www.apress.com). I'm sorry to say that I can't afford to offer you a reward for your help, besides my acknowledgment at the Web site.*

```
' --- Compiler input
compilerInput := sourceProgram | immediateCommand
' --- Immediate commands
immediateCommand := singleImmediateCommand (":" singleImmediateCommand)*
singleImmediateCommand := expression | explicitAssignment
' --- Source programs
sourceProgram := optionStmt
sourceProgram := sourceProgramBody
sourceProgram := optionStmt logicalNewline sourceProgramBody
optionStmt := Option ( "Base" ("0" | "1") ) | Explicit | Extension
sourceProgramBody := ( openCode | moduleDefinition ) +
openCode := statement [ logicalNewline sourceProgram ]
logicalNewline := Newline | Colon
statement := [UnsignedInteger | identifier Colon ] statementBody
statementBody := ctlStatementBody | unconditionalStatementBody |
                 assignmentStmt
ctlStatementBody := dim |
                    doHeader |
                    else |
                    endIf |
                    forHeader |
                    forNext |
                    if |
                    whileHeader |
                    loopOrWend
unconditionalStatementBody := circle |
                              comment |
                              data |
```

```
                                    end |
                                    exit |
                                    goSub |
                                    goto |
                                    input |
                                    print |
                                    randomize |
                                    read |
                                    return |
                                    screen |
                                    stop |
                                    trace
' --- The statements
' Assignment
assignmentStmt := explicitAssignment | implicitAssignment
explicitAssignment := Let implicitAssignment
implicitAssignment := lValue "=" expression
lValue := typedIdentifier [ "(" subscriptList ")" ]
subscriptList := expression [ Comma subscriptList ]
' Circle
circle := Circle ( expression Comma expression ) Comma expression
' Comment: note: NoNewLine is text that does not contain a newline
comment := Rem NoNewLine
comment := Apostrophe NoNewLine
comment := EmptyLine
' Data statement
data := Data constantList
constantList := constantValue [ Comma constantList ]
constantValue := number | string
number := [ sign ] unsignedNumber
sign := "+" | "-"
unsignedNumber := UnsignedInteger | UnsignedRealNumber
integer := [ sign ] UnsignedInteger
' Dim
dim := Dim dimDefinition
dimDefinition := identifier [ ( boundList ) ] [ asClause ]
asClause := As typeName
typeName := Boolean | Byte | Integer | Long | Single | Double | String | Variant
boundList := bound [ Comma boundList ]
bound := integer [ To integer ]
' Do loop header
doHeader := Do [ doCondition ]
' Do loop closure
doLoop := Loop [ doCondition ]
```

```
' Do condition
doCondition := While | Until expression
' else
else := Else
' End statement
end := End ' (followed immediately by newline)
' endIf
endIf := End If
endIf := EndIf
exit := Exit [ Do | For | While ]
' For header
forHeader := For lValue "=" expression To expression [ Step expression ]
' For next
forNext := Next lValue
' GoSub
goSub := GoSub (UnsignedInteger | identifier | expression )
' GoTo
goto := GoTo (UnsignedInteger | identifier | expression )
goto := UnsignedInteger
' If
if := If expression [ Then ] unconditionalStatementBody
if := If expression Then
' Input
input := Input lValueList
lValueList := lValue [ Comma lValue ]
' Loop or Wend
loopOrWend := Wend | ( Loop [ whileUntilClause ] )
whileUntilClause := ( WHILE | UNTIL ) expression
' Print
print := Print expressionList [ ";" ]
expressionList := expression [ Comma expressionList ]
' Randomize
randomize := Randomize
' Read data
read := Read lValueList
' Return from a GoSub
return := Return
' SCREEN n command (does nothing)
screen := Screen UnsignedInteger
' Stop
stop := Stop
' Trace
trace := "Trace Push"
trace := "Trace Off"
```

```
trace := "Trace Text"
          ("Source"|"Memory"|"Stack"|"Inst"|"Object"|"Line"|
           UnsignedInteger|
           "NoBox")*
trace := "Trace Headsup" ("Inst"|"Line"|UnsignedInteger)*
trace := "Trace HeadsupText"
          ( "Source" |"Memory" |"Stack" |"Inst" |"Object" |"Line" |
            UnsignedInteger | "NoBox" )*
trace := Trace Pop
' While loop header
whileHeader := While expression
' Do loop closure
wend := Wend
' --- Expressions
expression := orFactor [ orOp expression ]
orOp := Or
orOp := OrElse
orFactor := andFactor [ andOp orFactor ]
andOp := And
andOp := AndAlso
andFactor := [ Not ] notFactor
notFactor := likeFactor [notFactorRHS]
notFactorRHS := Like likeFactor [notFactorRHS]
likeFactor := concatFactor [likeFactorRHS]
likeFactorRHS := "&" concatFactor [likeFactorRHS]
concatFactor := relFactor [concatFactorRHS]
concatFactorRHS := relOp relFactor [concatFactorRHS]
relFactor := addFactor [ relFactorRHS ]
relFactorRHS := relOp relFactor [ relFactorRHS ]
addFactor := mulFactor [addFactorRHS]
addFactorRHS := mulOp mulFactor [addFactorRHS]
mulFactor := powFactor [mulFactorRHS]
mulFactorRHS := powOp powFactor [mulFactorRHS]
powFactor := ("+" | "-")* term
term := unsignedNumber |
        string |
        lValue |
        True |
        False |
        functionCall |
        ( expression )
functionCall := functionName "(" expressionList ")"
functionName := Abs | Asc | Ceil | Chr | Cos | Eval |
                Evaluate | Floor | Int |
```

293

```
                    Iif | Isnumeric | Lbound | Lcase | Left | Len |
                    Log | Max | Min | Mid | Replace | Right | Rnd |
                    Run | Sin | Sgn | String | Tab |
                    Trim | Ubound | Ucase
unsignedNumber:= ( UnsignedRealNumber | UnsignedInteger )
                    [ numTypeChar ]
typedIdentifier := identifier [ typeSuffix ]
typeSuffix := numTypeChar | CurrencySymbol
numTypeChar := PERCENT | AMPERSAND | EXCLAMATION | POUNDSIGN
identifier := Letter LettersNumbersUnderscores
string := DoubleQuote AnythingExceptDoubleQuote DoubleQuote
relOp := "<" | ">" | "=" | "<=" | ">=" | "=" | "<>"
addOp := "+"|"-"
mulOp := "*"|"/"|"\"|"Mod"
powOp := "**"|"^"
' --- Subroutines and functions
moduleDefinition := subDefinition | functionDefinition
subDefinition := Sub identifier [ formalParameterList ]
                    openCode logicalNewline "End" [ "Sub" ]
functionDefinition := Function identifier [ formalParameterList ]
                        openCode logicalNewline "End" [ "Function" ]
formalParameterList := ( formalParameterListBody )
formalParameterListBody := formalParameterDef
                             [ "," formalParameterListBody ]
formalParameterDef := [ ByVal | ByRef ] identifier ["()"] asClause
```

Built-In Functions

Table A-3 lists the quickBasicEngine built-in functions and describes their use.

Table A-3: The quickBasicEngine Functions

Function	Description
Abs(n)	Returns the absolute value of the number n, which is n when n is greater than or equal to 0, or $-n$ when n is less than zero.
Asc(c)	Returns the numeric code of the ASCII character c.
Ceil(n)	Returns the smallest integer that is greater than or equal to n. Note that when n is negative, this will still return the smallest integer greater than or equal to n; for example, while ceil(2.05) is 3, ceil(-2.05) is –2.
Chr(n)	Returns the character with the ASCII value in n as a string.
Cos(x)	Returns the cosine of x.

Table A-3: The quickBasicEngine Functions (continued)

Function	Description
Eval(*s*)	Evaluates the string *s* considered as an expression that is acceptable to quickBasicEngine. The evaluation is performed using the default properties of the quickBasicEngine class.
Evaluate(*s*)	Evaluates the string *s* considered as an expression that is acceptable to quickBasicEngine. The evaluation is performed using the properties of the quickBasicEngine instance performing the Evaluate function.
Floor(*n*)	Returns the largest integer that is less than or equal to *n*. Note that when *n* is negative, this will still return the largest integer greater than or equal to *n*; for example, while floor(2.05) is 2, floor(-2.05) is –3.
Iif(*a*,*b*,*c*)	Evaluates the expression in *a*. If the value is True (any number other than zero), returns the value of the expression in b. If the value is False (0), returns the value of the expression in *c*. Note that whether *a* is True or False, this function will fully evaluate the *b* and the *c* expressions.
Int(*n*)	Returns the value of *n*, rounded to the closest integer.
Isnumeric(*s*)	Returns True when *s* is any number; False otherwise.
Lbound(*a*)	Returns the lower bound of the array *a*.
Lcase(*s*)	Converts the string in *s* to lowercase.
Left(*s*, *n*)	Returns the substring of *n* characters in *s* commencing at position 1.
Len(*s*)	Returns the length of the string *s*.
Log(*s*)	Returns the natural logarithm of *s*.
Max(*n*, *m*)	Returns the larger of *n* and *m*.
Mid(*s*, *n*, *L*)	Returns the substring of characters in s commencing at position *n* for a length of *L*. If *L* is omitted, returns the substring of characters in *s*, commencing at position *n* and proceeding to the end of the string.
Min(*n*, *m*)	Returns the smaller of *n* and *m*.
Replace(*s*, *t*, *r*)	In the string *s*, replaces all occurrences of the target string *t* with the replacement string *r*.
Right(*s*, *n*)	Returns the substring of *n* characters in *s* commencing at position Len(s) – *n* +1 and ending at the end of *s*.

Table A-3: The quickBasicEngine Functions (continued)

Function	Description
Rnd	Returns a random value in the interval 0..1.
Run(*s*)	Where *s* consists of one or more executable commands, this function runs these commands. Their output, if any, will consist of printEvents. These printEvents will be available to the code that executes the Run function. In addition, the value of this function will be the value it leaves on the stack. If the stack on exit from this function is empty, the value of this function will be Nothing. The execution will use the options and settings of the quickBasicEngine instance that runs the Run command.
Sin(*x*)	Returns the sine of *x*.
Sgn(*x*)	Returns the "signum" of *x*, where the signum of *x* is 1 when $x > 0$; the signum of *x* is 0 when x = 0; and, the signum of *x* is –1 when $x < 0$.
String(*c*, *n*)	Creates *n* copies of the character *c*.
Tab	Returns the tab character.
Trim(*s*)	Removes trailing and leading spaces from the string *s*.
Ubound(*a*)	Returns the upper bound of the array *a*.

quickBasicEngine Reference Manual

We have to be simple simply for lack of time
—Jacques Derrida

This appendix documents the properties and methods (known jointly as the procedures) exposed by quickBasicEngine, as well as its references, with the exception of the utility DLLs: utility, windowsUtilities, collectionUtilities, and zoom. Full documentation of the utility DLLs is available in the source code for these tools.

We should be as simple as possible, but no simpler (as Al Einstein said) in the time available, as the French philosopher Jacques Derrida implies.

This is the original design document for the compiler. When I sit down to code, I first write a design document. It was kept up to date while coding, and even after flooding my laptop with a Starbuck's vente.

This document describes the standards followed by each class and the procedures exposed by each class. The following classes are described:

- qbOp

- qbPolish

- qbScanner

- qbToken

- qbTokenType

- qbVariable

- qbVariableType

- quickBasicEngine

This appendix is useful if you need to understand the compiler in detail or use its components. For example, the `qbScanner` object can be used to scan any language that is lexically the same as the language supported by `quickBasicEngine`.

Class Standards

Properties of each class start with an uppercase letter; methods start with a lowercase letter. Any method, which does not otherwise return a value, will return `True` on success or `False` on failure.

All classes except `qbOp` and `qbtokentype` have state in the form of variables in `General Declarations` that persist between procedures but which goes away when the class is destroyed. *Stateful* (as opposed to *stateless*) classes can be usable or not usable.

During the execution of the constructor procedure for the stateful class, it is unusable. On successful completion of the constructor, the class object instance becomes usable, and it remains usable until the class is disposed (or otherwise terminated) or a serious internal error is found. Serious internal errors include bugs in the code of the object, whether from errors in the original code or through modification, and "object abuse" (the use of the object after a serious error has been discovered and reported). When the object is not usable, most Public properties and methods will report an error when called and return a suitable default value.

All classes implement an informal interface known as the core methodology. It is informal because classes don't implement a file containing procedures in the methodology; instead, they tend to implement the core procedures shown in Table B-1 consistently.

Table B-1. Class Core Procedures

Procedure	Description
About	Shared, read-only property implemented to provide information about the class.
ClassName	Shared, read-only property implemented to provide the name of the class.
dispose	Method implemented to cleanly dispose all reference objects in the object state and mark the object as unusable.
inspect	Method implemented to test a series of assertions about object state, and to raise an error condition and mark the object unusable when any assertion fails.
mkUnusable	Method implemented to mark the object as not usable.

Table B-1. Class Core Procedures (continued)

Procedure	Description
Name	Read-write property implemented to assign and return an object instance name for identifying the object on debugging reports and elsewhere. By default, the object name will be *classNamennnn date time*, where *nnnn* is the object sequence number.
object2XML	Method implemented to return the state of the object as an XML tag.
toString	Method implemented to serialize part of the object's state and value.
Tag	Read-write property implemented to assign and return user data that is associated with the object in a specific application. Tag can be a reference object. If so, it is treated as an honored guest by its host object. While objects in this suite rather remorselessly destroy their own reference variables when they are destroyed in a form of electronic *suttee*, the Tag object isn't destroyed.
test	Method implemented by some objects as a self-test. It runs a series of tests on the object while placing the result in a strReport parameter passed by reference. In most cases, the test methods will either create an internal test object (so that tests do not disrupt the main object) or provide the option to control this.
Usable	Read-only property implemented to return True when the object is usable; False otherwise

The stateless object qbOp is of necessity fully threadable; multiple copies may run in multiple threads, and all procedures are Shared (Static in C# terms). Other than the qbOp object, the other objects are serially threadable. Multiple copies may coexist in parallel threads, but the same copy cannot run more than one non-Shared method in the same thread. quickBasicEngine is stateful but fully threadable.

Each serially threadable object organizes its state into a structure with the name TYPstate and an instance of the TYPstate called USRstate. quickBasicEngine, because it is fully threadable, organizes its state into an OBJstate object, which contains the USRstate. This makes it much easier to lock the state using Synclock.

Note that each method that doesn't otherwise need to return a value is nonetheless coded as a Boolean function, and returns True on success and False on an error. Although this standard produces, at times, some strange code (such as functions that always return True), it is maintained for consistency.

qbOp

The qbOp stateless class identifies the operators supported by the non-CLR Nutty Professor machine as a large enumerator, and it provides Shared conversion tools for enumerator values.

qbOp includes references to utilities.DLL.

qbOp is stateless and is fully threadable. Multiple instances can run simultaneously in multiple threads, and multiple procedures may be executed in the same instance in multiple threads.

Properties and Methods of qbOp

Table B-2 lists the properties and methods of the qbOp class.

Table B-2. qbOp Properties and Methods

Property/Method	Description
Public Shared ReadOnly Property About As String	Shared, read-only property that returns information about the class.
Public Shared ReadOnly Property ClassName As String	Shared, read-only property that returns the class name qbOp.
Public Shared Function isJumpOp (ByVal enuOpcode As ENUop) As Boolean	Shared, read-only property that returns True when the operator is a jump operator; False otherwise. Used to detect operators that include a label that the assembler must resolve.
Public Shared Function opCodeFromString(ByVal strOpcode As String) As ENUop	Shared method that returns the opcode enumerator for the opcode, where strOpcode is the case-independent op name.
Public Overloads Shared Function opCodeToDescription (ByVal strOpcode As String) As String	Shared method that returns the opcode's description, where strOpcode is an opcode specified as a string. The description will be in the format op(template): text. The template describes what the opcode requires on the stack. See the "Stack Template" section following this table.

Table B-2. qbOp Properties and Methods (continued)

Property/Method	Description
`Public Overloads Shared Function opCodeToDescription (ByVal enuOpcode As ENUop) As String`	Shared method that returns the opcode's description, where enuOpcode is an opcode specified as an opcode enumerator. The description will be in the format *op(template): text*. The template describes what the opcode requires on the stack. See the "Stack Template" section following this table.
`Public Shared Function opCodeToStackTemplate(ByVal enuOpcode As ENUop) As String`	Shared method that returns the template of expected operands for this opcode, where enuOpcode is an opcode specified as an enumerator. See the "Stack Template" section following this table for a description of the template.
`Public Shared Function opCodeToString(ByVal enuOpcode As ENUop) As String`	Shared method that returns the opcode's name only.

Stack Template

The template describes what an opcode requires on the stack. The template is a string containing the comma-separated list of expected stack values, from lower down in the stack to the top of the stack. The template is defined inside the op description statement in the `opCodeToDescription` method.

Each stack value must be one of the following:

- x: Any qbVariable is permitted at this position.

- s: Any scalar qbVariable is permitted.

- n: Any numeric qbVariable is permitted.

- i: Any numeric integer qbVariable is permitted.

- u: Operator expects the utility stack frame: stack(top) is an operand count: stack(top+1) is the name of a utility: stack(top+n+1)..stack(top+2) are the operands.

- <name>: Where *name* is the name of one of the values of the ENUvarType enumerator, this specifies that the stack value is restricted to the varType.

- a: An array index frame is expected at this location, in the form i(1), i(2)...i(n), *Count, array*, where i(*n*) is the index at dimension *n, Count* is the number of preceding indexes, and *array* is a qbVariable with the type array.

qbPolish

The qbPolish class represents one instruction to our non-CLR Nutty Professor machine.

References of qbPolish are qbOp.DLL, qbVariable.DLL, and utilities.DLL.

qbPolish is serially threadable. Multiple instances can run simultaneously in multiple threads, but errors will result if one object's procedures run in multiple threads and in parallel.

The qbPolish Instruction Data Model and State

The state of this class consists of an opcode, an operand, a comment, an index back to the source code responsible for the instruction (as stored by the qbScanner object inside qbParser), and the length of the source code.

The state of each qbPolish instance, which represents one instruction to the Nutty Professor machine, consists of the following.

- strName: Object instance name

- booUsable: Object usability switch

- enuOpCode: Operation code (see Chapter 8 for a list of the supported opcodes)

- enuOperand: Operand, which should be a .NET scalar

- strComment: Commentary about this instruction, which is set by the Comment property

- intStartIndex: Start index of the source code responsible for this instruction

- intLength: Length of the source code responsible for this instruction

qbPolish Inspection Rules

The following inspection rules are used by the `inspect` method as a check on errors in the source code, whether as delivered or as changed, or due to object abuse in the form of using the object after a serious user error has occurred:

- The object instance must be usable.

- The operation code can't be the Invalid enumerator value.

- The start index corresponding to the operation in the source code must be 1 or greater.

- The length of the source code corresponding to the operation must be 0 or greater.

- If the inspection fails, the object becomes unusable.

An internal inspection is carried out in the constructor (after the object construction steps are complete) and in the `dispose` method (before the reference objects in the state are disposed of).

Properties and Methods of the qbPolish Class

Table B-3 lists the properties and methods of the `qbPolish` class.

Table B-3. qbPolish Properties and Methods

Property/Method	Description
`Public Shared ReadOnly Property About As String`	Shared, read-only property that returns information about this class.
`Public Shared ReadOnly Property ClassName As String`	Shared, read-only property that returns the name of the class (qbPolish).
`Public Property Comment As String`	Read-write property that can define and return comments about the operation suitable for the assembler listing.
`Public Function dispose As String`	Method that disposes of the object and cleans up any reference objects in the heap. This method marks the object as unusable. For best results, use this method when you are finished using the object in code.

Table B-3. qbPolish Properties and Methods (continued)

Property/Method	Description
Public Function inspect(ByVal strReport As String) As Boolean	Method that inspects the object, checking for errors that result from blunders in the source code of this class or object abuse, not simple user errors. The report parameter should be a string, passed by reference; it is assigned an inspection report. See the "qbPolish Inspection Rules" section preceding this table.
Public Function mkUnusable As Boolean	Method that forces the object instance into the unusable state; it always returns True.
Public Property Name() As String	Read-write property that returns and can set the name of the object instance, which will identify the object in error messages and on the XML tag that is returned by object2XML. The name defaults to qbPolish*nnnn date time*, where *nnnn* is a sequence number.
Public Overloads Function object2XML() As String	Method that converts the state of the object to XML.
Public Overloads Function object2XML(ByVal booHeaderComment As Boolean) As String	Optional overload of object2XML that controls the commenting of the XML strings that are returned: object2XML(False) returns XML with no header comment.
Public Overloads Function object2XML(ByVal booHeaderComment As Boolean, ByVal booLineComments As Boolean) As String	Optional overload of object2XML that controls the commenting of the XML strings that are returned. The booHeaderComment parameter controls the generation of the block header comment. The booLineComments parameter controls the generation of a line of explanatory comment for each XML element.
Public Property Opcode() As ENUopcode	Read-write property that returns and can assign the instruction's opcode as one of the names listed in Chapter 8. See also opcodeFromString and opcodeToString.

Table B-3. qbPolish Properties and Methods (continued)

Property/Method	Description
Public Function opcodeFromString (ByVal strOpcode As String) As Boolean	Method that assigns the opcode from its name. It can be used instead of the Opcode property when the enumerator name is undefined in your project.
Public Overloads Shared Function opcodeToDescription As String	Shared method that obtains the description of the opcode.
Public Function opcodeToString() As String	Method that returns the opcode as a string. It can be used instead of the Opcode property when the enumerator name is undefined in your project.
Public Property Operand() As Object	Read-write property that returns and can change the Polish operand.
Public Property TokenLength() As Integer	Read-write property that returns and can change the length, in tokens, of the source code responsible for the Polish instruction.
Public Property TokenStartIndex() As Integer	Read-write property that returns and can change the token index from 1 of the source code responsible for the Polish instruction.
Public Function toString() As String	Method that converts the Polish operation to a string in the format *op operand: comment.* The string is always suitable for display; in particular, the operand is converted to a number or a quoted string.
Public ReadOnly Property Usable() As Boolean	Read-only property that returns True if the object instance is usable; False otherwise.

qbScanner

The qbScanner class scans input source code for the quickBasicEngine and provides, on demand, scanned source tokens and scanned lines of source code. This class uses "lazy" evaluation, scanning the source code only when necessary and when an unparsed token is requested.

References of qbScanner include collectionUtilities.DLL, qbToken.DLL, qbTokenType.DLL, and utilities.DLL.

qbScanner is serially threadable. Multiple instances can run simultaneously in multiple threads, but errors will result if one object's procedures run in multiple threads and in parallel.

The qbScanner class is ICloneable and IComparable; see its clone and compareTo methods in Table B-4.

The compareTo and normalize methods make format-independent comparison of source code possible. compareTo will ignore white space when comparing two scanned source code strings, and normalize will reduce white space to a standard form in preparation for comparing source code strings.

The qbScanner Data Model and State

The state of this class consists of raw source code, and a series of qbTokens indexed commencing at the start of the input code and accounting for all characters of source code, comments, and white space. See qbToken.vb for the data model of the token itself.

The state of the scanner consists of the following:

- strName: Object instance name

- booUsable: Object usability switch

- strSourceCode: Input source code

- intLast: Index of the last token parsed or zero when no tokens have been parsed

- objQBtoken(): Array of scanned qbTokens

- objQBtoken(): Array of pending qbTokens, maintained during the lookahead scan (see Chapter 5)

- intLineNumber: Current line number

- colLineIndex: Collection, relates line numbers to character positions. Its key is _lineNumber (underscore followed by a line number). Each entry contains a subcollection with two items: item(1) is the line number, and item(2) is the start index, from 1, of this line number.

- booScanned: Indicates whether the strSourceCode has been completely scanned

qbScanner Inspection Rules

The following inspection rules are used by the inspect method as a check on errors in the source code, whether as delivered or as changed, or due to object abuse in the form of using the object after a serious user error has occurred:

- The object instance must be usable.

- Each token in both the array of scanned tokens and the array of pending tokens must pass the inspect procedure of qbToken.

- The tokens in the scanned array must be in ascending order; gaps are acceptable but not overlaps.

- No token's end index may point beyond the end of the source code in either the scanned array or the pending array.

- The line number must be greater than or equal to 0.

- The format of the line number index collection positive integers must be valid. This is a collection of three-item subcollections. Item(1) must be a string containing the key of the index entry. Item(2) and item(3) must be positive integers. Item(2) cannot be zero.

- If the (nonnull) code is fully scanned, the first token's start index should be the same as the position of the first nonblank character in the source code. The last token's end index should be the same as the position of the last nonblank character.

- If the code is null and indicated as fully scanned, the scan count must be empty.

An internal inspection is carried out in the constructor (after the object construction steps are complete) and the dispose method (before the reference objects in the state are disposed). Note that the dispose inspection may be suppressed using the overload dispose(False).

Properties, Methods, and Events of the qbScanner Class

Table B-4 lists the properties, methods, and events of the qbScanner class.

Table B-4. qbScanner Properties, Methods, and Events

Property/Method/Event	Description
`Public Shared ReadOnly Property About As String`	Shared, read-only property that returns information about this class.
`Public Overloads Function checkToken (ByRef intIndex As Integer, ByVal strValueExpected As String, Optional ByVal intEndIndex As Integer = 0) As Boolean`	Method that checks the scanned tokens for strValueExpected. If it finds the expected value, it increments a token index. intIndex should be an Integer, passed by reference. The scan token at this index is checked. On success, this integer is incremented; on failure, it is unchanged. strValueExpected is compared to the source code, disregarding case differences. The optional parameter intEndIndex can be used to restrict the check to all tokens up to and including the token at the specified end index. See also checkTokenByTypeName.
`Public Overloads Function checkToken (ByRef intIndex As Integer, ByVal enuTypeExpected As qbTokenType. qbTokenType.ENUtokenType, Optional ByVal intEndIndex As Integer = 0) As Boolean`	Method that checks the scanned tokens for the type in enuTypeExpected. If it finds the expected token type, it increments a token index. intIndex should be an Integer, passed by reference. The scan token type at this index is checked. On success this integer will be incremented. The optional parameter intEndIndex can be used to restrict the check to all tokens up to and including the token the specified end index. See also checkTokenByTypeName.
`Public Overloads Function checkTokenByTypeName(ByRef intIndex As Integer, ByVal strTypeExpected As String, Optional ByVal intEndIndex As Integer = 0) As Boolean`	Method that checks the scanned tokens for strValueExpected. If it finds the expected token type (identified using its name), it increments a token index. intIndex should be an Integer, passed by reference. The scan token type at this index is checked. On success, this integer is incremented. The optional parameter intEndIndex can be used to restrict the check to all tokens up to and including the token the specified end index. See also checkToken.
`Public Function clear As Boolean`	Method that clears the source code and resets the scan.

Table B-4. qbScanner Properties, Methods, and Events (continued)

Property/Method/Event	Description
`Public Function clone As qbScanner`	Method that makes a clone of the scanner object. The clone is guaranteed only to have the same source code that will tokenize to the same source code and contain the same white space patterns. The clone, when passed to the `compareTo` method as exposed by the source object, returns `True`. This method implements `ICloneable`.
`Public Function compareTo(ByVal objScanner As qbScanner) As Boolean`	Method that compares the object instance with the scanner object passed in `objScanner`, returning `True` when the source code in the instance is identical, after tokenization, to the object code. The source code in the instance may have a different white space pattern from the source code in `objScanner`. The `qbScanner` clone always produces an object that returns `True` when compared to the source. (All objects that compare to a given object are token-identical, but not all are clones, because a clone will be white-space-identical in addition to being token-identical.) This method implements `IComparable`.
`Public Overloads Function dispose As String`	Method that disposes of the object and cleans up any reference objects in the heap. This method marks the object as unusable. This overload will always conduct an internal inspection of the object instance (using the `inspect` method), and an error is thrown if the inspection failed. For best results, use this method when you are finished using the object in code. See the next method for an overload that allows inspection to be skipped.
`Public Overloads Function dispose (ByVal booInspect As Boolean) As String`	Method that disposes of the object and cleans up any reference objects in the heap. This method marks the object as unusable. This overload inspects the object instance, unless `dispose(False)` is used. For best results, use this method when you are finished using the object in code.

Table B-4. qbScanner Properties, Methods, and Events (continued)

Property/Method/Event	Description
`Public Function findRightParenthesis (ByVal intIndex As Integer, Optional ByVal intEndIndex As Integer = 0) As Integer`	Method that searches for a balancing right parenthesis at the scanner position in i. On success, it returns the index of the token containing the right parenthesis. On failure, it returns one index past the last parenthesis with no other error indication. `intIndex` should normally point one character to the right of the left parenthesis to be balanced. The optional parameter `intEndIndex` can be used to restrict the search to all tokens up to and including the token at the specified end index.
`Public Overloads Function findToken (ByVal intIndex As Integer, ByVal strValueExpected As String, Optional ByVal intEndIndex As Integer = 0) As Integer`	Method that searches the scanned tokens left to right, starting at `intIndex`, for the expected value in `strValueExpected`, ignoring case differences. If it finds the expected value, it returns the scan index of the token. If it does not find the expected value, it returns 0. The optional parameter `intEndIndex` can be used to restrict the search to the token up to and including the token at the specified end index.
`Public Overloads Function findToken (ByVal intIndex As Integer, ByVal enuTypeExpected As qbTokenType. qbTokenType.ENUtokenType, Optional ByVal intEndIndex As Integer = 0) As Integer`	Method that searches the scanned tokens left to right, starting at `intIndex` for the expected token type. If it finds the expected type, it returns the scan index of the token. If it does not find the expected type, it returns 0. The optional parameter `intEndIndex` can be used to restrict the search to the token up to and including the token at the specified end index.
`Public Overloads Function findToken ByTypeName(ByVal intIndex As Integer, ByVal strTypeExpected As String, Optional ByVal intEndIndex As Integer = 0) As Integer`	Method that searches the scanned tokens left right, starting at `intIndex`, for the expected type named in `strTypeExpected`, ignoring case differences. If it finds the expected value, it returns the scan index of the token. If it does not find the expected value, it returns 0. The optional parameter `intEndIndex` can be used to restrict the search to the token up to and including the token at the specified end index.
`Public Function inspect(ByRef strReport As String) As Boolean`	Method that inspects the object. The report parameter should be a string, passed by reference; it is assigned an inspection report. See the "qbScanner Inspection Rules" section preceding this table.

Table B-4. qbScanner Properties, Methods, and Events (continued)

Property/Method/Event	Description
`Public Shared Function isInteger(ByVal strInstring As String) As Boolean`	Shared method that returns True when strInstring is an unsigned integer in the syntactical sense of containing no sign, no decimal part (including no 0 decimal part as in 1.0), and no exponent (including no meaningless exponent as in .1e0.).
`Public ReadOnly Property Line(ByVal intLine As Integer) As String`	Indexed, read-only property that returns the source code contained in the line numbered intLine (numbering starts at 1). Use of this property forces a complete scan. Continuation lines count as distinct lines.
`Public ReadOnly Property LineCount As Integer`	Read-only property that returns the total number of lines in the source code. Use of this property forces a complete scan. Continuation lines count as distinct lines.
`Public ReadOnly Property LineLength (ByVal intLine As Integer) As String`	Indexed, read-only property that returns the length of the source code contained in the line numbered intLine (numbering starts at 1). Use of this property forces a complete scan. Continuation lines count as distinct lines.
`Public ReadOnly Property LineStartIndex(ByVal intLine As Integer) As String`	Indexed, read-only property that returns the character starting index, from 1, of the source code contained in the line numbered intLine (numbering starts at 1). Use of this property forces a complete scan. Continuation lines count as distinct lines.
`Public Function mkUnusable As Boolean`	Method that forces the object instance into the unusable state; it always returns True.
`Public Property Name() As String`	Read-write property that returns and can set the name of the object instance, which identifies the object in error messages and on the XML tag that is returned by object2XML. The name defaults to qbScanner*nnnn date time*, where *nnnn* is a sequence number.

Table B-4. qbScanner Properties, Methods, and Events (continued)

Property/Method/Event	Description
`Public Overloads Function normalize()` `As String`	Method that returns the normalized form of the source code in the object instance.[1] It places one space between each token, and it removes all tokens at the start and end of the source code. It does not change the source code. The output of this method is not especially readable, and it actually inserts unneeded spaces between tokens. However, two normalized source code sequences will be character-identical, which means that normalization is a tool for comparing source code in different formats for logical identity.

`Public Overloads Function object2XML`
`(Optional ByVal booAboutComment As`
`Boolean = True, Optional ByVal`
`booStateComment As Boolean = True)`
`As String`
	Method that converts the state of the object to an XML string. The returned tag includes all source code and parsed tokens, so it may be unmanageably large for large source code files. See the next overload of this method for a way to truncate the source code and/or tokens. Two optional parameters are exposed: `booAboutComment:=False` suppresses a boxed comment at the start of the XML containing the value of this object's `About` property, and `booStateComment:=False` suppresses comments that describe each state value returned.

`Public Overloads Function object2XML`
`(ByVal intSourceTruncation As Integer,`
`ByVal intTokenTruncation As Integer,`
`Optional ByVal booAboutComment As`
`Boolean = True, Optional ByVal`
`booStateComment As Boolean = True)`
`As String`
	Method that converts the state of the object to an XML string. The returned tag includes all source code and all parsed tokens, so it may be unmanageably large for large source code files. Therefore, this overload allows a maximum source length to be specified in `intSourceTruncation`, and/or the maximum number of tokens to be specified in `intTokenTruncation`. Two optional parameters are exposed: `booAboutComment:=False` suppresses a boxed comment at the start of the XML containing the value of the object's `About` property, and `booStateComment:=False` suppresses comments that describe each state value returned.

---

1. Normalization shouldn't be confused with prettyprinting or packing, although it may save space.

Table B-4. qbScanner Properties, Methods, and Events (continued)

Property/Method/Event	Description
`Public ReadOnly Property QBToken(ByVal intIndex As Integer) As qbToken.qbToken`	Indexed, read-only property that returns the indexed scanned token as an object of type qbToken. It will cause a scan of tokens, up to and including token *i*, when the token is not available.
`Public Function reset() As Boolean`	Method that resets the scan. The reset method does not clear the source code; it merely undoes all parsing done prior to the reset. See also the `clear` method.
`Public Overloads Function scan() As Boolean`	Method that resets the scanner object and scans all characters in the source code as set by the SourceCode property.
`Public Overloads Function scan(ByVal strSourceCode As String) As Boolean`	Method that resets the scanner object, sets the SourceCode property to `strSourceCode`, and scans all characters.
`Public Overloads Function scan(ByVal lngEndIndex As Long) As Boolean`	Method that scans existing source code from a previous scan position to `lngEndIndex`, which must be the Long precision end index for the scan (last character to be scanned from 1). The scanner is not reset. Tokens are appended from the source code starting at 1 or the end of the previous scan, until a token that ends at or after `lngEndIndex` is scanned or the end of the source code is scanned, whichever comes first. A previous scan position exists unless the reset method has been executed, where the scan will start at 1. If your end value is not Long, use `CLng(end)` to convert it to the required type to avoid confusion with the overload `scan(intCount)`, which scans a specific number of tokens.
`Public Overloads Function scan(ByVal lngStartIndex As Long, ByVal lngEndIndex As Long) As Boolean`	Method that scans existing source code from `lngStartIndex` to `lngEndIndex`. The scanner is not reset. Tokens are appended from the source code starting at `lngStartIndex` until a token that ends at or after `lngEndIndex` is scanned or the end of the source code is scanned.

Table B-4. qbScanner Properties, Methods, and Events (continued)

Property/Method/Event	Description
`Public Overloads Function scan(ByVal intCount As Integer) As Boolean`	Method that scans existing source code from a previous scan position until `intCount` tokens have been found or the end of the source code is reached. The scanner is not reset. Tokens are appended from the source code starting at the scan position until `intCount` tokens have been scanned. A scan position exists unless the reset method has been executed. Immediately after a reset, the scan position will be 1. If your count value is not Long, use `CInt(count)` to convert it to the required type, to avoid confusion with the overload `scan(lngEndIndex)`, which scans to a specified end index.
`Public Event scanErrorEvent(ByVal strMsg As String, ByVal intIndex As Integer, ByVal intLineNumber As Integer, ByVal strHelp As String)`	Event that occurs when an error is detected by the scanner. `strMsg` is the error message, `intIndex` is the character at which the error was detected, `intLineNumber` is the line number, and `strHelp` contains additional information.[2]
`Public Event scanEvent(ByVal objQBtoken As qbToken.qbToken, ByVal intCharacterIndex As Integer, ByVal intLength As Integer, ByVal intTokenCount As Integer)`	Event that fires at completion of each successful scan of a token; useful for progress reporting. It passes the following to the delegate: `objQBtoken` is the token object (of type qbToken); `intCharacterIndex` is the character index, from 1, of the token; `intLength` is the length of the source code; and `intTokenCount` contains the number of tokens found so far, including this token.
`Public ReadOnly Property Scanned() As Boolean`	Read-only property that returns `True` when the source code has been fully scanned; `False` otherwise.
`Public Property SourceCode() As String`	Read-write property that returns and may be set to the source code for scanning. Assigning source code clears the array of tokens in the object state, but does not result in an immediate scan of the source code. Scanning occurs when the QBToken property is called and the token is not available.
`Public Overloads Function sourceMid (ByVal intStartIndex As Integer) As String`	Method that returns the source code that commences at the token at `intStartIndex` (a token index, not a character index).

---

2. At this writing, the only error detected occurs when unrecognizable characters are found.

Table B-4. qbScanner Properties, Methods, and Events (continued)

Property/Method/Event	Description
`Public Overloads Function sourceMid (ByVal intStartIndex As Integer, ByVal intLength As Integer) As String`	Method that returns the source code that commences at the token at `intStartIndex` and contains `intLength` tokens.
`Public Function test(ByRef strReport As String) As Boolean`	Method that tests the scanner and returns `True` when all tests are passed or `False` when any test fails. The by-reference string parameter r is set on success or failure to a test report. When the test fails, the object is marked unusable.
`Public Shared ReadOnly Property TestString() As String`	Shared, read-only property that returns the test string used in the `test` method. This string tests all tokens for valid results.
`Public Function token(ByVal intIndex1 As Integer) As String`	Method that returns the string value of the token indexed by `intIndex1`, where `intIndex1` is between 1 and `TokenCount`.[3]
`Public ReadOnly Property TokenCount() As Integer`	Read-only property that returns the number of tokens. Calling `TokenCount` causes a complete scan of the source code.
`Public Function tokenEndIndex(ByVal intIndex As Integer) As Integer`	Method that returns the character end index of the token at `intIndex`.
`Public Function tokenLength(ByVal intIndex As Integer) As Integer`	Method that returns the length of the token at `intIndex`.
`Public Function tokenLinenumber(ByVal intIndex As Integer) As Integer`	Method that returns the line number at which the token at `intIndex` starts.
`Public Function tokenStartIndex(ByVal intIndex As Integer) As Integer`	Method that returns the character start index of the token at `intIndex`.
`Public Function tokenType(ByVal intIndex As Integer) As qbTokenType. qbTokenType.ENUtokenType`	Method that returns the type of the token at `intIndex` as an enumerator of type `ENUtokenType`. See the "qbTokenType" section for the possible values of `ENUtokenType` enumerators.
`Public Function tokenTypeAsString (ByVal intIndex As Integer) As String`	Method that returns the type of the token at `intIndex` as a string. See qbTokenType for the possible values of `ENUtokenType` enumerators, which convert directly to string values.

---

3. At this writing, this method will result in a full scan of the input source code.

Table B-4. qbScanner Properties, Methods, and Events (continued)

Property/Method/Event	Description
Public Overloads Overrides Function toString() As String	Method that converts all tokens into a string containing their serialized values separated by newlines. Each value will be in the form `<type>@<startIndex>..<endIndex>: <lineNumber>:<sourceCode>`.
Public Overloads Overrides Function toString(ByVal intStartIndex As Integer) As String	Method that converts all tokens commencing with the token at intStartIndex into a string containing their serialized values separated by newlines. Each value will be in the form `<type>@<startIndex>..<endIndex>: <lineNumber>:<sourceCode>`.
Public Overloads Overrides Function toString(ByVal intStartIndex As Integer, intCount) As String	Method that converts intCount tokens commencing with the token at intStartIndex into a string containing their serialized values separated by newlines. Each value will be in the form `<type>@<startIndex>..<endIndex>: <lineNumber>:<sourceCode>`.
Public ReadOnly Property Usable() As Boolean	Read-only property that returns True if the object instance is usable; False otherwise.

qbToken

The qbToken class defines one scan token as used in quickBasicEngine, including its start index, length, type, and its line number.

References of qbToken include qbTokenType.DLL and utilities.DLL.

qbToken is serially threadable. Multiple instances can run simultaneously in multiple threads, but errors will result if one object's procedures run in multiple threads and in parallel.

The qbToken class is ICloneable: see its clone method.

The Token Data Model

For our purposes, the token consists of the following information: the token type, the start index (from 1) of the token in the source code, the length of the token, and its line number. See the "qbTokenType" section for the token types.

The token data model does not include the value of the token, because this would make the data structures in this class larger, by definition, than the source code. Instead, the user code is expected to use the start index and the length to get the raw source code.

qbToken Inspection Rules

The following inspection rules are used by the `inspect` method as a check on errors in the source code, whether as delivered or as changed, or due to object abuse in the form of using the object after a serious user error has occurred:

- The object instance must be usable.

- The type must be a valid enumerator value, other than Invalid.

- The start index must be greater than or equal to zero.

- The length must be greater than or equal to zero.

- The line number must be zero or greater.

If the inspection fails, the object becomes unusable.

An internal inspection is carried out in the constructor (after the object construction steps are complete) and the `dispose` method (before the reference objects in the state are disposed). The `dispose` inspection may be suppressed using the overload `dispose(False)`.

Properties and Methods of the qbToken Class

Table B-5 lists the properties and methods of the qbToken class.

Table B-5. qbToken Properties and Methods

Property/Method	Description
`Public Shared ReadOnly Property About As String`	Shared, read-only property that returns information about this class.
`Public Shared ReadOnly Property ClassName As String`	Shared, read-only property that returns the name of this class (qbToken).
`Public Function clone() As qbToken`	Method that creates a new and identical token object based on the instance (since tokens are ICloneable).

Table B-5. qbToken Properties and Methods (continued)

Property/Method	Description
`Public Overloads Function dispose As String`	Method that disposes of the object. This method marks the object as unusable.[4] This overload always conducts an internal inspection of the object instance (using the `inspect` method), and an error will be thrown if the inspection is failed. For best results, use this method when you are finished using the object in code. See the next method for an overload that allows inspection to be skipped.
`Public Overloads Function dispose (ByVal booInspect As Boolean) As String`	Method that disposes of the object. This method marks the object as unusable. This overload inspects the object instance unless `dispose(False)` is used. For best results, use this method when you are finished using the object in code.
`Public Property EndIndex() As Integer`	Read-write property that returns and can be set to the ending index, from 1, of the token. Changing this property changes the length of the token. This property is calculated from the start index and length of the token.
`Public Function fromString(ByVal strToString As String) As Boolean`	Method that sets the token to values created by the `toString` method. `strToString` must be in the format `<type>@<startIndex>..<endIndex>:<lineNumber>`. The line number, and the colon preceding the line number, are optional.
`Public Function inspect(ByRef strReport As String) As Boolean`	Method that inspects the object. The report parameter should be a string, passed by reference; it is assigned an inspection report. See "qbToken Inspection Rules" preceding this table.
`Public Property Length As Integer`	Read-write method that returns and may be set to the token length.
`Public Property LineNumber As Integer`	Read-write method that returns and may be set to the number of the line containing the token.
`Public Function mkUnusable As Boolean`	Method that forces the object instance into the unusable state. It always returns `True`.

---

4. In the specific case of qbTokens, at this writing, there are no reference objects in the state for cleanup. The dispose is provided for consistency, to allow for future growth and to mark the object as unusable.

Table B-5. qbToken Properties and Methods (continued)

Property/Method	Description
`Public Property Name() As String`	Read-write property that returns and can set the name of the object instance, which identifies the object in error messages and on the XML tag that is returned by `object2XML`. The name defaults to `qbTokennnnn date time`, where *nnnn* is a sequence number.
`Public Property StartIndex As Integer`	Read-write property that returns and may be set to the starting index, from 1, of the token in the source code. It may be set to 0, usually to indicate a nonexistent token.
`Public Function object2XML As String`	Method that converts the state of the object to an XML string.
`Public Property StartIndex() As Integer`	Read-write property that returns and may be set to the start index of the token in its source code (position numbering is from 1).
`Public ReadOnly Property TokenType() As ENUtokenType`	Read-only property that returns the type of the token as an enumerator of type `ENUtokenType`. For a list of the supported types, see the "qbTokenType" section.
`Public Function tokenTypeMatch (ByVal enuType As ENUtokenType) As Boolean`	Method that matches the token in the instance with `enuType`. It returns `True` when the token types are identical, or when the range of the instance is a part of the range of `enuType`. For example, if the instance is an unsigned real number and `enuType` is "unsigned integer" this method will return `True`.
`Public Function toString() As String`	Method that converts the token state into a string containing its serialized value in the form `<type>@<startIndex>..<endIndex>: <lineNumber>`. This state can always be assigned to a token index using the `fromString` method.
`Public Shared Property TypeCount`	Shared, read-only property that returns the number of distinct types defined, excluding null, invalid, and `ampersandSuffix`.
`Public Shared Property TypeCountActual`	Shared, read-only property that returns the number of distinct types defined, including null, invalid, and `ampersandSuffix`.
`Public Function typeFromString (ByVal strType As String) As Boolean`	Method that sets the type using `strType`, after leading and trailing blanks and case differences are ignored.
`Public Shared Function typeToEnum (ByVal strType As String) As ENUtokenType`	Shared method that returns the distinct `ENUtokenType` identified by a case-insensitive name, from which leading and trailing blanks are removed. If the prefix "`tokenType`" is not provided in `strType`, it will be added.

Table B-5. qbToken Properties and Methods (continued)

Property/Method	Description
Public Shared Function typeToIndex (ByVal strType As String) As Integer	Shared method that returns the distinct index value type identified by a case-insensitive name in `strType`, from which leading and trailing blanks are removed.
Public Function typeToString(ByVal enuType As ENUtokenType) As Integer	Method that returns the string value of the type assigned to the current instance.
Public ReadOnly Property Usable() As Boolean	Read-only property that returns `True` if the object instance is usable; `False` otherwise.

qbTokenType

The `qbTokenType` class merely defines the token types recognized by the `qbScanner` and `qbToken` classes.

Token Types

Table B-6 defines the token types in the `ENUtokenType` enumerator that is exposed by the `qbTokenType` class.

Table B-6. Token Types

Type	Description
tokenTypeAmpersand	Ampersand
tokenTypeApostrophe	Single quote
tokenTypeColon	Colon
tokenTypeComma	Comma
tokenTypeIdentifier	Identifier
tokenTypeNewline	Newline
tokenTypeOperator	Operator
tokenTypeParenthesis	Left or right parenthesis
tokenTypeSemicolon	Semicolon
tokenTypeString	String
tokenTypeUnsignedInteger	Unsigned integer (sign is always an op)
tokenTypeUnsignedRealNumber	Unsigned real number (sign is always an op)

Table B-6. Token Types (continued)

Type	Description
tokenTypePercent	Percent
tokenTypeExclamation	Exclamation point
tokenTypePound	Pound sign
tokenTypeCurrency	Dollar sign
tokenTypePeriod	Period
tokenTypeNull	Null value
tokenTypeInvalid	Invalid
tokenTypeAmpersandSuffix	Ampersand, preceded by an identifier

qbVariable

The qbVariable class represents the type, structure, and value of a quick basic scalar, an *n*-dimensional QuickBasic array, or a user data type.

References of qbVariable include collectionUtilities.DLL, qbScanner.DLL, qbTokenType.DLL, qbVariableType.DLL, and utilities.DLL.

This class implements IDisposable, ICloneable, and IComparable.

qbVariable is serially threadable. Multiple instances can run simultaneously in multiple threads, but errors will result if one object's procedures run in multiple threads and in parallel.

The qbVariable Data Model

Each type of QuickBasic variable has structure and data, as follows:

Scalar: Scalars are of type Boolean, Byte, Integer, Long, Single, Double, or String. The structure of a scalar is just its type. Data is the data associated with the variable. For a scalar, the data is represented by the corresponding .NET type with two important exceptions: QuickBasic Integers are represented by .NET Short integers, because .NET Integers are 32-bit, while QuickBasic Integers are 16-bit. QuickBasic Longs are represented by .NET Integers, because .NET Longs are 64-bit, while QuickBasic Integers are 32-bit.

NOTE *Mapping of QuickBasic variables to .NET variables is accurate unless the variable is Single or Double. Single and double precision are not (at this writing) mapped accurately, and Single and Double values will have a wider range than the corresponding QuickBasic values. This means that numerical results may differ when running old QuickBasic code using this object and* `quickBasicEngine`.

Variant: A `Variant` is a variable that contains (has a) nonvariant data item. The structure of a `Variant` is the type (not including the value) of what it contains. The structure of an ordinary `Variant` is "concrete," because it cannot be specified unless the accompanying contained nonvariant type is also specified. Variants actually contain an instance of this type (`qbVariable`) in their state, which provides the type and the data of the variant value. This `qbVariable`, however, is prevented from being itself a `Variant`, but it is allowed to be an array.

Array: An `Array` is a collection of entries with a nonvariant type. The structure of an array is its number of dimensions, and, in QuickBasic, upper and lower bounds, which can be almost any positive or negative numbers.[5] The structure of an array also includes the uniform (what we refer to as *orthogonal*) type of all the data in the array. This type can be an abstract `Variant` type that as a pure `Variant` type does not specify the contained type, because this will vary in an array. One-dimensional array data is represented by a collection of .NET objects. Two-dimensional arrays are represented by a collection that contains one or more orthogonal member collections.[6] In general, *n*-dimensional arrays are represented by fully orthogonal balanced trees of subcollections.

NOTE *The* `Array` *structure is sometimes referred to as a* dope *vector. Here, the dope concept is generalized to use* dope *as a synonym for the structure of any variable.*

---

5. The only semi-useful ability to start an array at a lower bound, other than one, was dropped by .NET.

6. These are *orthogonal* in the sense that each subcollection has an identical number of members.

User Defined Type (UDT): A UDT is also represented as a collection of entries. The structure of a UDT is the ordered collection of variables. In QuickBasic, this collection cannot be nested. It cannot contain, directly, definitions of further UDTs (as seen, for example, in Cobol). But it can contain UDTs defined elsewhere. UDTs contain a collection of qbVariables representing their components.

Unknown and Null: A variable can be an Unknown value or Null (represented by Nothing in .NET.). The structure of an Unknown or Null variable is just its "being-Unknown" or its "being-Nothing."

Containment, Identity, and Isomorphism in qbVariable

The containedVariable, isomorphicVariable, and stringIdentical methods support comparison of variables.

The variable a is "contained in" the variable b solely by virtue of its underlying type; if all potential values of a can be assigned to b, then a is contained in b. (See the "qbVariableType" section for more information.)

The variable a is isomorphic to b when the type of a is contained in b, the type of b is contained in a, and the values of a and b (after conversion to a string) are the same.

The conversion to a string is performed by calling the toString method for serializing the variable to type:value(s), and throwing away the material to the left of the colon as well as the colon. (toString is described in the next section.) The stringIdentical method will test two qbVariable objects for this type of identity.

In the case of scalar isomorphism, a and b will have identical type and identical value. But if a and b are arrays, they may differ in lowerBounds and upperBounds, while retaining all other common properties.

UDTs are never contained or isomorphic (at this writing).

The fromString Expression Supported by qbVariable

The state of the variable is represented in an expression accepted by the fromString method of this class and generated by the toString method, known as the fromString expression.

The fromString expression contains both the type and values of the variable in a string, in the form *type:value*.

If the *type* is present and the *value* is omitted, the variable will take on the default contents for the type.

If the *type* is omitted and the *value* is specified, the type will default to the narrowest QuickBasic type capable of containing the specified data. If the value string is null or an asterisk, the type is Unknown. If the value string is a number or quoted string, the type is the narrowest scalar QuickBasic type that can contain the value. If the value string is in parentheses, contains a comma-separated list, or both, the type is Array, and the array's entry type is determined by examining the values in the array. If they all convert to a single type, the array's type is this type. If they all convert to more than one type, the array's type is Variant. The type may not be omitted when a UDT is specified.

fromString Types

The type should be the variable type in the syntax supported by qbVariableType.fromString and one of the following values, depending of the overall type:

- For a scalar type, the type should be one of Boolean, Byte, Integer, Long, Single, Double, or String.

- For a Variant, the type should be Variant,*scalarType*,Variant,(*arrayType*) or Variant,(*userDataType*). The scalar type should be as described for a scalar type. The array type or UDT should be in parentheses and as described in the following items.

- For an Array, the type should be *Array*,*type*,*bounds*, where *type* is the name of a scalar type, the keyword Variant, or a parenthesized UDT definition. The type of variant arrays is specified "abstractly" and with no associated scalar type.

- For a UDT, the type should be *UDT*, *memberlist*, where the member list consists of one or more comma-separated and parenthesized member definitions. Each definition in the member list has the parenthesized form (*name*,*type*), where *name* is the member name and *type* is its type. The type must be scalar, abstract Variant, or Array.

- For the Unknown type, the type should be Unknown.

- For the Null type, the type should be Null.

fromString Values

The fromString expression value should specify the variable value(s). If the variable is a scalar or a Variant that does not contain an array, the value may be the scalar's value (compatible with its type) as True, False, a number, or a string, quoted using Visual Basic's conventions.

Alternatively the variable may be in "decorated" form as *type(value)*, where the value is True, False, a number, or a string.

The variable may be represented as an asterisk. This will assign the appropriate default value for the type.

If the variable is an array, the value should be the list of array values. This is a comma-separated list of scalar values (plain or decorated) for a one-dimensional array. This is a comma-separated list of parenthesized rows for a two-dimensional array. In general, this is a comma-separated list of array *slices* (arrays of one dimension lower) for *n*-dimensional arrays. Each value in the array may optionally be followed by a repeat count in parentheses. The entry value will be repeated until the end of the current slice or the indicated number of entries. The repeat count may be an asterisk to repeat to the end of the current array slice.

> **NOTE** *When the variable is not otherwise known to be an array (when, for instance, the variable type is omitted from the* fromString *expression), the use of a repeat count will make the variable into an array.*

For a UDT, the value should be the comma-separated list of member values. Each member that is a scalar or the scalar value of a Variant member should be its value in string form or in the decorated form *type(value)*. Each member that is an array should be the array's value, represented orthogonally (as described in the previous paragraph) and enclosed in parentheses. Each member that is a UDT should be the *nested* UDT specification, in parentheses.

For Unknown and Null types, *values* (and its preceding colon) should not be specified.

The syntax :*value* (colon and value without a type) may be used to change the value of the variable without altering the type. The value must be compatible with the existing type, unless the existing type is Unknown; in this case, the type will be changed to the narrowest QuickBasic type capable of containing the value.

Examples of fromString Expressions

This section presents examples of fromString expressions with various types and values.

> **TIP** *You can run the* qbVariableTest *executable (provided with the sample code) and try each example. Type it in the text box at the top of the screen and click Create to make sure the example creates the* qbVariable *object. Then click the toString button to verify that the* fromString *expression converts to the variable and type specified in the examples.*

```
Integer:4
```

specifies a 16-bit integer containing the value four.

```
Variant,Integer:4
```

specifies a variant that contains a 16-bit integer containing the value four.

```
Array,Integer,0,3:1,2,3,4
```

specifies a one-dimensional integer array.

```
Array,Integer,1,2,1,2:(1,2),(1,2)
```

specifies a two-dimensional integer matrix.

```
Array,Variant,1,2:Integer(1),Long(2)
```

specifies a one-dimensional variant array, and it uses decoration to be specific about the type.

```
32768
```

specifies a Long integer containing 32768.

```
:32767
```

assigns 32767 to a prespecified type. When set after the previous example, :32767 will preserve the type of Long integer. When assigned to an uninitialized variable, :32767 creates a 16-bit integer.

```
Array,Byte,0,1
```

specifies a Byte array that contains the Byte default values of 0. The toString will be Array,Byte,0,1:*.

```
Array,Byte,0,1:*,1
```

specifies a Byte array that contains the Byte default value of 0 followed by 1. The toString will be Array,Byte,0,1:*,1.

```
Array,Variant,0,1,1,2:(32767,"B"),(32768,1)
```

specifies a Variant array. The toString will be Array,Variant,0,1,1,2: (System.Int16(32767), System.String("B")), System.Int32(32768), System.Byte(1)). Note that values are decorated, because the array has variant entries.

```
UDT,(intMember01,Integer), (strMember02,Array,String,1,2), (typMember03,(udt,
(intMember01,Integer))) : 1,("A","B"), (udt,(intMember01,Integer):1)
```

specifies a UDT containing an integer, a string array, and an inner UDT.

fromString Values Returned as Random Variables

Some of the qbVariable methods return a random variable, with random type and value, as an expression that is valid input for the fromString method.

The fromString returned will have the following randomly selected characteristics.

- With 10% probability, it will be Unknown.

- With 10% probability, it will be Null.

- With 20% probability, the fromString will represent a scalar, and with equal subprobability this will be any of the types Boolean, Byte, Integer, Long, Single, Double, or String.

- With 20% probability, it will be an array, and this array will contain a variable that has 50% probability of being a Variant and will otherwise be a random scalar.

- With 20% probability, it will be a UDT, and this UDT will randomly contain 1..10 scalars, Arrays, Variants, and UDTs. Each type will have 25% probability.

- With 20% probability, it will be a Variant, and this Variant will contain a variable that has these type probabilities, with one exception: there is a 70% probability that the variable will be a scalar, and no probability that the variable will be a Variant.

fromString BNF Syntax in qbVariable

The lexical syntax of fromString expressions matches that of the quickBasicEngine itself: blanks can be freely used, and strings are delimited by double quotes (with doubled double quotes representing, inside strings, the occurrence of a single double quote).

Note that this object is responsible only for scanning and parsing the fromStringValue, which contains the value(s) of the variable. Parsing of the fromStringType occurs inside the qbVariableType object.

```
fromString := fromStringType
fromString := fromStringValue
fromString := fromStringWithValue
fromString := fromStringType COLON fromStringValue
fromString := COLON fromStringValue
fromStringType := baseType | udt
baseType := simpleType | variantType | arrayType
simpleType := [VT] typeName
typeName := BOOLEAN|BYTE|INTEGER|LONG|SINGLE|DOUBLE|STRING|
            UNKNOWN|NULL
variantType := abstractVariantType COMMA varType
varType := simpleType|(arrayType)
arrayType := [VT] ARRAY,arrType,boundList
arrType := simpleType | abstractVariantType | parUDT
parUDT := LEFTPARENTHESIS udt RIGHTPARENTHESIS
udt := [VT] UDT,typeList
typeList := parMemberType [ COMMA typeList ]
parMemberType := LEFTPAR MEMBERNAME,baseType RIGHTPAR
abstractVariantType := [VT] VARIANT
boundList := boundListEntry | boundListEntry COMMA boundList
boundListEntry := BOUNDINTEGER,BOUNDINTEGER
simpleType := [VT] typeName
typeName := BOOLEAN|BYTE|INTEGER|LONG|SINGLE|DOUBLE|STRING|
            UNKNOWN|NULL
variantType := abstractVariantType,varType
varType := simpleType|(arrayType)
arrayType := [VT] ARRAY,arrType,boundList
arrType := simpleType|abstractVariantType
abstractVariantType := [VT] VARIANT
boundList := boundListEntry | boundListEntry, boundList
boundListEntry := BOUNDINTEGER,BOUNDINTEGER
fromStringValue := ASTERISK | fromStringNondefault
fromStringNondefault := arraySlice [ COMMA fromStringValue ] *
arraySlice := elementExpression | ( fromStringNondefault )
elementExpression := element [ repeater ]
element := scalar | decoValue
scalar := NUMBER | VBQUOTEDSTRING | ASTERISK | TRUE | FALSE
decoValue := quickBasicDecoValue | netDecoValue
quickBasicDecoValue := QUICKBASICTYPE ( scalar )
netDecoValue := netDecoValue := [ SYSTEM PERIOD ] IDENTIFIER
                LEFTPARENTHESIS ANYTHING RIGHTPARENTHESIS
repeater := LEFTPAR ( INTEGER | ASTERISK ) RIGHTPAR
```

qbVariable Inspection Rules

The following inspection rules are applied by the `inspect` method as a check on errors in the source code whether as delivered or as changed, or object abuse in the form of using the object after a serious user error has occurred:

- The object instance must be usable.

- The variable type object `objDope` must pass its own inspection procedure. It must be `Unknown` or an array type. If the dope is `Unknown`, the `objValue` must be Nothing and the following tests are skipped.

- `objValue` must be one of the following:

  Nothing (when the type of the variable is `Unknown` or `Null`)

  One of the types that represents, in .NET, a QuickBasic type (`Boolean`, `Byte`, `Short`, `Integer`, `Single`, `Double`, or `String` (when the type of the variable is scalar)

  A collection—the type must be `Array` or `UDT`. If the type is `Array`, this must be an orthogonal collection that contains a balanced structure of elements representing an array. Each final element's type must either match the nonvariant type in the variable's `variableType`, or, when the variable's `variableType` is `Variant`, each final element's type must be the .NET representation of a QuickBasic scalar. If it consists of subcollections, each subcollection must be balanced and orthogonal. If the type is UDT, the collection must consist exclusively of `qbVariable` objects. Each must be a scalar, an `Array`, a `Variant`, or a UDT.

> **NOTE** *The collection must be orthogonal in that it must be a balanced tree. To be a balanced tree, the collection must either contain 0..n scalars or 0..n balanced subcollections.*

  A variant `qbVariable` that is either abstract (containing no value) or of a scalar or UDT type.[7]

---

7. At this writing, `qbVariable` does not support variants that contain arrays, although the `fromString` syntax allows their specification. This rule should be changed to allow variants that contain arrays when code is added to fully support this feature.

- The `toString` serialization of the variable must create a clone of the variable when used with `fromString`. However, `Variants`, `Arrays`, and UDTs are not subject to this rule

- The empirical dope of the variable must be consistent with its recorded type. The empirical dope (the type as determined by examination of the value) must be either the same as or contained in the type. Only scalars are subject to this rule.

- If the variable is a `Variant`, its `Variant` type must match the type of its entry as seen in the decorated value when the variable is serialized using `toString`. For example, `Variant,Byte:Integer(256)` is not valid.

Properties, Methods, and Events of qbVariable

Table B-7 lists the properties, methods, and events of the `qbVariable` class.

Table B-7. qbVariable Properties, Methods, and Events

Property/Method/Event	Description
Public Shared ReadOnly Property About As String	Read-only Shared property that returns information about the class.
Public Shared Function Class2XML As String	Shared method that returns information about the class as an XML tag.
Public Shared ReadOnly Property ClassName As String	Shared read-only property that returns the class name `qbVariable`.
Public Shared Function clearVariable As Boolean	Method that clears the variable. If it is a scalar, it is set to the default appropriate to its type, which is `False` for Booleans, 0 for numeric types, and a null string for strings. If the variable is a `Variant`, it is set to the default appropriate to its contained type. If the variable is an Array, each entry is set to the appropriate default. If the variable is a UDT, each member is cleared according to its type. If the variable is `Unknown` or `Null`, no change is made. See also `resetVariable`.
Public Function clone As qbVariable	Method that implements `ICloneable`. It creates a new `qbVariable` with identical type and value, returning it as the function value.

Table B-7. qbVariable Properties, Methods, and Events (continued)

Property/Method/Event	Description
`Public Function compareTo(ByVal objQBvariable2 As qbVariable) As Boolean`	Method that compares the object instance to qbVariable2 and returns True when the type and value of the variables in both are the same; False otherwise. This method is a wrapper for the private compareTo_ method, which implements IComparable.
`Public Overloads Function containedVariable(ByVal objVariable2 As qbVariable) As Boolean`	Method that returns True when the qbVariable object in objVariable2 is contained in the instance as described in the preceding section. If the object instance is a UDT or objVariable2 is a UDT, this method returns False.
`Public Overloads Function containedVariable(ByVal objVariable2 As qbVariable, ByRef strExplanation As True) As Boolean`	Method that returns True when the qbVariable object in objVariable2 is contained in the instance as described in the preceding section. If the object instance is a UDT or objVariable2 is a UDT, this method returns False. The strExplanation parameter is set to an explanation of why the containment relation is True or False.
`Public Function derefMemberName (ByVal strName As String) As qbVariable`	Method that is valid only for variables that are UDTs. strName should be the name of a UDT member, and this method returns the qbVariable object, contained directly or indirectly in the overall instance, identified by *n*. strName may be a simple member name. If it selects a member that is a UDT, strName may be simple, in which case, it returns the UDT. strName may also select submembers when periods separate names. For example, if a UDT contains UDT01, and UDT01 contains intVal, then this method returns the object corresponding to intVal when strName is udt01.intVal.
`Public Sub dispose()`	Method that disposes of the heap storage associated with the object (if any) and marks the object as not usable. For best results, use this method (or disposeInspect) when you are finished with the object.
`Public Function disposeInspect() As Boolean`	Method that disposes of the heap storage associated with the object (if any) and marks the object as not usable. For best results, use this method (or dispose) when you are finished with the object. This dispose method conducts a final object inspection. See "qbVariable Inspection Rules" preceding this table.

Table B-7. qbVariable Properties, Methods, and Events (continued)

Property/Method/Event	Description
`Public Property Dope() As qbVariableType`	Read-write property that returns and can change information about the variable as an instance of the class `qbVariableType`. The default `Dope` is the `Unknown` `qbVariableType`. It may be set to any `qbVariableType`. Changing this property usually clears the variable. If the variable is scalar or `Variant`, it is set to its appropriate default. If the variable is an `Array` or UDT, each entry is set to its default. However, when an array structure is changed to an isomorphic structure (same dimensions, identical element types, and same size at each dimension), setting `Dope` does not clear the array. Otherwise, the array is cleared.
`Public Function empiricalDope() As String`	Method that returns a reconstruction of the variable's type (including array bounds when the variable is an array) from its data exclusively.[8] This reconstruction is returned as a string acceptable to the `fromString` method of `qbVariableType`. If the variable is *not* an array, the `empiricalDope` will be identical to the variable's dope. If the variable is an array, the `empiricalDope` will be isomorphic to the array dope of the variable; dimensions and bound sizes will be the same, as well as the entry type; but lowerBounds of the `empiricalDope` will be 0.
`Public Function fromString(ByVal strFromstring As String) As Boolean`	Method that sets the type and the value of the variable to the value serialized in `strFromstring`. See the preceding section "The fromString Expression Supported by qbVariable" for the syntax requirements of `strFromstring`.
`Public Function inspect(ByRef strReport As String) As Boolean`	Method that inspects the object instance for errors resulting from bugs in the original code, bugs in the code as changed, or object abuse in the form of using the object after a serious error has already occurred. An internal inspection is carried out when the object is constructed and inside the `disposeInspect` method. If the inspection fails, the object is marked unusable. See the preceding section "qbVariable Inspection Rules."

---

8. Since a valid instance contains type information, this method is primarily a curio, for internal use and to clarify the concept of deriving a type from data only, which we need when changing the data of an array without, unnecessarily, changing its structure.

Table B-7. qbVariable Properties, Methods, and Events (continued)

Property/Method/Event	Description
`Public Function isANumber()` `As Boolean`	Method that returns `True` when the object instance is of scalar, numeric type including `Boolean`; `False` otherwise. This method will return `False` for strings that contain numbers.
`Public Function isAnUnsigned` `Integer() As Boolean`	Method returns `True` when the variable is an *unsigned* integer of any scalar type. The variable can be Boolean (but not `True`, since this converts to a signed integer), a string, or a real number type, as long as its syntactical representation as a string is that of an unsigned integer.
`Public Function isClear() As Boolean`	Method that returns `True` when the object instance contains the default value appropriate to its type; `False` otherwise.
`Public Function isomorphicVariable` `(ByVal objVariable2 As qbVariable)` `As Boolean`	Method that determines whether the variable `objVariable2` is an isomorph of the variable in the instance. See the preceding "Containment, Identity, and Isomorphism in qbVariable" section for the rules of isomorphism.
`Public Function isomorphicVariable` `(ByVal objVariable2 As qbVariable,` `ByRef strExplanation As String)` `As Boolean`	Method that determines whether the variable `objVariable2` is an isomorph of the variable in the instance according to the rules of the preceding section "Containment, Identity, and Isomorphism in qbVariable." This overload places an explanation of why `objVariable` is or is not an isomorph in its `strExplanation` parameter.
`Public Function isScalar() As Boolean`	Method that returns `True` when the object instance represents a scalar variable or a `Variant` that contains a scalar value.
`Public Shared Function` `mkRandomVariable() As String`	Shared method that returns a random variable with random type and value, as an expression that is valid input for the `fromString` method. See the preceding section "The fromString Expression Supported by qbVariable."
`Public Function mkUnusable` `As Boolean`	Method that forces the object instance into the unusable state. It always returns `True`.

Table B-7. qbVariable Properties, Methods, and Events (continued)

Property/Method/Event	Description
Public Shared Function mkVariable (ByVal strFromString As String) As qbVariable	Shared method that creates and returns a new qbVariable object with the specified type and value in strFromString. strFromString may be in the syntax *type:value* or the syntax *value*; but in the latter syntax, when the value is not a number, it must be quoted using Visual Basic conventions. This method may be used to make an array by explicitly specifying array type and members, as in mkVariable("Array,Integer,0,1:0,1"). Also see mkVariableFromValue.
Public Shared Function mkVariableFromValue(ByVal objValue As Object) As qbVariable	Shared method that creates and returns a new qbVariable object with the specified scalar value. The value operand may be any .NET scalar value of the type Boolean, Byte, Short, Integer, Long, Single, Double or String. When the value is a string, it should *not* be quoted. This method cannot create an array. For example, mkVariableFromValue("0,1") creates a string. It also cannot create a variant; the qbVariable will instead have the narrowest possible scalar, nonvariant type. For example, mkVariableFromValue(32768) creates a Long integer. Also see mkVariable.
Public Event msgEvent(ByVal strMsg As String, ByVal intLevel As Integer)	Event that provides general information. It exposes the strMsg and intLevel parameters. strMsg is a general information message. intLevel should contain a nesting level starting at 0 and is useful in indenting displays. To obtain the msgEvent, declare the qbVariable object WithEvents and write the event handler.
Public Property Name() As String	Read-write property that returns and can set the name of the object instance, which identifies the object in error messages and on the XML tag that is returned by object2XML. The name defaults to qbVariable*nnnn date time*, where *nnnn* is a sequence number. This property identifies the object instance. The VariableName property identifies its data.

Table B-7. qbVariable Properties, Methods, and Events (continued)

Property/Method/Event	Description
`Public Shared Function netValue2QBvariable(ByVal objNet As Object) As qbVariable`	Shared method that converts the .NET object objNet to a qbVariable. objNet may be Nothing or a .NET scalar of type Boolean, Byte, Short, Integer, Long, Single, Double, or String. If objNet is Nothing, the Unknown qbVariable is created and returned. If objNet is a .NET scalar, it is converted to a string, which is used as the fromString expression to create a new qbVariable. Therefore, the qbVariable returned will have the narrowest QuickBasic type possible given the value of the .NET scalar. An error will occur if the .NET value cannot be assigned to a QuickBasic type, such as when the .NET value is an Integer beyond the Long precision of QuickBasic (-2^31..2^31-1).
`Public Sub new`	Object constructor that creates the qbVariable and inspects its initial state.
`Public Sub new(ByVal strFromString As String)`	Overloaded object constructor that creates the qbVariable and inspects its initial state. It sets the type and the value of the new qbVariable to the strFromstring. For example, objQBvariable = New qbVariable ("Integer:4") creates the variable with type Integer and value 4.
`Public Overloads Function object2XML() As String`	Method that converts the state of the object to XML.
`Public Event progressEvent(ByVal strActivity As String, ByVal strEntity As String, ByVal intEntityNumber As Integer, ByVal intEntityCount As Integer, ByVal intLevel As Integer, ByVal strComments As String)`	Event that indicates progress through a loop inside one of the stateful procedures of qbVariable. strActivity describes the activity or goal of the loop. strEntity identifies the entity being processed. intEntityNumber is the entity sequence number from 1. intEntityCount is the number of entities. intLevel is the nesting level of the loop (starting at 0). strComments may supply additional information about the processing in the loop. To obtain the progressEvent, declare the qbVariable object WithEvents and write the event handler. See also progressEventShared.

Table B-7. qbVariable Properties, Methods, and Events (continued)

Property/Method/Event	Description
`Public Shared Event progressEvent Shared(ByVal strActivity As String, ByVal strEntity As String, ByVal intEntityNumber As Integer, ByVal intEntityCount As Integer, ByVal intLevel As Integer, ByVal strComments As String)`	Event that indicates progress through a loop inside one of the stateless procedures of qbVariable. `strActivity` describes the activity or goal of the loop. `strEntity` identifies the entity being processed. `intEntityNumber` is the entity sequence number from 1. `intEntityCount` is the number of entities. `intLevel` is the nesting level of the loop (starting at 0). `strComments` may supply additional information about the processing in the loop. See also `progressEvent`.
`Public Function stringIdentical (ByVal objValue2 As qbVariable) As Boolean`	Method that returns `True` when the value(s) of the instance is identical to the value(s) of the qbVariable object *o*; `False` otherwise. The instance and `objValue2` are converted to string format by the `toString` method. The type information (as well as the colon separator) is removed for the comparison.
`Public Property Tag() As Object`	Read-write property that returns and can be set to user data that needs to be associated with the qbVariable instance. `Tag` can be a reference object. If so, when the object is destroyed, the `Tag` object is not destroyed.
`Public Overloads Function test (ByRef strReport As String) As Boolean`	Method that runs tests on the object. It returns `True` to indicate success or `False` to indicate failure. The `strReport` parameter is set to a test report. The tests are carried out on an internal instance of the object, so their results do not affect the main instance.
`Public Overloads Function test (ByRef strReport As String, ByVal booMkObject As Boolean) As Boolean`	Method that runs tests on the object. It returns `True` to indicate success or `False` to indicate failure. The `strReport` parameter is set to a test report. The tests are carried out on an internal instance of the object if `booMkObject` is `True`; when `booMkObject` is `False`, the tests use the object instance and their results will affect the state of the object.
`Public Function toDescription() As String`	Method that returns a description of the value consisting of the description of its type, followed by either "is empty" or "contains nondefault values."
`Public Function toMatrix() As String`	Method that returns a multiline, multicolumn display of the array indexes and values suitable for display in a monospace font.

Table B-7. qbVariable Properties, Methods, and Events (continued)

Property/Method/Event	Description
`Public Function toString() As String`	Method that returns the type and value of the qbVariable, in the format described for `fromString`. If the variable is an array, the representation returned is packed, condensing series of identical elements using parenthesized repetition counts as described under `fromString`. The representation returns default values as asterisks if the value of a scalar variable contains the default value appropriate to its type, or each member in an array value contains the default; or if the value of a scalar variable contains the default value appropriate to its type, or each member in an array value contains the default. The variables in the output string are decorated (using *type(value)* syntax) when the variable type is either variant or variant array.
`Public Function toStringTypeOnly() As String`	Method that returns only the type of the variable in the serialized format acceptable to `fromString`.
`Public Function toStringType WithType() As String`	Method that returns a string in the form *type,toString*, where *type* is the string returned by `toStringTypeOnly` and *toString* is the string returned by `toString`.
`Public ReadOnly Property UDTmember (ByVal objMemberID As Object) As qbVariable`	Indexed, read-only property that returns the qbVariable object that corresponds to a member of a UDT. `objMemberID` may be an index between 1 and the value of `Dope.UDTmemberCount` for the object, or it may be a member name. When `objMemberID` is a member name, it may address submembers of nested UDTs if the path to the submember is a series of period-separated member names.
`Public ReadOnly Property Usable() As Boolean`	Read-only property that returns `True` if the object instance is usable; `False` otherwise.
`Public Overloads Function value() As Object`	Method that returns the value of the qbVariable as long as the object instance represents a scalar value, `Unknown`, or `Null` or a `Variant` that contains a scalar value, `Unknown`, or `Null`.
`Public Overloads Function value (ByVal intIndex As Integer) As Object`	Method that returns the value of the qbVariable when it is a one-dimensional array, at the entry indexed by `intIndex`.
`Public Overloads Function value (ByVal intIndex1 As Integer, ByVal intIndex2 As Integer) As Object`	Method that returns the value of the qbVariable when it is a two-dimensional array, at the entry indexed by `intIndex1` and `intIndex2`.

Table B-7. qbVariable Properties, Methods, and Events (continued)

Property/Method/Event	Description
Public Overloads Function value (ByVal strID As String) As Object	Method that returns the value of the qbVariable. If strID is a null string, the object instance must represent a scalar value, Unknown, or Null or a Variant with a value that is a scalar, Unknown, or Null. If strID is not a null string, it must be a comma-separated list of array indexes to access an array value or a UDT member name. If strID is a UDT member name, it may be a period-separated series of member names to get to UDT submembers.
Public Overloads Function valueSet (ByVal objValue As Object) As Boolean	Method that assigns the .NET value objValue to the qbVariable as long as the object instance represents a scalar value, Unknown, or Null or a Variant that contains a scalar value, Unknown, or Null.
Public Overloads Function valueSet (ByVal objValue As Object, ByVal intIndex As Integer) As Boolean	Method that assigns the .NET value objValue to the qbVariable when the object instance represents a one-dimensional array, at the entry indexed by intIndex.
Public Overloads Function valueSet (ByVal objValue As Object, ByVal intIndex1 As Integer, ByVal intIndex2 As Integer) As Boolean	Method that assigns the .NET value objValue to the qbVariable when the object instance represents a two-dimensional array, at the entry indexed by intIndex1 and intIndex2.
Public Overloads Function valueSet (ByVal objValue As Object, ByVal strID As String) As Boolean	Method that assigns the .NET value objValue to the qbVariable. If strID is a null string, the object instance must represent a scalar value, Unknown, or Null or a Variant with a value that is a scalar, Unknown, or Null. If strID is not a null string it must be a comma-separated list of array indexes to access an array value or a UDT member name. If strID is a UDT member name, it may be a period-separated series of member names to modify UDT submembers.

Table B-7. qbVariable Properties, Methods, and Events (continued)

Property/Method/Event	Description
Public Property VariableName As String	Read-write property that returns and can change the name of the variable. VariableName defaults to *typennnn*, such as int0001 or vntInteger0002. *type* is the three-character Hungarian prefix designating the variable type: boo, byt, int, lng, sgl, dbl, str, vnt, arr, typ, unk, or nul. For a variant or array, the prefix vnt or arr is followed by the propercase full name of the variant's contained type or the array's entry type. *nnnn* is the variable's sequence number. The name must conform to QuickBasic rules: from 1 to 31 characters long, start with a letter, and contain only letters, numbers, and the underscore. VariableName the variable and changes when it has not been assigned except by default or the variable Dope (type) is changed in any way. See also the Name property.

qbVariableType

This qbVariableType class represents the type of a quickBasicEngine variable, including support for an unknown type and Shared methods for relating .NET types to QuickBasic types.

References of qbVariableType include collectionUtilities.DLL, qbScanner.DLL, qbTokenType.DLL, and utilities.DLL.

qbVariableType is serially threadable. Multiple instances can run simultaneously in multiple threads, but errors will result if one object's procedures run in multiple threads and in parallel.

Note that this class implements IDisposable, ICloneable, and IComparable.

The Variable Types of the quickBasicEngine

The variable types supported by quickBasicEngine fall into these general classes:

- **Scalars:** Ordinary values with no structure. They can have the type Boolean, Byte, Integer, Long, Single, or String.

- **Variants:** Variables capable of containing variables including scalars and even arrays.

- **Arrays:** Variables with 1..*n* dimensions. In QuickBasic and this implementation, at each dimension, an array has flexible lower and upper bounds.

> **NOTE** *In QuickBasic and this implementation, variants cannot contain variants. The elegance of such an idea is totally outweighed by its uselessness. Flexible lower bounds are another nearly useless idea, but here they were a part of both QuickBasic and Visual Basic up to .NET.*

- **User Data Types (UDTs):** Variables that contain 1.. members, which may be a mix of scalars, Variants, or Arrays but cannot be nested UDTs.

- **Unknown:** As its name implies, the type we don't know. In this implementation, Unknown is assigned to the variable type in the constructor.[9]

- **Null:** A variable type primarily for assignment as the initial value of a Variant value.

When an Array, Variant, or UDT is represented, this qbVariableType class also contains the Variant's type, the Array type, and array dimensions or the collection of member types. These are delegates within the main object.

Table B-8 shows the types exposed by the qbVariableType object.

Table B-8. Types Exposed by qbVariableType

Type	Description
ENUvarType.vtBoolean	True or False. The default is False.
ENUvarType.vtByte	Unsigned integer in the range 0..255. The default is 0.
ENUvarType.vtInteger	Integer in the range –32768..32767. This is different from VB .NET and like VB 6. The Integer is a Short in VB .NET. The default is 0.
ENUvarType.vtLong	Integer in the range $-2^{31}..2^{31}-1$. This is different from VB .NET and like VB 6. The Long is an Integer in VB .NET. The default is 0.
ENUvarType.vtSingle	Real number in the Single precision range of VB .NET. This is not fully compatible with Microsoft's old QuickBASIC. The default value of Single is 0.

---

9. In a planned future EGN implementation of a language for symbolic computation (which will probably be called FOG), this will be used to actually calculate with mystery values.

Table B-8. Types Exposed by qbVariableType (continued)

Type	Description
ENUvarType.vtDouble	Real number in the Double precision range of VB .NET. This is not fully compatible with Microsoft's old QuickBASIC. The default value of Double is 0.
ENUvarType.vtString	String restricted to 64KB when quickBasicEngine is compiled with QUICKBASICENGINE_EXTENSION set to False. The string restricted to the VB .NET string limit when this compile-time symbol is True. The default value of string is the null string.
ENUvarType.vtVariant	Variant proto-object container for another value, which can be any type (including Array) except Variant itself. The default value of Variant is Nothing. Most variants will occur set to a contained type; but the abstract variant exists as a valid special state of this data type for variants inside arrays. This is a vtVariant variable type for which the Abstract property will return True.
ENUvarType.vtArray	Array of any dimensionality. It has no default. Unlike the Variant, an abstract array is not supported. This is because an array in this implementation of QuickBasic is always an array of a definite type specified for each entry, including a Variant type, which is abstract.
ENUvarType.vtUDT	UDT container for 1..n scalars, Variants and/or Arrays.
ENUvarType.vtUnknown	Default special value. No default for this "default" is defined.
ENUvarType.vtNull	Used primarily for certain Variants. It is a dummy, uninitialized value. There is no default.

Containment and Isomorphism of Variable Types

The containedType and isomorphicType methods of the qbVariableType class ensure that one type can be converted safely to another type.

Type *a* is contained in type *b* when:

- Type *a* and type *b* are scalars (Boolean, Byte, Integer, Long, Single, Double, or String) and all possible values of type *a* convert without error to type *b*.

- Type *a* and type *b* are arrays, and each dimension of type *b* contains the same number of elements as the corresponding dimension of *a*, or more elements. The array entry type of *a* is contained in the array entry type of *b* according to this overall definition. Note that lowerBounds of *a* and *b* may differ.

- *a* is a scalar, a Variant, or an Array, and *b* is a Variant.

Type *a* and type *b* are isomorphic types when *a* is contained in *b*, and *b* is contained in *a*. Scalar types are isomorphic only when identical, but array definitions may differ in lower bounds.

If either *a* or *b* is a UDT, Null, or Unknown, the types are never considered to contain each other.

The fromString Expression Supported by qbVariableType

The state of the variable type is represented in an expression accepted by the fromString method of this class and generated by the toString method, known as the fromString expression.

The fromString expression contains the type of a variable as the overall type name, extended (for Variants, Arrays, and UDTs) with additional type information:

- For a scalar type, the type should be one of Boolean, Byte, Integer, Long, Single, Double, or String.

- For a Variant, the type should be Variant,*scalarType*,Variant,(*arrayType*) or Variant,(*userDataType*). The scalar type should be as described in the previous item. The array type or UDT should be in parentheses and as described in the following items.

- For an Array, the type should be Array,*type*,*bounds*, where *type* is the name of a scalar type, the keyword Variant, or a parenthesized UDT definition. The type of variant arrays is specified "abstractly" and with no associated scalar type.

- For a UDT, the type should be UDT, *memberlist*, where the member list consists of one or more comma-separated and parenthesized member definitions. Each definition in the member list has the parenthesized form (*name*,*type*), where name is the member name and type is its type. The type must be scalar, abstract Variant, or Array.

- For the Unknown type, the type should be Unknown.

- For the Null type, the type should be Null.

The following are some examples of fromString expressions with various types.

Integer

specifies the 16-bit integer type.

Variant,Integer

specifies a variant that contains a 16-bit integer.

Array,Integer,0,3

specifies a one-dimensional integer array.

Array,Integer,1,2,1,2

specifies a two-dimensional integer matrix.

UDT,(intMember01,Integer), (strMember02,Array,String,1,2), (typMember03, (udt,(intMember01,Integer)))

specifies a UDT containing an integer, a string array, and an inner UDT.

Cache Considerations for qbVariableType

The qbVariableType object avoids excessive parsing of fromString expressions to create types by using a cache to save parsed types. The cache is a keyed Collection in Shared storage. Each item of this collection contains the clone of a preexisting variable type object; the key of each item is its fromString expression. The cache will contain a maximum of 100 entries, and the oldest entries are dropped when the cache is full.

Information about the cache, in the form of a list of its entries and its maximum size, is available with a special parameter of the object2XML method for converting the object state to an XML tag. See the object2XML method for more information.

fromString BNF Syntax in qbVariableType

The lexical syntax of fromString expressions matches that of the quickBasicEngine itself: blanks can be freely used, and strings are delimited by double quotes (with doubled double quotes representing, inside strings, the occurrence of a single double quote).

```
typeSpecification := baseType | udt
baseType := simpleType | variantType | arrayType
simpleType := [VT] typeName
typeName := BOOLEAN|BYTE|INTEGER|LONG|SINGLE|DOUBLE|STRING|
            UNKNOWN|NULL
variantType := abstractVariantType COMMA varType
varType := simpleType|(arrayType)
arrayType := [VT] ARRAY,arrType,boundList
arrType := simpleType | abstractVariantType | parUDT
parUDT := LEFTPARENTHESIS udt RIGHTPARENTHESIS
udt := [VT] UDT,typeList
typeList := parMemberType [ COMMA typeList ]
parMemberType := LEFTPAR MEMBERNAME,baseType RIGHTPAR
abstractVariantType := [VT] VARIANT
boundList := boundListEntry | boundListEntry COMMA boundList
boundListEntry := BOUNDINTEGER,BOUNDINTEGER
```

qbVariableType Inspection Rules

The following inspection rules are used by the inspect method:

- The object instance must be usable.

- The type must be compatible with the contained type and, when the type is Array, with the bounds. If the type is scalar (Boolean, Integer, Long, or String), the contained type must be Nothing. If the type is Variant, the contained type must be Null, a scalar, or Array. If the type is Array, the contained type must be Null, a scalar, or a Variant. If the type is UDT, the contained type must be a collection of scalar, Variant, or Array types.

- The type that is contained in the Variant or Array must pass its own inspection; each type in a UDT must likewise pass its own inspection.

- When the object is cloned, the clone must return the same toString value as the original object.

- When the fromString value of the object is used to set the value of a new instance, the compareTo method must indicate that the original instance and the new instance are identical.

An internal inspection is carried out when the object is constructed and inside the disposeInspect method. If the inspection fails, the object is marked as unusable.

qbVariableType has the capability, supported by the optional parameter booBasic of the inspect method, to carry out the default, extended inspection or a basic inspection. If basic inspection is in effect only the first three inspection rules are applied.

Properties, Methods, and Events of qbVariableType

Table B-9 lists the properties, methods, and events of the qbVariableType class.

Table B-9. qbVariableType Properties, Methods, and Events

Property/Method/Event	Description
Public Shared ReadOnly Property About As String	Shared, read-only property that returns information about the class.
Public ReadOnly Property Abstract As String	Read-only property returns True when the object instance represents a variant array.[10]
Public Function arraySlice() As qbVariableType	Method that creates a new variable type based on the type of the instance, which must be an array. The new type is created by removing the top-level lowerBound and the upperBound. The returned variable type is an array of one lower dimension, a Variant, or a scalar. When the instance type is not an array, this method returns a variable type of Unknown with no other error indication.
Public ReadOnly Property BoundList() As String	Read-only property that returns a null string when the instance type is not an array, or it returns the bounds of the array type as a comma-delimited list of lower and upper bounds. For each dimension in the array, the expression lower,upper is returned.
Public ReadOnly Property BoundSize (ByVal intDimension As Integer) As Integer	Indexed, read-only property that returns the size of an array variable at dimension *d* (upperBound − lowerBound + 1). An error occurs when the variable is not an array or the dimension is not defined.

10. Variant arrays do not have a contained type.

Table B-9. qbVariableType Properties, Methods, and Events (continued)

Property/Method/Event	Description
Public Shared Function changeArray Bound(ByVal strFromstring As String, ByVal intRank As Integer, ByVal intLU As Integer, ByVal intChange As Integer) As String	Shared method that modifies an array bound in a fromString expression, returning the modified fromString expression. strFromstring is the fromString expression of an array type, intRank is the dimension at which the bound should be changed. intLU is 0 to modify the lower bound or 1 to modify the upper bound. intChange is a positive value to increase the lower or upper bound or a negative value to decrease the bound.
Public Shared ReadOnly Property ClassName	Shared read-only property that returns the class name qbVariableType.
Public Shared Function clone As qbVariableType	Method that implements ICloneable. It creates a new qbVariableType with identical type information, returning it as the function value.[11]
Public Overloads Function compareTo(ByVal objQBvariableType2 As qbVariableType) As Boolean	Method that compares the object instance to qbVariableType2 and returns True when the types in both are the same; False otherwise. This method is a wrapper for the private compareTo_ method, which implements IComparable.
Public Overloads Function compareTo (ByVal objQBvariableType2 As qbVariableType, ByRef strExplanation As String) As Boolean	Method that compares the object instance to qbVariable2 and returns True when the types in both are the same; False otherwise. This method is a wrapper for the private compareTo_ method, which implements IComparable. This overload places an explanation of why the types are identical or different in its strExplanation parameter.
Public Shared Function contained Type(ByVal enuType1 As ENUvarType, ByVal enuType2 As ENUvarType) As Boolean	Shared method that returns True when the type identified by enuType1 is contained in the type identified in enuType2; False otherwise. See the preceding section "Containment and Isomorphism of Types."
Public Shared Function contained Type(ByVal enuType1 As ENUvarType, ByVal objType2 As qbVariableType) As Boolean	Shared method that returns True when the type identified by enuType1 is contained in the type identified in objType2; False otherwise. See the preceding section "Containment and Isomorphism of Types."

---

11. At this writing, the clone method runs slowly because it (1) serializes the type information using toString into a fromString expression for the type, and (2) uses fromString on the new object to parse and set the type. A Friend variant of clone is used internally. It copies the state directly, but this has not been fully tested and is not ready for prime time. It should be fully tested as a replacement for the original clone to make qbVariableType applications run faster.

Table B-9. qbVariableType Properties, Methods, and Events (continued)

Property/Method/Event	Description
`Public Shared Function contained Type(ByVal objType1 As qbVariableType, ByVal enuType2 As ENUvarType) As Boolean`	Shared method that returns `True` when the type identified in `objType1` is contained in the type identified by `enuType2`; `False` otherwise. See the preceding section "Containment and Isomorphism of Types."
`Public Shared Function contained Type(ByVal objType1 As qbVariableType, ByVal objType2 As qbVariableType) As Boolean`	Shared method that returns `True` when the type identified in `objType1` is contained in the type identified in `objType2`; `False` otherwise. See the preceding section "Containment and Isomorphism of Types."
`Public Function containedTypeWith State(ByVal enuType1 As ENUvarType, ByVal enuType2 As ENUvarType) As Boolean`	Method that returns `True` when the type identified by `enuType1` is contained in the type identified in `enuType2`; `False` otherwise. This method works the same way as the corresponding overload of `containedType`, but it creates the reusable containment matrix in the state of the object using it, which will result in faster processing.
`Public Function containedTypeWith State(ByVal enuType1 As ENUvarType, ByVal objType2 As qbVariableType) As Boolean`	Method that returns `True` when the type identified by `enuType1` is contained in the type identified in `objType2`; `False` otherwise. This method works the same way as the corresponding overload of `containedType`, but it creates the reusable containment matrix in the state of the object using it, which will result in faster processing.
`Public Function containedTypeWith State(ByVal objType1 As qbVariableType, ByVal enuType2 As ENUvarType) As Boolean`	Method that returns `True` when the type identified in `objType1` is contained in the type identified by `enuType2`; `False` otherwise. This method works the same way as the corresponding overload of `containedType`, but it creates the reusable containment matrix in the state of the object using it, which will result in faster processing.
`Public Function containedTypeWith State(ByVal objType1 As qbVariableType, ByVal objType2 As qbVariableType) As Boolean`	Method that returns `True` when the type identified in `objType1` is contained in the type identified in `objType2`; `False` otherwise. This method works the same way as the corresponding overload of `containedType`, with the difference that it creates the reusable containment matrix in the state of the object using it, which will result in faster processing.

Table B-9. qbVariableType Properties, Methods, and Events (continued)

Property/Method/Event	Description
`Public Function containedTypeWith State(ByVal objType1 As qbVariable Type, ByVal objType2 As qbVariable Type, ByRef strExplanation As String) As Boolean`	Method that returns `True` when the type identified in objType1 is contained in the type identified in objType2; `False` otherwise. See the preceding section "Containment and Isomorphism of Types." This method creates the reusable containment matrix in the state of the object using it, which will result in faster processing. This method also places an explanation of why or why not the state is contained in strExplanation.
`Public Overloads Function defaultValue As Object`	Method that returns the default value associated with the type in the object instance. For all scalars, this method returns `False` (for the type `Boolean`), `String` (for the type `String`) or 0 (for the numeric scalar types). For Variants, Null types, and UDTs, this method returns Nothing. For nonvariant arrays, this method returns the default type of the array's entry.
`Public Overloads Shared Function defaultValue(ByVal enuType As ENUvarType) As Object`	Shared method that returns the default value associated with the type specified in enuType. For all scalars, this method returns `False` (for the type `Boolean`), `String` (for the type `String`) or 0 (for the numeric scalar types). For Variants, Null types, and UDTs, this method returns Nothing. enuType may not specify an array.
`Public ReadOnly Property Dimensions() As Integer`	Read-only property that returns the number of dimensions associated with an Array. This property returns 0 with no other error indication when the variable is not an Array.
`Public Sub dispose()`	Method that disposes of the heap storage associated with the object (if any) and marks the object as not usable. For best results, use this method (or `disposeInspect`) when you are finished with the object.
`Public Function disposeInspect() As Boolean`	Method that disposes of the heap storage associated with the object (if any) and marks the object as not usable. For best results, use this method (or `dispose`) when you are finished with the object. This method conducts a final object inspection. See the preceding "qbVariable Inspection Rules" section.
`Public Function fromString(ByVal strFromstring As String) As Boolean`	Method that sets the variable type to the value serialized in strFromstring. See the preceding section "The fromString Expression Supported by qbVariableType" for the syntax requirements of strFromstring.

Table B-9. qbVariableType Properties, Methods, and Events (continued)

Property/Method/Event	Description
`Public Overloads Function innerType() As qbVariableType`	Method that returns Nothing when the object instance type is Null, Unknown, or scalar. For a Variant or an Array, this method returns the variable type of the value contained in the Variant or the Array entry. This overload of innerType may not be called when the object instance type is a UDT.
`Public Overloads Function innerType(ByVal objIndex As Object) As qbVariableType`	Method that returns the type of a member of a UDT. If the object instance type is not UDT, this method overload causes an error. objIndex may be the UDT member sequence number or the member name. If it is a member name, objIndex may identify submembers by separating distinct member names with periods.
`Public Function inspect(ByRef strReport As String, Optional ByVal booBasic As Boolean = False) As Boolean`	Method that inspects the object instance for errors. See the preceding section "qbVariableType Inspection Rules." The optional booBasic parameter can be passed as True to suppress the extended inspection rules identified in that section.
`Public Function isArray() As Boolean`	Method that returns True for all array types; False otherwise.
`Public Overloads Function isDefaultValue(ByVal objNetValue As Object) As Boolean`	Method that returns True when objNetValue is the default value for the object instance's type; False otherwise.
`Public Overloads Shared Function isDefaultValue(ByVal objNetValue As Object, ByVal enuType As ENUvarType) As Boolean`	Shared method that returns True when objNetValue is the default value for the type identified in enuType; False otherwise.
`Public Function isNull() As Boolean`	Method that returns True when the type is Null; False otherwise.
`Public Overloads Function isomorphicType(ByVal objType2 As qbVariableType) As Boolean`	Method that returns True when all values of the object instance type can be converted without loss of information or error to values of objType2 and all values of objType2 can be converted to the object instance type. For more on isomorphism, see the preceding section "Containment and Isomorphism of Variable Types."

Table B-9. qbVariableType Properties, Methods, and Events (continued)

Property/Method/Event	Description
`Public Overloads Function isomorphicType(ByVal objType2 As qbVariableType, ByRef strExplanation As String) As Boolean`	Method that returns True when all values of the object instance type can be converted without loss of information or error to values of objType2 and all values of objType2 can be converted to the object instance type. This overload of the isomorphicType method provides an explanation of why the types are or are not isomorphic.
`Public Function isScalar() As Boolean`	Method that returns True when the type is scalar; False otherwise. This method returns True only when the type is one of the scalar types Boolean, Byte, Integer, Long, Single, Double, or String. This method returns False for a variant with a scalar contained type.
`Public Shared Function isScalarType(ByVal enuType As ENUvarType) As Boolean`	Shared method that returns True when the type identified in enuType is scalar; False otherwise. This method returns True only when enuType is one of the scalar types Boolean, Byte, Integer, Long, Single, Double, or String.
`Public Shared Function isScalarType(ByVal strType As String) As Boolean`	Shared method that returns True when the type identified by name in strType is scalar; False otherwise. This method returns True one when strType is one of the scalar types Boolean, Byte, Integer, Long, Single, Double, or String.
`Public Function isUDT() As Boolean`	Method that returns True when the type is a UDT; False otherwise.
`Public Function isUnknown() As Boolean`	Method that returns True when the type is Unknown; False otherwise.
`Public Function isVariant() As Boolean`	Method that returns True when the type is Variant; False otherwise.
`Public Property LowerBound(ByVal intDimension As Integer) As Integer`	Indexed, read-write property that returns and can change the lower bound of an array at the dimension *d*, which starts at 1 for the major dimension. If the qbVariableType isn't an array or *d* is invalid, an error occurs. The lower bound may not be changed to a value that is greater than the upper bound, because this would leave the qbVariableType object in an invalid state. See redimension for a method that can change the lower and upper bounds of an array in one statement.

Table B-9. qbVariableType Properties, Methods, and Events (continued)

Property/Method/Event	Description
`Public Overloads Shared Function mkRandomArray() As String`	Shared method that creates a random array specifier (as its toString/fromString string in the form *Array,<type>, <dimensions>*), with one to three random dimensions. The array size at each dimension is restricted to 20 elements, and the lower and upper bounds of each dimension are random, in the range –5..5. The array will randomly be any one of the types Boolean, Byte, Integer, Long, Single, Double, String, or Variant. If it is Variant, it will randomly contain one of the scalar types.
`Public Overloads Shared Function mkRandomArray(ByVal strScalarTypes As String) As String`	Shared method that creates a random array specifier (as its toString/fromString string in the form *Array, <type>,<dimensions>*). This overload works in the same way as the previous one, but it allows the type to be restricted to one of a comma-separated list of type names made up of the types Boolean, Byte, Integer, Long, Single, Double, String, or Variant.
`Public Overloads Shared Function mkRandomDomain() As ENUvarType`	Shared method that creates a random variable type as one of Boolean, Byte, Integer, Long, Single, Double, String, Variant, Array, Unknown, or Null.
`Public Overloads Shared Function mkRandomDomain(ByVal booScalar As Boolean) As ENUvarType`	Shared method that creates a random variable type as one of Boolean, Byte, Integer, Long, Single, Double, String, Variant, Array, Unknown, or Null. If its booScalar parameter is True, this method won't return Variant, Array, Unknown, or Null.
`Public Overloads Shared Function mkRandomScalar() As String`	Shared method that creates a random variable type as one of Boolean, Byte, Integer, Long, Single, Double, or String.
`Public Overloads Shared Function mkRandomScalar(ByVal strTypes As String) As String`	Shared method that creates a random variable type as one of the types identified in the comma-delimited list in strTypes.
`Public Overloads Shared Function mkRandomScalarValue() As Object`	Shared method that creates a random scalar value in .NET form as one of Boolean, Byte, (16-bit Short) Integer, (32-bit) Long, Single, Double, or String.

Table B-9. qbVariableType Properties, Methods, and Events (continued)

Property/Method/Event	Description
Public Shared Function mkRandomType() As String	Shared method that returns a random QuickBasic type expressed as the fromString for that type. With 20% probability, this type will be one of Array, scalar, Variant, or UDT. With 10% probability, this type will be Unknown or Null.
Public Shared Function mkRandomUDT() As String	Method that creates a random UDT specifier (as its toString/fromString string). This UDT will have 1..10 members. Each member will be a random type selected with equal probability from scalar, Variant, Array, or UDT, except that not more than five nested UDTs are allowed.
Public Shared Function mkRandomVariant() As String	Shared method that creates a random value of the Variant type, containing a nonvariant type. The Variant is returned as a string in the form *type(value)*, where *type* is one of the QuickBasic scalar types Boolean, Byte, Integer, Long, Single, Double, or String; and *value* is the value, which will be True, False, a number, or a string. This notation is referred to as *decorated* notation.
Public Shared Function mkRandomVariantValue() As String	Shared method that creates a Variant type (containing a random scalar value). Note that this method cannot create a Variant that contains an array.
Public Shared Function mkType(ByVal enuType As ENUvarType) As qbVariableType	Shared method that creates a new qbVariableType based on the ENUvarType enumerator enuType, which may not be an Array but can be a Variant.
Public Function mkUnusable As Boolean	Method that forces the object instance into the unusable state. It always returns True.
Public Property Name() As String	Read-write property that returns and can set the name of the object instance, which identifies the object in error messages and on the XML tag that is returned by object2XML. The name defaults to qbVariableType*nnnn* date time, where *nnnn* is a sequence number.
Public Shared Function name2NetType (ByVal strSystemName As String) As String	Shared method that converts the system's name for a .NET type (such as System.Int32) to the generic name of one of the .NET types used to support QuickBasic variables (such as Integer). name2NetType will convert System.Int64 to Integer.
Public Shared Function netType2Name (ByVal strNetType As String) As String	Shared method that converts the generic name for a .NET type (such as Integer) to the system name of the .NET type (such as System.Int32).

Table B-9. qbVariableType Properties, Methods, and Events (continued)

Property/Method/Event	Description
`Public Shared Function netType2QBdomain(ByVal strType As String) As ENUvarType`	Shared method that returns the QuickBasic type used to represent the .NET scalar value as an ENUvarType. See also qbDomain2NetType.
`Public Shared Function netValue2QBdomain(ByVal objValue As Object) As ENUvarType`	Shared method that returns the narrowest QuickBasic type to which the .NET object in objValue converts without error as an ENUvarType enumerator. This method returns ENUvarType.vtUnknown when the .NET object does not convert to any QuickBasic type. It does not return Boolean, Array, or Variant. It returns one of Byte, Integer, Long, Single, Double, or String. It returns Null when the .NET value is Nothing. It returns Unknown (with no other error indication) when the .NET value converts to no other values. See also netValueInQBdomain.
`Public Shared Function netValue2QBvalue(ByVal objValue As Object) As Object`	Shared method that converts the .NET value in objValue to a .NET value in the narrowest .NET type that corresponds to a QuickBasic type.
`Public Shared Function netValue2QBvalue(ByVal objValue As Object, ByVal enuType As ENUvarType) As Object`	Shared method that converts the .NET value in objValue to the .NET type that corresponds to the QuickBasic type specified in enuType.
`Public Shared Function netValue2QBvalue(ByVal objValue As Object, ByVal strType As String) As Object`	Shared method that converts the .NET value in objValue to the .NET type that corresponds to the QuickBasic type identified by strType.
`Public Overloads Function netValueInQBdomain(ByVal objValue As Object) As Boolean`	Method that returns True when the .NET value in objValue may be converted without error to the variable type in the object instance.
`Public Overloads Shared Function netValueInQBdomain(ByVal enuType As ENUvarType, ByVal objValue As Object) As Boolean`	Shared method that returns True when the .NET value in objValue may be converted without error to the variable type identified by enuType.
`Public Shared Function netValueIsScalar(ByVal objValue As Object) As Boolean`	Shared method that returns True when the .NET value in objValue is one that can represent one of the QuickBasic scalar values.
`Public Sub new`	Object constructor that creates the qbVariableType and inspects its initial state.

Table B-9. qbVariableType Properties, Methods, and Events (continued)

Property/Method/Event	Description
`Public Sub new(ByVal strFromString As String)`	Overloaded object constructor that creates the qbVariableType and inspects its initial state. It sets the type to the `strFromstring`. For example, `objQBvariableType = New qbVariableType("Integer")` will create the variable type `Integer`.
`Public Shared Function object2Type (ByVal objValue As Object) As String`	Method that returns the corresponding `fromString` expression for its type for any .NET object. If `objValue` is a scalar with a .NET scalar type that corresponds to a QuickBasic type (`Boolean`, `Byte`, `Short`, `Integer`, `Single`, `Double`, or `String`), that type is returned. If `objValue` is a .NET `Long` but in the range –2^31..2^31–1, the `Long` type is returned. If `objValue` is any other value, `Unknown` is returned.
`Public Overloads Function object2XML(Optional ByVal booIncludeCache As Boolean = True) As String`	Method that converts the state of the object to XML. By default, information concerning the variable type cache won't be included in the output XML, but the optional parameter `booIncludeCache` may be passed as `True` to include the serialized cache information. See the previous section "Cache Considerations."
`Public Shared Function qbDomain2NetType(ByVal enuDomain As ENUvarType) As String`	Shared method that converts the type identified by `enuDomain` to the .NET type that is used to contain values of this type. The `enuDomain` cannot be `Unknown`, `Null`, or `Array`. The .NET type is returned as the string name of the type; it will be in the form `SYSTEM.type`.
`Public Function redimension(ByVal intDimension As Integer, ByVal intLowerBound As Integer, ByVal intUpperBound As Integer) As Boolean`	Method that redimensions an array type to the lower bound and upper bound specified. It doesn't allow the lower bound to be greater than the upper bound, but it does avoid the problem that occurs when you need to sequentially change the lower bound to a value that is higher than the upper bound, and the upper bound to a new valid value, or vice versa, using the `LowerBound` and `UpperBound` properties.
`Public Function scalarDefault() As Object`	Method that returns the default value applicable to the type. If the type is `Null` or `Unknown`, it returns Nothing. If the type is scalar, it returns the default for the scalar type. If the type is array, it returns the default for the array entry. If the type is concrete variant (a `Variant` with a known embedded type), it returns the default for the embedded type. If the type is abstract variant (a `Variant` with an unknown embedded type), it returns Nothing.

Table B-9. qbVariableType Properties, Methods, and Events (continued)

Property/Method/Event	Description
`Public ReadOnly Property StorageSpace() As Integer`	Read-only property that returns the total number of abstract cells occupied by the variable type. Scalar and Variant values occupy one cell. Arrays occupy the number of cells equivalent to their total size in array elements. Unknown values occupy 0 cells. Null values occupy 1 cell. UDTs occupy the sum of space occupied by their members.
`Public Shared Function string2enuVarType(ByVal strInstring As String) As ENUvarType`	Shared method that converts a string type name to an enuVarType enumerator. `strInstring` is one of vtBoolean, vtByte, vtInteger, vtLong, vtSingle, vtDouble, vtString, vtVariant, vtArray, vtUDT, vtNull, or vtUnknown. The prefix vt may be omitted, and the name is case-insensitive.
`Public Property Tag() As Object`	Read-write property that returns and can be set to user data that needs to be associated with the qbVariableType instance. Tag can be a reference object. If so, the Tag object isn't destroyed when the object is destroyed.
`Public Overloads Function test(ByRef strReport As String) As Boolean`	Method runs tests on the object, and returns True to indicate success; False otherwise. The strReport reference parameter is set to a test report. The test consists of four phases: a series of random fromString expressions are built and used to create new qbVariableType objects,[12] the defaultValue method is tested to make sure it provides valid defaults, the testing type containment methods are run for a series of known results, and finally, the various "domain-mapping" methods (which convert .NET values and types to QuickBasic values and types) are tested. If the test fails, the object instance is marked as not usable. A test method will be exposed by this object, unless the compile-time symbol QBVARIABLETYPE_NOTEST is set explicitly to True in the project properties for qbVariableType.[13]
`Public Shared ReadOnly Property TestAvailable() As Boolean`	Shared method that returns True if the version of qbVariableType, running this method, was compiled with the compile-time symbol QBVARIABLETEST_NOTEST either omitted or set to False.

---

12. Of course, these new qbVariableType objects are inspected for validity when created.

13. Set the compile-time symbol QBVARIABLETYPE_NOTEST to True in the project to suppress the generation of the test method.

Table B-9. qbVariableType Properties, Methods, and Events (continued)

Property/Method/Event	Description
Public Event testEvent(ByVal strDesc As String, ByVal intLevel As Integer)	Event that is fired during the execution of the test method for testing stages and testing events. strDesc describes the stage or event, and intLevel is a nesting level that starts at 0. To obtain this event, the qbVariableType instance must be declared WithEvents, a handler for the testEvent must be supplied, and the compile-time symbol QBVARIABLETEST_NOTEST must be omitted or set to False.
Public Event testProgressEvent (ByVal strDesc As String, ByVal strEntity As String, ByVal intEntityNumber As Integer, ByVal intEntityCount As Integer)	Event that is fired during the execution of the test method. It reports progress inside loops. strDesc describes the loop goal. strEntity describes the entity being processed in the loop. intEntityNumber is the number of the entity. intEntityCount is the total number of entities. To obtain this event, the qbVariableType instance must be declared WithEvents, a handler for the testEvent must be supplied, and the compile-time symbol QBVARIABLETEST_NOTEST must be omitted or set to False.
Public Overloads Function toContainedName() As String	Method that returns the name of the type contained in a Variant or the entry type of an Array. If the type in the object instance does not represent a Variant or an Array, this method returns a null string.
Public Overloads Function toContainedName(ByVal objIndex As Object) As String	Method that returns the name of the type contained in a UDT at the indexed member, where objIndex may be the position (from 1) of the member or the name of the member. Submembers of member UDTs can be accessed as a series of period-separated names.

Table B-9. qbVariableType Properties, Methods, and Events (continued)

Property/Method/Event	Description
`Public Function toDescription() As String`	Method that returns a readable description of the variable type. For a scalar, it returns the scalar type name, such as `Integer`. For an abstract variant, it returns "Abstract Variant."[14] For a concrete variant, it returns "Variant containing *desc*," where *desc* is the description of the contained type. For a one-dimensional array, it returns "1-dimensional array containing *n* elements from *m* to *p*: each element has the type *desc*." For a two-dimensional array, it returns "2-dimensional array with *n* rows (from *m* to *p*) and *q* columns (from *r* to *s*): each element has the type *desc*." For an *n*-dimensional array, it returns "*n*-dimensional array with these bounds: *list*: each element has the type *desc*." For a UDT, it returns "UDT; *list*," where *list* is a list of scalar, `Array`, and `Variant` descriptions. For an Unknown type, it returns "Unknown type." For a `Null` type, it returns "Null type."
`Public Function toName() As String`	Method that returns the name of the variable type in the object instance. Unlike `toString`, it returns only `Variant`, `Array`, or UDT.
`Public Overrides Function toString() As String`	Method that returns the type in the `qbVariableType`, in the format described for `fromString` in the preceding section "The fromString Expression Supported by qbVariableType." If the variable is an array, the representation returned is packed, condensing series of identical elements using parenthesized repetition counts. The representation returns default values as asterisks if the value of a scalar variable contains the default value appropriate to its type, or each member in an array value contains the default. The variables in the output string are decorated (using *type*(*value*) syntax) when the variable type is either `Variant` or `Variant Array`.

---

14. An *abstract variant* is a variant with an unknown contained type.

Table B-9. qbVariableType Properties, Methods, and Events (continued)

Property/Method/Event	Description
Public Function toStringVerify (Optional ByVal booVerify As Boolean = False) As String	Method that returns the type and value of the qbVariableType, in the format described for fromString in the preceding section "The fromString Expression Supported by qbVariableType." Setting toStringVerify (booVerify:=True) causes the object to try to create an object using the synthesized toString, and the object will then verify that the created object clones the original object. If this test fails, an error is thrown and the object marks itself as unusable.
Public ReadOnly Property UDTmemberCount() As Integer	Read-only property that returns the number of members when the object instance represents a UDT. If the object instance does not represent a UDT, an error occurs.
Public Function udtMemberDeref (ByVal strMemberName As String) As Integer	Method that "dereferences" strMemberName, because it converts it to the index (from 1) of the corresponding UDT member in the variable type instance. If the object instance does not represent a UDT, an error occurs.
Public Function udtMemberName(ByVal objIndex As Object) As String	Method that "dereferences" objIndex, which is normally the index (from 1) of a UDT member, and this method converts objIndex to the member name. The index may also be the actual member name in which case this method performs no useful work.
Public Function udtMemberType (ByVal objIndex As Object) As qbVariableType	Method "dereferences" objIndex, which will be either the index (from one) of a UDT member, or a member name, and this method returns the type at the indexed UDT member.
Public Property UpperBound(ByVal intDimension As Integer) As Integer	Indexed, read-write property that returns and can change the upper bound of an array at the dimension *d*, which starts at 1 for the major dimension. If the qbVariableType isn't an array or *d* is invalid, an error occurs. UpperBound may not be changed to a value that is less than LowerBound, because this would leave the qbVariableType object in an invalid state. See redimension for a method that can change the lower and upper bounds of an array in one statement.
Public ReadOnly Property Usable() As Boolean	Read-only property that returns True if the object instance is usable; False otherwise.
Public Overloads Shared Function validFromString(ByVal strFS As String) As Boolean	Method that returns True when strFS contains a valid fromString expression; False otherwise. Validity is determined by creating a qbVariableType, which is then destroyed.

Table B-9. qbVariableType Properties, Methods, and Events (continued)

Property/Method/Event	Description
`Public Overloads Shared Function validFromString(ByVal strFS As String, ByRef objTest As qbVariableType) As Boolean`	Method that returns True when strFS contains a valid fromString expression; False otherwise. All overloads of validFromString determine validity by actually creating a qbVariableType, and this overload returns the variable created.
`Public ReadOnly Property VariableType() As ENUvarType`	Read-only property that returns the type inside the object instance. VariableType is the main variable type. See also VarType.
`Public Shared ReadOnly Property VariableTypeList() As String`	Shared, read-only property that returns a space-delimited list of all the variable types supported: Boolean Byte Integer Long Single Double String Variant Array Unknown Null.
`Public ReadOnly Property VarType() As ENUvarType`	Read-only property that returns the type *contained* inside the object instance type. For Variants, this is the type of the Variant's value. For Arrays, it is the entry type. For everything else, this property returns ENUvarType.vtUnknown, with no other error indication. VarType is the contained variable type. See also VariableType.
`Public Shared Function vtPrefixAdd(ByVal strName As String) As String`	Shared method that adds the vt prefix to strName, unless it is present, and returns the result.[15]
`Public Shared Function vtPrefixRemove(ByVal strName As String) As String`	Shared method that removes the vt prefix from strName, when it is present, and returns the result.

quickBasicEngine

The quickBasicEngine class does all scanning, parsing, and interpretation for this version of QuickBasic. It may be dropped in to a .NET application, and it will provide the ability to evaluate immediate Basic expressions, as well as compile and run Basic programs.

References of quickBasicEngine include collectionUtilities.DLL, qbOp.DLL, qbPolish, qbScanner.DLL, qbToken, qbTokenType.DLL, qbVariable, qbVariableType, and utilities.DLL.

---

15. Variable type enumerator names are prefixed by vt.

`quickBasicEngine` is fully thread-safe. See the documentation header in the source code for instructions on modifying the source code while maintaining the thread safety of this code.

Note that this class implements `ICloneable` and `IComparable`.

The quickBasicEngine Data Model and States

The state of the `quickBasicEngine` class consists of all source code for a program, its scanned representation, and the names and the structured values of all variables found in the code. It also includes various processing details, such as the trivial queue maintained for the legacy `Read Data` instruction.

> **NOTE** *No explicit parse tree is built, because this is unnecessary. Parse information is available just-in-time through the* `parseEvent`, *which is fired for each distinct grammar symbol.*

At any time, instances of this class are usable or nonusable, and one of the following states:

- **Ready to run:** When the object is fully initialized, and after normal procedures have terminated, it is Ready to run.

- **Running (*n* threads):** When the object is running normally, it is Running. It may be simultaneously running procedures in more than one thread.

- **Stopping:** When the user has requested a stop, through the `stopQBE` method, but threads are still running, the object is Stopping.

- **Stopped:** When the user has requested a stop, through the `stopQBE` method, and no threads are still running, the object is Stopped.

The usability and running states, and the number of running threads, are available through methods and properties.

At the end of a successful `New` constructor, the instance becomes usable and Ready to run. A successful or failed execution of `dispose` makes the object unusable.

A serious internal error, such as failure to create a resource, or using the object after a serious error is reported makes the object not usable. The `mkUnusable` method may also be used to force the object into the unusable state. The `Usable` property tells the caller whether the object is usable.

Usability makes run status moot because an unusable instance won't run. It should be disposed, a new instance should be created, and the processing that created the error should not be repeated.

The stopQBE method places the object in a Stopping state immediately, and it puts the object in a Stopped state when all running threads have terminated. While an unusable object cannot be made usable, a Stopped object can be restored to active duty using the resumeQBE method.

When the object instance is Stopped, the state of the engine becomes immediately Stopping as an atomic operation. Then the following occurs:

- Any executing For or Do loop in the engine, which issues loop events, is exited as soon as the loop event is issued.

- If the interpreter is running, the interpreter is exited after an undefined amount of time, after the object is stopped. The time is the duration from the issuance of stopQBE and the point at which the interpreter arrives at the head of its For loop.

- No Public procedure will execute, and all Public procedures will return default values, until Stopped is set to False.

The resumeQBE method places the object in the Ready state if the object is stopped. The resume method has no effect when the object is already Ready or is in the Running or Stopping states.

The getThreadStatus method returns the run status as one of ready, running, stopping, or stopped.

When the quickBasicEngine is Running, the runningThreads method returns the number of threads that are running methods and properties as a number between 1 and *n*. When quickBasicEngine is Stopped or Ready, runningThreads returns 0.

Inspection Rules of the quickBasicEngine

The following inspection rules are used by the inspect method:

- The object instance must be usable.

- The scanner object must pass its own inspection.

- The collection of qbPolish instructions must contain qbPolish objects exclusively. If the collection contains fewer than 101 objects, each object must pass the qbPolish.inspect inspection; if more 100 objects exist, a random selection of objects is inspected.

- The collection of `qbVariable` variables must conform to its expected structure; see the source code for details.

- The subroutine and function index must conform to its expected structure; see the source code for details.

- The constant expression index must conform to its expected structure; see the source code for details.

- If the inspection is failed, the object becomes unusable.

An internal inspection is carried out in the constructor and inside the `dispose` method.

Properties, Methods, and Events of quickBasicEngine

Table B-10 lists the properties, methods, and events of the `quickBasicEngine` class.

Table B-10. quickBasicEngine Properties, Methods, and Events

Property/Method/Event	Description
Public Shared ReadOnly Property About As String	Shared, read-only property that returns information about the class.
Public Function assemble() As Boolean	Method that assembles the Polish tokens, replacing symbolic labels with numeric addresses and removing comment lines inserted by the compiler. Assembly is a two-pass process: pass one converts the dictionary mapping labels to addresses, and pass two replaces the labels.
Public Function assembled() As Boolean	Method that returns True if the current source code has been assembled already; False otherwise.
Public Property AssemblyRemovesCode() As Boolean	Read-write property that returns and may be set to True to remove remarks inserted by the compiler and label statements inserted during assembly, or False to suppress this removal. By default, this removal occurs. Setting this property to False does not change the effect of QuickBasic code, only its efficiency.
Public Shared ReadOnly Property ClassName	Shared read-only property that returns the class name: quickBasicEngine.
Public Function clear() As Boolean	Method that resets the engine to a start state by ensuring all reference variables are cleared. You don't need to execute it in the normal case, as long as you use dispose to responsibly clean up the compiler.

Table B-10. quickBasicEngine Properties, Methods, and Events (continued)

Property/Method/Event	Description
`Public Function clearStorage() As Boolean`	Method that sets all variables in the current program to the default value for their type.
`Public Shared Function clone As quickBasicEngine`	Method that implements ICloneable and returns a clone of the instance object. The clone consists of identical code (including comments and white space patterns) and identical run mode options, including optimization, but it may not be in the same state as the cloned object. The clone is always n the initial, unexecuted state. When passed to the compareTo method, the clone returns True.
`Public Event codeRemoveEvent(ByVal objQBsender As qbQuickBasicEngine, ByVal intOpIndex As Integer)`	Event that is triggered whenever code is removed from the compiled set of qbPolish tokens: objQBsender identifies the quickBasicEngine, and intOpIndex identifies the index of the operation removed.
`Public Shared Function codeType (ByVal strCode As String) As String`	Shared method that returns the type of strCode as a string. immediateCommand is returned when the code is a valid expression. program is returned when the code is a valid executable program. Otherwise, invalid is returned.
`Public Function compareTo(ByVal objQBE As quickBasicEngine.qbQuick BasicEngine) As Boolean`	Method that compares the instance object to the quickBasicEngine identified in objQBE, and returns True when objQBE clones the instance. objQBE clones the instance when the source code of objQBE and that of the instance are identical, except for white space, and all global options such as the ConstantFolding property are the same. The compilation and assembly of the two objects and their storage values may differ. The compareTo method implements the IComparable interface.
`Public Function compile() As Boolean`	Method that compiles the source code to unassembled interpretive code. This method won't proceed to assembly on a successful compile, it will scan code that has not been scanned already.
`Public Function compiled() As Boolean`	Method that returns True if the current source code has been compiled already; False otherwise.

Table B-10. quickBasicEngine Properties, Methods, and Events (continued)

Property/Method/Event	Description
`Public Event compileErrorEvent(ByVal objQBsender As qbQuickBasicEngine, ByVal strMessage As String, ByVal intIndex As Integer, ByVal intContextLength As Integer, ByVal intLinenumber As Integer, ByVal strHelp As String, ByVal strCode As String)`	Event that is triggered by errors in the source code. `objQBsender` identifies the `quickBasicEngine` reporting the error. `strMessage` is the error text, which might have more than one line. `intIndex` is the index of the character at which the error occurs. `intContextLength` is the length of the error's context (the source code probably responsible for the error). `intLineNumber` is the line number of the error. `strCode` is the line of source code at which the error occurs.
`Public Property ConstantFolding() As Boolean`	Read-write property that returns and may be set to `True` or `False`, to control constant folding. When `ConstantFolding` is `True`, all expressions and subexpressions in the source code that consist exclusively of constants and operators are evaluated by the compiler, not at runtime.[16] When `ConstantFolding` is `False`, all subexpressions in the source code that consist exclusively of constants and operators are compiled normally to code.
`Public Property DegenerateOpRemoval() As Boolean`	Read-write property that returns and may be set to `True` or `False` to control the removal of degenerate operations. When `DegenerateOpRemoval` is `True`, all operations known to have no effect at compile time (including addition of the constant 0 and multiplication by the constant 1) are removed. When `DegenerateOpRemoval` is `False`; all degenerate operations generate code for runtime evaluation.
`Public Overloads Function dispose As String`	Method that disposes of the object and it cleans up any reference objects in the heap. This method marks the object as unusable. This overload always conducts an internal inspection of the object instance (using the `inspect` method), and throws an error if the inspection is failed. For best results, use this method when you are finished using the object in code. See the next method for an overload that allows inspection to be skipped.
`Public Overloads Function dispose (ByVal booInspect As Boolean) As String`	Method that disposes of the object and cleans up any reference objects in the heap. This method marks the object as unusable. This overload inspects the object instance unless `dispose(False)` is used. For best results, use this method when you are finished using the object in code.

16. This can speed up runtime. For example, in `a+1+1` when `ConstantFolding` is `True`, the subexpression 1+1 is evaluated by the compiler. This example is contrived (as in stupid) but many code and business rule generators may yield such contrived, stupid examples.

Table B-10. quickBasicEngine Properties, Methods, and Events (continued)

Property/Method/Event	Description
`Public Shared ReadOnly Property EasterEgg() As String`	Shared, read-only property that returns the quickBasicEngine's Easter egg of dedicatory, ceremonial language and quotes, setting a dignified, high-toned atmosphere.
`Public Overloads Shared Function eval(ByVal strExpression As String) As qbVariable.qbVariable`	Shared, "lightweight" method that evaluates the string *s* as a single expression in QuickBasic notation or as a series of statements (separated by colons), followed by a colon and then a final expression. For example, *s* may be a series of `Let` assignment statements that set variable values, followed by an expression. The value of the expression is returned as a `qbVariable` object. This method creates a new `quickBasicEngine` with all of the default values and default properties, and the evaluated string is executed using default values and default properties. See also `evaluate`.
`Public Overloads Shared Function eval(ByVal strExpression As String, ByRef strLog As String) As qbVariable.qbVariable`	Shared, "lightweight" method that evaluates the string *s* as a single expression in QuickBasic notation or as a series of statements (separated by colons), followed by a colon and then a final expression. This overload works like the previous overload, but it places the evaluation event log in the `strLog` string, passed by reference. See the `EventLog` property for details on the format of event logs. See also `evaluate`.
`Public Overloads Shared Function eval(ByVal strExpression As String, ByRef booError As Boolean) As String`	Shared, "lightweight" method that evaluates the string *s* as a single expression in QuickBasic notation or as a series of statements (separated by colons), followed by a colon and then a final expression. The value of the expression is returned, as a string. The reference parameter `booError` is set to `True` on any error (and a null string is usually returned). `booError` is set to `False` on an error-free evaluation. The `eval` method creates a new `quickBasicEngine` with all of the default values and default properties, and the evaluated string is executed using default values and default properties. See the `EventLog` property for details on the format of event logs. See also `evaluate`.

Table B-10. quickBasicEngine Properties, Methods, and Events (continued)

Property/Method/Event	Description
`Public Overloads Function evaluate (ByVal strExpression As String) As qbVariable.qbVariable`	Shared, "heavyweight" method that evaluates the string strExpression as a single expression in QuickBasic notation or as a series of statements (separated by colons), followed by a colon and then a final expression. For example, strExpression may be a series of Let assignment statements that set variable values, followed by an expression. The value of the expression is returned as a qbVariable object. The evaluate method uses the current state of the object running the evaluation. See also eval.
`Public Sub evaluate(ByVal strExpression As String, ByRef objValue As qbVariable)`	Shared, "heavyweight" method that evaluates the string strExpression as a single expression in QuickBasic notation or as a series of statements (separated by colons), followed by a colon and then a final expression. For example, strExpression may be a series of Let assignment statements that set variable values, followed by an expression. The value of the expression is returned in objValue as a reference parameter. The evaluate method uses the current state of the object running the evaluation. This version of evaluate is provided primarily to allow threads to easily use it through the standard call. See also eval.
`Public Overloads Shared Function evaluate(ByVal strExpression As String, ByRef strLog As String) As qbVariable.qbVariable`	Shared, "heavyweight" method that evaluates the string strExpression as a single expression in QuickBasic notation or as a series of statements (separated by colons), followed by a colon and then a final expression. For example, strExpression may be a series of Let assignment statements that set variable values, followed by an expression. The value of the expression is returned as a qbVariable object. The evaluate method uses the current state of the object running the evaluation. This overload places the evaluation event log in the strLog string, passed by reference. See the EventLog property for details on the format of event logs. See also eval.
`Public ReadOnly Property Evaluation() As qbVariable.qbVariable`	Read-only property that returns the result of the most recent evaluate method or Nothing when no such result exists.
`Public Function evaluationValue() As qbVariable.qbVariable`	Method that returns the result of the most recent evaluate method, or Nothing when no such result exists.

Table B-10. quickBasicEngine Properties, Methods, and Events (continued)

Property/Method/Event	Description
`Public ReadOnly Property EventLog()` `As Collection`	Read-only property that returns a `Collection` of items, each of which represents an event raised by a `RaiseEvent` in the QuickBasic engine. The event log is populated only when the `EventLogging` parameter is set to `True`. This property is useful in finding events issued by a `quickBasicEngine` that has not been defined using `WithEvents`. Each item in the event log is a three-item subcollection: item(1) identifies the event, item(2) is the event date and time, and item(3) is a list of the event operands. In item(3), each operand is separated by a newline and is in the format *name=value*.
`Public Overloads Function` `eventLog2ErrorList() As String`	Method that returns a list suitable for display in a monospaced font (such as Courier New) of all compiler and interpreter error events in the object instance event log.

`Public Overloads Shared Function`
`eventLog2ErrorList(ByVal colEventLog`
`As Collection) As String`
	Shared method that returns a list suitable for display in a monospaced font (such as Courier New) of all compiler and interpreter error events in the object instance event log passed as `colEventLog`. `colEventLog` must be in the format described for the `EventLog` property.

`Public Overloads Function` `eventLogFormat() As String`	Method that formats the event log in the object instance in a way best viewed in a monospace font such as Courier New, and returns the formatted log as a string.

`Public Overloads Function`
`eventLogFormat(ByVal intStartIndex`
`As Integer) As String`
	Method that formats the event log in the object instance in a way best viewed in a monospace font such as Courier New, and returns the formatted log as a string. The returned log starts at `intStartIndex`.

`Public Overloads Function`
`eventLogFormat(ByVal intStartIndex`
`As Integer, ByVal intCount As`
`Integer) As String`
	Method formats the event log in the object instance in a way best viewed in a monospace font such as Courier New, and returns the formatted log as a string. The returned log starts at `intStartIndex` and contains at most `intCount` entries.

`Public Overloads Shared Function`
`eventLogFormat(ByVal colEventLog`
`As Collection) As String`
	Shared method that formats the event log passed as `colEventLog` in a way best viewed in a monospace font such as Courier New, and returns the formatted log as a string.

`Public ReadOnly Property` `EventLogging() As Boolean`	Read-write property that returns and may be set to `True` or `False` to control the generation of event logs.

Table B-10. quickBasicEngine Properties, Methods, and Events (continued)

Property/Method/Event	Description
`Public Overloads Function getThreadStatus() As String`	Method that returns the thread status, while discounting its own effect, as one of the strings Initializing, Ready, Running, Stopping, or Stopped. The value returned is non-deterministic, because while getThreadStatus discounts its own effect, the status may change while it is executing.[17] See also runningThreads.
`Public Function inspect(ByRef strReport As String, Optional ByVal booBasic As Boolean = False) As Boolean`	Method that inspects the object instance for errors. An internal inspection is carried out when the object is constructed and inside the disposeInspect method. If the inspection fails, the object is marked as unusable. See the preceding section "quickBasicEngine Inspection Rules." The optional booBasic parameter can be passed as True to suppress the extended inspection rules.
`Public Property InspectCompiler Objects() As Boolean`	Read-write property that returns and may be set to True when objects created by the compiler need to be inspected when disposed. Its default is False. Set this option to True when testing the compiler and modifications as a way to be sure that objects don't include buggy code. Setting this option will slow the compiler down. When this option is True, the following compiler object types will be inspected when they are disposed: The scanner, each variable that is created during compilation and interpretation (including its type), and the quickBasicEngine.
`Public Function interpret() As Object`	Method that interprets the compiled code (it will scan, compile, and assemble the source code as needed). This method will return an Object. If the stack is empty at the end of interpretation, this method returns True. If the stack contains one entry at the end of interpretation, it returns that entry, which will be a qbVariable. If the stack contains multiple entries at the end of interpretation, it returns False. This method does QuickBasic input and output by means of events. See interpretInputEvent and interpretPrintEvent for details.

---

17. For this reason, getThreadStatus should be used for entertainment purposes only; for example, to display the nondeterministic status in a GUI.

Table B-10. quickBasicEngine Properties, Methods, and Events (continued)

Property/Method/Event	Description
Public Event interpretErrorEvent (ByVal objQBsender As QuickBasicEngine, ByVal strMessage As String, ByVal intIndex As Integer, ByVal strHelp As String)	Event that is triggered when an error occurs in the interpreter. objQBsender identifies the quickBasicEngine. strMessage is the error message (which may contain multiple lines). intIndex identifies the position of the Polish instruction causing the error. strHelp may contain additional error information.
Public Event interpretInputEvent (ByVal objQBsender As QuickBasicEngine, ByRef strChars As String)	Event that is triggered when an Input statement is executed and the interpreter needs input. The event handler should usually prompt through the GUI for input and place the input characters in strChars. objQBsender identifies the quickBasicEngine that requires the input.
Public Event interpretPrintEvent (ByVal objQBsender As QuickBasicEngine, ByVal strOutstring As String)	Event that is triggered when a Print statement is executed. The event handler should usually display the output string as-is, or the Print statement may be in use to return results to a business rules interface.
Public Event interpretTraceEvent (ByVal objQBsender As qbQuickBasicEngine, ByVal intIndex As Integer, ByVal objStack As Stack, ByVal colStorage As Collection)	Event that is triggered prior to each interpreter execution of each Polish opcode. objQBsender identifies the quickBasicEngine. intIndex is the index of the Polish opcode. objStack is the stack prior to executing the opcode. colStorage is the variable collection prior to executing the opcode. The Shared stack2String method is available for serializing the stack, and the Shared storage2String method is available for serializing variable storage.
Public Event loopEvent(ByVal objQBsender As qbQuickBasicEngine, ByVal strActivity As String, ByVal strEntity As String, ByVal intNumber As Integer, ByVal intCount As Integer, ByVal intLevel As Integer, ByVal strComment As String)	Event that is triggered inside loops inside the quickBasicEngine. objQBsender identifies the quickBasicEngine. strActivity identifies the loop activity. strEntity identifies the entity being processed. intNumber identifies the number of the current entity. intCount identifies the total number of entities. intLevel identifies the nesting level starting at 0. strComment may provide additional information about the loop.
Public Function mkUnusable As Boolean	Method that forces the object instance into the unusable state. It always returns True.
Public Event msgEvent(ByVal objQBsender As qbQuickBasicEngine, ByVal strMessage As String)	Event that is triggered by general messages inside the quickBasicEngine. objQBsender identifies the quickBasicEngine. strMessage is the message.

Table B-10. quickBasicEngine Properties, Methods, and Events (continued)

Property/Method/Event	Description
`Public Function msilRun() As Object`	Method that translates the interpretive Nutty Professor code into MSIL, generates a simple dynamic assembly, and runs the code. This method returns the final stack value as a function value, which is a .NET value.[18] If Polish operations exist that cannot be translated, this method throws an error and returns Nothing. If the MSIL code leaves an empty stack, this method throws an error and returns Nothing.
`Public Property Name() As String`	Read-write property that returns and can set the name of the object instance, which will identify the object in error messages and on the XML tag that is returned by `object2XML`. The name defaults to `quickBasicEnginennnn date time`, where *nnnn* is a sequence number.
`Public Sub new`	Object constructor that creates the `quickBasicEngine` and inspects its initial state.
`Public Overloads Function object2XML (Optional ByVal booAboutComment As Boolean = False, Optional ByVal booStateComment As Boolean = True) As String`	Method that converts the state of the object to XML. By default, the About information of this class is not included in the returned tag, but it can be included using `booAboutComment:=True`. By default, line-by-line comments describing each state variable are included in the returned tag, but they can be suppressed using `booStateComment:=False`.
`Public Event parseEvent(ByVal objQBsender As qbQuickBasicEngine, ByVal strGrammarCategory As String, ByVal booTerminal As Boolean, ByVal intSrcStartIndex As Integer, ByVal intSrcLength As Integer, ByVal intTokStartIndex As Integer, ByVal intTokLength As Integer, ByVal intObjStartIndex As Integer, ByVal intObjLength As Integer, ByVal strComment As String, ByVal intLevel As Integer)`	Event that is triggered when a terminal or nonterminal grammar category is parsed. `objQBsender` identifies the `quickBasicEngine`. `strGrammarCategory` identifies the grammar category. `booTerminal` is True (grammar category is a terminal) or False. `intSrcStartIndex` is the start index of the code corresponding to the grammar category as a character index from 1. `intSrcLength` is the character length of the code corresponding to the grammar category. `intTokStartIndex` is the start index of the code corresponding to the grammar category as a token index from 1. `intTokLength` is the token length of the code corresponding to the grammar category. `intObjStartIndex` is the start index of the output Polish code corresponding to the grammar category from 1. `intObjLength` is the length of the Polish code corresponding to the grammar category. `strHelp` may contain additional information about the parse. `intLevel` is the parse nesting depth from 0.

---

18. At this writing, only a few Polish opcodes are translatable to MSIL.

Table B-10. quickBasicEngine Properties, Methods, and Events (continued)

Property/Method/Event	Description
`Public Event parseFailEvent(ByVal objQBsender As qbQuickBasicEngine, ByVal strGrammarCategory As String)`	Event that is triggered when the parser has attempted to parse a grammar category and failed. This doesn't necessarily indicate an error. `objQBsender` identifies the quickBasicEngine. `strGrammarCategory` identifies the grammar category.
`Public Event parseStartEvent(ByVal objQBsender As qbQuickBasicEngine, ByVal strGrammarCategory As String)`	Event that is triggered when the parser starts a parse attempt. `objQBsender` identifies the quickBasicEngine. `strGrammarCategory` identifies the grammar category.
`Public ReadOnly Property PolishCollection() As Collection`	Read-only property that returns the collection of qbPolish objects corresponding to the compiled code. This collection may be Nothing if there is no compiled code.
`Public Function reset() As Boolean`	Method that resets the quickBasicEngine.
`Public Function resumeQBE() As Boolean`	Method that puts the quickBasicEngine in the Ready state when it is in the Stopped state. If the object is in any other state, resume has no effect and results in no error. For best results, clear the quickBasicEngine after resuming it.
`Public Overloads Function run() As Boolean`	Method runs the immediate command or program in the quickBasicEngine. The code will be scanned, compiled, and/or assembled as needed.
`Public Overloads Function run(ByVal strRunType As String) As Boolean`	Method that runs the immediate command or program in the quickBasicEngine. The run type of immediateCommand or program may be specified in strRunType.
`Public Function runningThreads() As Integer`	Method that returns the number of threads that are running procedures inside the quickBasicEngine as a number between 0 and *n*. This method includes its own thread. The value returned is nondeterministic, because the status may change while it is executing. The value will always be one or greater because runningThreads includes its own thread. See also getThreadStatus.
`Public Function scan() As Boolean`	Method that scans the source code.
`Public Event scanEvent(ByVal objQBsender As qbQuickBasicEngine, ByVal objToken As qbToken.qbToken)`	Event that is triggered when the scanner has found the next token. `objQBsender` identifies the quickBasicEngine. `objToken` identifies the token.
`Public Function scanned() As Boolean`	Method that returns True when the current source code has been scanned; False otherwise.

Table B-10. quickBasicEngine Properties, Methods, and Events (continued)

Property/Method/Event	Description
Public Function scanner() As qbScanner	Method that returns the qbScanner object associated with the source code. If no scanner has been created, it may return Nothing.
Public Property SourceCode() As String	Read-write property that assigns and returns the current source code. When it is assigned, storage is emptied of all variables, and the indicators showing that lexical analysis, compile, and assembly are complete are set to False.
Public Shared Function stack2String (ByVal objStack As Stack) As String	Shared method that formats a stack of qbVariables such as the stack returned by the interpretEvent. The formatted stack is best viewed in a monospace font such as Courier New.
Public Function stopQBE As Boolean	Method that puts the quickBasicEngine in the Stopped state when it is in the Ready or Running state. If the object is in the Stopped state already, it has no effect and results in no error. If the object is in the Running state, (1) any executing For or Do loop is exited as soon as the loop event is issued, (2) if the parser is running, the compiler is exited when the next grammar category is recognized, (3) if the interpreter is running, the interpreter is exited as soon as the interpreter's loop event is issued.
Public Shared Function Storage2String(ByVal colStorage As Collection) As String	Shared method that formats a collection of qbVariables such as is returned by the interpretEvent as the interpreter storage. The formatted storage is best viewed in a monospace font such as Courier New.
Public Property Tag() As Object	Read-write property that returns and can be set to user data that needs to be associated with the quickBasicEngine instance. It's a kind of post-it note. The Tag can be a reference object. If so, the Tag object is not destroyed when the object is destroyed.
Public Overloads Function test(ByRef strReport As String) As Boolean	Method that runs tests on the object. It returns True to indicate success or False to indicate failure. The strReport reference parameter is set to a test report.
Public Overloads Function test (ByRef strReport As String, ByVal booEventLog As Boolean) As Boolean	Method that runs tests on the object. It returns True to indicate success or False to indicate failure. The strReport reference parameter is set to a test report. The booEventLog parameter may be specified as True to get an event log inside the report.

Table B-10. quickBasicEngine Properties, Methods, and Events (continued)

Property/Method/Event	Description
`Public Shared ReadOnly Property TestAvailable() As Boolean`	Shared method that returns True if the version of quickBasicEngine running this method was compiled with the compile-time symbol QBVARIABLETEST_NOTEST either omitted or set to False.
`Public Event testEvent(ByVal strDesc As String, ByVal intLevel As Integer)`	Event that is fired during the execution of the test method for testing stages and testing events. strDesc describes the stage or event, and intLevel is a nesting level that starts at 0. To obtain this event, the quickBasicEngine instance must be declared WithEvents, a handler for the testEvent must be supplied, and the compile-time symbol QBVARIABLETEST_NOTEST must be omitted or set to False.
`Public Event testProgressEvent(ByVal strDesc As String, ByVal strEntity As String, ByVal intEntityNumber As Integer, ByVal intEntityCount As Integer)`	Event that is fired during the execution of the test method. It reports progress inside loops. strDesc describes the loop goal. strEntity describes the entity being processed in the loop. intEntityNumber is the number of the entity. intEntityCount is the total number of entities. To obtain this event, the quickBasicEngine instance must be declared WithEvents, a handler for the testEvent must be supplied, and the compile-time symbol QBVARIABLETEST_NOTEST must be omitted or set to False.
`Public Event threadStatusChangeEvent (ByVal objQBsender As qbQuickBasicEngine)`	Event that is raised when the number of threads running quickBasicEngine code changes or the quickBasicEngine is stopped. objQBsender is the handle of the sender quickBasicEngine.
`Public Event userErrorEvent(ByVal objQBsender As qbQuickBasicEngine, ByVal strDescription As String, ByVal strHelp As String)`	Event that is triggered when there is an error in using the procedures of this object, as opposed to an error in the QuickBasic source code. objQBsender identifies the quickBasicEngine. strDescription identifies the error (and it may contain more than one line). strHelp identifies additional help information.

END START
—Fragment of IBM 1401 assembler code

This is the end.
—Jim Morrison, The Doors

The rest is silence.
—Shakespeare, Hamlet

Of that which we cannot speak of thereupon must we be silent.
—Wittgenstein

That's all folks.
—Porky Pig

In my end is my beginning.
—T. S. Eliot

Index

Symbols

ASPToday is a unique solutions library for professional ASP Developers, giving quick and convenient access to a constantly growing library of **over 1000 practical and relevant articles and case studies**. We aim to publish a completely original professionally written and reviewed article every working day of the year. Consequently our resource is completely without parallel in the industry. Thousands of web developers use and recommend this site for real solutions, keeping up to date with new technologies, or simply increasing their knowledge.

Exciting Site Features!

Find it FAST!
Powerful full-text search engine so you can find exactly the solution you need.

Printer-friendly!
Print articles for a bound archive and quick desk reference.

Working Sample Code Solutions!
Many articles include complete downloadable sample code ready to adapt for your own projects.

ASPToday covers a broad range of topics including:

- ▶ ASP.NET 1.x and 2.0
- ▶ ADO.NET and SQL
- ▶ XML
- ▶ Web Services
- ▶ E-Commerce

- ▶ Security
- ▶ Site Design
- ▶ Site Admin
- ▶ SMTP and Mail
- ▶ Classic ASP and ADO

and much, much more…

To receive a FREE two-month subscription to ASPToday, visit **www.asptoday.com/subscribe.aspx** and answer the question about this book!

forums.apress.com

FOR PROFESSIONALS BY PROFESSIONALS™

JOIN THE APRESS FORUMS AND BE PART OF OUR COMMUNITY. You'll find discussions that cover topics of interest to IT professionals, programmers, and enthusiasts just like you. If you post a query to one of our forums, you can expect that some of the best minds in the business—especially Apress authors, who all write with *The Expert's Voice*™—will chime in to help you. Why not aim to become one of our most valuable participants (MVPs) and win cool stuff? Here's a sampling of what you'll find:

DATABASES
Data drives everything.

Share information, exchange ideas, and discuss any database programming or administration issues.

INTERNET TECHNOLOGIES AND NETWORKING
Try living without plumbing (and eventually IPv6).

Talk about networking topics including protocols, design, administration, wireless, wired, storage, backup, certifications, trends, and new technologies.

JAVA
We've come a long way from the old Oak tree.

Hang out and discuss Java in whatever flavor you choose: J2SE, J2EE, J2ME, Jakarta, and so on.

MAC OS X
All about the Zen of OS X.

OS X is both the present and the future for Mac apps. Make suggestions, offer up ideas, or boast about your new hardware.

OPEN SOURCE
Source code is good; understanding (open) source is better.

Discuss open source technologies and related topics such as PHP, MySQL, Linux, Perl, Apache, Python, and more.

PROGRAMMING/BUSINESS
Unfortunately, it is.

Talk about the Apress line of books that cover software methodology, best practices, and how programmers interact with the "suits."

WEB DEVELOPMENT/DESIGN
Ugly doesn't cut it anymore, and CGI is absurd.

Help is in sight for your site. Find design solutions for your projects and get ideas for building an interactive Web site.

SECURITY
Lots of bad guys out there—the good guys need help.

Discuss computer and network security issues here. Just don't let anyone else know the answers!

TECHNOLOGY IN ACTION
Cool things. Fun things.

It's after hours. It's time to play. Whether you're into LEGO® MINDSTORMS™ or turning an old PC into a DVR, this is where technology turns into fun.

WINDOWS
No defenestration here.

Ask questions about all aspects of Windows programming, get help on Microsoft technologies covered in Apress books, or provide feedback on any Apress Windows book.

HOW TO PARTICIPATE:
Go to the Apress Forums site at **http://forums.apress.com/**.
Click the New User link.